THE MOST IMPORTANT PERSON ON EARTH

OTHER BOOKS BY DR. MYLES MUNROE

The Spirit of Leadership
The Principles and Power of Vision
The Principles and Power of Vision
Study Guide
Understanding the Purpose and Power of Men
Understanding the Purpose and Power of Men
Study Guide
Understanding the Purpose and Power of Woman
Understanding the Purpose and Power of Woman
Study Guide
Understanding the Purpose and Power of Prayer
Understanding the Purpose and Power of Prayer
Study Guide

AVAILABLE IN SPANISH

Entendiendo el Propósito y el Poder de la Mujer
Entendiendo el Propósito y el Poder de los Hombres
Entendiendo el Propósito y el Poder de la Oración
El Espíritu de Liderazgo
Los Principios y el Poder de la Visión

THE Most IMPORTANT PERSON ON EARTH

DR. MYLES MUNROE

WHITAKER
HOUSE

THE MOST IMPORTANT PERSON ON EARTH:
The Holy Spirit, Governor of the Kingdom

Dr. Myles Munroe
Bahamas Faith Ministries International
P.O. Box N9583
Nassau, Bahamas
e-mail: bfmadmin@bfmmm.com
websites: www.bfmmm.com; www.bfmi.tv; www.mylesmunroe.tv

ISBN: 978-0-88368-986-8
Printed in the United States of America
© 2007 by Dr. Myles Munroe

Whitaker House
1030 Hunt Valley Circle
New Kensington, PA 15068
www.whitakerhouse.com

Library of Congress Cataloging-in-Publication Data

Munroe, Myles.
The most important person on earth : the Holy Spirit, Governor of the
Kingdom / Myles Munroe.
p.   cm.
Summary: "Explores how the Holy Spirit is the most important Person on earth because
he is the presence and power of heaven in the world, bringing true life and transforming
individuals, societies, and nations"—Provided by publisher.
Includes bibliographical references and index.
ISBN-13: 978-0-88368-986-8 (trade hardcover : alk. paper)
ISBN-10: 0-88368-986-3 (trade hardcover : alk. paper) 1. Holy Spirit. I. Title.
BT121.3.M86 2006
231'.3—dc22   2006030325

1 2 3 4 5 6 7 8 9 10 11 12 ᵾᴊ 15 14 13 12 11 10 09 08 07

DEDICATION

To the human spirit searching for its source.

To the leaders of nations grappling with the challenges of our twenty-first century world.

To the desperate heart of the present generation looking for meaning and hope.

To the BFMI and ITWLA family, who stand with me in my passion to help humanity rediscover the kingdom.

To my wife, Ruth, and my greatest investment on earth, my daughter, Charisa, and son, Chairo.

To the King eternal, immortal, the all-wise God and Creator of all things.

To His Excellency the Heavenly Governor, who is the source of truth and life.

CONTENTS

PREFACE

The greatest dream in the heart of every human being is of a perfect world. The greatest desire and pursuit of all humankind is the power to achieve this dream. We all want power, which is the ability and capacity to control circumstances and destiny.

Our experience does not often meet our dreams and desires, however. Consider...

√ The chaotic aftermath of a presidential assassination attempt.

√ Rescue and recovery following the devastation of a powerful hurricane.

√ Countries struggling with overwhelming poverty and the pandemic of AIDS.

Whenever there's a crisis, people want to know, "Who's in charge?" They want to find out who has the authority and the ability to solve the problems, bring stability, and maintain a peaceful and prosperous life.

9

When Ronald Reagan was shot early in his first term as president, the press wanted to know who was running the country while he was in surgery and recovery. His secretary of state was criticized for his hasty choice of words, "I'm in control here," because he wasn't next in the line of presidential succession. He may have had the *ability*, but he didn't have the legal *authority*, to be in charge.

When hurricane Katrina hit New Orleans, bringing suffering and death to that region of the United States, both federal and local officials came under fire for their alleged poor response to the crisis. They had the *authority*, but seemed to be lacking the *ability*, to address the urgent needs.

Some nations struggle with perpetual poverty and the uncontrolled spread of disease. Those with illegitimate governments, which have seized control and squander the wealth and the lives of their people, do not have the *authority*, the *ability*, or the *desire* to deal with the critical problems facing their nations.

It often seems as if the state of the world today is one of ongoing crises, so that many people are asking, "Who's in charge?" We want to know how to solve our global problems, such as terrorist attacks, war, crime, hunger, AIDS, flu epidemics, and economic instability. Who has the necessary authority, ability, and desire to address them?

Individuals, nations, and even corporations are trying to tackle some of these problems, but it is often difficult to make substantive changes.

The United Nations is limited in its authority and power to carry out its resolutions and programs, and it is currently under scrutiny for a lack of effectiveness.

Our inability to find real solutions to problems is often mirrored in our personal lives, as well. When financial setbacks arise, our personal dreams are dashed, or our children seem bent on self-destruction, we ask ourselves, in effect, "Who's in control?" We certainly don't feel as if we are. We long to create order and peace and well-being in our families once more. We desire the authority and the power to change our circumstances.

This is why I'm convinced that the number one desire of all people in every situation of life—global or personal—is for *power*. Power is *the ability to influence and control circumstances.*

Power is the principle issue of humanity. People may not express it in exactly that way, but ultimately they desire the ability to manage and shape their circumstances, reverse personal and family setbacks, and build a better life for themselves. This is why a person who wants to be a millionaire is not really seeking money. He's seeking power. He wants the capacity to control what he eats, where he lives, what he drives, and how he will conduct his life.

Yet both the richest person and the poorest person on the planet have this desire. The principle issue of humanity applies to both CEOs and homemakers. It makes no difference what nationality or ethnicity a person may have; everyone desires to influence his life and the world around him. And the frequent lack of this influence is frustrating and painful.

The chaos in our world and the uncertain nature of our individual lives reveals the absence of authority and power that can address our deepest needs and most critical issues. This is the reason many of us admire and try to emulate the talented, powerful, and influential; this is also why we seek to cultivate a sense of hope and faith in the noble qualities of humanity.

We want to believe in our ability to overcome the odds. For example:

√ Every year, major news magazines, such as *Time* and *Newsweek,* attempt to identify the "person of the year."

√ Many people venerate globally respected humanitarian awards, such as the Nobel Peace Prize and Templeton award.

√ The public loves TV programs such as *Who Wants to Be a Millionaire?, Deal or No Deal, Survivor,* and especially *American Idol.*

In fact, *American Idol* has spun imitations in almost forty countries. It is a universal desire, crossing national, cultural, and ethnic lines, to be recognized as the "best" and to have a life of wealth and influence. People want to become stars in the media or athletics or business or religion because stars have influence, and influence brings you power over situations and other people. These shows are successful because many are looking for ways to escape the human quicksand of cultural, social, and economic control. We long for power because life can be so uncertain, fearful, and painful.

Perhaps it is also this inherent desire and drive to control our circumstances that spawns the creation of superhero characters, such as Superman, Batman, Wonder Woman, the Fantastic Four, the X-Men, and the Jedi Knights of *Star Wars.* All these characters fulfill our deep psychological fantasy to possess the ability to control life, destiny, and situations at will. I believe that the massive success of many of the blockbuster movies that glorify these imaginary figures in contrast to the lesser success of more real-life movies is proof that our desire for power and control is universal and naturally human. We desire control over crisis.

It is also interesting to note that some of our most successful superheroes have their origins in another world or distant planet. This may indicate that, deep in the heart of mankind, there is an unconscious awareness that the solution to our earthly dilemma cannot come from our planet itself. Rather, our help must come from another realm, and our future lies somewhere beyond our world. There is more truth to this than we might want to admit.

There are solutions for the problems and crises in our families, communities, businesses, nations, and world. As a planet under siege, we need help from a higher authority, help from a greater world that has the ability to address our needs. We need someone from that world who has experience in bringing light into darkness, life into barrenness, and order out of chaos. If we could identify that person, and he came to earth to solve all our problems, he would naturally be called the most important person on earth.

Only one person has those qualifications. Actually, he is already here on earth. We must meet him, come to understand him, and discover his purpose, intent, program, and strategy to enable us to regain our authority and power, and to influence life on earth as we were meant to.

INTRODUCTION

Human beings of all ages, genders, nationalities, and ethnic groups are on a search for purpose and significance. Consider:

√ the multitude of religions in the world that seek to explain our existence.

√ the large and growing number of books on the "self-help" shelves in bookstores.

√ the enormous emphasis in Western countries on self-actualization.

√ the scientific community's continual pursuit of the origins of life.

√ the ongoing struggle of Third-World peoples to gain freedom and a sense of identity for their nations and themselves.

We seek to understand why we are here, the significance of the world we live in, and how we can fulfill our personal potential. We want to know if our individual lives have any real meaning in the vast expanse of history and time.

Why do we struggle with these questions? Why don't we already know the answers to them?

What makes us so introspective and continually longing to find meaning for ourselves and our world?

"RETURN TO MANUFACTURER"

Wouldn't it be wonderful if all human beings were born with "manufacturer's instructions" tied to their wrists, explaining who they are and how they work? (Of course, even if we did, most of us would probably skip the instructions and try to figure out life as we went along!)

I believe human beings do come with the equivalent of operating instructions that give us answers to our deepest questions about ourselves and our world. Some of this information has been placed within us; the rest has been given to us by our Creator or "Manufacturer" in written form. The reason we're filled with such uncertainty and confusion about life is that we've lost our connection to these original instructions. We haven't stopped to recognize our internal programming, or to read our life manual in order to understand our personal potential or how we work. This is why we can't see the purpose of the world itself and how it is supposed to function.

When we try but fail to solve what is broken in our lives and in our world, it is because our Manufacturer's labels have become faded, and we haven't read this crucial instruction: "Do not try to repair yourself. Return to Manufacturer."

It is the Manufacturer who...

√ has the original blueprints.

√ knows how to repair what is broken inside us.

√ can provide the replacement piece for what is missing in our lives.

When we rediscover the Manufacturer's original intent, we come to understand our purpose, our potential, and the significance of our role in this world.

KINGDOM GOVERNMENT

The mind of our Manufacturer didn't invent the fragmented life we have today, with its divisions among nations and people groups, its strife among families, its double-mindedness and double standards, its abuse and waste. He conceived of an orderly but energetic life in which every person could reach his fullest potential in conjunction with others for the greatest good of individuals and the community of human beings.

The original blueprint of the Creator was for a *kingdom government on earth* as an extension and reflection of his own greater, spiritual kingdom. This earthly government was to be a thriving colony with humanity as (1) its citizens, and (2) its local vice governors representing the home kingdom. Our mandate was to transform the colony into the nature of the kingdom.

The character of the initial colony was both peaceful and productive because of the generous nature of its Creator and Sovereign. His interests are the welfare, fruitfulness, and fulfillment of his citizens. His is a *perfect* government, a benevolent rule.

INTER-REALM CONNECTION

The key to the success of this plan was the establishment of an *inter-realm connection* and ongoing relationship between the home kingdom and the colony of earth. This connection was completely effective because it was direct—from Sovereign to individual citizens—through a super-natural communication that allowed the citizens to know the desires and plans of the King. That connection was the very Spirit of the Sovereign living within humanity—his Holy Spirit.

To understand this inter-realm connection, we have to look at the concept of *supernatural*, and we must address the various misconceptions people have when they hear the term *Holy Spirit*. I am not talking about some kind of "force," "mist," or "feeling," but a Person. I am referring to the Creator "extending himself" to us in personal interaction, a Person-to-person communication.

THE CONCEPT OF THE SUPERNATURAL

The word *supernatural* does not exist in Scripture, but it does describe a concept clearly presented there. Supernatural simply means "outside" or "above" the natural; it is spiritual rather than physical. The supernatural world is above our natural world. Paul of Tarsus, the first-century theologian, defined this concept as *invisible* or *unseen*:

ROMANS 1:20

Since the creation of the world God's *invisible* qualities—his eternal power and divine nature—have been clearly seen, being understood from what has been made.

2 COR. 4:18

So we fix our eyes not on what is seen, but on what is *unseen*. For what is seen is temporary, but what is *unseen is eternal*.

The supernatural realm is therefore an invisible or unseen world that is distinct from our physical one. It is what the incomparable young rabbi, Jesus of Nazareth, was referring to when he said, "My kingdom is not of this world....But now my kingdom is from another place."

When someone "experiences" the supernatural world of the Creator-King, it refers to his encounter with the kingdom of his Sovereign. The key to his interaction with the unseen kingdom is the Holy Spirit communicating the King's mind and heart to him so he can carry it out on earth.

The nature of this relationship between the unseen world of the kingdom government and the seen world of the physical earth underscores the incalculable value of the one who makes the connection between these two realms possible, the Holy Spirit.

THE CONCEPT OF THE KINGDOM

To fully appreciate the invisible kingdom government, we must realize that the *idea* of "kingdom" didn't originate on earth with the ancient civilizations of Babylon and Egypt. It didn't come from earth at all. The concept of kingdom is rooted in the desire of the Creator to design and sustain both the unseen and seen realms in order to express, represent, and manifest his nature.

Ideas are one of the most powerful forces in existence. We see how the greatest ideas transcend generations and serve as the source of people's creative activity and the motivation for their productivity. Ideas are the starting point of all that is created. An idea becomes a full-fledged, viable concept when it is envisioned and executed. The concept of an ideal kingdom is so beautiful that only a Creator-King of a certain nature could have envisioned and established it. We need to understand the King and kingdom out of which we come.

The word *king* refers to the person or personality who influences and oversees the productive development and profitable service of everything under his care, for the fulfillment of his noble desires and the benefit of all those living in his realm. The environment, territory, and authority over which he presides are his "domains" or "realms." A king effectually relating to his domains is the essence of the concept of kingdom.

Kingdom is thus the perfect example of the divine, creative act of the Creator. The first realm of his dominion is described as heaven. Heaven is the original kingdom; it was the origin of kingdoms. No kingdom existed before it, and nothing natural can be adequately compared to it. It is the first real kingdom because the first King created it. The kingdom of heaven is the only perfect prototype of kingdoms in existence.

When our Creator-King desired to extend his perfect kingdom from the invisible realm to the visible realm, the result was the creation of the physical universe and the appointment of planet earth as the destination for a unique extension of his divine being. Paul of Tarsus attempted to communicate this divine process of creation and extension when writing to people in the city of Colossae: "By him all things were created: things in heaven and on earth, visible and invisible, whether thrones or powers or rulers or authorities; all things were created by him and for him."

The kingdom of heaven and its colony of earth exist through the will of our Creator-King. It is therefore impossible to comprehend humanity's purpose without understanding the kingdom concept and how we are meant to live it out on earth. An inter-realm connection through the Holy Spirit is what enables us to fulfill our very purpose as human beings.

The kingdom government is the ultimate answer to our search for personal significance and the meaning of the world around us.

We can no longer ignore the fading writing on our Manufacturer's label. Let us return to the initial intent of our Creator-King, so we may understand the original blueprints of both kingdom and colony.

PROLOGUE

I n the beginning was the King's Word. His Word was himself and was inseparable from him. His Word was with
him from the start. Everything that exists came into
being through the King's Word; no other source of life exists.
In his Word was life, and this life manifested the knowledge
of the King and his kingdom to the darkened and confused
minds of humanity. But although the light of this knowledge
shines brightly, those who choose to remain in a darkened
state cannot see it.

In the beginning, the King created a colony for his kingdom. The colony was raw and undeveloped, and there was no
life there. The King's Governor was poised to bring order and
kingdom influence to the colony through the King's Word...

PART 1

THE PROGRAM OF CELESTIAL EXPANSION

CHAPTER ONE
THE POWER OF INFLUENCE

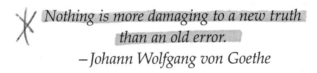

Nothing is more damaging to a new truth than an old error.
— *Johann Wolfgang von Goethe*

I found myself sitting between kingdom and colony.

I was the guest of the United States ambassador to the Bahamas for an official state function at his residence. Also attending this function were both the Premier of the Turks and Caicos Islands, and His Excellency, the royal governor of the Turks and Caicos Islands.

This group of islands lies off the southeastern coast of my country of the Bahamas. At the writing of this book, the Turks and Caicos is a colony of Great Britain. The colony is overseen by the royal governor, who was appointed by Queen Elizabeth II of Great Britain. He is the highest authority in that colony. The Premier, however, is an elected official, approved by the Crown, who heads the local government.

The Premier was the special guest of the American ambassador. The ambassador had also invited other members of the diplomatic corps, as well as distinguished governmental officials and guests from around the world. Previous to this gathering, I had already become well acquainted with the Premier. At his invitation, I had visited his beautiful island territory to address governmental and civic leaders in a special national event, and we had become good friends.

During the state function at the United States ambassador's residence, I also came to know the royal governor fairly well because I was seated between him and the Premier for over three hours during the proceedings. While the Premier is a native-born Turks and Caicos Islander, His Excellency the Governor is pure British. When he spoke, you knew immediately that he was not from the islands.

As I conversed with these two distinguished leaders, one on either side of me, I realized once again the principle of kingdoms and their impact on their colonies. It refreshed my perspective and reminded me of my personal experience as a citizen of a former colony of the kingdom of Great Britain. There I sat between the crown and the colony, the governor and the administrator, the authority and the power. The governor was sent from the kingdom to live in the colony, among the people, to represent the Queen and execute her wishes and will in the colony. His primary purpose was to maintain the kingdom's influence and presence in that territory.

THE KINGDOM LIFE

Years of research have led me to the conclusion that the practical outworking of kingdoms points us to truths and principles that transcend the mere political fortunes of individual empires. Seeing how they function actually:

√ provides us with a deep understanding of our own nature as human beings,

√ reveals the key to our remarkable life purpose, and

√ enables us to exercise our full potential in the world.

These things have tremendous implications for the human race personally, professionally, socially, and politically; for our families, communities, nations, and the world.

I am in a somewhat unique position to discuss the nature of kingdoms and their colonies, having grown up in a land that was a British colony for nearly two hundred years, and having witnessed its peaceful transition to independence. I well remember what it meant to live under a monarch—both the mind-set of a kingdom and its functioning and procedures. Yet I also understand what it means to live in an independent nation, having eagerly followed our transition to self-government as a young person. My close acquaintance with these two ways of governing has been extremely beneficial to me as I have explored the nature of kingdom and what it means for every person on this planet.

> *The success of your life depends upon how well you live out the kingdom life.*

My investigation into the concept of kingdom has convinced me that the success of your life and mine depends upon how well we understand and live out what I will call the *kingdom life*. I am not referring to a political system or to any particular national government, but to a way of understanding and living everyday life.

AN ANTI-KINGDOM PERSPECTIVE

The concept of kingdom may seem antithetical to the contemporary mind. Empires and their colonies seem outdated in the twenty-first century, just fading remnants of the past. Many nations today have representative governments. A number of former colonies and protectorates have gained their independence. Opportunities for self-government have expanded greatly throughout the world, and we rightly celebrate the political freedoms and opportunities these changes have brought. Human history has seen enough tyrannical kingdoms and dictators to want to move on to a different form of government.

Democracy is essentially humanity's reaction to perverted kingdoms. The founders of the United States rebelled against what they considered an oppressive government, and the very genetics of contemporary Western society are anti-kingdom. Because of the strong influence of political and social ideas of independence and freedom, this perspective has permeated the world and affects many areas of our thinking, not just the governmental realm. It shows up in how we view and conduct ourselves in personal relationships, business, media, education, and even religion because our cultural experiences produce our definitions. This is why the concept of kingdom is dismissed by most people today as irrelevant, and is even considered out-and-out frightening by others.

In the light of these developments, however, many people no longer understand what life in an authentic and uncorrupted kingdom entails. I believe this lack of understanding has hindered them in the way they've approached their lives. Most of us have forgotten why kingdoms historically had such a profound impact on people and nations for thousands of years, some of which is still being felt. They haven't recognized what the concept and history of kingdoms reveal that is vital to us today.

I therefore want to present to you, step-by-step, how the practical working of the kingdom life answers essential questions about our human existence, purpose, and fulfillment. We have approached our personal goals and problems, as well as our national and global crises, from many vantage points, but not often from this perspective. Democracies are valuable political institutions for us today, but I'm referring to something that transcends our contemporary politics and government—something that speaks to the basis of our very being as humans. It has significance for people of all nations, religions, and creeds. It lies at the heart of the existence of every person on earth, *whether Christian, Buddhist, Hindu, Muslim, Jew, agnostic, or atheist.*

Just as I found myself sitting between kingdom and colony, you and every other person on the planet are, in a sense, supposed to find yourselves in a relationship between kingdom and colony, and to experience that dynamic in your own lives.

KINGDOM POWER

The character of this kingdom is, again, nothing like the political kingdoms of the past and present that seek to force others under their control based on territorial power, greed, or religious doctrine. Those kingdoms enslave. But the very nature of humanity, as well as the personal and corporate progress of the world, are designed to develop and thrive from the outworking of this kingdom.

I mentioned in the preface to this book that the principal issue of humanity is power, defined as "the ability to influence and control circumstances." We all want to direct and influence our lives in a positive and fulfilling way. The nature of this kingdom speaks directly to this need.

Understanding our association with this kingdom begins with an exploration of what all human kingdoms have shared in common and how they were different from the contemporary experience of government most of us are familiar with today. Then we can move to the larger context of what these qualities reveal about our human existence and purpose.

THE NATURE OF KINGDOM GOVERNMENT

I define a kingdom as **"the governing authority and influence of a sovereign ruler who impacts his territory through his will, purpose, and intentions, which are manifested in the culture, lifestyle, and quality of his citizenry."** A king must have his dominion, or his territory. We call it his "king-dominion" or his kingdom. You cannot be a king without having territory; you have to be ruling over something. And you cannot be a king without having kingdom citizens who live and work in the kingdom.

> *In a true, traditional kingdom, all power is vested in the monarch.*

In a true, traditional kingdom, all power is vested in the monarch. The king actually, personally *owns* the country, including the people. In contrast, a president or prime minister in a representative government doesn't own the country; he governs it on behalf of the people.

The king implements his vision for the kingdom. There is no congress or parliament to discuss which laws they're going to create. There is only the monarch, and he has immediate access to his handpicked, trusted council, who carry out his wishes. The job of these advisors is to take the will of the king, translate it into the law of the land, and make sure it is enacted throughout the kingdom.

> *The king implements his vision for the kingdom based on his personal will.*

A kingdom is therefore the governing influence of a king over his territory, impacting and influencing it with his *personal will.* In a kingdom, the king's personal interest becomes policy, and the king's personal will becomes law.

The effectiveness of a kingdom and its power is therefore its ability to influence and control the territory according to the vision of the king.

The Goal of the Kingdom: Ruling and Gaining Territory

Most kingdoms throughout history have sought to take additional land, sometimes at some distance from the home country, because the power of a king is related to the territory he owns. The more territory a king had, the greater he was respected by other kingdoms, especially if the territories had abundant natural wealth. The home country of the king was his *domain,* and the outlying territories were his *colonies.*

Once a colony was gained, the sovereign's number one goal was to exercise his personal influence over it.

31

THE TRANSFORMATION OF COLONIES INTO THE KINGDOM

A colony is comprised of "a group of emigrants or their descendants who settle in a distant land but remain subject to the parent country."[1] The word *colony* comes from the Latin word *colonia*, derived from *colere*, meaning "to cultivate."[2] In this sense, a colony is:

√ the presence of a distinct cultural citizenry in a foreign territory that is governed by the laws and customs of its home country.

√ established to influence the territory for the home government.

This means that a colony's purpose was essentially to:

1. be an extension of the home country in another territory.
2. establish a prototype of the original country in another territory.
3. represent the values, morals, and manners of the home country.
4. manifest the culture and lifestyle of the original nation.

When a kingdom takes a territory, therefore, its goal is to make that territory exactly like the kingdom. The purpose is not only to gain lands, but also to transform these lands so that they mirror the country in its mind-set and lifestyle, its characteristics and culture. In this way, the kingdom not only extends its power, but it also expands the influence of its very nature.

The Roman Empire had a specific way of ensuring the permanency and effectiveness of kingdom influence over its colonies. When the Romans conquered a region, they planted a group of about three hundred of their own citizens, as well as a larger number of those allied with the empire, and a number of settlers, within it to serve as a type of military outpost. These constituted a "colony of Romans citizens" (*colonia civium Romanorum*) or a "little Rome." A colony of Roman citizens was free from taxation and military duty. It had its own constitution based on the Roman constitution and was allowed to elect its own senate and other offices of state. The original inhabitants had to adhere to this new government and its constitution.[3] These "little Romes" brought the culture and values of the Roman empire throughout Europe and northern Africa.

A striking picture of the power and influence of kingdoms over a territory and the lifestyle of its inhabitants can be seen in the various nations of the Caribbean and West Indies. You can always tell who controlled a colony by studying its culture. The Bahamas, Jamaica, Trinidad, and Barbados are former colonies of

> *A kingdom's goal is to make its colony exactly like the kingdom.*

the United Kingdom. Cuba was a colony of Spain. Haiti was a colony of France. The cultures of all these islands are distinctly characteristic of the countries that claimed them.

You can still see the kingdoms' influence in the daily lives of the peoples' customs. If you visited the Bahamas, you'd see the influence of Great Britain in our narrow streets, our driving on the left-hand side of the road, and our habit of drinking tea. When I was a young boy attending school, my classmates and I grew up singing "God Save the Queen." We were being taught to be a "little Britain." Similarly, if you went to Cuba, you might think you were in Spain as you observed its architecture and food. Significantly for their cultures, each of these former colonies speaks the language of the kingdom that conquered it.

Most kingdoms in the colonial period had to fight for new territory because there was a limited amount of land in the world. Under European control, the Bahamas was initially claimed by the Spaniards. The French tried to conquer it, but the Spaniards held them off. Finally, the British won out over the Spanish. If the British Empire hadn't won, I might be speaking Spanish today. So even though the Bahamas, Haiti, and Cuba are all part of a chain of islands, whoever controlled the domain controlled the language and culture of the people. If you really want to investigate the power of kingdoms, study the island of Hispaniola, home of both the Dominican Republic and Haiti. Two kingdoms grabbed the same island, and there's a line right down the middle of the island; one side speaks French, while other side speaks Spanish.

THE MOST IMPORTANT PERSON IN THE COLONY

The transformation of a colony into the culture of the kingdom didn't happen automatically. A purposeful development was involved. The king didn't usually directly extend his influence to his colony by physically going there. He administrated his will through his personal representative, called a governor or regent. He sent his representative to physically live in the colony in his place. Therefore, the royal governor was the *presence of the absent king* in the colony.

With the governor in the colony, you didn't need the physical presence of the king to experience and be changed by the king's influence. I mentioned that the British monarchs who influenced the English-speaking Caribbean nations didn't frequently visit their colonies. Yet, in the Bahamas, we all learned to speak English, drink tea, wave the Union Jack, and sing the songs of Britain. We became part of the United Kingdom. And the royal governors were the direct instrument of that transformation.

The governor was therefore the most important person in the colony. We get a greater appreciation for why this was true when we look at his purpose.

THE GOVERNOR'S PURPOSE

The governor's purpose was sixfold:

1. *Relationship*: The governor was the guarantee that the kingdom could always have access to the colony. The inter-relationship between king and colony was totally dependent on him.

2. *Communication*: Anything the king wanted the colony to know or to receive, he would send through his governor, his avenue of communication.

3. *Representation*: The governor was the chief representative of the king and his kingdom in the colony. He also represented the colony to the king.

4. *Interpretation*: The governor understood intimately the king's desires, ideas, intent, purposes, will, and plans; therefore, he was the only one who could effectively interpret these things for the colony.

5. *Power*: The governor was the only one empowered with the authority and ability to execute the king's desires and commands for the colony.

6. *Partnership*: The governor was effectively the king's partner in rulership.

35

THE GOVERNOR'S QUALIFICATIONS AND ROLES

The qualifications and roles of a governor were significant in terms of kingdom and colony:

1. *The governor was appointed by the king.*

Unlike the governors of representational governments, the royal governor was not voted in; he was appointed by the king.

2. *The governor came only from the kingdom, never the colony.*

Governors were never chosen from the indigenous peoples of the colonies. They were always appointed from the home countries. Why? A governor had to be steeped in the *original culture* of the kingdom. He had to be a person who knew the kingdom and understood the heart, mind, desires, will, and intent of the king in carrying out the kingdom's purposes in the territory.

3. *The governor represented only the king.*

Again, the difference between the governors of colonies and the governors many of us are familiar with in representative governments is like night and day. Every state in the United States has a governor who is voted in by the people and can also be voted out by them. He or she is ultimately accountable to the people of the state, not to the federal government or its leaders. In contrast, the royal governor was responsible and accountable to the king alone in his allegiance, attitude, actions, and responsibility.

4. *The governor only expressed the mind and will of the king.*

The governor was not there to promote his own personal policies or agendas. He was to take the vision and will of the king and communicate that to the people, translating it into policy and law.

5. *The governor was responsible for converting the colony into the kingdom.*

Once more, it was the governor's job to oversee and carry out the transformation of the colonies according to the character of the kingdom. The governor was "planted" in the colony to sow the seeds of the home country into the culture of the new territory. Colonization was for the purpose of *conversion*—to exchange the culture of the territory for the culture of the kingdom. Whatever was happening in the kingdom was supposed to happen in the colony, as well.

6. *In converting the colony, the governor transferred the kingdom's culture, values, nature, language, and lifestyle to the people.*

The governor made sure that every subject of the kingdom took on the kingdom culture in language, attitude, dress, food, and so forth. The colonists were even to take on the history of the kingdom as if it were their own, which in fact it now was, because they had become a part of the chronicles of the nation. The subjects were to take on the mind-set and lifestyle of the kingdom until, if you visited the territory, you would think you were in the home country itself.

7. *The governor prepared the subjects for citizenship.*

When a king took over a colony, the people essentially became his possessions. The inhabitants of the colony did not automatically become citizens; they were called *subjects*. For example, when the Bahamas was a colony, the people were not citizens of Great Britain. We couldn't vote, and we didn't have other rights of British citizens.

In a kingdom, citizenship was a privilege. Who became a citizen was the king's prerogative, and he personally granted it. The reason citizenship wasn't automatic is that, once a person was appointed a citizen, he had special benefits and protections in the kingdom. In the Roman Empire, citizenship was a high honor and privilege involving many rights. In the first century, Paul of Tarsus was arrested in Jerusalem by the Roman commander for allegedly disturbing the peace. He was about to be whipped when he declared to a nearby centurion that he was a Roman citizen. Immediately, the soldiers' attitude toward him changed. The following exchange dramatically reveals the power of kingdom citizenship in the Roman Empire, especially if you were *born* a citizen:

Citizens have special benefits and protections in a kingdom.

ACTS 22: 25-29

As they stretched him out to flog him, Paul said to the centurion standing there, "Is it legal for you to flog a Roman citizen who hasn't even been found guilty?" When the centurion heard this, he went to the commander and reported it. "What are you going to do?" he asked. "This man is a Roman citizen." The commander went to Paul and asked, "Tell me, are you a Roman citizen?" "Yes I am," he answered. Then the commander said, "I had to pay a big price for my citizenship." "But I was born a citizen," Paul replied. Those who were about to question him withdrew immediately. The commander himself was alarmed when he realized that he had put Paul, a Roman citizen, in chains.

Once you are a citizen, your privileges, rights, and demands upon the throne change. The king is responsible for taking care of you. Therefore, the governor's role of preparing subjects for citizenship was a tremendous responsibility. If the governor believed a subject was ready to be a citizen or especially deserved citizenship, he recommended the subject to the king. Since the governor lived in the colony and knew the subjects firsthand, the king accepted the suggestions of the governor in this regard.

8. *The governor lived in a residence built by the government of the home country.*

A kingdom would build a residence in its colonies specifically for its royal governors to live in. This emphasized that the governor, the chief representative of the kingdom in the colony, was not just a visitor; he lived there, he was there to stay, and this was his legal residence. The British built a governor's mansion in Nassau, the capital of the Bahamas, specifically for the royal governor to live in, which today is called the Government House. Great Britain similarly built governors' houses in Jamaica, Trinidad, Barbados, and in every colony where it ruled.

9. *The governor's presence in the colony was evidence that the kingdom itself was in the colony.*

As long as the governor lived in the colony, the kingdom itself was present. The first time the Bahamas was declared a British colony was when a royal governor drove out the remaining Spanish garrisons, solidifying its ownership by the kingdom of Great Britain.

10. *The governor left if the colony declared independence.*

Either by force or recall, the royal governor would leave a colony if it declared independence and the kingdom was no longer officially governing. In the American Revolution, the royal governors of the colonies were forced to withdraw from their posts. When the Bahamas received independence, it was through negotiation with Great Britain, and the governor was recalled because he no longer had a legal right to be there.

THE VALUE OF THE GOVERNOR

In kingdom terms, then, the governor was the most powerful and important person in the colony. Because he introduced the kingdom's culture, language, and lifestyle—every unique aspect of the kingdom—to the colony, he had great value for the kingdom and its larger purposes. To summarize, the governor was valuable:

1. *As the presence of the government.* Without him, the kingdom would not exist in the colony.

2. *For representing the government.* If he wasn't there, the king would not be adequately or effectively represented.

3. *For the enablement of the colony.* He was the one with the authority and ability to supply power and resources to the colony.

4. *For protection.* As long as the kingdom was represented in a colony by the governor, the king was obligated to protect the territory from outside threats and danger.

5. *For his ability to know and communicate the mind of the king.* The governor represented the king's interests and will to the colony and made sure they were carried out.

6. *For enabling the colony's citizens and subjects to fulfill the will of the kingdom.* The colony received its instructions only through the governor and therefore was dependent on him for its effectiveness. The citizens and subjects would not be able to carry out their kingdom mandate without the governor's guidance and empowerment.

THE INFLUENCE OF ANOTHER KINGDOM

These were the main features of a kingdom-colony relationship, including the pivotal role of the governor in the process of transforming colonies into the home country. This brings us back to the kingdom I mentioned earlier in this chapter, which transcends our human governments and speaks to the basis of our very nature and existence as human beings. This kingdom has properties that are similar to, but go beyond, those of the traditional earthly kingdoms we've been looking at.

Two millennia ago, a startling young teacher described this transcendent kingdom. When Jesus of Nazareth began traveling and speaking around Palestine, the first thing he is recorded as saying is, "The time has come....The kingdom of God is near." MARK 1:15

This statement intrigues me and brings up several questions for us to explore in terms of kingdom:

√ What "time" was he speaking about? And why then?

√ What was the nature of the kingdom he was referring to?

He was announcing the imminent return of a kingdom and its influence on earth. Notice that he didn't proclaim the entrance of a new religion, nor did he announce the beginnings of a democratic form of government. We have to ask:

√ Why would he use this particular governmental reference at the beginning of his public life?

√ What did it signify about his message and purpose?

√ If the influence of a kingdom was entering the world, what new culture would emerge for the citizens of earth?

To understand the context of these thought-provoking statements and their implications, we need to go back to the first book of Moses, the book of Genesis, to the origins of this kingdom. For this wasn't the first time the transcendent kingdom had entered the world and impacted its inhabitants...

CHAPTER TWO

THE ADAMIC ADMINISTRATION

The principle and purpose of delegated authority is accountability and responsibility.

T he first government on earth came from a kingdom outside it. The world was governed in a way similar to the colonies we have been looking at. Yet the transcendent kingdom had significant differences:

√ The territory of earth was created by the home country rather than taken by force. It was not anyone else's possession beforehand.

√ There were no inhabitants on earth at first, which was designed with them in mind; it was specifically prepared for those who would live here.

√ The original inhabitants were not of a different culture from the home country but were actually the offspring of the King himself.

The similarities are these:

√ The home country desired to expand the realm of its influence by bringing the nature, mind-set, and purposes of the kingdom to the colony of earth.

√ The King's Governor was present in the colony to oversee the transformation process. He was to guide the King's children—his local governors—who were to convert the colony into a replica of the kingdom.

Let's take a closer look at the creation of this colony of earth.

THE ORIGINAL GOVERNMENT

The first book of Moses begins with these words: "In the beginning God [the Creator-King] created the heavens and the earth [the physical universe]." The Creator-King is described by first-century theologian Paul of Tarsus as "the blessed and only Ruler, the King of kings and Lord of lords, who alone is immortal and who lives in unapproachable light, whom no one has seen or can see." The eternal King of an unseen kingdom conceptualized and made the entire physical universe. By creation rights, it is his property.

> *By creation rights, the physical universe is the property of the Creator-King.*

It would be impossible to grasp the vastness of the unseen kingdom that encompasses our universe—especially when we consider that the physical realm in which the earth exists is too immense for us to comprehend. Our universe is so enormous that we're still trying to find out where it ends. Astronomers have discovered billions (some say up to 200 billion) of galaxies in the observable universe. It is estimated that each of these galaxies has tens or hundreds of billions of stars. Multiply billions of galaxies by billions of stars in each galaxy and you have a staggering number of stars in the universe.[1] If these sheer numbers were not enough to astound us, consider the way they are held together. As NASA records,

> Almost every object in space orbits around something. The planets orbit the Sun; our Moon and the moons of other planets orbit their planets; comets orbit the Sun....Even the Sun is orbiting around the center of our galaxy....
>
> An orbit is the result of a precise balance between the forward motion of an object in space (such as a planet or moon) and the pull of gravity from the body it orbits. An object in motion will stay in motion unless something pushes or pulls on it. This is Isaac Newton's First Law of Motion. Without gravity, an Earth-orbiting satellite would go off into space along a straight line. With gravity, it is pulled back toward the Earth. There is a continuous tug-of-war between the one object's tendency to move in a straight line and the tug of gravity pulling it back.[2]

The universe exists in remarkable balance. This is why the Scripture says, in essence, that only a fool thinks, *Nobody is keeping this universe in order.* Clearly, an orderly government of vast ability and power maintains our universe.

EXPANDING THE INVISIBLE KINGDOM

HEB 11:3

One of the New Testament writers said, "The universe was formed at God's command, so that what is seen was not made out of what was visible." The King of the *invisible* world

45

decided to create a *physical* world. He did this for the purpose of expanding his heavenly domain as an extension of himself and his government. He created the physical universe so there would be additional territory to rule and to transform into the expression of his nature and desires. Returning to our definition of *kingdom*, we can say that the invisible kingdom is the governing influence of God over the territory of earth, impacting and influencing it with his will, his purpose, and his intent. Heaven is God's kingdom or home country, and earth is his colony.

We see various types of governing influence in our everyday human experience, not just in a political context:

√ An artist extends the domain of his mind and heart by expressing himself in physical paintings or sculptures, which can have an impact on those who view them.

√ A writer expresses the vision of his inner world through the printed word, and these words can influence the thoughts and attitudes of those who read them.

√ A businessman transforms his entrepreneurial concepts into specific companies that reflect his personal philosophy and provide new products and services that change the way others live.

All these are examples of individuals enlarging their personal influence in the world.

What people create, express, or build is usually a reflection of their personalities and outlook. Therefore, as we look at the Creator-King's desire to extend the influence of the invisible kingdom to earth, it is natural for us to want to know the nature of this King and his kingdom. What influence did he want to bring to earth?

THE NATURE OF THE KING: A PERFECT GOVERNMENT

The nature of the invisible kingdom becomes especially significant when we learn that the inhabitants of earth are to have this very nature themselves. The first book of Moses records these words of the Creator-King:

GEN 1:26-27

> "Let us make man in our image, in our likeness, and let them rule ["have dominion"] over the fish of the sea and the birds of the air, over the livestock, over all the earth, and over all the creatures that move along the ground." So God created man in his own image, in the image of God he created him; male and female he created them.

Human beings were not made as machines or as beings with no direct relationship to the Creator. They were drawn out his own person: "Let us make man in our *image,* in our *likeness,* and let them *rule*...over all the earth."

After creating the universe by his own divine prerogative, the Creator chose one planet amid all the planets of the universe as the practical and unique extension of his influence—earth. Then he extended rulership of earth to those made in his own image, his royal "children."

> *A perfect government does not exist for itself; it exists for its citizens.*

The original Hebrew word for "image," *selem,* "means 'image' in the sense of essential nature."[3] The Hebrew word for *likeness* is *demuth,* which "signifies the original after which a thing is patterned."[4] These words define and describe our

47

design, capacity, potential, and value as human beings made to reflect the personhood of our Creator.

The nature of our Creator-King was recorded by Moses as "the compassionate and gracious God, slow to anger, abounding in love and faithfulness." The only way a kingdom can function perfectly is if it is ruled by a perfect king who will not betray his citizens through corruption or oppression. If he does, he is not a true king but a tyrant and dictator. Since a king is the source and owner of everyone and everything in his kingdom, the key to a true kingdom is benevolence. A perfect government does not exist for itself; it exists for its citizens.

THE NATURE OF EARTH'S CITIZENS

Being made in the image and likeness of the Creator-King means that human beings possessed his spiritual nature, characteristics, and essential specifications. We were designed to be like, act like, and function like the Ruler of the invisible kingdom.

> *We were designed to be like, act like, and function like the Ruler of the invisible kingdom.*

After the Creator gave us his own nature, he (1) gave us physical bodies so we could function in the physical world he had created and prepared specifically for us, and (2) breathed His very Spirit *into* us, animating and empowering us to fulfill our calling on earth. Moses recorded, "The LORD God formed the man from the dust of the ground and breathed into his nostrils the breath of life, and the man became a living being."

The Creator-King formed man, Adam, from the dust of the earth, which means that this human "product" was present

in the world but wasn't yet alive. His body and brain we?
but they were dormant. We couldn't say that Adam was "dead"
because there was no death at that time. He was what we could
call an "un-living being." It was when the Creator breathed
into him the breath of life that Adam became a living being.

That breath of the Spirit ignited life in Adam in three distinct ways: (1) in the invisible spirit of man, which, being made
in the image of God, is eternal; (2) in the soul of man—meaning the total human consciousness of his mind, will, and emotions; and (3) in his physical body, which became a living vessel
housing the spirit and soul. Man's soul and body gave him an
awareness of his earthly environment, while the Spirit of God,
dwelling within man's spirit, gave him a consciousness of his
Creator-King and the ability to communicate directly with the
heavenly government.

So the Spirit gave life to all aspects of Adam as a human
being. The same was true in the creation of Eve, the first
woman. When God imparted his Spirit to human beings,
humanity experienced the reception of the Spirit of God for
the first time. The Creator's Spirit was our heavenly "Governor" on earth, who proceeded from the King and dwelled with
us in the colony of earth, enabling us to receive, know, and
carry out his will, much as the royal governors guided and led
the people of the colonies.

The statement, "Let us make man in our own image," does
not refer to *looking* alike, but *being* alike. The intent of the Creator-King was to express his nature through humanity. That
nature was to be communicated through man's spirit and manifested through his soul—mind, will, and emotions—eventually
finding expression through his physical body. In this way, human
beings were created by God to live from the "inside out."

Human beings were created to express the *nature* of God—in other words, what he is like naturally. (We might say "supernaturally-naturally," since the Creator-King is a purely spiritual Being.) A human being can relate to and reflect the nature of the Creator only if he possesses his essential image and has his Spirit living within him.

Paul wrote, "The God who made the world and everything in it is the Lord of heaven and earth and does not live in temples built by hands," and "Do you not know that your body is a temple of the Holy Spirit, who is in you, whom you have received from God?" The Creator-King does not live in any type of building, whether church, temple, shrine, or mosque. His only true residence on earth is within his human creation. When his Spirit fills our bodies, we are his dwelling place. In this way, through the creation of humanity, the King built his own royal residence to settle in and from which to govern the colony of earth.

> *Humanity is really a royal family whose Father is the King of a vast and eternal kingdom.*

ROYAL CHILDREN AND FULL CITIZENS

Adam and Eve were the offspring or children of the Creator-King. Humanity is therefore really a royal family whose Father is the King of a vast and eternal kingdom. Human beings were not subjects but had full status of *citizens* of the kingdom, having been given free access to everything on earth.

Then God blessed them, and God said to them, "Be fruitful and multiply; fill the earth and subdue it; have dominion over the fish of the sea, over the birds of the air, and over every living thing that moves on the earth."

The only exception to their complete access to the earth was a restriction on one part of their garden home, which was under the jurisdiction of the King alone. He told them, "You are free to eat from any tree in the garden; but you must not eat from the tree of the knowledge of good and evil, for when you eat of it you will surely die." We will talk more about this restriction in the next chapter.

GEN 3: 16-17

ASSIGNMENT AS VICE GOVERNORS

When the King gave Adam and Eve dominion over the earth, he was delegating authority to humanity. They were made local rulers in the territory of earth under the heavenly Governor. Humanity was like a "little Rome," established on earth for the purposes of the kingdom of heaven and given the assignment of making the earth like the home country. As such, they were like the *patroni* of the Roman colonies who founded and guided the colony on behalf of the kingdom.[5] But while the Roman *patroni* were limited to about three members, each member of humanity to be born on earth was given the mandate of dominion. The earth was to be colonized by all members of the human race. I call this assignment the "Adamic Administration."

To have *dominion* means to govern, to rule, to control, to manage, to lead, to affect, and to impact. Human beings are essentially spiritual beings who live in physical bodies to carry out their governing responsibilities in the material world of the colony of earth. When the Creator-King said, "Let them have dominion," he was saying, "Let them have 'kingdom' over the earth. Let them influence the earth on behalf of my country of heaven." Humanity's job was to execute heaven's policies, legislation, and oversight on earth—to cultivate the life of the heavenly kingdom, manage the earth's natural resources, rule over the animals, govern wisely and justly, and keep everything in order. All these things have to do with the administration of the territory.

THE ROLE OF THE HEAVENLY GOVERNOR

It is important to note that since human beings were made in the image of the Creator-King and given the assignment of administering the earth, the key to their effective rulership was a benevolent governing that had the best interests of the kingdom and its citizens at heart. Only a perfect colonial government could work in a perfect kingdom.

I emphasized earlier that, in a colony, in order for delegated authority to function, it had to have an open channel of communication to the king, as well as the power to perform its responsibilities in accordance with the king's wishes. This is why the Governor—the very Spirit of the King himself—was given to humanity.

The Governor came from the King and was the only one who could suitably transform the colony into the home country. He knew the King's heart, mind, desires, will, and intent, and he was committed to carrying out the King's purposes in the territory. Paul wrote, "For who among men knows the thoughts of a man except the man's spirit within him? In the same way no one knows the thoughts of God except the Spirit of God." In addition, human beings were made in the image and likeness of the King, *with his own personal presence living within them,* so they would be able to transform the colony of earth in to an extension of the invisible kingdom. Who could better implement the transformation process than those who had the very nature of the King and were guided by the very Spirit of the King? In this way, the earth would be intimately related to the home country in nature and purpose.

We see therefore that *the Creator-King's intent was to rule the seen world from the unseen world.* He desired to rule the visible world through the spirit of man. And the Holy Spirit, as Governor of the human spirit, was humanity's bridge to the home kingdom; he was the direct channel of communication between the spirit of man and the government of heaven.

> *The Holy Spirit is humanity's bridge to the home kingdom.*

It was the presence of the Holy Spirit within human beings that gave them the *authority* and *ability* to have dominion over their environment. I mentioned earlier that the primary issue of humanity is one of power, the ability to influence and control life's circumstances. We desire this ability because we were designed to fulfill our original assignment as vice governors on earth. One of the psalmists wrote, "The highest heavens belong to the LORD, but the earth he has given to man."

RULERSHIP OVER A NEW TERRITORY

Let's look at humanity's assignment from one other perspective. A prince or princess who is the king's heir doesn't succeed to the throne if the king is still alive. The only way this might occur (apart from a king abdicating his throne) is for the king's heir to go to another territory to rule. This has happened in history, although rarely. Therefore, while the heir is in the same territory as the king-father, he or she remains a prince or princess. Yet if the heir lives in a foreign country or territory, he or she can rule as sovereign, while the king-father still rules the home country. So, if a king wanted his children to have the same power, authority, glory, and rulership that he possessed, he had to send them to a different territory or territories to rule.

The King of the invisible realm of heaven is eternal. He cannot die. No one will ever succeed him on his heavenly throne. Yet because he delighted in humanity, his children whom he had made in his own image, he wanted them to rule a territory of their own in his name.

This was not a last-minute idea. He prepared the earthly colony before he created the first man and woman. He designed the perfect physical environment for his children to rule in. The first book of Moses recounts the creation of the earth, sea, and animals—which human beings were to rule over as vice governors—prior to the creation of humanity. Then, we read, "The LORD God took the man and put him in the Garden of Eden to work it and take care of it." The natural world, as distinct from the encompassing invisible realm, was an entirely new realm over which humanity could legally have dominion.

The message of the creation of humanity is therefore very practical. It is not about "religion" as we tend to think of it; it is not about rituals. It describes the government of an eternal King and kingdom and the King's royal children whom he made his local governors on earth through the authority and power of his own Spirit. It is about the rule of a King over his territory and the transformation of that territory into the manifestation of his kingdom.

CHAPTER THREE

DECLARATION OF INDEPENDENCE

The greatest threat to kingdom privileges and benefits is an independent spirit.

T he territory of earth had been created and the colony established. The King's children were provided with a rich home and given authority to rule and prosper on earth in behalf of the King. However, something happened to disrupt the home country's plan of expanding the realm of its heavenly kingdom on earth. A rebellion that started in the home country spread to the colony.

A BREACH OF TRUST

THE PLOT: OVERTHROW

The rebellion had been instigated by one of the King's top generals, named Lucifer. He had attempted a coup of the heavenly kingdom and been banished from the presence of the King, along with his followers. This disgraced former aide was bent on revenge and still craved the power to rule a kingdom. He thought that if he could gain control over the King's own children, he could insult the King, thwart the purposes of the heavenly kingdom, and usurp the colony.

THE PLAN: DETACHMENT

Lucifer's plan was to sever the relationship between the King's children and their Father and separate the citizens of the colony from their true government. So he went to the colony in disguise, where the King's children had just begun to rule, and infiltrated their government using craftiness and deceit.

THE STRATEGY: AN INDEPENDENT SPIRIT

His strategy to accomplish this broken relationship was to promote a spirit of rebellion and independence. Subtly questioning the integrity and goodwill of the King, he seduced the King's children to disregard their Father's authority over the colony and encouraged them in an act of insurrection. The following is an account of this incident from the first book of Moses:

> Now the serpent...said to the woman, "Did God really say, 'You must not eat from any tree in the garden'?" The woman said to the serpent, "We may eat fruit from the trees in the garden, but God did say, 'You must not eat fruit from the tree that is in the middle of the garden, and you must not touch it, or you will die.'" "You will not surely die," the serpent said to the woman. "For God knows that when you eat of it your eyes will be opened, and you will be like God, knowing good and evil." When the woman saw that the fruit of the tree was good for food and pleasing to the eye,

and also desirable for gaining wisdom, she took some and ate it. She also gave some to her husband, who was with her, and he ate it. Then the eyes of both of them were opened, and they realized they were naked.

The children of the King went against his explicit instructions, which he had instituted for their protection. The renegade general had planted doubts about the motivation of the King, and distrust grew in their hearts. They immediately turned their backs on all their Father had given them and instead believed the lie placed before them. The children's response was contrary to the nature and desires of the King. It was also a corruption of their own nature, which had been made in his likeness. What seemed to be a harmless act to their benefit was actually a disaster; it represented a series breach of faith and departure from the heart and will of the King. If they could not be trusted with even the simplest aspect of their assignment in the colony, how could they transform the earth into the culture of the kingdom of heaven? Especially now that their minds and hearts were shown to be aligned with the King's bitter enemy?

> *Adam and Eve violated the legal contract heaven had established with human beings.*

THE RESULT: TREASON

The King's own children had declared, "I don't want to be under the kingdom's jurisdiction anymore; I don't want to be under the King of kings; I don't want to be subjected to heaven's government." Yet the earth is heaven's property. When Adam and Eve rebelled and declared independence, they violated the legal contract the government of heaven had established with human beings. Many people think of "sin" as things a person does. Yet it is both deeper and more specific than that. Sin is rebellion against the essential nature and authority of the heavenly government.

By their rebellion, the children not only took something that wasn't theirs, but they also handed it over to someone who didn't deserve it and would never be qualified for it. Lucifer, the unfaithful former general of heaven, would never transform the world into the heavenly kingdom. He would transform it into something completely opposite, a kingdom of darkness.

RENOUNCED ALLEGIANCE AND EXPATRIATION

How did the King react to his children's breach? Although he knew what they had done, he gave them a chance to admit their fault. Instead, they blamed each other, as well as the one who had enticed them to revolt. Like many rebellious children exposed for disobedience, they seemed sorry only to have been caught. The King had no choice but to remove them from the garden; they were banished from the special home that had been provided them because they no longer had the nature necessary to live there, and were no longer able to care for it properly.

The first book of Moses says, "After [the Creator-King] drove the man out, he placed on the east side of the Garden of Eden cherubim and a flaming sword flashing back and forth to guard the way to the tree of life." The word *drove* used here means "to drive out from a possession; especially to expatriate or divorce." It is significant that we find the concept of *expatriate* here, which means "to renounce allegiance to one's native country." Adam and Eve virtually cut themselves off from their own King-Father and home country. Having to drive them out of the garden was as painful to their Father as experiencing a wrenching divorce after the betrayal of a loved one.

Adam and Eve had committed high treason. The King had given them authority under delegated power, but they had instead abused that authority to cut the territory off from the government of heaven.

THE RECALL OF THE GOVERNOR

Although they were removed from the magnificent garden, their former rule, and their previous kingdom life-style, their rejection of the King and his nature led to something far worse. The King had previously alerted them, "You are free to eat from any tree in the garden; but you must not eat from the tree of the knowledge of good and evil, for *when you eat of it you will surely die*." This was

> *Adam and Eve lost their essential source of life as human beings—the King's Spirit.*

the only area on earth over which the King claimed jurisdiction because he knew its misuse would lead to death.

The death the King referred to was not an immediate, bodily death. Adam and Eve did not physically die right away, but they lost their *essential source of life* as human beings—the King's Spirit. Remember that the Spirit of the King gave life to their spirits, souls, and bodies. When they rejected the King, they also rejected and lost his Spirit. The Governor alone was their dynamic connection between the seen and the unseen realms. Therefore, their spirits and souls were cut off from the home country, and their physical bodies began to die a slow death. They were still physically alive for a time, but spiritually and soulically, they were dead to the King and his kingdom.

We saw earlier that, whenever a colony becomes independent from the mother country, the governor is either forced out, or the kingdom withdraws him. Likewise, when Adam and Eve declared independence, the Governor had to be recalled to the heavenly kingdom. I saw a striking illustration of this circumstance the night governing power in the Bahamas was transferred from Great Britain to the new independent government. The Bahamian people had said, "We no longer want to be connected with Britain, as far as direct government control is concerned," and we won our freedom.

Thousands of emotionally charged Bahamians gathered at Clifford Park a few hours before midnight on the evening before independence. The official change in government was scheduled for 12 a.m. on July 10, 1973. Prince Charles, as the representative of the crown, was present, as well as our premier, whose title would soon change to prime minister. There were various ceremonies, and the musical group that I had founded was invited to sing as representatives of the youth of the nation.

At 11:50 p.m., the Union Jack was still flying on the flagpole in the middle of the park. The symbol of the kingdom of Great Britain signified that we were still under England's rule. At 11:59, one of our law enforcement officers stood at that pole and began to lower the flag. Another officer was next to him, pulling up the new flag of the independent Bahamas. We were witnessing a change of kingdoms firsthand. The lower the British flag got, the closer we came to no longer having a royal governor. The higher the new flag got, the closer our premier came to becoming prime minister. When the British flag reached the bottom and the Bahamian flag reached the top, it was over. Early the next morning, the royal governor left the governor's house, got on a plane, and departed from the Bahamas. The queen had recalled him. He no longer had the authority or legal right to be there.

While I've described a joyful period in the national life of Bahamians, it was not a jubilant time for the citizens of earth when they rejected the heavenly government. Again, they had not thrown off foreign rule from their lives. They had rejected their own homeland and their beloved King-Father, who desired to give them the riches of his kingdom. As Adam raised the "human independence flag," the flag of the heavenly kingdom was simultaneously being lowered until humanity was severed from the King and his kingdom.

> *Human beings rejected their homeland and their beloved King-Father.*

I mentioned that the governor of the Bahamas had to vacate the governor's house when he was recalled to the home country. On the colony of earth, the *human beings themselves were the house the heavenly Governor had lived in.* So when humanity declared independence from their King-Father, this house became a hostile and unclean environment, and the Governor could no longer dwell there. He was recalled to the home country.

EXISTENCE WITHOUT THE GOVERNOR

What was life like for Adam and Eve after they turned their backs on the kingdom and lost the presence of the

Governor? Their act of rebellion is often referred to as "the fall" because of the extreme change in the quality of human existence they experienced. It was like a prince falling from a luxurious royal coach into a muddy ditch and then having to live there. Independence, in a human political sense, is a positive concept to us. The American Revolution, in which America declared independence from Great Britain in 1776, is celebrated with fireworks and family gatherings. Yet humanity's independence from heaven's kingdom is nothing to celebrate. It's something to mourn because it's the worst thing that ever happened to human beings, whereas the kingdom was the best thing we could have been given.

> *Humanity's independence from the kingdom was the worst thing that ever happened to them.*

We can begin to comprehend the value of the Governor on earth by looking at what existence without him is like.

LOSS OF THE KINGDOM

The loss of the Governor meant the loss of the environment of the kingdom on earth. Since the Governor was the evidence of the presence of the kingdom, his absence inevitably meant the absence of the kingdom presence. Earth's environment changed to the antithesis of the heavenly kingdom.

CUT OFF FROM TRUE LIFE

Although human beings were designed to live from the *inside out*, this situation was now reversed. Since they had lost the Holy Spirit, which was their connection with their Father, they now had to live from the *outside in*. They became totally dependant on their five physical senses. The physical world—which could give them only a limited perspective on life's realities—imposed itself on their inner world. I believe this is why one of the first words we read about Adam and Eve after their rebellion is the word "realized" or "knew." Suddenly, they *realized* they were naked. Does this imply they didn't know this before? I don't think so. I believe it implies this: nakedness is an external consciousness rather than something that is spiritually discerned. The body and its senses, rather than the spirit, took over humanity's focus in life. Human beings no longer had a *spiritual* perspective at their essence but a *sensual* one.

> *A perspective based only on the senses inevitably leads to confusion.*

A perspective based *only* on the senses inevitably leads to confusion. Humanity began to depend on the soul—the mind, will, and emotions informed by the senses—to interpret life. From then on, what we saw, heard, touched, tasted, and smelled became the dominant components in our human experience. Consequently, we began to interpret our Creator-King mainly from our physical senses, as well. For example, the field of science attempts to understand the unseen world only from the seen world. This approach is dangerous because human beings were never intended to interpret the physical world from itself but from the spiritual reality of the kingdom.

I am not saying that science is "bad." Neither am I saying that the intellect is evil, but only that it has been moved out of its proper position. The intellect is a wonderful gift created by God. It must be in its right position, however, for it to effectively execute its purpose and fulfill its potential. The things that are seen were made from things that are not seen, and the only way to truly understand something is to relate to how it was made and who made it. The Spirit of the Creator is the only avenue we have for fully understanding ourselves and the physical world since he is the Source, Author, and Manufacturer of creation.

We must grasp the deep significance of this truth: Having the Spirit of the King is not only vital for our relationship with the invisible King, but also for understanding our own humanity. Only through the Governor can we know why we are really here and how to interpret the world in which we live; in other words, how to truly *see* our environment. *The Governor is the key to our being fully human.* We can't express the King's nature unless we are in relationship with him, and the Governor provided that relationship.

Only the Governor knows the mind of the King. We can't really be what we were born to be as human beings unless we have a vital connection to his original intent. The Governor is our reference to ourselves; he is the key to our self-understanding. To be true and complete human beings, we must somehow become reconnected to and re-indwelled by the Holy Spirit.

LOSS OF AUTHORITY AND POWER

We not only lost communication with the home country through the loss of the Governor, but we also lost the power and authority he provided. Remember that power is the ability to control and influence circumstances. One of the first things the King said to Adam after his rebellion was, in effect, "From now on, you will have to fight the earth in order to get food." Beforehand, he had said, "Rule over...all the earth." Now the King had to sadly inform him,

Cursed is the ground because of you; through painful toil you will eat of it all the days of your life. It will produce thorns and thistles for you, and you will eat the plants of the field. By the sweat of your brow you will eat your food until you return to the ground, since from it you were taken; for dust you are and to dust you will return.

The King wasn't only speaking of literal thorns. He was saying, "It's going to be hard for you to provide for yourself. You're going to have to sweat for it." Before that, Adam's work was not exhausting. He had authority and dominion over the natural world. It worked for him, rather than the other way around.

RAMIFICATIONS OF SELF-GOVERNMENT

The Governor had been humanity's connection with the home country, enabling human beings to fulfill their authority and dominion on earth. When he left, the earth basically became an independent nation. A colony without a governor results in self-government. Again, to our contemporary minds, *independence* and *self-determination* are positive words. We celebrate freedom and self-government. But again, this was not the triumph of freedom over tyranny. This was not removing the shackles of foreign occupation. It was like rejecting your beloved family, your home country, and your billion-dollar inheritance all at once. To paraphrase the wise King Solomon, "Some paths in life *seem* right, but they lead to death."

There's nothing more dangerous and threatening to a kingdom than a spirit of independence. For human kingdoms, this translates into a loss of power and wealth and probably some pride. For the heavenly kingdom, however, it meant the spiritual death of beloved children who were meant to carry on the family name and legacy. For the children, it meant the introduction of fear, a survival mind-set, and the knowledge of the inevitability of death.

When you are an independent person, you have to survive by your own wits. Likewise, when a country becomes an independent nation, it has to totally pay its own way. When the royal governor left the Bahamas on the morning of July 10, we were totally on our own—in our political and economic life, in caring for our infrastructure, and all aspects of governance. Likewise, humanity was left to fend for itself. Yet human beings weren't designed to function using only their senses. They weren't supposed to live like orphans left to survive in a hostile world on what they can scrape by on, or convicts left to scratch out an existence on a remote, punitive island. Human beings were designed to thrive and prosper and use the heights of their creativity through the guidance and power of the Holy Spirit. The recall of the Governor was a devastating loss to the inhabitants of earth.

A REBELLIOUS STATE

Humanity's declaration of independence and subsequent loss of the Governor left human beings in a state of rebellion. The government of earth, as exercised in the life of every human being, became essentially one of rebellion that did not have the purposes of the kingdom at heart. Every person has been born into this state since the initial rebellion. Theologian Paul of Tarsus put it this way: "For all have sinned and fall short of the glory of God." We all fall short of the essential nature of God and everything that makes him praiseworthy. He is the perfect King; his kingdom is the perfect government. Yet we have distorted the image of that perfection within us. And all our efforts to execute government on earth in personal and corporate ways have fallen deeply short as well.

A Culture of Darkness and Death

When a country becomes independent after being a colony, it usually elects or appoints its own governor. This governor does not teach the people about the culture of the former home country, but only its own. Similarly, when the heavenly government recalled the Governor, human beings stopped learning the culture of heaven and created their own culture, which they passed along to their children. We stopped living heaven's values and began to have our own independent ideas about life.

> *The recall of the Governor was a devastating loss to the inhabitants of earth.*

We must ask ourselves: How well are we doing? What has the nature of our culture become? One of the first things that took place after earth lost the Governor was that a man was murdered by his older brother. What a way to start a new culture! Instead of the kingdom of heaven defining and transforming earth, a kingdom and culture of darkness came upon it and began to spread. Adultery, incest, abuse, and domestic violence are all parts of this culture of darkness; it destroys young and old, strong and weak. We are still experiencing crime upon crime, brother killing brother. Wherever the Governor of the King does not rule, you will find murder and other instances of man's inhumanity to man. The abuse and destruction afflict families, communities, businesses, and government—the whole realm of human existence.

All this transpired because human beings listened to the treacherous lies of a rebellious former aid to our King-Father, who wanted to usurp the colony for himself. Jesus of Nazareth described Lucifer as the "father of lies" and a "murderer." He also said, "The thief comes only to steal and kill and destroy."

When this disgraced former general took authority over the territory of earth, the natural result was devastation and death. His intent as the illegal governor on earth was not to bring freedom. It was to steal people's lives so he could ultimately destroy them. He is a foreign ruler who has taken over the colony of earth and desires to destroy the original culture of the inhabitants. He rules over a destructive kingdom of darkness in which human beings have become either his willing or unwilling accomplices.

> *A kingdom and culture of darkness came upon the earth and began to spread.*

What have we done to this planet? From the time of humanity's rejection of the King and the loss of the Governor, human beings have been attempting to dominate the King's colony without the mind and heart of the King. Trying to run the planet without the King's nature has led to a breakdown in human authority and power to address vital issues. It is the source of the world's poverty, genocide, terrorism, political corruption, drug addiction, broken homes, and every kind of evil that can be named. We have created a state of rebellion and confusion. This world is a disaster without the Governor.

THE PROMISE OF THE KING

The colony of earth crumbled under the absence of the Governor. Without his presence, the human race lost its dignity and sense of responsibility; it became confused and chaotic. The people experienced a living death. Even though many people still struggle to do good, this is the essence of the culture of earth today. As the descendants of Adam and Eve, we are unable to rule on behalf of the heavenly kingdom because we abdicated our rule to Lucifer's culture of darkness.

Yet, remarkably, immediately following humanity's rebellion and the loss of the Governor, the King promised the *return* of the Governor and the restoration of earth as a territory loyal to the kingdom of heaven. The most important promise the government of heaven ever made to humanity was the return of the Governor because he is what every human being needs for true life. He is what the entire world needs, or the territory would forever remain in a state of chaos and death.

Even in the immediate aftermath of the rebellion, the King gave an indication of how he would restore the Governor. He told Lucifer, "I will put enmity between you and the woman, and between your offspring and hers; he will crush your head, and you will strike his heel." The King's plan was to send an Offspring, to be born in the colony, who would restore kingdom influence to the colony. He would crush the power of the realm of darkness, take back the kingdom authority that was stolen, and restore power and authority to those to whom it was first given—humanity. We would be reinstated as local rulers on behalf of the heavenly kingdom once again. This would happen because the King would reappoint the Governor to the colony of earth.

SEEKING THE GOVERNOR

I believe that the bottom line in every person's search for power and meaning in life is this: they are actually seeking the return of the Governor, though they may not realize it. Many people feel they are missing something in their lives yet aren't sure what it is. They try to fill the emptiness with a variety of things: money, relationships, parties, drugs, sex, alcohol, work, sports, or vacations. In fact, I believe that every person, whether he is Christian, atheist, Hindu, Buddhist, Muslim, Shintoist, Scientologist, animist, or even Satanist ultimately desires the same thing. He wants to fill what is missing in his life, and only the presence of the Governor in his life can accomplish this. A human being without the Governor is dysfunctional because he's never complete; his very purpose requires the presence of the Holy Spirit.

Therefore, if a message were sent from the kingdom of heaven to earth regarding the fulfillment of the King's promise—the restoration of the Governor—that message would not be a religion. Neither would it be a self-help method by which human beings could use their own abilities to solve their problems. It would be a message about the kingdom and the return of the King's Spirit.

CHAPTER FOUR

THE PROMISE OF THE GOVERNOR'S RETURN

When the end becomes the means, and the minor becomes the major, then injustice is inevitable.

B efore looking more closely at the King's plan to restore the Governor, let's review some major points regarding the kingdom of heaven and its plan for the colonization of earth:

√ The King of the eternal and invisible kingdom desired to extend his own nature and influence to the physical realm of earth, which he had created. The kingdom of heaven is his governing influence over the world, impacting and influencing it with his will, his purpose, and his intent. Heaven is God's kingdom or home country, and earth is his colony.

√ Human beings were created in the image of the King and were given the Spirit of the King to live within them. The King's Spirit gave life to their spirits, souls, and bodies.

√ Human beings were designed to function like their Creator-King. The presence of the Spirit of the King within human beings guaranteed that they would have his character and nature. It also assured that they would be able to rule on earth as he would rule in the heavenly kingdom, having his very nature of love, mercy, kindness, and forgiveness.

√ The King did not desire to rule the earth directly, but to cultivate his colony through his children, who also functioned as his local governors. They were to exercise dominion over the earth under the direction of the chief Governor, the Spirit of the King.

√ Adam and Eve's declaration of independence cut humanity off from the King and caused the Governor to be recalled by the kingdom of heaven.

√ The departure of the Governor meant the departure of the heavenly government and its direct influence over the colony of earth.

√ After humanity rebelled against the authority of the heavenly government, the King immediately promised to restore the Governor to his children.

√ The most important promise the Creator-King ever made to human beings was the promise that the Governor would return to live within them, because he is the key to life.

√ The restoration of the King's Spirit to humanity is central to the restoration of his kingdom on earth.

All the above leads us to this conclusion: **The principal purpose of the redemptive program of the Creator-King, in his dealings with humanity throughout human history, was the restoration of the Governor to the colony of earth.**

In light of this, let's consider the theme of the sacred literature of the Old or First Testament, also known as the Jewish canon of Scripture. Some say its theme is the creation of a monotheistic religion. Others say it's the story of the rise and fall of the ancient Hebrew nation. Still others see it as the record of various traditions and rituals. If we look at it in any of these terms, however, we miss its crucial essence.

THE THEME AND SIGNIFICANCE OF THE SCRIPTURES

What is the significance of the Scriptures? Why do we have the accounts of Noah, the patriarchs Abraham, Isaac and Jacob, and the story of the nation of Israel? What was the purpose of all the blood sacrifices? Why is there a record of priests, prophets, and the lineage of kings?

While its events revolve around the people and nation of Israel, the theme of the Old Testament is universal: it is the restoration of the key to *humanity's* existence, the reestablishment of true life for *every human being* on the planet. The record of the people and events depict the unfolding of the King's plan to restore his Spirit within

> *The theme of the Old Testament is the restoration of the key to humanity's existence.*

human beings so they can be and do what they were originally intended to; so they can fulfill their remarkable purpose and potential once again.

The first two chapters of Genesis explain the heavenly government's plan for expanding the kingdom to earth. The third chapter describes the interruption of this plan, and the immediate promise of restoration. From the third chapter all the way through the last book of the Old Testament, the King's plan for the return of his Governor to earth is revealed. All the situations, people, and programs we read about serve these ends:

1. They are a continual reminder of the promise of the Governor's restoration.

2. They depict the King's intervention in the lives of specific families on earth to preserve a lineage for the Offspring who would restore the Governor.

3. They depict a prototype of the restoration of the kingdom of heaven on earth.

4. They expose the fact that only the Governor himself can reconnect the earthly colony to its heavenly government.

5. They foretell the coming of the Offspring who will personally reconcile the children-citizens to the King and authorize the return of the Governor.

In other words, after humanity's rebellion, the King's intent was essentially this: "My purpose in creating the world was disrupted, and I'm going to correct it. My Spirit can no longer live in the earthly residence I created. I will therefore restore my Spirit to humanity so my kingdom can function on earth again."

Everything depicted in the Old Testament about the intervention of God in the lives of human beings was ultimately a means to this end. God was revealing to humanity, in effect, "Here's the program: Your rebellion has put you in a hopeless situation. I am therefore going to come to the earth personally, and I will provide a way of restoring purity of heart and wholeness to you, so that the Governor can come to live in you again. Second, I will reappoint the Governor to the colony of earth to live within you once more and carry out my desire to transform the earth into a reflection of my kingdom."

HUMANITY'S NEED FOR HOLINESS

The Old Testament emphasizes the fact that when Adam and Eve lost the Holy Spirit, humanity became *unholy*. I think this word has so many religious images connected with it that we don't really know what it means anymore. We find its essence by looking at what the Creator-King told the nation of Israel: "You will be for me a kingdom of priests and a holy nation." In this instance, he is using the word *holy* in relation to a *nation*. He's obviously not talking about wearing a cross or a liturgical robe or entering a religious order.

So what does the concept mean? There are two related connotations of the word that I want to emphasize here: one of them is "pure," and the other is "devoted" or "dedicated."[1]

These words signify, first of all, something that is *set apart* specifically and purely for a certain use. In this sense, holiness can be applied to many things. For example, I could set apart my favorite cup and say, "This may only be used by me for drinking hot tea, nothing else." I've sanctified it by setting it apart and dedicating it for a specific purpose. Thus, the word *pure* in this context means something beyond just "clean." It has to do with being *pure in use*.

In relation to human beings, the King said his people needed to be "holy unto me." How can you be holy unto a person? Holiness, in this connection, means, "I am devoted only to you. Not only am I dedicated to you, but my loyalty to you is not tainted by any other loyalties. I have no ulterior motives."

Next, let's look at what it means for the Creator-King to describe himself as a "holy" God. Does it mean he's devoted to himself alone? No, it means that he is *true* to himself. He is faithful and consistent in who he is, what he desires, what he says, and what he does. I associate the word *holy* with *integrity*. The King is fully "integrated" or unified. His nature is so pure that he can never have an ulterior or deceitful motive. This is why the King cannot lie. This is also why the King-Father can never disagree with the King-Son, who is the Offspring who came to restore the Governor; and this is why neither of them can disagree with the Governor. The three persons of the Creator-King are one or *integrated*.

Having personal holiness therefore means "to be one with yourself." When Jesus of Nazareth told his disciples, "Be perfect [holy], just as your [King-Father] is perfect," he was saying, "Be one with yourself, as your King-Father is one with himself." Here is the practical application: if you say that you will do something, you do it. If you promise something, you fulfill it. If you are truly holy, you can never say something and then do something contrary to it. Your public behavior is the same as your private behavior. Nothing the King does is ever in conflict with his nature so that he has to hide it. You don't have to hide anything unless you are saying or doing something that is contrary to what you say you are. Adam and Eve had been totally integrated before they disobeyed the King and then lied about it, destroying the trust he had placed in them.

> *Holiness is associated with integrity. It means "to be one with yourself."*

The central issue of the Old Testament is that, when Adam and Eve rebelled, the Holy Spirit had to leave humanity because human beings were no longer pure in motive or integrated in themselves, and consequently were no longer set apart for God or in agreement with him. The Governor is a pure Spirit and could not live in intimate relationship with humanity in that environment.

STAGES OF THE KING'S PLAN

When human beings cut themselves off from the Governor, the King was faced with a supreme challenge. Human beings needed to live in his presence, and to have his presence within them. However, their current state would not permit this. If he wanted to restore the Governor to his children and continue his purpose of having the earth reflect his kingdom, something had to happen to change their state of being.

The King's plan to fully restore the Governor unfolded in stages:

1. He implemented a program that allowed the Governor to come *upon* people, although not *within* them, so as not to violate his integrity. *His Spirit could come upon any person who chose to submit to the influence of the heavenly government.* Since the Governor had been recalled and was therefore "illegal" on earth, he would come and rule in someone's life when that person yielded to his prompting and direction. This wasn't the same influence over the entire world that was in place before the rebellion; it was what we might call "selective rulership" or "rulership by submission."

2. The sacrificial system, which the Hebrew people practiced, and which we will talk more about shortly, allowed the Governor to work on earth through a special nation of people who were meant to be a prototype of the return of the kingdom to the whole world.

3. The King himself would come to earth to restore integrity to humanity, and thus provide a way for the Governor to again live *within* human beings on a permanent basis.

Understanding the Creator-King's program to restore humanity puts the entire Old Testament in the proper light. It is not a group of stories strung together or a handbook of rituals. It is about the King initiating his restoration program.

In Genesis, when the King said that the Offspring would come and "crush the head" of the serpent, this was actually the first promise that he himself was coming to earth—incarnated as a human being—and would defeat humanity's deceiver, reconcile his people to himself, and restore the Governor. The prophet Isaiah wrote, "For to *us* a child is born, to *us* a son is given, and the government will be on his shoulders. And he will be called Wonderful Counselor, Mighty God, Everlasting Father, Prince of Peace."

In this sense, Christmas really began in the third chapter of Genesis. The King-Father was preparing the earth to receive the King-Son. And the old sacrificial system would be replaced by a permanent sacrifice made by the King-Son himself. The New Testament writer to the Hebrews, quoting Psalm 40, wrote, "Sacrifice and offering you did not desire, but a body you prepared for me." From Genesis 4 onward, therefore, the King-Father was working to set apart and preserve a lineage dedicated to his Son's eventual coming to earth. Let's take a fresh look at the Old Testament from this perspective.

INFLUENCE OVER EARTH'S ENVIRONMENT

The Governor's presence on earth through the submission of individuals to the heavenly government was always accompanied by the manifestation of kingdom influence over the earth's environment. In other words, when the King made himself known to people, and they responded by yielding to him and his redemptive purposes, miraculous things would happen on earth. Yet what we call "miracles" were not extraordinary from the point of view of the kingdom of heaven. They were *natural* outcomes of the influence of the heavenly government in the lives of those yielded to the King.

NOAH AND THE FLOOD

After the rebellion of Adam and Eve, the culture of the world became so evil that it had to be virtually destroyed in order to preserve a lineage for the coming Offspring. This is why the Creator-King came to a man named Noah and instructed him to build an ark to save himself and his family from the flood that would destroy the rest of the earth's inhabitants. His message was essentially this: "Noah, the people of the world have become totally wicked, and

> *"Miracles" were natural outcomes of the influence of heavenly government.*

I need to preserve a pure lineage. Therefore, I'm going to start over again with you and your family because you have a heart that is obedient toward me."

Notice that the King's words to Noah after the flood were almost exactly the same as the ones he had first spoken to Adam: "Then God blessed Noah and his sons, saying to them, 'Be fruitful and increase in number and fill the earth.'" The King was continuing the same program with Noah's family that he had begun with Adam and Eve; he did not change his original purpose for humanity on earth because of the rebellion. Instead, he was working out his plan to restore it. Noah was not the actual source of the restoration but was part of the pure (set apart) lineage that needed to be preserved for the coming of the Offspring. The worldwide deluge and the survival of Noah and his family on the ark were the result of the kingdom manifesting its influence through the faith Noah placed in the King and his ultimate purposes for humanity.

ABRAHAM

Ten generations later, Noah had a descendant named Abraham, and the King's plan of preparing a lineage and a body for himself started to take more specific shape. He told Abraham that even though he and his wife were old, they would have a child. This child would be the beginning of a great nation, which in turn would be a prototype of what the kingdom of heaven on earth was supposed to look like. Moreover, one of his descendents would be the promised Offspring.

Sarah's ability to conceive and bear a son in her old age was a result of Abraham and Sarah's willingness to cooperate with the purposes of the heavenly government. Although they did not fully understand the plan, their relationship with the Creator-King brought about the next stage in his redemptive purposes for earth.

Both Noah and Abraham believed and obeyed the King's instructions. Belief and obedience were the means of their holiness or righteousness before him. *Righteousness* refers to "right standing" or "right alignment" with evident authority, and Noah and Abraham lined themselves up with the government of heaven.

THE TRIBES OF ISRAEL

Abraham had his miracle child, Isaac. Isaac had twin sons, Esau and Jacob, and Jacob was chosen as the one to carry on the lineage. Jacob's name was later changed to Israel, which means "Prince with God." He was the heir of the promise of the coming Offspring. Jacob had twelve sons, and each son's family grew and became a large tribe; this was the origin of the twelve tribes of Israel. The Creator-King chose Jacob's son Judah as the one through whom the special lineage would be carried on, even though all the tribes were destined to play a part in the unfolding drama.

THE ISRAELITES: A KINGDOM OF PRIESTS AND A HOLY NATION

Eventually, the twelve tribes moved to Egypt because of a famine in their homeland. They were preserved through the heavenly government's intervention in the life of another son of Jacob's, named Joseph, who became the Egyptian pharaoh's second-in-command. But the tribes eventually become slaves of Egypt under a different pharaoh. After several hundred years, the Creator-King called a man named Moses, of the tribe of Levi, to free the Israelites as part of his plan to preserve a lineage for the birth of the Offspring.

All the events we read about in the life of Moses show the manifestation of kingdom influence on earth through Moses' submission to the purposes of the kingdom government. For example, Moses' ability to bring the plagues of locusts and flies was an example of a human being exercising dominion over "all the creatures that move along the ground" through the power of the King's Spirit. The same is true for the miracle of the parting of the Red Sea that allowed the Israelites to cross over on foot and escape the pursuing Egyptians. Moses was the heavenly government's instrument to bring about many manifestations of kingdom influence on earth during his lifetime.

I want to reemphasize that Abraham, Isaac, Jacob, Moses, and the Israelite nation were not preserved in order to create a religion. The nation of Israel was an instrument in the hand of the King's unfolding purposes to reconcile the whole world to himself and to restore the Governor—it was not an end in itself. The Israelites were called and set apart as a special nation so they could rediscover the King and his ways for the purpose of becoming a nation with a holy (dedicated) purpose. As we will shortly see, they were to be "a kingdom of priests and a holy nation" to help fulfill the King's plan of restoration for the world.

The Hebrew word for "kingdom" in this context is *mamlakah,* which means "dominion" or "rule."[2] Here we return to the theme of earthly dominion. *Kingdom* indicates governing responsibility, while the role of the priest was to help people become realigned with the heavenly government. In essence, priestly work involves lining up with true authority, and kingdom work has to do with executing rulership under that authority. The Creator-King wanted a *kingdom* or nation of priests on earth. He wanted the entire nation of Israel to be properly aligned with him, all the time, the way Adam and Eve had been when they still had the Spirit of the Creator living within them. Every human being was meant to be a priest—personally aligned with the Creator-King—and a ruler—having dominion over the earth.

God had told the Israelites when they came out of Egypt that, if they continued to believe and obey him, he would make them the greatest nation in the world. He gave them instructions for living, called the law. This was a comprehensive picture of how they were supposed to think and act as a kingdom of priests and rulers living in integrity. If they did so, he would provide for them and protect them; they would have everything they needed, and they would never be defeated by their enemies. The nation as a whole was to be a prototype of what the King would do for all who were submitted to his Governor and were ruling their homes, communities, and nations under his guidance.

Sadly, the nation of Israel didn't live up to its high purpose. The people rejected the laws of the King, just as Adam and Eve had. They were no longer in alignment with him. Consequently, they failed to be an example to other nations of the kingdom of heaven on earth. Although there were times when the people returned to their King, they rejected him over

> *The Creator-King wanted a kingdom or nation of priests on earth.*

and over again throughout their history as a nation. Whenever this happened, the King allowed other nations, which didn't acknowledge him, to overrun them so they would see their need and return to him. Throughout the Old Testament, we read how the nation was often overtaken by other peoples, such as the Canaanites, Moabites, and Hittites.

THE MEANING OF THE LAW

When the Israelite people first came out of Egyptian slavery, they had forgotten much about the King and his ways. They had lost a clear conception of his nature and will. They didn't know about Abraham's personal relationship with the King, but had only a vague idea that Abraham was their forefather. This is when God instructed Moses to tell them who they were and what their true purpose was as a nation of kings and priests:

This is what you are to say to the house of Jacob and what you are to tell the people of Israel: "You yourselves have seen what I did to Egypt, and how I carried you on eagles' wings and brought you to myself. Now if you obey me fully and keep my covenant, then out of all nations you will be my treasured possession. Although the whole earth is mine, you will be for me a kingdom of priests and a holy nation." These are the words you are to speak to the Israelites.

With these words, the King established his relationship to the Israelites, and their relationship to him. Then he instructed Moses to tell the whole nation to meet him at the mountain where they were encamped. He wanted to give them his laws directly. He didn't want to give them to just one person who would pass them along to the people; he wanted the whole nation to hear them because all of them were to be rulers and priests. When they came to the mountain, and the King descended to talk to them, they were afraid of the display of his power and greatness. Moses told them not to be afraid but to reverence the King. But instead, the people wanted Moses to serve as their mediator.

Again, the King gave the law so the people would know what it meant to live according to his nature. Yet his ultimate desire was not to have his laws recorded merely on stone or even paper. He wanted them to exist in the spirit of their minds. He revealed his ultimate plan with these words, which he gave to his prophet Jeremiah: "This is the covenant I will make with the house of Israel after that time....I will put my law in their minds and write it on their hearts. I will be their God, and they will be my people." This is a direct reference to the eventual return of the Governor to live within humanity.

For now, however, Moses received the written code, the laws and principles of the kingdom, or the "kingdom standards," to give to the people. Their King wanted them to understand how his Spirit thought and how his kingdom worked so they could stay in alignment with him. If the nation obeyed the King's laws, they would attract his Spirit because they would be living in holiness and be in harmony with his nature.

When Moses came down from the mountain after meeting with the King, the people agreed to obey the law. As we saw, however, this didn't last long. Joshua, Moses' second-in-command, eventually took the people into the land the King had promised them. What we consider amazing miracles at this time, such as the parting of the waters of the river Jordan, the collapse of the walls of the city of Jericho, and the sun standing still and not setting for about a full day during a battle, were merely evidence of kingdom influence over the physical universe. Yet even with all these demonstrations of the presence of the kingdom of heaven among them, the people turned away from the will of the King. They began to intermarry with citizens outside the prototype kingdom and took on the traits of nations that did not acknowledge the King. They gradually became alienated from him and unaligned with his kingdom purposes.

> *The Creator-King gave the law so the people would know how to live according to his nature.*

THE PRIESTHOOD AND SACRIFICES

This is where the priesthood comes in. I don't believe God's real desire was to have a specific group of people called priests. Remember that he wanted a *kingdom* or nation of priests. But in order for the Israelites to remain his prototype nation, he provided a way for them to be restored when they rebelled against him and violated his kingdom standards.

Since they had forsaken their calling to be a nation of priests, the King appointed Aaron, Moses' brother, and Aaron's sons, who were of the tribe of Levi, to be the nation's priests. Their descendents would succeed them as priests. He also told Moses to set aside certain other men of the tribe of Levi to assist the priests in their duties. The priests were to keep themselves aligned with the King. They performed rituals of sacrifice prescribed by the King, which served to atone for (cover over) their rebellion and position the nation of Israel in alignment with the heavenly government again. In this way, the Governor could reveal the will of the King to the people, and his kingdom culture could come on earth through them. The result was that they would bring all other nations back to the King through their example. Therefore, all the sacrifices, the rituals involving the blood, the incense that was burned, the various components of the tabernacle, and later the temple—all these things were for the purpose of realigning the people with God so they could be what they were originally called to be.

The rituals that the priests performed involved the sacrifice of animals because the culture of rebellion, murder, and death that human beings had created needed to be paid for. So did individuals' infractions of the King's law. The first-century writer of the book of Hebrews wrote, "The law requires that nearly everything be cleansed with blood, and without the shedding of blood there is no forgiveness." In the system of sacrifices, therefore, the blood atoned for the violations against the kingdom law that the people had committed.

THE PROMISE OF THE GOVERNOR'S RETURN

When we read about all the intricacies of priestly dress and practice, the systems of worship, and the specific details of the animal sacrifices, we tend to be caught up in the particulars and miss their overall meaning. The ultimate goal of the King's program was not the priests, the robes, the incense, the showbread, the goblets, and the inner and outer courts. Some people almost seem to consider these things as mystical religious icons. Instead, they were a means to an end. They were God's provision (his temporary program) for realigning the people with him so that his Spirit, the absent Governor, could come back to them and intervene on the earth.

The ultimate goal of the entire Old Testament ritualistic program was designed, motivated, and developed for this purpose: when the high priest went in to the innermost chamber of the tabernacle (later, the temple), the sacrifices would be accepted on behalf of the people, and the Spirit of God would be able to come and dwell between

> *Temporary sacrifices brought the Governor into the people's presence but not into them.*

the cherubim on the mercy seat (or atonement cover) there because the requirements for holiness had been fulfilled.

Everything that came in the presence of the Spirit had to be holy because he is a *holy* Spirit. The sacrificial blood would cleanse both the people and the high priest who would stand in the immediate presence of the Governor in the inner room of the tabernacle, called the "Holy of Holies." As a result of these sacrifices, a most beautiful thing occurred. The Spirit came back. The Governor was on earth! All the temporary sacrifices brought the Governor into the people's *presence*, but not into *them*. He could not enter into human beings at that time because the permanent sacrifice had not yet been made.

The animal sacrifices had to be offered again and again because the people were continually rebelling against the authority of heaven, and the sacrifices were a temporary method of atonement that allowed the heavenly government to intervene in their lives, even though it couldn't change their rebellious *nature*.

Whenever the people of Israel were aligned with the King and his Spirit was with them, they won every battle, had no sickness among them, and experienced peace. Why? They were living as true human beings again. They were living as they were intended to live—above their environment and circumstances.

Great lengths had to be taken by the priests just to ensure the Governor's presence in the inner chamber of the tabernacle or temple so the people could be at peace, prosper, and fulfill their role as the prototype nation. When the people disobeyed God, the Holy Spirit left them, and their lives became chaotic again. When they received forgiveness through the sacrifices and again obeyed God, the Holy Spirit would return, and they would have success.

The sacrificial system served its purpose, even though it was inadequate to fully solve humanity's dilemma of separation from the heavenly kingdom. It actually emphasized the incompleteness of the temporary cleansing to keep the people aligned with God. They were "sprinkled" with the blood because the blood of animals cannot permanently cleanse a person from the inside out. The intent of the hearts of men and women are basically and continually evil. The unholy (nonintegrated, non set apart) state of the human heart and its potential for evil are always under the surface and always emerge in one way or another.

Yet this program was the Creator-King's temporary provision for working with human beings, whom he couldn't yet dwell within—because of their unholiness—but still needed to influence. He created his own environment of holiness through the sacrificial system in order to work among his people without violating his purity and integrity. The prophets, priests, and kings of the nation of Israel would receive the Spirit of the King *upon* them for specific instances where they would speak or act on earth in behalf of the King.

Many people like to study and teach all the intricacies of the Old Testament rituals; some even make quite a bit of money off books and products expounding on such things as the "ten keys to the tabernacle." I've found that many people are (at best) missing the main purpose of these things, and other people are (at worst) exploiting people by overemphasizing them. They were not ends in themselves. We must always remember that their whole purpose was to be a means of bringing the governing influence of heaven back to earth for the benefit of humanity.

THE KINGS

Because the Israelites wanted to be just like the other nations around them, having the same standards and lifestyle, they had asked for their own earthly king. The King had told them, in effect, "No, you really don't want an earthly king. A king will just oppress you with taxation and forced labor. I am your King, who provides everything for you and gives you what is good." He was trying to tell them, "You are *not* like other nations. You are supposed to be an example to them. You're supposed to be the prototype for my kingdom."

Human kings were not the King's ultimate plan for his people. He wanted a whole *nation* of kingdom rulers who would be directed by him. This idea reflects his ultimate goal of having every citizen on earth be a local governor, exercising authority under the chief Governor. Yet the Israelites insisted on having a king, so he gave them what they wanted.

The people's desire for a king indicated a lack of alignment with the King and complete misunderstanding of their calling. After they told the prophet Samuel they wanted a king, "the LORD told [Samuel]: 'Listen to all that the people are saying to you; it is not you they have rejected, but they have rejected me as their king.'" They were rejecting their heavenly King once more.

Yet the King used the institution of kings to further his redemptive purposes. The second king over Israel, David, was a man who desired what the heavenly government desires. Kingdom influence was manifested in his life in many ways. His amazing slaying of the giant Goliath when he was still a youth was an example of a human being exercising kingdom dominion over a pawn of the kingdom of darkness. When David said to Goliath, "You come against me with sword and spear and javelin, but I come against you in the name of the LORD Almighty," he was saying, "I come to you under the authority of the government of heaven."

> *Human kings were not the Creator-King's ultimate plan: He wanted a nation of kingdom rulers.*

Ultimately, the King used the line of Israelite kings to preserve the lineage for his Son's coming to earth. The Offspring would be a descendant of David.

THE PROPHETS

However, most of the nation's kings, who were supposed to represent the King's justice on earth, became corrupt. The priesthood also become corrupt. The very ones who were supposed to align the nation to the King had become unaligned themselves. So the King raised up people from within the Israelite nation, at various times, who could speak to both priests and kings on behalf of the heavenly kingdom.

A distinct pattern is emerging: The nation of Israel was raised up as a prototype to address the need of a rebellious people called *humanity*. The priesthood came about when those who were meant to be a "kingdom of priests and a holy nation" failed to fulfill their corporate calling. The institution of kings was established when the people rejected the Creator-King as their ruler. The King therefore raised up individual voices—the prophets—who called upon the kings, priests, and people to change their ways and come back into alignment with him.

The prophets would begin their assignments by saying something like, "The word of the Lord came to me." Where does the word of the Lord come from? It comes from his Spirit. The Spirit would come upon the prophet, and the prophet would tell the king and the priests to correct themselves so they could correct the nation.

In other words, the prophet's job was to bring the earthly king back to the Creator-King so the king could execute the heavenly government's justice and help bring the nation back to the law and ways of the Creator-King. He was also to bring the priests back in alignment so they could help bring the people and nation back in alignment. In this way, the nation could return to being the prototype of the kingdom of heaven. The nation could then correct the *nations* of the world, for the ultimate purpose of redeeming the whole earth.

The prophets manifested the influence of the kingdom on earth in many ways. For example, because the prophet Elijah was submitted to the King, the heavenly government used him to bring back to life the son of a woman who was also submitted to the kingdom. We should not really be surprised at this particular administration of the kingdom, since the King's Spirit originally gave life to humanity and can also restore that life. The heavenly government was manifested in the life of the prophet Daniel when he received special communication through the Governor regarding the future of the Israelite people and when he escaped harm after being thrown into a den of ravenous lions. His "miracle" of preservation was, again, an example of the dominion of the kingdom of heaven over the earth.

However, how did the leaders and people usually react to the prophets? They would ignore, criticize, threaten, or kill them! Eventually, the people were so disobedient as a nation that they were perpetually unaligned; the result was that the Spirit left the temple prior to the people's captivity in Babylon. The Israelites had only the trappings of their old way of life. The prototype nation was essentially gone, setting up the next phase of the plan for the complete restoration of the kingdom on earth.

The King spoke through his prophets, saying, "I'm not going to keep sending word to you through other people. I'm going to come there myself to bring you back to me!"

Governmental Messages about the Coming King Who Would Restore the Governor

The entire Old Testament is therefore about the repetition of the promise of the Governor's return, and the evidence of heavenly kingdom influence selectively manifested through the prototype nation and individuals who were submitted to the kingdom. Over the centuries, specific prophets, as well as other leaders such as Moses and David, spoke messages from the King announcing that he himself would reestablish his kingdom in the colony of earth, paving the way for the restoration of the Governor to humanity. For example, the prophet Isaiah said,

> For to us a child is born, to us a son is given, and the government will be on his shoulders. And he will be called Wonderful Counselor, Mighty God, Everlasting Father, Prince of Peace. Of the increase of his government and peace there will be no end. He will reign on David's throne and over his kingdom, establishing and upholding it with justice and righteousness from that time on and forever.

The King of the eternal, invisible kingdom was going to reclaim his property. When the colony was regained, he would set up his government on earth again and recommission his Spirit as Governor once more. Jesus told a parable about himself that describes the King's desire to implement his plan of extending his influence on earth, and of the resistance of most the earth's inhabitants to him until he himself came to rectify the situation:

> There was a landowner who planted a vineyard. He put a wall around it, dug a winepress in it and built

a watchtower. Then he rented the vineyard to some farmers and went away on a journey. When the harvest time approached, he sent his servants to the tenants to collect his fruit. The tenants seized his servants; they beat one, killed another, and stoned a third. Then he sent other servants to them, more than the first time, and the tenants treated them the same way. Last of all, he sent his son to them. "They will respect my son," he said. But when the tenants saw the son, they said to each other, "This is the heir. Come, let's kill him and take his inheritance." So they took him and threw him out of the vineyard and killed him. Therefore, when the owner of the vineyard comes, what will he do to those tenants?... The kingdom of God will be...given to a people who will produce its fruit.

THE MANDATE OF THE COMING KING

The last book of the Old Testament ends with the prophet Malachi giving this message from the heavenly government about the coming King of heaven: "He will turn the hearts of the fathers to their children, and the hearts of the children to their fathers." This was the mandate of the Offspring, whom the prophets referred to as the "Messiah," to reconcile the children of Adam and Eve to their Creator-King. When this was accomplished, the Governor could be restored to his earthly residence within them.

> *The King of the eternal kingdom was going to reclaim his property.*

THE GOVERNOR'S RETURN IS FOR ALL HUMANITY

The prophet Joel gave one of the major messages from the heavenly kingdom regarding the Governor's return:

Afterward, I will pour out my Spirit on all people. Your sons and daughters will prophesy, your old men will dream dreams, your young men will see visions. Even on my servants, both men and women, I will pour out my Spirit in those days.

Joel was saying, in effect, "I see a day coming when we aren't going to have to read or study the law in order to know how to obey the King because his Spirit will come upon young and old, and they will obey the King as naturally as they formerly disobeyed him." No longer would there be a need for "selective rulership," with only certain individuals being influenced by the Governor. All of humanity had lost the Spirit, and Joel was saying the Spirit would be poured out on "all people"—male, female, Israelite and non-Israelite, free and slave. Earthly prejudices related to gender, race, or social status would disappear in the face of the Governor's return.

The Holy Spirit is not just meant for people of a certain "religion" or nationality. The whole world lost the presence of the Governor within them, and the King wants everyone in the world to receive him into their lives again through the provision of the Offspring. The Governor is the key to life for *all* of humanity.

THE ERA OF THE KING'S COMING

The idea of the Spirit's coming upon the *people* probably seemed incredible to the Israelites when they heard Joel's message. In their experience, the Holy Spirit would only come upon the priests, the prophets, and some of the kings. Or, he would dwell between the cherubim on the mercy seat in the Holy of Holies in the temple. Joel referred to the time of the Spirit's coming as "the day of the LORD." The word "*day*" in this context means "era" or "age." Therefore, the day of the Lord would be the era or the time when the King came to earth.

The word "*LORD*" here is the Hebrew word for "self-Existent or Eternal" one.[3] The message of these prophets was, "Animal sacrifices and other rituals can't restore humanity to its relationship with the King, so the King himself is coming." When he came to earth, his Spirit would also return. The Governor would come upon young and old men, young and old women. More than that, he would once more be able to dwell *within* humanity.

The prophet Malachi was the last prophet to promise the King's return before the King himself came. The heavenly government gave him this message:

> "See, I will send my messenger, who will prepare the way before me. Then suddenly the Lord you are seeking will come to his temple; the messenger of the covenant, whom you desire, will come," says the LORD Almighty.

The first messenger mentioned would *prepare* the way. The second messenger, "the messenger of the covenant," was the one who would "turn the hearts of the fathers to their children, and the hearts of the children to their fathers." This messenger was referred to as "the Lord you are seeking." What was his covenant message? It was the restoration of the Spirit to humanity, which had been promised since the initial rebellion.

ANNOUNCING THE ARRIVAL OF THE KING

When we turn the page of the Scriptures from Malachi in the Old Testament to Matthew in the New Testament, we encounter the messenger who prepared the way for the King's coming:

> In those days John the Baptist came, preaching in the Desert of Judea and saying, "Repent, for the kingdom of heaven is near." This is he who was spoken of through the prophet Isaiah: "A voice of one calling in the desert, 'Prepare the way for the Lord, make straight paths for him.'"

"The kingdom of heaven is near." In other words, the King's government was imminent because the King had come to earth. What was the theme of this message? *The Governor.* John said, "I baptize you with water for repentance. But after me will come one who is more powerful than I, whose sandals I am not fit to carry. He will baptize you with the Holy Spirit and with fire."

The King would *baptize* them with his Spirit, thus *aligning them with the kingdom.* The Spirit's coming would no longer be a temporary appearance but a permanent one. The Governor would be like a consuming fire, burning out every false mind-set and philosophy that alienated the citizens from the heavenly kingdom. He would correct all their confusion and satisfy all their hunger to know and fulfill their purpose in life. At last, they would be permanently reconnected to the King and his kingdom. The earth would be a colony of holiness and power again because its inhabitants would finally have the Spirit of holiness and power living within them once more.

Part 2

The Return of the Governor

CHAPTER FIVE

THE REBIRTH OF A KINGDOM

*The greatest motivation of the human spirit is
to control its environment.*

The King's goal was to cause his children to be integrated, set apart, and devoted to him—so that his Spirit could live within them once more. This would be the work of the Offspring, the one called the Messiah by the prophets. The Offspring was first mentioned in Genesis 3 and was revealed by the prophets Isaiah, Malachi, and others to be the King of heaven himself. While the First or Old Testament emphasizes the promise of the coming King, the New Testament reveals the rebirth of the kingdom on earth through his arrival.

The rebirth of the kingdom signified the recolonization of earth. Recolonization is unheard of in human history, or is at least very rare. Once a people declare independence, they don't go back to the home country. The plan that the King was unfolding was therefore unprecedented.

101

THE BIRTH OF THE KING ON EARTH

The King, of course, needed to remain in the heavenly kingdom as its ruler and sustainer. At the same time, he had to come to earth to provide for the return of the Governor. The Spirit of the King was directly involved in his coming to earth. Luke the physician, the writer of the gospel bearing his name, wrote,

> God sent the angel Gabriel to Nazareth, a town in Galilee, to a virgin pledged to be married to a man named Joseph, a descendent of David. The virgin's name was Mary. The angel went to her and said, "Greetings, you who are highly favored! The Lord is with you." Mary was greatly troubled at his words and wondered what kind of greeting this might be. But the angel said to her, "Do not be afraid, Mary, you have found favor with God."

The angel's statement, "You have found favor with God," shows us that Mary was yielded to the heavenly government and the purposes of the King, and this is why she was chosen for this crucial assignment in the intervention of the heavenly kingdom on earth. The angel continued,

> You will be with child and give birth to a son, and you are to give him the name Jesus. He will be great and will be called the Son of the Most High. The Lord God will give him the throne of his father David, and he will reign over the house of Jacob forever; his kingdom will never end. "How will this be," Mary asked the angel, "since I am a virgin?" The angel answered, *"The Holy Spirit will come upon you, and the power of the Most High will overshadow you. So the holy one to be born*

*will be called the Son of God....*For nothing is impossible with God." "I am the Lord's servant," Mary answered. "May it be to me as you have said."

Again, we see evidence of Mary's submission to the heavenly government: "I am the Lord's servant....May it be to me as you have said."

In this passage is a fact of vital significance: the Spirit conceived God the Son or the King-Son, whose earthly name was Jesus, in the womb of Mary. Mary was what we might call a surrogate mother for the eternal and invisible God's entrance into the physical world as a human being. Also, the King-Son was filled with the Spirit when he was conceived. This means that the Governor returned to earth

> *The King-Son was fully divine and fully human, yet not infected by man's rebellious nature.*

at this time within the person of Jesus. The Governor was resident in the body of Jesus until the rest of humanity could be prepared to receive him as well, through Jesus' provision. At that time, the King-Son would reappoint the Governor to the earth in order to restore kingdom influence throughout the world and to give back kingdom citizenship to humanity.

The King-Son was both fully divine (as God the Son) and fully human (as the man Jesus). Yet he was not infected by the rebellious nature of humanity. The womb of a woman is designed in such a way that the blood of a mother and her unborn child never mix. Jesus' blood was pure; his life was pure. As we read in the third book of Moses, "The life of every creature is its blood." Like Adam before the rebellion, Jesus and everything about him was set apart and devoted to the King-Father.

The Governor Gave the King so the King Could Give the Governor

The King-Son had to be born of the Spirit and filled with the Spirit, so that he could deliver the Governor to the people of earth in fulfillment of the promise. John the Baptist announced to the world the arrival of the King-Son who would restore the Spirit, and he said about Jesus, "The one who *comes from heaven* is above all....For the one whom God has sent speaks the words of God, for *God gives the Spirit without limit* [to him]," and "He will baptize you with the Holy Spirit and with fire." Jesus told his disciples,

> If you love me, you will obey what I command. And I will ask the Father, and he will give you another Counselor to be with you forever—the Spirit of truth. The world cannot accept him, because it neither sees him nor knows him. But you know him, for he lives with you and will be in you. I will not leave you as orphans; I will come to you. Before long, the world will not see me anymore, but you will see me. Because I live, you also will live. On that day you will realize that I am in my Father, and you are in me, and I am in you.

Therefore, *the Governor gave the King-Son to the earth so the King-Son could send the Governor to the earth after he returned to the heavenly kingdom.* They worked in harmony to achieve this ultimate purpose.

The King-Son Was Completely Filled with the Governor

The King-Son not only was filled with the Spirit at his conception, but he also continued to be filled with the Spirit throughout his entire lifetime. As John the Baptist said, "God gives the Spirit without limit [to him]." This was the first time a human being was filled with the Holy Spirit since before the rebellion of Adam and Eve. The Holy Spirit within Jesus was limitless in presence and power.

In preparation for the King's appearance on earth, John had been baptizing people who desired to be realigned with the kingdom. Then, just before Jesus began his public ministry, he also went to John for baptism.

> The next day John saw Jesus coming toward him and said, "Look, the Lamb of God, who takes away the sin of the world! This is the one I meant when I said, 'A man who comes after me has surpassed me because he was before me.' I myself did not know him, but the reason I came baptizing with water was that he might be revealed to Israel." Then John gave this testimony: *"I saw the Spirit come down from heaven as a dove and remain on him.* I would not have known him, except that the one who sent me to baptize with water told me, 'The man on whom you see the Spirit come down and remain is he who will baptize with the Holy Spirit.' I have seen and I testify that this is the Son of God."

John made these declarations about Jesus: (1) he was the one who would take away the sin of the world (making it possible for the citizens to be fully aligned with the heavenly kingdom); (2) the Spirit came down from heaven and *remained* on him (Jesus had the total sanction of the King-Father); and (3) he was the Son of God (he came directly from the King-Father and was one with him). Paul wrote, "In Christ all the fullness of the Deity lives in bodily form." God the Father, God the Son, and God the Spirit are one. The King expresses himself in three unique dimensions, which he revealed in the plan to restore humanity.

Jesus therefore possesses a dual nature—he is fully God and fully human. God the Father is the King, and Jesus Christ is the King who came in human form. The New Testament book of John says, "In the beginning was the Word, and the Word was *with* God, and the Word *was* God." Yet the King's coming as a man wasn't just a convenient way in which to coordinate his rule on both heaven and earth. His mission was to restore holiness to men and women so they could again be a suitable environment for the Holy Spirit to dwell in. As we will see, the only way he could do this was to become a human being himself.

> *Jesus was the fulfillment of the King's plan to send His Son to earth to restore the heavenly government here.*

THE ERA OF THE KING ON EARTH

In a previous chapter, I stated that Jesus began his public ministry by saying, "The time has come....The kingdom of God is near," and I posed these questions:

√ What "time" was he speaking about? And why then?

√ What was the nature of the kingdom he was referring to?

The "time" was the "day of the LORD," or the era when the King-Son would come to earth to restore the Governor to humanity. The purpose and nature of the kingdom was (1) the reconciliation of the earth's inhabitants to the King-Father, so that it was possible once more for human beings to be his children, and (2) the reign of heaven returning to earth through the Governor's presence and power operating in the lives of the King's children.

The inhabitants of the colony of earth had been ransacking the King's territory—stealing, lying, abusing, killing one another, living their lives outside the nature of the kingdom. Therefore, as the Son and heir of the King of heaven, Jesus was coming to reclaim his Father's territory. His arrival on earth marked "the day of the LORD" prophesied by Joel.

The King-Son came to reclaim his Father's property two thousand years ago as a baby born in Bethlehem. Christmas is not about a beggar coming; it's about an owner arriving. He came to reclaim the earth because, as the psalmist David, king of Israel, wrote, "The earth is the Lord's, and everything in it." He came to recover all of creation as its legal owner.

> *Through Jesus, human beings can be restored as vice governors in the world.*

The King-Son didn't come to earth to plead with Lucifer to return his property. He treated him as a thief, saying, "The thief comes only to steal and kill and destroy; I have come that they may have life, and have it to the full." He also said, "How can one enter a strong man's house and plunder his goods, unless he first binds the strong man? And then he will plunder his house." The King-Son came to *bind* the strongman, Lucifer, so he could retake the house and give it back to the children of the household. Therefore, the man Jesus was the fulfillment of the King-Father's remarkable plan to send his Son to earth to restore the heavenly government here.

Paul called Jesus the "last" or Second Adam. The King-Son came to fulfill what the first Adam had failed to do. He lived a life in total harmony with the King-Father, his kingdom, and the kingdom's purposes on earth. Jesus taught his disciples to pray, "Our Father in heaven, hallowed be your name, *your kingdom come, your will be done on earth as it is in heaven.*"

As the Second Adam, Jesus came to rescue us from being dominated by the kingdom of darkness led by Lucifer and to restore us to the home kingdom. He went through his life and death on earth so we could be reconciled to the King as his children.

Through Jesus, human beings can be restored as vice governors in the world, earthly kings who rule under the direction of the Spirit of the King—the Royal Governor. The kingdom of heaven is therefore *a family of kings.* This is what the nation of Israel was meant to demonstrate as a prototype: "a kingdom of priests and a holy nation." Although the Governor is equal to the King-Father and the King-Son, the Scriptures never refer to him as a King in relation to humanity, but as our Counselor or Comforter. This is because his role is to sustain and perpetuate the will and work of the heavenly kingdom in the lives of the inhabitants of earth.

THE KING-SON REINTRODUCED THE KINGDOM OF HEAVEN TO HUMANITY

Jesus' first declaration in his public ministry was essentially his mission statement: "Repent, for the kingdom of heaven is near." He continually repeated this same message for three-and-a-half years during his entire ministry on earth. Throughout the written record of his life in the New Testament writings of Matthew, Mark, Luke, and John, we find him restating his central theme of *the kingdom of heaven.* Sometimes, he would use the phrase *the kingdom of God.* While these phrases are essentially the same, you could say that the kingdom of heaven is the *place,* while the kingdom of God is the *influence.* The kingdom of heaven is the headquarters, the invisible country where the King-Father resides. The kingdom of God is the influence of that country on its territories. Here is a sample of the King-Son's other statements concerning the kingdom:

√ Jesus went throughout Galilee, teaching in their synagogues, preaching the good news of the kingdom, and healing every disease and sickness among the people.

√ "But if I drive out demons by the Spirit of God, then the kingdom of God has come upon you."

√ "The kingdom of heaven is like a king who wanted to settle accounts with his servants...."

√ "The kingdom of heaven is like a landowner who went out early in the morning to hire men to work in his vineyard...."

√ "The kingdom of God will be...given to a people who will produce its fruit."

Lucifer (also called the devil or Satan) knew that the King-Son had come to overthrow him to restore the heavenly kingdom on earth. He therefore tried to tempt Jesus away from his mission by appealing to his natural human desire to exercise dominion over the earth. Notice that Lucifer tried to get Jesus to substitute the kingdoms of the world for the kingdom of heaven, which is basically the same thing with which he had tempted Adam and Eve. This would allow Lucifer to maintain his oppressive domination and destruction of the earth. Yet the King-Son was totally loyal to the kingdom. He countered Lucifer's temptation by rebuking him with the words of the King-Father, which were first given to the Israelites after they came out of Egypt. The New Testament book of Matthew records,

> The devil took him to a very high mountain and showed him all the kingdoms of the world and their splendor. "All this I will give you," he said, "if you will bow down and worship me." Jesus said to him, "Away from me, Satan! For it is written: 'Worship the Lord your God, and serve him only.'" Then the devil left him.

BAPTISM INTO KINGDOM PHILOSOPHY

Jesus' temptation by the devil occurred right after his baptism by John. Many people are confused about the true nature of baptism and why Jesus himself was baptized. While baptism is treated as a religious ritual by many people, it is actually a very practical act that is related to the will of the King and his desire for the colony of earth.

When a person was baptized, he was signaling that he aligned his thoughts and actions with his master teacher.

CHANGING ONE'S THINKING AND LIFESTYLE

At the time Jesus lived on earth, various rabbis, teachers, and groups (such as the Sadducees) baptized their followers. Baptism in this context meant you were publicly declaring you believed in a particular teacher and his philosophy. In fact, to a large degree, this was the significance of the baptism of John, which John referred to as a "baptism of repentance." Our contemporary connotation of the word *repentance* doesn't really convey John's meaning. In its essence, repentance does not mean crying or wailing over wrongdoing. It simply means to change your mind, to reverse your way of thinking and acting.[1] When a person was baptized, he was signaling that he was changing his thinking and actions and aligning them with the views and life of the teacher he had committed himself to follow.

This type of teacher-student relationship was not uncommon. The Old Testament makes references to "the company of the prophets," also called the "schools of the prophets." These particular prophets were closely associated with the well-known prophets Elijah and Elisha, supporting them and learning from them. In New Testament times, the Pharisees, the Sadducees, and the Herodians had disciples. Outside the biblical world, we note similar teacher-learner arrangements among the Greek philosophers Socrates, Plato, and Aristotle and their followers. A philosopher, of course, is someone who sets forth his own ideas about life. Philosophers attract people who want to learn their ideas and imitate their lifestyles, and these become their students or disciples. The Greek word we translate as *disciple* means "learner" or "pupil."[2] Disciples were personally trained by their masters in the masters' philosophies and belief systems, perhaps traveling with them as they learned to think and act like their masters.

JOINING A SCHOOL OF THOUGHT

When you became a student of a philosopher or other teacher, you joined what is called his school of thought. Schools were not originally associated with buildings. They were essentially the ideas unique to a teacher. They were the teacher's philosophical concepts and ways of thinking, which he passed along to his followers.

From this perspective, the significance of baptism is not the water or even the act of being baptized—it has to do with the *transformation* of your way of thinking and living. When you were baptized in the name of your master teacher, you were saying, "I am choosing you above every other available teacher, philosopher, rabbi, and leader, and I am publicly declaring that I am submitting to your school of thought. I'm going to be associated with you *only*, so that whenever people see me, they're going to know, 'He belongs to that teacher.'"

> *Jesus is the Master Teacher; the kingdom is the embodiment of his teaching.*

As I mentioned, at the time of Jesus, there were a number of teachers and philosophers, and all had their own schools of thought and their own disciples. In that culture, a man couldn't begin such a school until he was thirty years old because this was the age at which a young man could be officially designated as a master teacher.

Therefore, when the Creator of heaven and earth himself came to earth as a man, he entered the culture of the day and presented himself in a way that the people would understand the life-changing nature of his message and its requirement of total commitment to him. It was at age thirty that Jesus began his public ministry, became the ultimate Master Teacher, and welcomed those who desired to follow him. *The kingdom* was the embodiment of his teaching.

JESUS' MESSAGE WAS IN HARMONY WITH JOHN'S MESSAGE

Note that John the Baptist had been presenting the same message about the kingdom. Jesus was fully aware of John's message when he went to him for baptism. Many people are at first surprised to read of the King-Son submitting to a master teacher for baptism. Yet he did this to demonstrate to the people of the world that his teaching was not independent of John's; rather, he was in total harmony with it. In fact, Jesus himself was the *fulfillment* of the teaching of John who, as the faithful prophet of the King-Father, was proclaiming the message of the kingdom and preparing the way for the King-Son's appearance in the world.

John had been gaining a number of disciples, and when people came to him with a sincere desire to repent (to change their thinking and lifestyle from the kingdom of darkness to the kingdom of heaven), he baptized them. Yet when Jesus went to him for baptism, John was taken aback and said, in essence, "You should be the teacher, not me!" John recognized Jesus as the King who would send the Governor to earth. In fact, John had said to the people earlier, "After me will come one more powerful than I, the thongs of whose sandals I am not worthy to stoop down and untie. I baptize you with water, but he will *baptize you with the Holy Spirit*."

Jesus, however, replied to John, "Let it be so now; it is proper for us to do this to fulfill all righteousness." He was saying, "I understand your reluctance to act as master teacher to me. However, in order to demonstrate to the world that I am aligned with the kingdom of heaven, I need to be identified with it through baptism. I need to publicly declare that I belong to the school of the kingdom of heaven, that I am fully integrated with the mind and ways of the kingdom."

THE KINGDOM SCHOOL TRANSFERRED TO JESUS

When a master teacher was no longer able to teach, he would decide which of his disciples would succeed him. Whoever was chosen to take his place would automatically gain his students. Jesus had to be a part of John's school in order to take over leadership of it. And John turned the whole school over to Jesus; he released his disciples to him, indicating that Jesus was the one they should follow because he was the King who would restore them to the kingdom. The New Testament book of John records,

> *We are followers of Jesus when we identify with his life and message and submit to him as Master Teacher.*

> The next day John was there again with two of his disciples. When he saw Jesus passing by, he said, "Look, the Lamb of God!" When the two disciples heard him say this, they followed Jesus. Turning around, Jesus saw them following and asked, "What do you want?" They said, "Rabbi" (which means Teacher), "where are you staying?" "Come," he replied, "and you will see." So they went and saw where he was staying, and spent that day with him. It was about the tenth hour. Andrew, Simon Peter's brother, was one of the two who heard what John had said and who had followed Jesus.

Most importantly, we should note that the King-Father had appointed Jesus as the ultimate Master Teacher of the kingdom school. After Jesus submitted to John's baptism to show that he was immersed in the philosophy of the kingdom and in alignment with it, what happened to him? The *Holy Spirit*—the Governor—descended on him. The New Testament book of Matthew says,

> As soon as Jesus was baptized, he went up out of the water. At that moment heaven was opened, and he saw the Spirit of God descending like a dove and lighting on him. And a voice from heaven said, "This is my Son, whom I love; with him I am well pleased."

The King-Father was confirming, "This one has the Holy Spirit; he is my Son, and he is fully integrated with my thoughts and ways. He is the one who will restore my Spirit to the earth." Later on, the King-Father affirmed that Jesus was the one whom his disciples were to listen to above all others, when he said, as documented in the book of Mark and elsewhere in the New Testament, "This is my Son, whom I love. Listen to him!"

Jesus had many disciples or students, but he chose twelve to be in full-time traveling work with him and to learn from him in an intense training relationship. Among these were the notable apostles Peter, James, and John. When Jesus called various of his disciples, saying, "Follow me," he was inviting them to join the school of the kingdom of heaven.

We are followers of Jesus when we have decided to identify with the life and message of the King-Son and submit to him as our Master Teacher. Jesus said, "No one can serve two masters. Either he will hate the one and love the other, or he will be devoted to the one and despise the other. You cannot serve both God and Money." Although this statement was about money, it also has broader application. In the context of baptism, it tells us, "You cannot be in two schools. You cannot have two philosophies that are in contradiction to one another."

BAPTISM WITH FIRE

Water baptism aligned and identified Jesus' followers with his kingdom teaching. But what had John meant when he said that Jesus would "baptize...with the *Holy Spirit* and with *fire*"? The baptism with the Holy Spirit, which we will talk about in more detail in later chapters, is the consummation of identification with the King and his kingdom, as well as a reception of the *power* of the heavenly kingdom. The Holy Spirit is the personification of the heavenly government. To be baptized in this way means you are immersed in kingdom philosophy and lifestyle, and that it has total influence over your thoughts and actions.

The word *philosophy* is derived from the Greek word *philosophos,* which is a combination of two smaller Greek words. *Philos* means "fond" or "beloved," and *sophos* means "wise." So *philosophos* means a fondness for or a love of wise things.[3] Disciples of kingdom philosophy are to fall in love with the mind and will of the King, so that his mind and will become theirs, and their actions mirror his. As the wise King Solomon wrote, "As a person thinks within himself, so he is."

> *The only way to live the life of the kingdom is to be submerged in the mind-set of the King.*

This process of transformation into kingdom thinking and lifestyle is absolutely necessary because the Creator-King has declared this about the rebellious inhabitants of earth: "My thoughts are not your thoughts, neither are your ways my ways....As the heavens are higher than the earth, so are my ways higher than your ways and my thoughts than your thoughts." Our thoughts and ways need to become realigned with the Creator-King's, and we do this by identifying completely with kingdom thinking, submitting to the Master of the kingdom, and being baptized into his power.

The way to fully live out the life of the kingdom, therefore, is to be baptized with the Spirit. We are to be totally submerged in the Creator-King's frame of reference and mind-set so that we always think his thoughts, live his thoughts, and manifest his life.

The New Testament book of Luke tells us that, following his baptism by John, Jesus was "full of the Holy Spirit,...and was led by the Spirit in the desert, where for forty days he was tempted by the devil." When he emerged from that experience, having overcome each temptation, Luke further records, "Jesus returned to Galilee in the power of the Spirit," and the book of Matthew adds, "From that time on Jesus

> *The message of the kingdom and the power of the Spirit are intimately connected.*

began to preach, 'Repent, for the kingdom of heaven is near.'" The message of the kingdom and the fullness and power of the Spirit are intimately connected.

THE KING-SON DEMONSTRATED THE INFLUENCE OF THE KINGDOM ON EARTH

The King-Son not only spoke the message of the kingdom, but he also lived it out. His entire life on earth was evidence of kingdom rulership. Everything Jesus said or did was the administration of the King-Father's will through the power of the Governor within him. He spoke about this reality with statements such as these:

√ My teaching is not my own. It comes from him who sent me.

√ These words you hear are not my own; they belong to the Father who sent me.

√ My Father is always at his work to this very day, and I, too, am working.

√ I and the Father are one.

√ I tell you the truth, the Son can do nothing by himself; he can do only what he sees his Father doing, because whatever the Father does the Son also does. For the Father loves the Son and shows him all he does.

√ Do not believe me unless I do what my Father does. But if I do it, even though you do not believe me, believe the miracles, that you may know and understand that the Father is in me, and I in the Father.

√ If God were your Father, you would love me, for I came from God and now am here. I have not come on my own; but he sent me.

√ I came from the Father and entered the world; now I am leaving the world and going back to the Father.

In the Old Testament accounts we reviewed in the previous chapter, we saw that what we call miracles were actually evidence of kingdom influence on earth. The same thing applies to the miracles Jesus performed. The administration of the kingdom could be seen whenever Jesus healed someone who was sick (power over the effects of humanity's rebellion), delivered someone who was possessed by an agent of Lucifer (power over the kingdom of darkness), fed thousands by multiplying small amounts of food (power over the natural world), or raised people from the dead (power to give life). These acts were confirmation of heavenly dominion over the environment of earth; they were demonstrations of kingdom power over circumstances. Jesus was saying, in essence, "What you see is what the heavenly government is doing. I'm just manifesting it."

THE KING-SON DIED TO REDEEM AND RESTORE HUMAN BEINGS TO THE KING-FATHER AND HIS KINGDOM

The King-Son's mission on earth was not only to deliver the message and demonstrate the influence of the kingdom, but also to provide a way for human beings to reenter the kingdom and be reconciled to the King-Father. The children's separation from the Father because of their rebellion had to be addressed. And the only way their holiness (integrity or internal wholeness and devotion to the Father) could be restored was through a sacrifice.

As we saw, the Old Testament animal sacrifices of the tabernacle and temple were only temporary. Animal sacrifices were not equitable blood payment for the rebellion and the culture of hatred and death that human beings had brought to earth. Animal sacrifice did not have the power to change the perpetually evil hearts of the world's inhabitants. Only human blood could make restitution for the rebellion and bloodshed of humanity. Instead of making the people pay for their rebellion with their own blood, however, the Father sent the Son to earth as a human being to pay for it with his blood. The Son took the punishment for all the inhabitants of earth, which allowed them to be reconciled to the kingdom. This was the ultimate reason for his incarnation.

The King-Son could reconcile the inhabitants to the King-Father because he was holy. Again, in his humanity, Jesus was like other human beings in all ways except one—he had no rebellion in him or double-mindedness toward the kingdom. He was fully integrated, devoted, and set apart for the King-Father. He lived within a human body because he wanted to go through every aspect of human experience—he desired to feel what we feel and experience everything about being human, without the rebellion. **Jesus demonstrated by his life what it meant to be a human being with the Governor living within. He was true humanity rightly related to the King-Father and his kingdom.**

Jesus' death on the cross at the place called Calvary (meaning "Skull") was the plan of the Father to provide for the return of the Governor. It was not a mistake, but part of the program. The earthly temple with its sacrifices would no longer be needed because the heavenly temple had arrived in Jesus' own body; the Holy Spirit was present within *him*. Again, Jesus was able to be the ultimate sacrifice because he was fully aligned with the King and lived a perfect life. Jesus explained the nature of his death before he died:

> The reason my Father loves me is that I lay down my life—only to take it up again. No one takes it from me, but I lay it down of my own accord. I have authority to lay it down and authority to take it up again. This command I received from my Father.

The King-Son laid down his life in payment for the rebellion of all humanity, past and present. When this was paid, the Father gave him authority to take up his life again, and he was raised from the dead. The Author of life chose to die because of his love for the human beings whom he had created; he desired to rescue them from the kingdom of darkness so they could live within the kingdom of heaven once more. Paul described our entrance to the kingdom through the King-Son's sacrifice as walking in "newness of life":

> Do you not know that as many of us as were baptized into Christ Jesus were baptized into His death? Therefore we were buried with Him through baptism into death, that just as Christ was raised from the dead by the glory of the Father, even so we also should walk in newness of life.

Some people wish they could go back to the day Jesus died and prevent his death. We would all want to spare anyone from that kind of death. However, his dying was necessary to fulfill the Father's restoration plan. Jesus' death wasn't forced upon him; he chose it for the express purpose of saving the world and releasing the Governor to the earth again. Once more, before he was crucified, Jesus made his choice very clear, saying,

> I am the good shepherd; I know my sheep and my sheep know me—just as the Father knows me and I know the Father—and I lay down my life for the sheep. I have other sheep that are not of this sheep pen. I must bring them also. They too will listen to my voice, and there shall be one flock and one shepherd.

Jesus told his followers beforehand that he was going to die to pay for the rebellion of humanity, even though they didn't comprehend it at the time. He said, "This is what is written [was predicted by the King's prophet]: The Christ will suffer and rise from the dead on the third day."

Jesus therefore wasn't killed as a tragic mistake. He gave up his life in sacrifice so we could be cleansed vessels for the Governor to live in. He kept moving forward with the restoration plan until everything was set in place for our reconciliation with the Father. Just before he died, he said, "It is finished." The enemies of Jesus didn't finish him. He gave up his life when he was finished with his mission. Just before his arrest, he prayed,

> Father, the time has come. Glorify your Son, that your son may glorify you. For you granted him authority over all people that he might give eternal life to all those you have given him. Now this is eternal life: that they may know you, the only true God, and Jesus Christ, whom you have sent. I have brought you glory on earth by completing the work you gave me to do. And now, Father, glorify me in your presence with the glory I had with you before the world began.

Again, Jesus wasn't a helpless victim of jealous enemies. He is the King of glory who overcame both sin and death. Notice that he prayed to the Father, "I have brought you glory on earth by completing the work you gave me to do." The Old Testament prophet Habakkuk had foretold, "The earth will be filled with the knowledge of the glory of the LORD, as the waters cover the sea." Because Jesus completed the work of restoration, the glory (nature) of the kingdom of heaven was released and began to spread throughout the earth.

> *Because Jesus completed the work of restoration, the kingdom was released on earth and began to spread.*

THE KING-SON DESTROYED THE SPIRIT OF INDEPENDENCE AND REBELLION IN THE COLONY

Jesus' death at Calvary, the blood that he shed on the cross, and his resurrection from the dead were required in order to break the spirit of rebellion in humanity. I use the word *spirit* because rebellion is really an attitude or nature within every human being. It's something we're born with; it is ingrained within us. This spirit is antagonistic to the kingdom of heaven. It couldn't be wished away or ignored. It had to be *broken*. And Jesus did break this power, allowing the earth's inhabitants to instead yield to

> *In the kingdom of heaven, trust in the King-Son is the only way to experience life.*

the Holy Spirit. Paul wrote, "For the sinful nature desires what is contrary to the Spirit, and the Spirit what is contrary to the sinful nature. They are in conflict with each other, so that you do not do what you want. But if you are led by the Spirit, you are not under law."

Breaking a spirit of independence is very difficult, but this is what Jesus accomplished. He gave us the ability to say to the Father, as he himself said at the most difficult point in his earthly life, "Not my will, but yours be done." He provided for the spirit of rebellion to be replaced with a spirit of yieldedness to the kingdom. He gave us the ability to obey the will of the Father. In fact, Jesus said that submitting to him was the same thing as submitting to the Father, since he and the Father are one. "If you love me," he said to his followers, "you will obey what I command. And I will ask the Father, and he will give you another Counselor [the Governor] to be with you forever."

Can you imagine anyone in American politics telling the voters, "Do everything I say"? They would think he was crazy because we're taught not to trust anyone like that. But Jesus came to bring back the *perfect* government. In the kingdom of heaven, trust in the King-Son is the only way to experience life. In the kingdom of heaven, independence from the King-Son brings death, as Jesus explained to his disciples:

> Remain in me, and I will remain in you. No branch can bear fruit by itself; it must remain in the vine. Neither can you bear fruit unless you remain in me. I am the vine; you are the branches. If a man remains in me and I in him, he will bear much fruit; apart from me you can do nothing. If anyone does not remain in me, he is like a branch that is thrown away and withers; such branches are picked up, thrown into the fire and burned.

Jesus was destroying the idea of independence and rebellion, showing that this leads to deadly consequences. In contrast, dependence on him leads to life because "apart from [him] you can do nothing." We are to be dependent on him so that he can help us be what we were created to be. Paul discovered this truth firsthand. Jesus told him, "My grace is sufficient for you, for my power is made perfect in weakness." Paul's response was to say, "When I am weak, then I am strong [in the power of the kingdom]."

The key, then, to being freed from the grip of rebellion, restored to wholeness and devotion to the King-Father, and released in the power and life of the Spirit is to acknowledge and receive the cleansing that the King-Son accomplished for us when he paid for our rebellion through his death. His was the ultimate sacrifice for the rebellious nature of humanity. It was a sacrifice for *all* of humanity. It is available for *all* people. Yet each human being must make a personal decision to commit to Jesus' kingdom school and enter into the kingdom by accepting his sacrifice to break the spirit of rebellion and by desiring to realign with the King. As he does this, he will receive the nature of the kingdom within.

"He Lives with You and Will Be in You"

This brings us back to what Jesus told his followers about the Governor, the Spirit of the King: "He lives with you and will be in you." Jesus' followers had seen the demonstration of the Governor's power lived out in his life. The Governor's works were manifested on the earth, but no other human being besides Jesus had the Spirit living within. Jesus was promising the disciples that, through his sacrifice, the Governor would be coming back to live within them, also, just as had been promised since Genesis 3 when the rebellion occurred. This would not only *align* them with the nature and thinking of the kingdom, but it would also *empower* them to live it out just as Jesus had lived it out on earth. Soon, the Governor would be taking up his official residence again in the citizens of the kingdom on earth, as the prophet Joel had foretold.

The King-Son's Ultimate Reason for Coming to Earth

After his resurrection, Jesus told his disciples, "I am going to send you what my Father has promised." The King-Son was restating the essential reason for his ministry. This next statement may shock a few people, but I believe it is vital for us to

125

understand: the promise of the Father was not Jesus' sufferings, his death on Calvary, or even his resurrection. Over the centuries, the Christian church has emphasized these aspects of Jesus' ministry to the point that I believe the ultimate reason he endured them has been obscured.

Through the years, people—especially religious people—have changed the meaning of the Father's promise to humanity. Christianity has become the celebration of what Jesus did rather than a reception of the reason He did it. We have declared a message that Jesus never gave. We've changed the promise into one of leaving this earth and going to heaven, when what we're called to is restored *dominion* over the earth through the indwelling Spirit.

The result is that we have worshipped Calvary, rather than benefiting from it. Jesus' sufferings, death, and resurrection were the means to an end—the reconciliation of humanity to the King, and, ultimately, the restoration of the Spirit to humanity. They were not ends in themselves. We've made the process the purpose. The promise of the Father was the reappointment of the Spirit *as a result* of these things. The entire reason for the King-Son's coming into the world was to break the stronghold of Lucifer, destroy the grip of rebellion from human beings, and reconnect them to their King-Father so that the Governor could be restored to them.

> *In order to fulfill their purpose on earth, human beings need the Spirit.*

The Spirit is what all human beings need in order to be realigned with the King and fulfill their purpose on earth. We should note that John the Baptist never emphasized the blood or death or resurrection of Jesus. He emphasized the Holy Spirit, because John was expressing the specific reason for his coming: "He will baptize you with the Holy Spirit and with fire." Humanity is not in need of a "religion." We don't need rituals and traditions. We need this promise of the Father to be a reality in our lives.

We must come to truly understand that the Holy Spirit is the heavenly government personified. He is the source of the power of the kingdom in our lives. The Old Testament experience of the priests and prophets was only a shadow of what was to come. At that time, the Holy Spirit couldn't live in human beings; he could only be among them. But now, Jesus was saying, "The Spirit of truth...lives *with* you and will be *in* you."

As I said earlier, every miracle of Jesus, every healing, every act of dominion—whether it was walking on water, casting out demons, or cleansing a leper—was not for entertainment or for making an impression; nor was it for the purpose of creating a religion or providing interesting material for preaching. These things were for the purpose of producing *evidence* to the world that the Spirit of the kingdom had returned to earth and would soon live within humanity again.

Just before Jesus died, he gave his disciples many instructions, and these instructions had important information about the Governor. He was trying to tell them, in effect, "Everything I'm about to suffer is all because of my purposes concerning the Holy Spirit in your lives and in the lives of those who will believe in the future." He told them, in essence, "I'm going to leave you, but don't panic or worry. The Governor is going to come back; he will be with you forever, and he'll never forsake you."

A striking illustration of the Governor's return occurred at the moment of Jesus' death. The curtain in the temple separating the people from the Holy of Holies tore in two from top to bottom, signaling that Jesus had made provision for human beings to be holy and receive the Spirit once more. The Spirit no longer had to be separated from them, dwelling only between the cherubim on a mercy seat that had been sprinkled with the blood of animals. Because of Jesus' ultimate blood sacrifice, the Spirit could once more be at home *within human beings*, giving them direct access to the King.

THE GOAL OF THE KING

The King's desire to restore the Holy Spirit to humanity, therefore, is what made the entire redemptive program of Jesus Christ necessary. The principle goal and primary purpose of Jesus' coming into the world was to deliver the Governor of heaven to the colony of earth. *Everything* else was a means to that end. He didn't come to bring us to heaven. He came to bring heaven to earth. This is why our Master Teacher taught us to pray, in what we call The Lord's Prayer, that the King-Father's influence, will, intent, and laws be done on earth—the colony—as they are in heaven—the home country.

THE ROMAN EMPIRE AS A TYPE OF THE HEAVENLY KINGDOM

The best time in history for the concept of the heavenly kingdom to be fully communicated to the inhabitants of earth was during the time of the Roman Empire, and this is a major reason why the King-Son, the Messiah, was born at that time. It was not a random choice by the King; it was the perfect time. Paul wrote,

When the *time had fully come,* God sent his Son, born of a woman, born under law, to redeem those under law, that we might receive the full rights of sons. Because you are sons, God sent the Spirit of his Son into our hearts, the Spirit who calls out, "Abba, Father." So you are no longer a slave, but a son; and since you are a son, God has made you also an heir.

The structure and functioning of the Roman Empire (though not its moral nature) at the time of Jesus served as a type of the kingdom of heaven. For those living under its rule in Palestine, the analogy would have been obvious. Caesar was the emperor or king in Rome, and he was a type of the heavenly King.

Caesar sent Pilate to be his procurator or governor over the region of Judea, to oversee it and create the culture of the Roman Empire there. Similarly, Jesus said that when he returned to the Father, the Governor would be released to earth, enabling the inhabitants to fulfill the will of the King on earth once more, making it into a replica of the kingdom of heaven. Jesus told his disciples, "When the Counselor comes, whom I will send to you from the Father, the Spirit of truth who goes out from the Father, he will testify about me," and "I am going to send you what my Father has promised; but stay in the city until you have been clothed with power from on high."

Political concepts familiar to the people of the time were present for them to come to understand that Jesus was talking about the return of the Governor to earth to enable them to fulfill the will and work of the kingdom of heaven. Interestingly, Jesus' enemies recognized that his message was about a kingdom, not a "religion." This kingdom demanded full loyalty to the King-Father through the King-Son. Because Jesus' enemies did not want to submit to the authority of the heavenly government, they sought to kill him. They told Pilate that Jesus was a threat to the political order of the day, saying, "We have no king but Caesar." In this way, they pressured Pilate into choosing between killing an innocent man and appearing to support a king other than Caesar. He caved to the pressure and allowed Jesus to be crucified. He was responsible for his choice, even though Jesus' death was part of the heavenly restoration plan. Every person essentially faces the same choice. Allegiance to the kingdom of heaven does not allow for any person or anything to take the place of the King.

THE RELEASE AND RECEPTION OF THE GOVERNOR

After the King-Son's life on earth, a process unfolded by which the Governor was given to his followers. First, of course, the Holy Spirit dwelled within the body of Jesus—the first human being to have the Spirit within him since Adam and Eve. When Jesus died on the cross, eyewitness and disciple John recorded that he "gave up his spirit." Although this term can be a description for taking one's last breath, I believe it also has a deeper significance here. The Greek word for "give up" means to "yield up."[4] Therefore, I think this term means that Jesus also *released* the Holy Spirit back to the Father in heaven at his death.

When Jesus was resurrected, he was raised by the power of the Spirit, and the Spirit again dwelled in him. Paul wrote, "And if the Spirit of him who raised Jesus from the dead is living in you, he who raised Christ from the dead will also give life to your mortal bodies through his Spirit, who lives in you." Just as the King-Son was raised from death by the Spirit, and the Spirit dwelled in him, those who enter the kingdom through the King-Son's sacrifice will also receive the Spirit.

At Jesus' resurrection, then, the Spirit was now poised to return to humanity and rescue lives that had lived in rebellion, confusion, and despair under the kingdom of darkness. Just as the Spirit brought life out of emptiness and order from chaos at the creation of the earth, he would transform the earth once more into a colony of heaven through the return of the king-dom in the lives of its citizens.

CHAPTER SIX

A KING'S LOVE FOR HIS CITIZENS

Love is the nature of the King and his kingdom.

LOVE'S VOLUNTARY LIMITATION

To fully understand the nature of the kingdom we have an opportunity to enter, we must see that the King-Son's motivation for coming to earth was unqualified love for its inhabitants. He loved the people of the world so much that he voluntarily limited himself in significant ways in order to restore them to the kingdom. The New Testament writer John penned one of the best-known statements from the gospel writings: "For God so loved the world that he gave his one and only Son, that whoever believes in him shall not perish but have eternal life." Love is the nature of the King-Father and the King-Son.

Jesus is the perfect representation of God in human form. He came to show us what God is like and to take away our fear of Him, enabling us to call him not only our King, but also our Father again, because we have the same Spirit within us.

THE GOVERNOR'S LIMITATION

The King-Son's voluntary limitation of himself was prompted by the limited way in which the Governor had been able to work with the earth's inhabitants since the rebellion of humanity. As we noted earlier, the Governor could only come *upon* people in Old Testament times to do the work of the kingdom in specific instances; he could not work from *within* them yet. When the Son came to earth as the man Jesus, the Spirit could now live on earth within his body. Yet the Governor still could not dwell in all of humanity. The King-Father's plan was for the Governor to eventually be released into all human beings who would receive him through the provision of the King-Son.

THE KING-SON LIMITED HIMSELF IN ORDER TO BECOME UNLIMITED

Jesus' teachings were filled with seeming paradoxes that contain great truths. For example, he taught that in order to live eternally, one had to die to oneself; in order to be strong in kingdom power, one had to be weak in oneself. He lived out a paradox by voluntarily limiting himself so that he could become unlimited in the lives of his followers—those who became children of the King and received the Governor within them. Jesus limited himself in the following ways. He...

√ emptied himself so that we could be full; became poor so that we could be rich.

√ placed himself under the restrictions of a world of space and time so that we could be connected to the eternal kingdom.

√ subjected himself to law so he could free those under it.

134

√ submitted to physical death so we could have eternal life.

Paul wrote to the kingdom citizens in Philippi that Jesus,

> being in the form of God, did not consider it robbery
> to be equal with God, but made Himself of no reputa-
> tion, taking the form of a bondservant, and coming in
> the likeness of men. And being found in appearance
> as a man, He humbled Himself and became obedient
> to the point of death, even the death of the cross.

All the above are demonstrations of the King-Son's powerful love for the inhabitants of earth. He did these things so
that he could send the Governor back to us—and *in* us—without limitations. The Holy Spirit *continues the ministry of Jesus* on
earth. Jesus told his disciples,

> And I will ask the Father, and he will give you another
> Counselor to be with you forever—the Spirit of truth.
> The world cannot accept him, because it neither sees
> him nor knows him. But you know him, for he lives
> with you and will be in you.

Let's take a closer look at the ways in which the King-Son
limited himself for our sakes.

LIMITED HIMSELF FROM GLORY

In a letter to the followers of Jesus in Corinth, Paul wrote,
"For you know the grace of our Lord Jesus Christ, that though
he was rich, yet for your sakes he become poor, so that you
through his poverty might become rich." The King-Son emptied himself of his heavenly power, glory, and riches to live as
a physical, earthly being dependent on the King-Father for
everything through the Spirit. Jesus said, "I tell you the truth,

the Son can do nothing by himself; he can do only what he sees his Father doing, because whatever the Father does the Son also does."

When the Son became a man, he temporarily set aside his former glory. Just before his death, Jesus prayed, "Father, glorify me in your presence *with the glory I had with you before the world began.*" Only three of Jesus' disciples were given a glimpse of this glory when he was on earth, when he was "transfigured" by the Father for a short time:

> Jesus took with him Peter, James and John the brother of James, and led them up a high mountain by themselves. There he was transfigured before them. His face shone like the sun, and his clothes became as white as the light. Just then there appeared before them Moses and Elijah, talking with Jesus. Peter said to Jesus, "Lord, it is good for us to be here. If you wish, I will put up three shelters—one for you, one for Moses and one for Elijah." While he was still speaking, a bright cloud enveloped them, and a voice from the cloud said, "This is my Son, whom I love; with him I am well pleased. Listen to him!"

The effect of this experience on Peter, James, and John was overwhelming. The Son had set aside this magnificent glory to fulfill his mission on earth.

LIMITED HIMSELF TO TIME AND SPACE

The eternal King-Son also allowed himself to become restricted by time. He who owns the universe limited himself to a small region on a small planet during an earthly life of thirty-three years, where he could be in only one place at a time. He lived there, died there, rose again there, and even ascended to heaven from there. Eternity allowed itself to be limited within time, so that those in time could be reconnected to the eternal kingdom.

Limited Himself under Law

Paul wrote, "When the time had fully come, God sent his Son, born of a woman, born *under law, to redeem those under law,* that we might receive the full rights of sons." The law of Moses and the sacrificial system had been instituted for those who were disconnected from the King. Jesus had full access to, and total communion with, the heavenly Father; yet he submitted himself to all the requirements of the law so that he could perfectly fulfill them. Then, when we receive his perfect sacrifice on our behalf, we are enabled to obey God through the indwelling Holy Spirit. The book of the prophet Ezekiel says,

> I will give them an undivided heart and put a new spirit in them; I will remove from them their heart of stone and give them a heart of flesh. Then they will follow my decrees and be careful to keep my laws. They will be my people, and I will be their God.

Jesus also submitted himself to the laws of nature in this physical world. Can you imagine God having a tired body? Being thirsty? Hungry? The God who created the whole world and all its oceans, lakes, and rivers had to ask someone else for a drink of water. The God who made the trees and their ability to bear fruit had to stop to pick fruit to eat. The God whom the psalmist said "neither slumbers nor sleeps" had to rest. In fact, Jesus was once so tired that he kept sleeping in the middle of a violent storm! He temporarily submitted himself to physical limitations in order to give back dominion power to humanity.

LIMITED HIMSELF BY DEATH

The Author of life had to look into the eyes of death. He met it face-to-face and submitted to it. Then he conquered it, taking away its sting from humanity. The prophet Isaiah said it pleased the King-Father for the King-Son to suffer and die. Why would it please him to have the Son experience agonizing suffering and death? Again, it is because he didn't want the earth's inhabitants to experience spiritual death as a result of their rebellion, and therefore the King-Son willingly died in our place. He allowed himself to be limited in a physical human body, and to be limited by the experience of death, because only another human being could be a viable substitute for humanity. Paul wrote, "The wages of sin is death, but the gift of God is eternal life through Jesus Christ our Lord." Jesus had no sin, but he took all our sins on himself, and that is why he—the perfect man, the Second Adam—died.

> *The King-Son's limitation of death brought unlimited life for us!*

Yet Jesus was resurrected, never to be limited by death again. In the same way, when we enter into the kingdom, we receive eternal life, and death can't keep our bodies in the grave forever. Again, Paul wrote, "By his power God raised the Lord from the dead, and he will raise us also." The Son's limitation of death brought unlimited life for us! Death has no ultimate claim on us because Jesus paid the punishment of death for us. As Paul said, "God made him who had no sin to be sin for us, so that in him we might become the righteousness of God"—so that we could receive eternal life and be in right standing with the kingdom again.

This is another clear difference between the heavenly King and the human leaders we are familiar with. You don't hear of presidents or prime ministers dying in office for the purpose of freeing their citizens. A leader may be assassinated for standing up for a cause or because of someone's hatred or insanity. But to *choose* to die for his citizens? This is unheard of in our experience. Remember the words of the disciple John: "For God so loved the world that he gave his one and only Son, that whoever believes in him shall not perish but have eternal life." Jesus compared his sacrifice for humanity to a shepherd laying down his life for his sheep: "I am the good shepherd; I know my sheep and my sheep know me—just as the Father knows me and I know the Father—and I lay down my life for the sheep." His death was a demonstration of pure love for his people.

The Promise of Unlimited Kingdom Influence

Jesus' limiting of himself made possible the return of unlimited kingdom influence on earth. I've heard some people say longingly that they wish Jesus Christ was on earth today. They believe that if he were, and they met him personally, their lives would be different. Perhaps you wish for the same thing. I used to, also. But I've come to see that this is a bad wish; it's not in our best interests. The transformation of our lives is possible *because* Jesus is no longer physically on earth.

Why is this so? First, let's consider the logistics of it. If Jesus was physically here, and you wanted to visit him, you'd have to pay for the plane fare to Palestine. After you arrived, you'd have to make your way through all the crowds just to try to get near him. And then, you couldn't expect him to spend all his time with you. Think of the millions or billions of people who would also want to meet with him every day. Even so, we seem to hold on to the idea that Jesus' physical presence on earth is what we need. This is because we haven't realized that the Governor is now available to all people at all times.

> *When the Governor came, he would be with them continually, in all situations.*

Jesus' disciples made the same error we do. When the King-Son told his followers he was leaving earth to go back to the King-Father in the heavenly home country, they became depressed. They had become attached to Jesus' physical presence in their lives, and they were afraid to lose it. Yet let's look at Jesus' response to this perspective:

> Now I am going to him who sent me, yet none of you asks me, "Where are you going?" Because I have said these things, you are filled with grief. But I tell you the truth: it is for your good that I am going away. Unless I go away, the Counselor will not come to you; but if I go, I will send him to you....In a little while you will see me no more, and then after a little while you will see me.

Jesus was saying that he *had* to return to heaven so that he could send the Governor to be with them always. They would not see Jesus after he went away, but when he sent the Governor from heaven shortly thereafter, they would be indwelled with the Holy Spirit, who would guide them into all truth and remind them of everything Jesus had said to them.

When the Governor came, he wouldn't be with them only in a limited way, such as Jesus had to be when he was ministering to someone else or alone praying to the Father. He would be with them continually, day and night, in all situations. Before, if Jesus was in Samaria, he couldn't be in Galilee. If he was in Jerusalem, he couldn't be in Bethany.

We should be glad that he has returned to heaven because now the kingdom can be all over the world at the same time through the Holy Spirit, who lives in all kingdom citizens. Jesus assured his disciples, in essence, "My going away is for your good. The Governor is *with* you now, but he will be *in* you." It wasn't Jesus' purpose to physically remain on the earth because this would have stopped the King's plan of restoration right before its culmination in the return of the Governor.

When Jesus was arrested and crucified, Lucifer thought he had won the victory over the King that he had been looking for. Actually, he was being set up for total defeat. If Jesus hadn't gone to the cross and been resurrected, we would still be trapped in rebellion and in the kingdom of darkness. If Jesus hadn't returned to the heavenly home country and sent the Governor to fill us, the kingdom of God would not have been able to fully return to the earth. Jesus had said, in effect, "If I go to the cross, I will be able to draw all people to me and into the kingdom. I will be able to release billions of people into their original purpose of kingdom rulership and dominion."

Jesus limited himself, in the many ways that he did, out of self-sacrificial love and devotion to the estranged children of the King. He made reconciliation and restoration possible for all the inhabitants of the world.

A Priceless Gift for Humanity

We have seen all along that the most important person on earth is the Holy Spirit, the Governor of the heavenly kingdom.

He is a priceless gift to humanity, and it delighted the King-Father to restore the Governor to us. Luke the physician recorded Jesus as saying to his disciples, "If you then, though you are evil [controlled by the kingdom of darkness], know how to give good gifts to your children, how much more will your Father in heaven [Ruler of the kingdom of light] give the Holy Spirit to those who ask him!" He also said, "Your Father has been *pleased* to give you the kingdom."

In the next chapter, we will see how the Governor returned to earth.

CHAPTER SEVEN

RESTORING THE CONNECTION

The future of a plant is staying attached to the soil.

T he King-Son had promised his disciples concerning the Governor, "He lives with you and will be in you." He would connect them to the Father through the Spirit. After his resurrection, the work of *preparing* humanity to receive the Governor was complete. The spirit of rebellion and independence from the kingdom was broken. Any human being who personally received the sacrifice of Jesus, applying it to his own life, was now cleansed and qualified to be a residence for the Governor.

THE BREATH OF JESUS

Jesus' life, ministry, death, and resurrection therefore led up to his most important act on earth: the giving of the Governor. Shortly after his resurrection, Jesus came to the room where his disciples had gathered, and said, "'As the Father has sent me, I am sending you.' And with that he breathed on them and said, 'Receive the Holy Spirit.'"

Note that Jesus *breathed* on them. Does that act seem familiar? It was very similar to what the Creator did when he first made Adam a living being: "The LORD God formed the man from the dust of the ground and breathed into his nostrils the breath of life, and the man became a living being." But in this life-giving act, the King-Son specifically explained what this meant. He didn't just say, "Receive the breath of life." He said, "Receive the Holy Spirit."

The breath of life *is* the Holy Spirit; the Governor *is* the life of humanity. Without Him, even though our bodies may be physically alive for a limited length of time, we are dead to the kingdom, to the heavenly influence we were created to live in, and to the Creator-King himself.

In other words, when the Creator first breathed into Adam, he was essentially saying, "*Ceive* the Holy Spirit." Now, Jesus was saying to his disciples, as the first human beings (besides himself) to be filled with the Spirit, "Re-ceive the Holy Spirit." In the English language, we don't use the word *ceive* as a verb, but the English word *receive* comes the Latin *re-* (again) and *capere* (to take).[1] When Adam rebelled, he lost the Spirit he had been given. So when Jesus brought the disciples together after the resurrection, he was saying, in effect, "Humanity, take the Spirit *again*, as Adam did." He was giving human beings back what they had lost.

> *The return of the Holy Spirit is the most important act of redemption in God's plan for humanity.*

In breathing on his disciples, Jesus reconnected humanity to the kingdom of heaven. He was literally bringing his disciples into identity with heaven's government. He was renewing human beings' standing and authority in the kingdom. They were restored to their original assignment as vice governors of earth. So the disciples of Jesus were the first human beings after Jesus to receive the Governor resident within them again.

The return of the Holy Spirit is the most important act of redemption in God's program for humanity. At that moment, the kingdom of God returned to earth because the Spirit lived within humanity once more!

Note that, after his resurrection, Jesus' message continued to be the kingdom. Luke the physician wrote,

> In my former book...I wrote about all that Jesus began to do and to teach until the day he was taken up to heaven, after giving instructions through the Holy Spirit to the apostles he had chosen. After his suffering, he showed himself to these men and gave many convincing proofs that he was alive. He appeared to them over a period of forty days *and spoke about the kingdom of God.*

Some people question whether the kingdom of heaven is on earth right now. The answer is absolutely yes. In order to understand why, we have to remember the nature of kingdoms. Wherever the Governor is, the kingdom is present. Wherever the Spirit of the King is, the kingdom is. The Governor is the presence of the absent King. Luke recorded Jesus' response when he was asked about this very question:

> Once, having been asked by the Pharisees when the kingdom of God would come, Jesus replied, "The kingdom of God does not come with your careful observation, nor will people say, 'Here it is,' or 'there it is,' because the kingdom of God is within you."

145

The kingdom of God is within you when the Governor is resident within you. And when the Governor is resident within you, the kingdom of heaven is present on earth. Jesus told his followers, "I tell you the truth, some who are standing here will not taste death before they see the kingdom of God come with power." According to Luke's account in his second book, Acts, about one hundred twenty disciples were present when the Governor was poured out and fully reinstated on earth.

WAITING FOR THE FIRE

Jesus' purpose was to reintroduce the government that had been recalled from earth by humanity's rebellion. After he had completed his mission of providing a way for the inhabitants to be holy again, he returned to the heavenly kingdom. The ascension of Jesus was evidence of his finished work on earth, indicating that all was in readiness for the Governor's full return. The gospel of Mark records, "After the Lord Jesus had spoken to [his disciples], he was taken up into heaven and he sat at the right hand of God." I believe he reported to the Father at this time that everything was in place for the Governor to be poured out on the inhabitants of earth. Jesus had instructed his disciples about how they would receive this power from the Governor. On various occasions, he made these statements to his disciples:

> And I will ask the Father, and he will give you another Counselor to be with you forever—the Spirit of truth. The world cannot accept him, because it neither sees him nor knows him. But you know him, for he lives with you and will be in you.

> The Counselor, the Holy Spirit, whom the Father will send in my name, will teach you all things and will remind you of everything I have said to you.

I am going to send you what my Father has promised; but stay in the city until you have been clothed with power from on high.

On one occasion, while he was eating with them, he gave them this command: "Do not leave Jerusalem, but wait for the gift my Father promised, which you have heard me speak about. For John baptized with water, but in a few days you will be baptized with the Holy Spirit....But you will receive power when the Holy Spirit comes on you; and you will be my witnesses in Jerusalem, and in all Judea and Samaria, and to the ends of the earth."

Jesus had already breathed the Spirit on his disciples. They had received the Governor into their lives and were connected to the kingdom. But they still needed to be connected to the kingdom's *power*, which the King would soon send them. This is what John meant when he said Jesus would baptize them with the Holy Spirit and with fire. After Jesus returned to the heavenly kingdom, the "fire" would come, and his mission of both reconnection and restored power would be fully realized.

The disciples were connected to the kingdom, but they needed to connect to the kingdom's power.

In other words, Jesus was saying, "For the last three-and-a-half years, I have been telling you that the influence of the heavenly government is coming. Every time I talked about the kingdom, I was referring to the Governor's influence in your lives and on the world. Now, stay here in Jerusalem because you're about to receive the fullness of the promise my Father made to you."

147

Jesus told them they would be clothed with power from "on high." This point is vital: we are to receive our power from the heavenly country, from a place *outside* this world, because this world is controlled by the kingdom of darkness. Again, the King-Son sent the Governor to earth *from the throne of the Father,* just as a royal governor was sent to a colony from the throne of the king to carry on the work of the sovereign there.

THE HOLY SPIRIT POURED OUT AT PENTECOST

After Jesus ascended to heaven, his disciples, along with over one hundred other followers, met together and awaited the coming of the Governor. His arrival occurred on the day of Pentecost, which means "fiftieth" in Greek.[2] Pentecost was a harvest feast held on the fiftieth day after the Passover feast. Jesus appeared to his followers over a period of forty days after his resurrection, and they waited ten days from his ascension for the coming of the Spirit. These fifty days bring us exactly to the day of Pentecost. Luke the physician recorded,

> When the day of Pentecost came, they were all together in one place. Suddenly a sound like the blowing of a violent wind came from heaven and filled the whole house where they were sitting. They saw what seemed to be *tongues of fire* that separated and came to rest on each of them. All of them were filled with the Holy Spirit and began to speak in other tongues [languages] as the Spirit enabled them.

When Jesus' followers were *filled* with the Holy Spirit, they were given power to speak in the variety of languages spoken by the Jewish people who had come to Jerusalem, from a number of countries, to celebrate the feast of Pentecost. The heavenly government gave them the ability to communicate the message that the kingdom of God had fully come so that people of many nations could hear this momentous news. Their speaking in these languages was an evidence that they were connected to the King and their assignment to bring the kingdom of heaven to earth. As recorded in the book of Mark, Jesus had previously told his disciples, "And these signs will accompany those who believe: In my name they will…speak in new tongues…."

Luke reported that the people who heard them said, in essence, "Why are you speaking like this; what is going on with you?" The disciple Peter responded,

> Fellow Jews and all of you who live in Jerusalem, let me explain this to you; listen carefully to what I say. These men are not drunk, as you suppose. It's only nine in the morning! No, this is what was spoken by the prophet Joel: "In the last days, God says, I will pour out my Spirit on all people. Your sons and daughters will prophesy, your young men will see visions, your old men will dream dreams. Even on my servants, both men and women, I will pour out my Spirit in those days, and they will prophesy."…God has raised this Jesus [King-Son] to life, and we are all witnesses of the fact. Exalted to the right hand of God, he has received from the Father [King-Father] the promised Holy Spirit [Governor] and has poured out what you now see and hear.

Once again, we see the promise of the Father announced; but this time, the news was that the promise was now fulfilled in the return of the Governor. Peter was telling them they were witnessing the influence of the government of heaven through the arrival of the Holy Spirit.

When Jesus' disciples received the Holy Spirit, and then were filled by the Spirit when he was poured out at Pentecost, this signaled a seismic change on earth. The way was now open, for all people who received the cleansing Jesus provided, to receive the presence and power of the Governor. What separates the kingdom of heaven from all other philosophies, belief systems, and religions is that its citizens have within them the Holy Spirit. Religions have doctrines, tenets, and lists of *do*s and *don't*s, but they don't have the indwelling Spirit.

THE POWER OF ABSENCE

As we saw in the previous chapter, while the Holy Spirit once dwelled only in Jesus, now He is able to dwell in millions of people throughout the world. He's back home in the colony so that the whole planet can be filled with the glory of the King. Now that he has been poured out, he can be all over the world at the same time. He lives in people of all races and skin colors. He lives in both men and women. The physical Jesus had only two hands with which to bless children and break bread for the hungry and relieve the sick. Now, through the Spirit dwelling in the lives of his followers, there are millions of hands doing the work of the kingdom. While Jesus' ministry was once limited to the area of Palestine, it can now be in Australia, China, the United States, the Bahamas, and all over the world at the same time. His purpose is to spread the kingdom of God on earth through a multitude of people, in a multitude of ways, in all spheres of life.

For example, if the Spirit lives within you, then, when you are at your job, the heavenly government is also present there. He wants you to bring about his influence in your workplace by your kingdom value system, attitude, forgiveness, love, and patience. If anyone asks you, "Why are you so different?" your answer can be the same as Jesus': "My kingdom is not of this world." The King wants you to represent his kingdom in the midst of the kingdom of darkness, so others can be reconciled to the heavenly government, also.

GREATER WORKS ON EARTH

John recorded this statement by Jesus, which he made shortly before his death and resurrection: "I tell you the truth, anyone who has faith in me will do what I have been doing. He will do even greater things than these, *because I am going to the Father.*" How could we do greater works than Jesus did on earth?

> *If the Spirit lives within you, then wherever you are, the heavenly government is present.*

The word *greater* here has to do with magnitude, not quality.[3] We could never improve on the quality of the works of Jesus. But when we are aligned with the mind and will of the Father, and his purposes are foremost in our lives, Jesus promised, "And I will do whatever you ask in my name, so that the Son may bring glory to the Father." The nature of the heavenly government will be spread throughout the colony, and this will bring due honor to the King of both heaven and earth. All who have received his Spirit will collectively multiply his works in the world.

The power of the Governor is that he makes the reality of heaven on earth possible. This is why *everybody* needs the Holy Spirit. He is the only one who can connect us to King and, through us, dispel the kingdom of darkness with his kingdom of light. He is the most important person on earth.

Chapter Eight

Reinstating the Governor

A puzzle remains a puzzle until all the parts are in place.

Our entrance into the kingdom of heaven, also called the "new birth," results in the restoration of our legal authority as rulers on earth. Then, our baptism in the Holy Spirit results in the restoration of our power or ability to carry out that authority. Understanding these two concepts will enable us to be effective as we live out the culture of the kingdom on earth, for both have to do with the reinstatement of the Governor to his place and role in the lives of human beings.

Let us now take a closer look at these two concepts, comparing the new birth to a well of water, and the baptism in the Spirit to the power of a moving river.

The New Birth:
Reinstating the Authority of the Kingdom

John the disciple recorded these words of Jesus regarding the restoration of the Governor within humanity: "Whoever drinks the water I give him will never thirst. Indeed, the water I give him will become in him *a spring of water welling up* to eternal life." Water in this context is a symbol of the Holy Spirit. The reality of the new birth is that there is now a continuous reservoir of God's Spirit within us. Picture a spring forever bubbling up with fresh, clean, life-giving water. As we continually drink deeply from this water of the Spirit within us, we will constantly be connected to the life of the kingdom.

Let's look more closely at how the Governor restores the life of the kingdom to us through the new birth.

RECONNECTS HUMAN BEINGS TO THE GOVERNMENT

When we initially receive the breath of the Holy Spirit— the return of the Governor within us—we are given what theologian Paul of Tarsus referred to several times in his writings as a "deposit" showing that we now belong to the King and that he gives us an inheritance in his heavenly kingdom:

> Now it is God who makes both us and you stand firm in Christ. He anointed us, set his seal of ownership on us, and put his Spirit in our hearts as a deposit, guaranteeing what is to come.

> Now it is God who has made us for this very purpose and has given us the Spirit as a deposit, guaranteeing what is to come.

> And you also were included in Christ when you heard the word of truth, the gospel of your salvation. Having believed, you were marked in him with a seal, the promised Holy Spirit, who is a deposit guaranteeing

our inheritance until the redemption of those who are God's possession—to the praise of his glory.

RESTORES HUMAN BEINGS' CITIZENSHIP IN HEAVEN

Whereas, before, we were merely inhabitants of the earth, we have become children of the King and full citizens in the realm. Paul wrote, "Consequently, you are no longer foreigners and aliens, but fellow citizens with God's people and members of God's household." Our citizenship in heaven has been conferred on us by the King himself, with the full rights and privileges that encompasses.

REINSTATES THE KINGDOM ON EARTH THROUGH HUMANITY

Because the Governor is resident in the kingdom citizens who live on earth, the kingdom of God itself is on earth. This reinstatement first occurred with the King-Son's coming to live as a human being in the world, and first returned to fallen humanity when Jesus breathed the Holy Spirit on his disciples. The heavenly government has representatives on earth again through the new birth. The more inhabitants of earth who enter the kingdom of heaven, the more the kingdom influence should be felt in the world.

RESTORES INTER-REALM COMMUNICATION AND ACCESS TO THE UNSEEN WORLD

The new birth restores two-way communication from heaven to earth and earth to heaven. It is what I earlier called inter-realm communication. Humanity had perfect communication with the King-Father in the beginning, but we lost it when we lost the *means* of that communication, the Governor.

With the reestablishment of our relationship with the King, he is now able to have direct access and contact with us, and we are able to have direct access and contact with him. The new birth means that we have admittance to the unseen world in which the King dwells, and even have *influence* there as we pursue the purposes of the kingdom. This is what Jesus meant by the following statement, which we noted earlier:

> I tell you the truth, whatever you bind on earth will be bound in heaven, and whatever you loose on earth will be loosed in heaven. Again, I tell you that if two of you on earth agree about anything you ask for, it will be done for you by my Father in heaven. For where two or three come together in my name, there am I with them.

RESTORES THE NATURE OF THE KING WITHIN HUMANITY

This concept is what Jesus taught to Nicodemus, the Pharisee, who was trying to understand the meaning of the new birth. Jesus told him, "I tell you the truth, no one can enter the kingdom of God unless he is born of water and the Spirit. Flesh gives birth to flesh, but the Spirit gives birth to spirit. You should not be surprised at my saying, 'You must be born again.'"

This account is the only reference to the term "born again" in the Scriptures, yet the expression has become almost a catchphrase today so that we have lost its meaning. Being born again means that we have received the Governor and have therefore been given a new nature that enables us to be citizens in the territory of the kingdom. We become "imitators of God" once more, as Paul wrote: "Be imitators of God, therefore, as dearly loved children and live a life of love, just as Christ loved us and gave himself up for us as a fragrant offering and sacrifice to God." Because we are children of the King, we have his nature in our spiritual "DNA" and can now reflect it in the world.

THE BAPTISM IN THE HOLY SPIRIT:
REINSTATING THE POWER OF THE KINGDOM

The new birth, or conversion, prepares us for heaven—for reconnection with the heavenly government and restored relationship with the King. The baptism in the Spirit, on the other hand, prepares us for earth—for our restored dominion assignment to make the earth into a replica of heaven. I want to contrast these encounters with the Spirit because they are distinct experiences.

Just before the King-Son returned to the Father in the heavenly government, he told his disciples, "You will receive power when the Holy Spirit comes on you." The Greek word translated as *power* here is *dunamis,* which means "miraculous power."[1] Remember our earlier discussion about what we call "miracles." They are merely the manifestation of the influence of the kingdom of heaven on earth. So this power comes directly from another world, the heavenly government, to enable us to exercise authority on behalf of the King in the world.

> *The new birth prepares us for heaven. The baptism in the Spirit prepares us for earth.*

The book of John records these words of Jesus: "If anyone is thirsty, let him come to me and drink. Whoever believes in me, as the Scripture has said, *streams of living water will flow from within him.*" John added, "By this he meant the Spirit, whom those who *believed* in him were *later* to receive. Up to that time the Spirit had not been given, since Jesus had not yet been glorified."

The Spirit already dwells within us at conversion. The baptism in the Holy Spirit is our yielding to the King and allowing him to release in power what is already inside us. While the new birth is like a continuous well, the baptism is like a forceful river; it is like waterpower that is harnessed as energy to run equipment, such as in a mill, for the betterment of humanity and its needs.

Let's look at how the baptism in the Holy Spirit restores to our lives the power we lost at humanity's rebellion.

RESTORES THE POWER OF DOMINION

While the new birth restores us to the heavenly government, the baptism gives us the ability to carry out the authority that the government has given back to us. Remember that power refers to our ability to influence and control circumstances. This is the power we must have to exercise dominion over the physical earth and the various situations we will encounter in the world.

RESTORES HUMANITY'S ABILITY TO REPRESENT THE GOVERNMENT

It is one thing to be recommissioned as a representative of the heavenly government, but it's another to demonstrate proof that you have been sent by that government. The baptism gives you the power to prove the claims of your King. This is where the gifts of the Spirit become important. As we will see in chapter thirteen, the context of the gifts is governmental administration on earth. The Governor empowers us to fulfill the assignments given to us by the heavenly government. So the gifts are not some strange supernatural manifestations but very practical endowments.

Jesus said, "If I drive out demons by the Spirit of God, then the kingdom of God has come upon you." He was saying that driving out demons was *evidence* that the heavenly kingdom had returned to earth. The same is true for all the gifts of the Spirit, whether we are talking about faith, healing, or miracles. The gifts are evidence of the presence, authority, and power of the government of God on earth. This is what Jesus was referring to when he answered John the Baptist's questions about

> *The power of the baptism presents the reality of the kingdom.*

whether he was indeed the King-Son who had come to earth to bring back the Governor. The book of Matthew records,

> When John heard in prison what Christ was doing, he sent his disciples to ask him, "Are you the one who was to come, or should we expect someone else?" Jesus replied, "Go back and report to John what you hear and see: The blind receive sight, the lame walk, those who have leprosy are cured, the deaf hear, the dead are raised, and the good news is preached to the poor."

Jesus was giving John proof that he had come from the heavenly government and was exercising kingdom dominion in the earth. He referred to everything in terms of the kingdom, and since this was also John's message, Jesus knew he would understand his reference.

ENABLES HUMAN BEINGS TO PROVE THE KING'S CLAIMS AND DEMONSTRATE THE KINGDOM'S PRESENCE

The book of Matthew also records this statement of Jesus: "And this gospel of the kingdom will be preached in the whole world as a *testimony* to all nations." The word *testimony* generally refers to speaking as a witness to the truth about a situation. The word in the original Greek in the above statement means "something evidential, i.e. evidence given."[2] Exercising power through the baptism is a means of presenting the truth to the world about the reality of the kingdom and its purposes.

GIVES HUMAN BEINGS THE ABILITY TO DISPLAY THE GLORY OF THE KING AND HIS KINGDOM

The power of the baptism enables us to demonstrate both the characteristics and works of the almighty Creator of heaven and earth. The psalmist King David wrote,

> The heavens declare the glory of God; the skies proclaim the work of his hands. Day after day they pour forth speech; night after night they display knowledge. There is not speech or language where their voice is not heard. Their voice goes out into all the earth, their words to the ends of the world.

The glory of God as demonstrated in nature transcends language. People of all races and nations and backgrounds see it; it is a continual and articulate testimony to the Creator of the world. In a similar way, the works that kingdom citizens do through the power of the Governor transcend human language and culture. If you were to go to another country where you don't speak the language, and the Governor were to use you to bring healing to a man who had been paralyzed for years, it wouldn't matter if he could understand your words; he would understand your action. The word *glory* refers to the essential nature of something. The man would come to realize that it is the nature of the King to be concerned about his personal needs, and that he has the power to meet them. He would be open to hearing about this King and his kingdom. As Jesus told his disciples, "Let your light shine before men, that they may see your good deeds *and praise your Father in heaven.*"

GIVES HUMAN BEINGS THE ABILITY TO DEMONSTRATE HEAVENLY CITIZENSHIP

In line with this, the power demonstrated through the baptism proves that we are citizens of a heavenly kingdom. It is like a passport; it both identifies us as belonging to the King and gives us credibility in carrying out the work of the kingdom. Just *trying* to do the works of the kingdom is not enough; you must have the authority to back up your work. This is what the sevens sons of Sceva, written about in the book of Acts, found out the hard way. They noticed Paul driving out demons in the name of Jesus, so they thought they would try it, too. But they weren't a recognized authority of the heavenly kingdom:

> Seven sons of Sceva, a Jewish chief priest, were doing this [trying to expel demons in Jesus' name]. One day the evil spirit answered them, "Jesus I know, and I know about Paul, but who are you?" Then the man who had the evil spirit jumped on them and overpowered them all. He gave them such a beating that they ran out of the house naked and bleeding. When this

161

became known to the Jews and Greeks living in Ephesus, they were all seized with fear, and the name of the Lord Jesus was held in high honor.

Paul was an authorized citizen of heaven, and his authority in the heavenly kingdom was respected and obeyed by agents of the kingdom of darkness. The power of the heavenly kingdom is never to be used lightly, but only by those authorized by the King through his indwelling Spirit.

RECEIVING THE GOVERNOR IN YOUR LIFE

In coming chapters, I will be discussing more about the power that comes through the baptism in the Holy Spirit. Right now, I would like you to consider how to receive the Governor in your own life, because this first step will reconcile you to the King-Father and enable you to receive the authority of his kingdom.

Reconciliation through the new birth is the best news you could ever hear! It means you can approach the King without fear. Jesus has paid the penalty for your rebellion and independent spirit. When Jesus' disciple Peter spoke to the crowds who had gathered on the day of Pentecost, and explained to them what was happening, the people asked him what their response should be. He answered, "Repent and be baptized, every one of you, in the name of Jesus Christ for the forgiveness of your sins. And you will receive the gift of the Holy Spirit." Therefore, to receive the new birth, you are to...

First, *repent*. Change your mind about how you have been living and desire to live by the standards of the heavenly kingdom.

Second, *receive the forgiveness provided through Jesus' sacrifice.* One of the greatest problems of humanity today is a heavy weight of guilt for the wrong things we have done, for the actions we have committed that are contrary to the nature of the King and his kingdom. To forgive means to release from accountability and guilt. So, in order to live in the freedom of the kingdom, you must accept the forgiveness provided for you through Jesus, and then walk, as Paul wrote, in "newness of life."

Once you have gone through the above steps, you will *receive the gift of the Holy Spirit* within you. This is the "deposit" and proof of your entrance into the kingdom. Offer thanks to your King-Father for giving you this priceless gift.

Note that we are also instructed to *be baptized in water.* Being baptized in water in the name of Jesus shows that you are submitted to Jesus' kingdom school, acknowledges that your allegiance and identification from this time on is to him as your Master Teacher, and demonstrates that you have received full forgiveness for your rebellion.

The new birth means you no longer have to try to figure out life on your own. The King has removed that burden and stress from you. Just as a colony relies on the kingdom to build its roads, supply its water, and so forth, a kingdom citizen has all his needs supplied as he puts the priorities of the King first in his life. This is why Jesus said,

> Do not worry, saying, "What shall we eat?" or "What shall we drink?" or "What shall we wear?" For the pagans [people outside the heavenly kingdom] run after all these things, and our heavenly Father knows that you need them. But seek first his kingdom and his righteousness, and all these things will be given to

you as well. Therefore do not worry about tomorrow, for tomorrow will worry about itself.

This is the kingdom life: seeking the good of the kingdom first and allowing the King to provide for all your needs as you serve him in the authority and power he gives you through the heavenly Governor.

CHAPTER NINE

RESULTS OF RECONNECTION

The success of a fish is staying in water.

Without the Governor, a person cannot be a citizen of the heavenly kingdom. In his gospel, John documented this statement of Jesus: "I tell you the truth, no one can enter the kingdom of God unless he is born of water and the Spirit. Flesh gives birth to flesh, but the Spirit gives birth to spirit."

A person may do many beneficial things and be involved in a number of good causes and even have a religious background, but if he doesn't have the Spirit of the kingdom, he's not in the kingdom. The King of heaven is not interested in religious practices and rituals. Just as DNA pinpoints the identity of a person, the Spirit of God within a person identifies him as a citizen of the kingdom. There is no margin of error.

Yet when you are connected to the King through his Governor, an entirely new and remarkable life opens up for you. Before we discuss specific ways in which we are trained by the Governor in the lifestyle of the kingdom, and to partner with him in exercising dominion over the earth, let's review the initial transformation and benefits that occur when we receive the Governor into our lives.

RESTORED RELATIONSHIP WITH THE KING-FATHER

The first result of reconnection is a restored relationship with the King-Father. When human beings declared independence from the heavenly government, we cut ourselves off from our source of life; we became broken and confused, and this is why life on earth today is filled with such destruction, violence, grief, and lost potential. The earth is like somebody who has big plans—but no money to pay for them.

When the Governor enters a person's life, he connects that person to his source of life and gives him a relationship with his Creator—not just as his King, but also as his heavenly Father. He belongs to the King's immediate household now, with all the rights and privileges of a member of the heavenly royal family.

When we become realigned to our King-Father, we are acknowledging, "I came from you, and I must be sustained by you; I depend on you." We place the obligation for our sustenance upon God. As the prophet Isaiah said, the government is on the King's shoulders. He is responsible for leading his people. The names by which he is called indicate not only his responsibility, but also his ability, toward us, such as Wonderful Counselor, Mighty God, Father Who Lives Forever, Prince of Peace.

ENTRANCE INTO A NONDISCRIMINATORY, NONPARTISAN KINGDOM

The second result of reconnection is entrance into a nondiscriminatory and nonpartisan kingdom. Earlier, we looked at the words of the prophet Joel, who described the coming of the promise of the Father:

And afterward, I will pour out my Spirit on all people. Your sons and daughters will prophesy, your old men will dream dreams, your young men will see visions. Even on my servants, both men and women, I will pour out my Spirit in those days.

This was the prophecy that Peter quoted on the day of Pentecost. For the people listening to Peter's comments, this would have been a radical change from the life they knew. For the coming of the Governor affirmed the worth and value to the kingdom of every citizen on earth, whether male or female, young or old. In the past, it had only been the high priest who could be in the presence of God's Spirit in the Holy of Holies, and only after he had been cleansed by the blood of sacrifice. In addition, only males could be priests. Yet here was Peter, quoting Joel, saying that the Spirit would be poured out on *all* people.

No longer would people have to go through priests to receive forgiveness from God. No longer would they depend only on prophets to deliver the word of the Lord to them. The Spirit would be poured out on them, and they would have direct access to the King himself.

Today, many people still engage in customs that I call "pre-Lord's Day practices." These are practices that the coming of the Governor has made obsolete. For example, some people believe they can have their sins forgiven only if they confess them to a priest. That's basically the way it was in the day of Joel. Only one person could go in to the presence of God in the Holy of Holies and enable you be in right standing with God again, and that was the priest. Joel was saying, however, that there would be a day when the King-Son was going to make this program obsolete because his sacrifice would make full atonement for our rebellion and sin. Everybody who received forgiveness through his substitutionary death would be able to come in to the King-Father's presence. No one would have to enter in to the Holy of Holies because the Holy of Holies would be *in* them in the person of the Governor! Nothing else—not our penitence, our memorization of Bible verses, our chanting, or our going to church meetings makes us acceptable to God. Only the King-Son's sacrifice cleanses us from *all* sin and enables the Governor to reside within us.

In addition, under the previous system, no woman would have imagined ever being a priest. Yet Joel told us that when the day of the Lord arrived, the King was going to give the Governor to everybody, regardless of gender. He said, "Your sons and daughters will prophesy." Why were "daughters" mentioned? This was to show the nature and extent of the kingdom. Joel prophesied, in effect, "I see the day coming when the King will arrive on earth, and he will destroy our categorizing of people according to gender." Both sons and daughters would prophesy, which means they would begin to speak the mind and heart of the home country to the colony of earth. The Greek word translated as *prophesy* means to "foretell events," "tell forth," or "speak under inspiration."[1] It means to speak forth on behalf of God. Both men and women are meant to communicate heaven's thoughts. Paul wrote,

> You are all sons of God through faith in Christ Jesus, for all of you who were baptized into Christ have clothed yourselves with Christ. There is neither Jew nor Greek, slave nor free, male nor female, for you are all one in

Christ Jesus. If you belong to Christ, then you are Abraham's seed, and heirs according to the promise.

The next statement in Joel is, "Your young men will see visions, your old men will dream dreams." He didn't say, "Young *priests* will see visions" or "Old *priests* will dream dreams." All people who have the Governor are eligible. It doesn't matter if you are a child, a teenager, a middle-aged person, or a senior citizen, you can receive the Governor into your life, and he will

> *Human cultural discrimination disappears in the kingdom of heaven.*

involve you in kingdom purposes. There's no age discrimination in the kingdom of heaven.

Then, just in case we missed the point, Joel said, "Even on my servants, both men and women, I will pour out my Spirit in those days." The King repeated himself, as if to say, "All the human cultural prohibitions regarding gender, age, and social status have disappeared. When I pour out my Spirit on the territory of earth, everybody can be filled."

Again, the King desires to pour out his Spirit on *all people*. Everyone on earth needs the Governor. Those without the Holy Spirit feel the lack of him, whether they realize it or not, and are inadvertently seeking him as they try to fill the void in their lives. The atheist is ultimately seeking the Holy Spirit. So are the agnostic, the Buddhist, the Hindu, and the Muslim.

When the Spirit was poured out on the day of Pentecost, Peter told the people,

> Repent and be baptized, every one of you, in the name
> of Jesus Christ for the forgiveness of your sins. And

you will receive the gift of the Holy Spirit. The promise is for you and your children and for all who are *far off—for all whom the Lord our God will call.*

Later, in his second letter to kingdom followers of Jesus, Peter wrote, "The Lord is not slow in keeping his promise, as some understand slowness. He is patient with you, not wanting anyone to perish, but everyone to come to repentance." All human beings lost the Holy Spirit when humanity rebelled, but God desires everyone to be reconciled to him and to be filled with the Governor. Some people seem to want to hoard the knowledge of the Governor for themselves. Yet the Holy Spirit is meant for every human. Receiving him into your life doesn't make you better than anyone else. It makes you a *steward* of kingdom authority and power. Paul wrote, "For it is by grace you have been saved, through faith—and this not from yourselves, it is the gift of God—not by works, so that no one can boast."

We should want others to receive the Spirit, as well, especially since the kingdom is to cover the whole earth. The power to live a life in alignment with the kingdom is everybody's privilege, because the King-Son died to give all people that right. John the disciple, in his first letter to new kingdom citizens, wrote, "He is the atoning sacrifice for our sins, and not only for ours but also for the sins of the whole world." Telling others about realignment with the Father through Jesus, and the promise of the Father, then, gives other people the opportunity to receive the precious gift of the Spirit.

RESTORED ABILITY TO INFLUENCE

Third, reconnection gives us a restored ability to influence the world around us. Remember our definition of power from earlier in this book? It is the ability to influence and control circumstances. This is what governments are largely about, and this is what the coming of the Governor to earth means.

A governor's job in a colony was to influence its way of life and to regulate activities in it. The world had been influenced and dominated by the kingdom of darkness since humanity's first rebellion, and it was only through the power of the Governor that life on earth could be set right again. As Paul wrote to first-century kingdom followers, "The kingdom of God is...[a matter of] righteousness, peace and joy in the Holy Spirit, because anyone who serves Christ in this way is pleasing to God and approved by men." The Governor gives us the kingdom authority we need to influence the colony of earth so that it reflects the nature of the King.

DELEGATED-AUTHORITY AND ABILITY-AUTHORITY

As we began to discuss in the previous chapter, there are two kinds of kingdom authority: (1) legal or delegated-authority, and (2) ability-authority. One gives you the right to do something. The other gives you the power and wherewithal to back up the authority by accomplishing the mandate.

The royal governor in a colony had delegated-authority, which was given to him by the king. When I was at the reception with the royal governor of the Turks and Caicos islands, the governor was really the only physical evidence in the colony that the queen was present there. Yet everyone treated him with great respect, bowing, shaking his hand, and calling him "Your Excellency." Why? Because, in the Turks and Caicos, he *was* the government of Great Britain. He was the monarchy. He was backed up by the authority of the kingdom of Great Britain.

The royal governor in colonial times also had ability-authority, which meant he was empowered by the king to *act*. A king gave ability-authority by providing people and material support that the Governor needed to fulfill his assignment. The governor was therefore backed up with the resources of the kingdom. This is a vital point because if you have delegated authority but not ability-authority, you probably won't see much accomplished. The power to act means that whatever the governor needed, the king made available to him. For example, in the days when Jesus lived on earth, Pilate, as Rome's procurator in Palestine, had the Roman army as a resource to back up his authority.

> *If you have delegated-authority but not ability-authority, you won't see much accomplished.*

Yet, with the kingdom of God, the heavenly King grants legal authority and ability-authority that have more influence than any human institution or power. When Jesus was brought before Pilate, the Roman governor threatened Jesus with death, essentially saying, "I have the authority to take your life or to give it to you." Pilate was a governor, but he didn't comprehend that Jesus was a King with all the power of the heavenly government within him. He had infinitely more power than Pilate had. At his arrest, Jesus told Peter that he could have called twelve legions of angels [warriors of the King] to rescue him. Jesus therefore replied to Pilate, in effect, "You would have no authority over me unless it was given to you by the heavenly government. I have at my disposal all the resources of my kingdom to execute whatever I need on earth. However, my purpose is not to free myself but to reconcile humanity to the Father through my sacrifice." His being handed over by Pilate to be crucified wasn't about a lack of power on his part; he was fulfilling his kingdom mission on earth.

After his resurrection, Jesus told his followers that, as King, he had the power to give them both delegated-authority *and* ability-authority to carry out their work of realigning people with the kingdom. His words are recorded in the book of Matthew:

> All authority in heaven and on earth has been given to me. Therefore go and make disciples of all nations, baptizing them in the name of the Father and of the Son and of the Holy Spirit, and teaching them to obey everything I have commanded you. And surely I am with you always, to the very end of the age.

The Greek word for *authority* used here is "in the sense of ability" and the "power to act."[2] We saw earlier that, when Jesus told his disciples, "You will receive power when the Holy Spirit comes on you," the word for *power* is *dunamis*, which means "miraculous power," "force," "might," and "strength."[3] His followers would have all the resources of heaven to carry out their assignment. This ability-authority would come with the outpouring of the Governor in their lives at Pentecost.

POWER IN THE NAME

The authority of a royal governor was in the name of the sovereign of the country he was serving. He used that name to exercise authority in getting things done. His own name had no real weight; he had to speak in the name of the monarch.

The King-Son operated on earth in terms of authority, and he showed us how we are to use his name in exercising dominion. He said, "I did not speak of my own accord, but the Father who sent me commanded me what to say and how to say it." The Governor also functions on earth in the same way. When Jesus was about to return to the heavenly kingdom, he said of the Spirit,

> But the Counselor, the Holy Spirit, whom the Father will send in my name, will teach you all things and will *remind you of everything I have said to you.*

> But when he, the Spirit of truth, comes, he will guide you into all truth. *He will not speak on his own*; he will speak only what he hears, and he will tell you what is yet to come. He will bring glory to me by taking from what is mine and making it known to you. All that belongs to the Father is mine. That is why I said the Spirit will take from what is mine and make it known to you.

We are therefore to act in the *name* of Jesus, the King-Son to whom all authority has been given by the Father, when we work on behalf of the kingdom. When Jesus was ready to leave to go back to the Father, he said in this regard,

> Now is your time of grief, but I will see you again and you will rejoice, and no one will take away your joy. In that day you will no longer ask me anything. I tell you the truth, my Father will *give you whatever you ask in my name.* Until now you have not asked for anything in my name. Ask and you will receive, and your joy will be complete....In that day you will ask in my name. I am not saying that I will ask the Father on your behalf. No, the Father himself loves you because you have loved me and have believed

that I came from God. I came from the Father and entered the world; now I am leaving the world and going back to the Father.

Under colonial rule, the royal governor of the Bahamas had a seal with the name of Elizabeth II on it. It was a sign to those who saw it that the one who used it was backed up by the authority and power of Great Britain. Whatever he sealed in the Bahamas was sealed in Great Britain, also. He had been given that authority by the queen.

Remember that Jesus gave his followers a similar authority when he said, "I will give you the keys of the kingdom of heaven; whatever you bind on earth will be bound in heaven, and whatever you loose on earth will be loosed in heaven." If we are rightly aligned with the King, the Governor confirms that we

> *We are to act in the name of Jesus when we work on behalf of the kingdom.*

are legal agents of the kingdom by backing us up with the power of the heavenly government.

RESTORED DOMINION

In one sense, the Governor returning is not really the ultimate issue of the King's purpose on earth. It is his intent that *humanity* should again have dominion in the world. This was his plan in the beginning, and the plan of redemption was put into effect to reclaim that purpose. I believe that we keep missing this point and stopping short of where the King wants us to be. Again, we aren't reclaimed for the kingdom just to go to heaven. We have been reclaimed for our assignment of earth.

Some Christians spend their lives focused only on Jesus' sacrifice on the cross and haven't understood that God wants them to receive the promised outpouring of the Spirit in their lives. Others have received the promised baptism in the Holy Spirit but do not fully understand its relationship to kingdom life. All of us need to move on to the main point: exercising rulership on earth for the kingdom of God. This was God's original assignment for humanity, and it is not temporary but eternal. Once Lucifer and the kingdom of darkness are totally defeated by the King of heaven, we will have what is, in essence, "Genesis II." The King has promised that there will be a new heaven and earth, in which we will fully reflect the glory of the heavenly kingdom. Below are statements from both Peter and John about this new kingdom environment:

> But in keeping with his promise we are looking forward to a new heaven and a new earth, the home of righteousness.

> Then I saw a new heaven and a new earth, for the first heaven and the first earth had passed away, and there was no longer any sea. I saw the Holy City, the new Jerusalem, coming down out of heaven from God, prepared as a bride beautifully dressed for her husband. And I heard a loud voice from the throne saying, "Now the dwelling of God is with men, and he will live with them. They will be his people, and God himself will be with them and be their God. He will wipe every tear from their eyes. There will be no more death or mourning or crying or pain, for the old order of things has passed away." He who was seated on the throne said, "I am making everything new!"

A TRANSFORMED OUTLOOK ON LIFE

Fourth, it is impossible to really be in the kingdom of God and not experience change. There is a realignment of the proper functioning of a person's spirit, soul, and body because anyone who has the Spirit of God has become truly human again.

For example, a major transformation occurs in the way we think. As we saw earlier, before the rebellion, Adam's intellect was a servant of his spirit. Afterward, when his spirit became dead to the kingdom of God, his intellect and senses took over and became dominant. All human beings who are not aligned with the King and have not received his Spirit find themselves in this same situation.

> *It is impossible to really be in the kingdom of God and not experience change.*

This is why, when the Governor comes to live within a person, the Governor immediately attacks the false mind-set with which the person has been influenced by the kingdom of the world. This is also why we are instructed by the Scriptures—what we can call the Constitution of the kingdom of heaven—with admonitions such as the following:

> For the sinful nature desires what is contrary to the Spirit, and the Spirit what is contrary to the sinful nature. They are in conflict with each other.

> Live by the Spirit, and you will not gratify the desires of the sinful nature.

> We demolish arguments and every pretension that sets itself up against the knowledge of God, and we

take captive every thought to make it obedient to Christ.

All these statements refer to the critical conflict between the mind-set of the kingdom of heaven and the mind-set of the kingdom of darkness.

Our outlook is to be transformed by a thorough understanding and reception of the mind and ways of the King, and through being receptive to the Governor's instructions and leading in our lives. If we try to deal with life from the mind-set we're used to, we'll fall back on thinking that is not in line with the kingdom. We need the Governor to teach us the ways of the King.

The Governor changes our inner culture by teaching us a new way to live. He reveals to us the thoughts and ways of the King so that we may understand and follow them. Remember that the King declared, "My thoughts are not your thoughts, neither are your ways my ways....As the heavens are higher than the earth, so are my ways higher than your ways and my thoughts than your thoughts." The word *ways* here means "a road (as trodden); figuratively a course of life or mode of action."[4] In other words, it's talking about lifestyle, and we need to change our mind-set if we are to have the same lifestyle as the King in order to help rule the earth. Then we will be able to live according to the heavenly government, rather than in the old culture of the kingdom of darkness.

We talked earlier about how a colony's citizens were made to learn the history of the kingdom they were now under. In a similar way, the King wants you to forget your former life outside his kingdom. He wants you to build a new history for yourself in the kingdom of heaven. Our history as the human race and as individuals is one of rebellion, fallenness, distorted

178

and lost purpose, and death. But when we are born anew into the kingdom of heaven, we have a history of being redeemed. We now have purpose and potential again. Our history is one of *life*—eternal life. The Governor encourages us to thoroughly learn our history, so that we can say, as Paul said, "If anyone is in Christ, he is a new creation; the old has gone, the new has come!'"

This means that we are supposed to be educated completely out of our history of sin. The book of Hebrews records, "'This is the covenant I will make with them after that time, says the Lord. I will put my laws in their hearts, and I will write them on their minds.' Then he adds, 'Their sins and lawless acts *I will remember no more*.'" The King is saying, "Look, your sins are blotted out. Just remember that you were rescued from the kingdom of darkness."

The kingdom's history of "righteousness, peace and joy in the Holy Spirit" is your own. Whenever Lucifer accuses you, saying, "You're a sinner," you can reply, "I was redeemed by the blood of the King-Son. He cleansed and washed away my wrongdoing."

The book of Hebrews continues, "Let us draw near to God with a sincere heart in full assurance of faith, having our hearts sprinkled to cleanse us from a guilty conscience." Even our *consciences* are cleansed by the blood of our Redeemer. Again, if another person brings up your past, you can say, "You're talking about someone who is dead. I've been raised in newness of life!" So the Governor teaches you your new kingdom history, for this is the will of the King for your life.

Paul wrote, "Do not conform any longer to the pattern of this world, but be transformed by the renewing of your mind." Your mind is to be transformed so that you will no longer have a mind-set filled with rebellion, guilt, depression, fear, confusion, and frustration, but rather righteousness, peace, and joy in the Holy Spirit.

Remember that the Governor is the presence and nature of the kingdom of God on earth. This means that if you receive the Holy Spirit, you should be able to say, as Jesus did, "He who has seen me has seen the Father." We will explore our transition into the Governor's culture in more detail in chapter eleven.

NEW COURAGE AND CONFIDENCE

Jesus' disciple John taught first-century kingdom citizens what he had learned from the Master Teacher: "You, dear children, are from God and have overcome [the kingdom of darkness], because the one who is in you [the Governor] is greater than the one who is in the world [Lucifer and his followers]." When the Spirit lives within you, heaven is your home country, and you have its authority and power. There is nothing or no one in the world who has more power and resources than the King. Therefore, you don't need to be threatened by anyone on earth who tries to intimidate or harm you. Luke the physician recorded Jesus' teaching on this:

> My friends, do not be afraid of those who kill the body and after that can do no more. But I will show you whom you should fear: Fear him who, after the killing of the body, has power to throw you into hell. Yes, I tell you, fear him. Are not five sparrows sold for two pennies? Yet not one of them is forgotten by God. Indeed, the very hairs of your head are all numbered. Don't be afraid; you are worth more than many sparrows. I tell you, whoever acknowledges me before men, the Son

of Man will also acknowledge him before the angels of God.

The fear of man is a snare to us as kingdom citizens because it will cause us to live by a mind-set and standards other than the kingdom's. We won't be acting in authority and power but in worry and timidity. Paul wrote that the King has not given us the spirit of fear but of power, love, and a sound mind. We can be composed in all circumstances

> *When the Spirit lives within you, heaven is your home country, and you have its power.*

because we know that the King lives within us through the presence of the Governor.

RECONNECTION TO LIFE'S PURPOSE

When the Governor comes to live within a person, he helps connect him to the assignment for which he was born. The prophet Joel talked about old men dreaming dreams, young men seeing visions, and sons and daughters prophesying the King's will. I define a dream as something you can see being accomplished in the future, even though you may not live to see it fully completed. A vision is something you can see to do, which you can complete in your lifetime.

Paul wrote, "For we are God's workmanship, created in Christ Jesus to do good works, which God prepared in advance for us to do." We are newly created when the Governor comes to dwell in us. We can therefore start over in the kingdom to do good works, which the King planned for us to accomplish even before we were born. The Governor gives back to older people the dreams for the future they thought they had lost.

He gives young people visions for their lives to help them stop wasting their time and energy on useless things. He makes us all rulers in the realms of our particular giftings.

Some people mistake the meaning of the Governor's presence in their lives. As we have seen, they think he came just to make them "feel good," or that he came to give them abilities that they can use to draw attention to themselves. Instead, he came to give us a vision or a dream of something that only we can help accomplish, because he has given it to us as our special work on earth. He came to give us *power* so that this particular work can be realized.

In addition, you can be cleansed and receive the Governor, but not understand that he wants to give you power for *living* the kingdom life. You therefore spend all your time fighting against attitudes and desires that are contrary to the kingdom, instead of overcoming them through the authority and power of the Spirit, so that you can do the important work for which you were born. His power should work through you so you can show evidence that your life is under the influence of the kingdom. The Governor came to empower you for *work*. He is here to impact the earth for heaven through *your* vision or dream.

COMMUNICATION WITH THE HEAVENLY GOVERNMENT

Finally, but very importantly, the return of the Governor gives us the ability to communicate with the heavenly government. We can bring the kingdom of heaven to earth and have dominion over it only if we are receiving clear instructions from the King. A kingdom can function in delegated authority only if the purpose, will, and intent of the King are being transmitted to that delegated authority.

What the King intends for earth is to be transmitted by the Governor to his vice governors, and to be executed on earth through their rulership. Whenever the Governor is not present, or the communication of the Governor is *ignored*, the practical rulership of the King is absent on earth. Some presence of the government has to exist. This is why the Holy Spirit is the key to the kingdom of heaven on earth. The Governor is the agent of the revelation of God's mind to the earth through humanity's dominion.

ACCESS TO THE KING

Let me try to illustrate how vital the Governor is to our communication with the King. In the colonial period in the Bahamas, if anybody, and I mean *anybody*, whether members of Parliament, local commissioners, or the bishop, wanted to go to Great Britain to see the queen, they couldn't get close to her without going through the royal governor first. This was true even for the premier of the colony.

A similar process applies in our relationship with the King-Father. Some people think they can have access to the heavenly throne because of their level of education or how wealthy they are, or how much they have done for the poor. We can't have an audience with the King-Father, however, unless we go through the King-Son, who opened the way for us by his substitutionary death, and unless we do so through the power of the Governor, who is our means of speaking with and hearing from the Father.

When you went to the governor in the Bahamas for permission to see the queen, the governor would send a message concerning you to England, and if the governor in Nassau cleared you, you were in. Likewise, when the King-Son clears you, and when you are relying on the Governor to communicate your requests and desires, you can go straight to the King-Father's throne room in the inner courts of the palace. As the writer of the book of Hebrews wrote, "Let us then approach the throne of grace with confidence, so that we may receive mercy and find grace to help us in our time of need."

I've heard that when John F. Kennedy was the president of the United States, he was sitting in the Oval Office having a meeting with his cabinet. They were discussing the most dangerous situations in the world at that time, the Bay of Pigs issue with Cuba and the Soviet Union's nuclear weapons. This was the most serious meeting they had held up to that point in the administration. The story goes that the door suddenly swung open, and a little boy ran across the room, around the cabinet members, and landed in the lap of the president. All the important members of the cabinet were suddenly silent. This little boy looked up at his father—the most powerful leader in the world—and said, "Daddy, who are these people?" And President Kennedy said, "These are my Cabinet, son." The boy looked at this powerful group of men; then he pointed to his father and said, "This is my daddy." At that moment, it didn't matter who the president was meeting with. The son had complete access to the father. And the same is true in our relationship with our King-Father.

> *We can bring the kingdom of heaven to earth only if we are able to receive clear instructions from the King.*

HEARING THE WILL OF THE KING

When a king wanted to communicate with his citizens, the Governor was also involved in this process. For example, any time the queen came to the Bahamas to visit, she didn't announce her visit directly to the people. She told the royal governor, and he told the people. In a similar way, whenever the King of heaven is going to do anything on earth, he communicates it through the Governor, who tells it to us. As Paul wrote, "Who among men knows the thoughts of a man except the man's spirit within him? In the same way no one knows the thoughts of God except the Spirit of God." The presence of the Governor in our lives enables us to hear and know the will of the King for us.

Hearing from the King is actually a very practical thing for a kingdom citizen, and was modeled for us by Jesus. The New Testament tells us that Jesus often went off by himself to hear the King-Father's instructions. Prayer was his means of dealing with government business. You have to be able to receive instructions from the heavenly government before you can accurately represent it. Jesus said to his disciples, "*When you pray....*" Prayer, therefore, is not an option; it is daily government communication. We need to ask the King, with the help of the Governor, "What do you want done today?" And we have to be ready to listen and respond.

KEEPING IN RIGHT RELATIONSHIP

Worshipping the King is another form of communication with the heavenly government. Many people have made worship into a ritual, when it's really about keeping in right relationship with the King. It is a means by which we remain in constant connection and communion with our Sovereign and honor his government.

Worship protects us from establishing our own kingdoms on earth, rather than the heavenly government's, because we acknowledge and confirm to him that his desires and will are paramount. We affirm that his government's interests are the ultimate reason for our existence.

The significance of our connection to the kingdom through the Governor will become even clearer in coming chapters as we explore the nature and role of the Holy Spirit and his impact on the culture of our individual lives, as well as the culture of earth.

PART 3

UNDERSTANDING THE GOVERNOR

CHAPTER TEN

THE NATURE OF THE GOVERNOR

A person left to himself will self-destruct.

We have seen that the presence of the Governor is essential for transforming the world into the kingdom of heaven. It is now vital that we consider in more depth the nature of the Holy Spirit because, though the Governor is the most important person on earth, he is also the most misunderstood and ignored.

People who are not yet in the kingdom don't understand the Holy Spirit's indispensable role in their lives because they've been led to believe that he is mysterious and unknowable. Or they think he is a kind of apparition because of our modern connotation of the word *spirit* and the use of the term *Holy Ghost* for Holy Spirit in the King James Version of the Bible. Even people who have received the Governor have misconceptions regarding who he is. I said earlier that some think he's a sensation or a thrill whose purpose is to make them feel good. Let's explore the nature of the Governor beginning with what he is *not*.

WHAT THE HOLY SPIRIT ISN'T

NOT AN "IT"

The Holy Spirit is not an "it" or a "thing." Some people refer to him as a nonpersonal object, saying, "Do you feel it?" or "Do you have it?" The Holy Spirit is a person with a personality. We will discuss more of his personal characteristics in the next section.

NOT A UNIVERSAL "FORCE" OR "COSMIC MIND"

The Holy Spirit is also not a kind of force or cosmic mind that we can "tap into" to receive the power and knowledge of the universe. He is not the sum total of the consciousness of the inhabitants of earth. To some people, these metaphysical ideas have become synonymous with God's Spirit. However, no one can control the Holy Spirit or "siphon off" his knowledge or power. Neither is he part of our consciousness. He is a distinct Being who grants us knowledge and power when we have a relationship with the King and are yielded to the will of the kingdom. Instead of demanding it or taking it for granted, we are to be grateful for the power with which he works in our lives to further the purposes of the kingdom and to strengthen us as children of the King.

NOT A CLOUD OR MIST

Some people think of the Holy Spirit as just a kind of smoke or mist or cloud that comes in to a place and sometimes causes people to fall down on the floor. I'm not saying that there aren't legitimate times when the Holy Spirit will manifest his presence in a physical way, but I believe that people who are always looking for such manifestations are susceptible to imaginings and fabrications.

Rather than referring to the Spirit as a kind of ethereal mist, Jesus talked about the Spirit using the word *he*. In fact, this statement of his could not be clearer:

> But when *he*, the Spirit of truth, comes, *he* will guide you into all truth. *He* will not speak on his own; *he* will speak only what *he* hears, and *he* will tell you what is yet to come. *He* will bring glory to me by taking from what is mine and making it known to you.

Jesus could have said, "When the Holy Spirit comes." He kept repeating the word *he*, however, as if he wanted to make sure we knew the Holy Spirit is not just a force or cloud.

Not a Feeling or Sensation

The Holy Spirit is also not just a "feeling." Again, I think we have often relegated him to a kind of strange, goose-pimple-raising experience. I think part of the reason for this is that some people come to corporate worship experiences so pent up with frustration about their lives that, when they can't take it anymore, but they sense an accepting environment, they run around screaming, roll on the ground, and call it the Holy Spirit. They are simply releasing tension.

You don't need to make noise to experience the Holy Spirit. You don't need loud drums and cowbells and screaming, shouting, and clapping. If you read the Bible carefully, most of the time when the Spirit manifested himself, it was in quietness, not feelings. The prophet Elijah had this experience:

> A great and powerful wind tore the mountains apart and shattered the rocks before the LORD, but the LORD was not in the wind. After the wind there was an

earthquake, but the LORD was not in the earthquake. After the earthquake came a fire, but the LORD was not in the fire. And after the fire came a gentle whisper. When Elijah heard it, he pulled his cloak over his face and went out and stood at the mouth of the cave. Then a voice said to him, "What are you doing here, Elijah?"

Let me add this statement, however: The Holy Spirit is not a feeling, but his presence can certainly affect your emotions as you experience his peace, joy, and comfort.

WHO IS THE HOLY SPIRIT?

THE HOLY SPIRIT IS GOD EXTENDED

The most important thing we must know about the nature of the Holy Spirit is that he is God. I like to use the term "God extended." He is God extended to a person and/or situation to work the purpose and will of his kingdom in the person's life or in the circumstance.

ONE WITH GOD

Earlier, we talked about the fact that Jesus is fully God, even though he is also fully human. God the Son became Jesus of Nazareth for the purpose of his redemptive task in the world. His dual nature never diminished His oneness and equality with the Father. The Scripture says that Jesus, "being in the form of God, did not consider it robbery to be equal with God, but made Himself of no reputation, taking the form of a bondservant, and coming in the likeness of men."

You don't need to grasp for something that you already have. Jesus is equal with God, even though he is distinct in personality and function from God the Father and God the Spirit. The Scripture tells us that Jesus was sent from the Father through the Spirit. The heavenly messenger told Mary, the mother of Jesus, "The Holy Spirit will come upon you, and the power of the Most High will overshadow you. So the holy one to be born will be called the Son of God." And Jesus spoke of his oneness with the Father, saying, "I and the Father are one," and "If anyone loves me, he will obey my teaching. My Father will love him, and *we* will come to him and make *our* home with him."

> *The Holy Spirit is God, and he is equal to the Father and the Son.*

The word *Father* in relation to God doesn't mean father the way one is related to a human father, or in the sense of someone who is "greater" or "older." God is not "older" than Jesus Christ. Jesus is eternal, as God the Father is eternal. Rather, the word *Father* refers to God's being the Source from which Jesus was sent.

Likewise, the Holy Spirit is God, and he is equal to the Father and the Son. John wrote in his gospel, "God is spirit, and his worshipers must worship in spirit and in truth." Jesus spoke of the Spirit as "*another* Counselor" who would continue his work on earth. So God is one, but he expresses himself in three distinct personalities and dimensions.

Jesus told his disciples, "When the Counselor comes, whom I will *send to you from the Father*, the Spirit of truth who *goes out from the Father*...." Both Jesus and the Spirit proceeded from the Father to accomplish the work that needed and still needs to be done on earth. Jesus was sent by the Father to redeem us; the Spirit was sent by Jesus to empower us. Jesus was sent to restore us; the Spirit was sent to release us into a new kingdom life.

I like to describe the concept of the triune God by the analogy of water. Water, in its liquid state, is like God the Father; it is the natural source. If you were to take some water and freeze it, it would become solid ice. Ice is like Jesus, the Word who became flesh; he was tangible, someone who could be seen, heard, and touched. If you were to take the same ice, put it in a pot, and heat it to boiling, it would become steam. Steam is like the Holy Spirit, the invisible influence that generates power. Ice and steam can return to their original liquid state. All three are in essence water, although in different forms.

RECEIVES THE SAME HONOR AS GOD

Another confirmation that the Holy Spirit is God is Jesus' statement about the consequences of blaspheming him. "I tell you the truth, all the sins and blasphemies of men will be forgiven them. But whoever blasphemes against the Holy Spirit will never be forgiven; he is guilty of an eternal sin." The only sin Jesus said you can never be forgiven of is a sin against the Holy Spirit. Why did he say this? I believe that he was saying it is the Holy Spirit who (1) convicts people of their need to be cleansed from sin by the work of Christ, and (2) who enables us to be spiritually reborn and brings us into the heavenly kingdom. Therefore, if someone totally hardens himself to the Spirit and his work, he won't be drawn to forgiveness through Christ, and he won't be able to receive the regenerating work of the Spirit in his life.

Jesus Christ cleanses us, the Father forgives us, and the Spirit renews us. The writer of the book of Hebrews wrote, quoting Psalm 95, "As the Holy Spirit says: 'Today, if you hear his voice, do not harden your hearts as you did in the rebellion.'" In other words, if you hear his voice, if you feel his conviction, if you hear him saying, "It's time," then do not harden your heart because there is going to come a day when he will stop calling you. The Scriptures speak about God as longsuffering or patient; it doesn't say that he is *forever*-suffering. He will allow foolishness for a long time, but only for so long.

The term *apostate* refers to someone who has entered a state where he can't hear the Spirit of God anymore. You don't want the Holy Spirit to stop convicting you. If the Holy Spirit convicts you about your need to repent, receive forgiveness, and enter the kingdom of God, you should run to him! Why? Because that means you are still in good relationship with him, and he is able to talk to you. Don't let your pride prevent you from responding because you wonder what people will say. You should rather worry that the Spirit will stop talking!

> *The Holy Spirit convicts people and enables them to be spiritually reborn.*

I hope that you will listen to the most important person from heaven, who is the most important person on earth! He is vastly more important than angels, which many people hope to see. Angels, however, work for the government, but he *is* the government.

THE HOLY SPIRIT IS A PERSON WITH QUALITIES, CHARACTERISTICS, AND A WILL

So the Holy Spirit is first of all "God extended." Second, as we have seen, the Holy Spirit is a *person*. A person has qualities and characteristics that distinguish him from others, so that he is a separate being. The Governor has a distinct personality, characteristics, and will. As the Representative of heaven, the Resident Governor in the colony, his main desire is for us to fulfill the King's purposes on earth.

Jesus described the person and work of the Holy Spirit, revealing at various times that among his characteristics are his abilities to teach and guide. A feeling or a force cannot be a governor. A mist can't teach or guide. Most citizens of the kingdom have no real relationship with the Governor because they haven't realized they have someone invaluable dwelling in them. Some*one*.

THE SPIRIT HAS SPIRITUAL SENSES

The Holy Spirit also has "senses" that are part of his personality. By this, I mean that he has spiritual senses similar to the way human beings have physical senses. Spiritually speaking, the Holy Spirit sees, hears, feels, and smells or discerns in his dealings with the earth and its inhabitants.

THE SPIRIT HAS FEELINGS OR EMOTIONS

Paul wrote, "Do not grieve the Holy Spirit of God, with whom you were sealed for the day of redemption." We can grieve the Spirit when we actively resist him, behave in ways that are contrary to the kingdom of heaven, or neglect him.

I want to focus on the area of neglect. Think about this: When you ignore someone, he generally stops talking to you. And the more you ignore him, the more he will ignore you. For example, if you don't acknowledge me, eventually I will come to the conclusion that I'm not important to you and that you don't have any regard for me. Or, if you keep ignoring me when I talk to you, then, eventually, I should have a little sense to say, "He really doesn't want to listen to me." Jesus said that the Holy Spirit will teach us all things. I used to be a teacher in the classroom, and let me tell you, there is no worse experience for a teacher than to have a group of students who have no interest in learning.

We must realize that the Holy Spirit is a person who knows when we are ignoring him. If we disregard his teaching and leading, we aren't treating him with the respect and devotion he deserves. We also miss opportunities to learn and serve in the kingdom. And it is not only we who are negatively affected by this. Suppose the Governor prompts you five times to bring food to a neighbor. Finally, he stops speaking to you about it. Two things happen: You miss a blessing, and your neighbor may go hungry.

Or suppose the Governor prompts you during the night to get up and pray for someone, but you say, "I'm tired, and I've had a long day, so I need to sleep." The Holy Spirit says, "Yes, but someone is in need of help, and I need a human vessel through whom to intercede because this is the way the kingdom of heaven works on earth." You think, "That's just my imagination; I'm tired." So you stay in bed and no longer sense his prompting. You find out the next day that someone was in a dangerous or troubling situation, and your prayers were urgently needed.

We listen to other people more than we listen to the Spirit of God. We seek other people's advice more than we seek his. Sometimes, he withdraws our sense of his presence in order to get our attention.

Some people have not heard the voice of the Holy Spirit for a long time. Why? They get up in the morning and don't acknowledge him at all before plunging into the day. They never refer to him when they make decisions, invest their finances, work at their jobs, run their businesses, or go to school. Therefore, he's quiet toward them.

You literally have to learn to fellowship with and listen to the Holy Spirit. He speaks to us through the Scriptures, through our thoughts, and through promptings and impressions. We need to practice hearing his voice and not ignore him, but acknowledge him as a person who is intimately interested in who we are, what we do, and how we fulfill our role in the kingdom.

> *You have to learn to fellowship with and listen to the Holy Spirit.*

THE GOVERNOR'S NATURE EXPRESSED TO US

Let us now look at how the Governor attends to us in fulfillment of his nature. The Scriptures describe and define particular roles and responsibilities of the Holy Spirit on earth. Again, in all his works, the Governor acts only according to the word of the King. "The Spirit of truth," Jesus said, "...will not speak on his own; he will speak only what he hears, and he will tell you what is yet to come. He will bring glory to me by taking from what is mine and making it known to you."

COUNSELOR AND COMFORTER

Jesus told his disciples,

But the Counselor, the Holy Spirit, whom the Father will send in my name, will teach you all things and will remind you of everything I have said to you.

And I will ask the Father, and he will give you another Counselor to be with you forever.

The Greek word for *Counselor* in both these statements is *parakletos,* which means "an intercessor, consoler," "advocate, comforter."[1] Some Bible translations use the word "Helper." It refers to one who comes right alongside us to assist us. Jesus promised his followers that he would return to be with them in the person of the Governor to enable them to live the life they were called to: "In a little while you will see me no more, and then after a little while you will see me."

I've heard people say, "I want to become a believer [citizen of the kingdom], but I'm not strong enough. When I have enough strength to stop doing this and start doing that, I'm going to commit to the kingdom." These people still haven't made a commitment because they think they have to be strong *first.* You may be struggling with the same issue because you're trying to change yourself on your own. The King is telling us, "Look, if you're going to learn kingdom culture, you need help from the home country." Receiving the Governor into your life will enable you to change. He will show you how to transform your thinking and how to live.

Likewise, some of you are discouraged because, even though you are citizens of the kingdom of heaven, you feel as if you keep falling back into the attitudes and actions of the kingdom of darkness. But the Governor says to you, "I'm going to help you up again." This is his job! He won't give up on you.

Jesus emphasized the King's commitment to you through his analogy of a shepherd who leaves his ninety-nine sheep in the fold while he goes off to look for the one that is lost. This doesn't give us a license to keep going back to the behavior of the kingdom of darkness. Once we're in the kingdom of heaven, we're not supposed to keep returning to our old ways intentionally. Some people purposely do what is contrary to the kingdom, and then they want to be automatically forgiven by the King. This does not reflect a true transformation into a kingdom citizen. If we really desire to live by heavenly standards, even though we sometimes may slip up, the Governor will help us to live them out. He wants us to succeed.

GUIDE AND TEACHER

Jesus also said about the Governor,

> But when he, the Spirit of truth, comes, he will guide you into all truth. He will not speak on his own; he will speak only what he hears, and he will tell you what is yet to come.

As we have seen, governors were placed in colonies not just to give information, but also to train the citizens to think, act, and live the standards, the customs—the entire culture—of the home country. This involved both general teaching and individual training.

Because the governor of a colony was sent from the throne of the sovereign, he knew the sovereign's intent. In the same way, the Governor from heaven is the only one who can enable us to understand the truth of the statements that Jesus made and the instructions he left for us. The Holy Spirit is the only one who can reconnect us to original information about the King and his kingdom. He protects us from error and from others' opinions that are not according to the mind of the King.

One of the jobs of a governor in a colony is to interpret for the citizens what the sovereign means by the words he delivers to them. We saw in the last section that the Holy Spirit is called the Counselor. The word *counsel* has to do with one who interprets law, and the Governor reveals and explains the laws of the King to us, bringing those words to life.

The prophet Isaiah said of Jesus, "The Spirit of the LORD will rest on him—the Spirit of wisdom and of understanding." We, too, have this Spirit of wisdom and understanding living within us. Knowledge is information, and wisdom is how to apply it. In other words, wisdom is the proper use of knowledge. The Governor shows us how to take our knowledge and apply it to life. He is the one who makes us practical people in the world. In some religious circles, this has been reversed. The Holy Spirit is considered to be the one who makes people act in strange ways. However, the Governor couldn't be more sensible. He shows us how to apply our knowledge to family, business, community, national, and worldwide issues.

> *The Governor shows us how to apply spiritual knowledge to all aspects of our lives.*

HELPER AND ENABLER

When the King-Son was on earth, he quoted from the prophet Isaiah concerning himself,

> The Spirit of the Lord is on me, because he has anointed me to preach good news to the poor. He has sent me to proclaim freedom for the prisoners and recovery of sight for the blind, to release the oppressed, to proclaim the year of the Lord's favor.

When a sovereign declared what he wanted for a colony, it was the governor's job to make sure it happened, encouraging the citizens to work toward its fulfillment. As the Holy Spirit carries out the will of God in the world, we are to be in unity with his desires and intent for the earth in carrying out our role as vice governors over the territory. We are not here to establish *our* kingdoms. We are here to establish the kingdom of our Sovereign, whom we represent.

IN FULFILLING THE PURPOSES OF THE KINGDOM

The above passage from the book of Isaiah emphasizes the focus of the kingdom on earth: telling the inhabitants about the promise of the Father, freeing them from the kingdom of darkness, and showing them the nature of the kingdom and how to enter in to it. It is the Governor who helps us to do all these things.

It is the King's ultimate purpose, as spoken through the prophet Habakkuk, that "the earth will be filled with the knowledge of the glory of the LORD, as the waters cover the sea." We can take this statement as an instruction concerning the kingdom. Again, the glory of God refers to the nature of God. Jesus said that, under the Governor's direction, we are to "go and make disciples of all nations, baptizing them in the name of the Father and of the Son and of the Holy Spirit, and teaching them to obey everything [Jesus has] commanded." In this way, the prophecy will be fulfilled.

The Governor calls upon us to bring the culture of the kingdom into the foreign culture that has taken over the earth—the culture of the kingdom of darkness. We saw earlier that to disciple means to teach kingdom philosophy and values, so that the students are immersed in the mind-set of the King. The term *nations* is the Greek word *ethnos*, referring to races or people groupings.[2] Every special grouping of people on earth is to be converted into kingdom culture.

The royal governor of the Bahamas used to appoint local commissioners, or council people, from the colony, and he would empower them do different improvement projects, such as fixing the roads. Likewise, the Governor empowers us to do good works in the world on behalf of the government. As Paul wrote, "For we are God's workmanship, created in Christ Jesus to do good works, which God prepared in advance for us to do."

In Reconnecting to Our Gifts

Every human being is born with gifts from God, but in order for these gifts to reach their maximum potential in service for the kingdom, they need to be reconnected to their original source. No one really knows the true essence of his gifts unless he reconnects with the Spirit of the Creator. Moreover, the Governor activates our gifts to a level that we wouldn't naturally bring them. Paul wrote, quoting the prophet Isaiah, "'No eye has seen, no ear has heard, no mind has conceived what God has prepared for those who love him'—but God has revealed it to us by his Spirit. The Spirit searches all things, even the deep things of God."

> *The Governor calls us to bring the culture of the kingdom into the culture of darkness.*

The Governor reconnects you to the source of your gifts so that you can understand what you have been given—not just the value of your gifts, but also the magnitude of them. In other words, no one's intellect alone can discern or understand the gifts that the King has placed within him for the purposes of the kingdom. This is why, if you want to know what the Spirit of God really created inside you, you have to connect to the Governor.

Paul also said, "We have not received the spirit of the world but the Spirit who is from God, that we may understand what God has freely given us." This statement tells us that we don't even realize what we *have* until the Holy Spirit reveals it to us. This truth is vital for fulfilling your purpose and potential. There are things about yourself that you will never know unless the Holy Spirit reconnects you to the deep things in the mind of the Creator and enables you to use your gifts most effectively.

Paul likewise wrote, "The man without the Spirit does not accept the things that come from the Spirit of God, for they are foolishness to him, and he cannot understand them, because they are spiritually discerned." Without the Governor, we can never recognize what has been placed deep within us. We cannot know who *we* are without the Spirit of God. This is why many of us are living far below our potential.

We should note here that there are gifts we are born with and additional gifts that we are given when we receive the Spirit. I believe there is a distinction between these two types of gifts, and we'll talk more about "gifts of the Spirit" in coming chapters. However, the gifts I'm referring to here are the gifts you were born with to fulfill a specific purpose on earth for the kingdom. And the Holy Spirit empowers us to execute these gifts. This empowerment is not necessarily to give us the ability to *do* them because that ability already exists within us. Rather, he empowers us by revealing them to us fully and even introducing us to gifts we didn't even know we had. Moreover, he shows us how to use them for the kingdom rather than for selfish purposes because the gifts our King gives us are always given to benefit other people.

CONVICTER

Jesus told his disciples concerning the Governor,

When he comes, he will convict the world of guilt in regard to sin and righteousness and judgment: in regard to sin, because men do not believe in me; in regard to righteousness, because I am going to the Father, where you can see me no longer; and in regard to judgment, because the prince of this world now stands condemned.

The word *world* in the above statement is not referring necessarily to people but to a *system* or *mind-set*. It's the system based on the kingdom of darkness that influences the behavior of humans. Therefore, it is the Governor who convicts those outside the kingdom that they need to be forgiven and connected to their Father in the heavenly government. He also convicts the citizens of the kingdom of attitudes and actions that are contrary to the nature of the kingdom. It is the Governor who works through our consciences so that we will choose to live according to kingdom standards.

We should realize that the Holy Spirit is not given to us to "take over" our lives. He prompts us, but he never forces us. In other words, he makes all the citizens *conscious* of the expectations, the standards, the laws, the regulations, and the customs of the kingdom, and he also convinces them of the benefits of these things.

The King-Father is not in the business of controlling his citizens. He wants his children to *desire* what he desires. He respects our wills. The Governor shows us what the Father's will is and helps us to fulfill it as we look to him for wisdom, strength, and power.

DRAWER TO GOD

In accordance with being Convicter and Convincer, the Holy Spirit is heaven's divine attraction to the throne of the King. As the Governor works in people's lives, he draws them to the Father in a gentle way. Again, he is not overbearing. The prophet Hosea gave a beautiful illustration of this approach when he recorded these words of the King to his people: "I led them with cords of human kindness, with ties of love."

> *The King wants his children to desire what he desires.*

COMMUNICATOR

A true governor would never communicate anything to the people that violated the king's wishes. Likewise, as we have seen, the Holy Spirit communicates only what comes from the heavenly throne. Jesus said, "He will not speak on his own; he will speak only what he hears, and he will tell you what is yet to come."

This statement reminds me of a practice we observed when the Bahamas was still under the kingdom of Great Britain. Every year, the people would gather at Clifford Park in Nassau to hear the royal governor read a document, sent from the queen in England, known as The Speech from the Throne. To ensure that everyone heard the speech, the whole country had a holiday; everything was shut down.

The royal governor would sit in a chair, surrounded by local government officials, and he would read the mind of the queen of England for our colony. That speech became the plan and the mandate for the new year. We were gathered together to be reminded of the sovereign's desires for the kingdom and the colony, and her expectations from the colony. It was a review of the laws, customs, and standards of the kingdom, and it also expressed her plans for the future of the colony.

Similarly, the Holy Spirit regularly brings us The Speech from the Heavenly Throne as we set aside the busyness of life to listen to him. The Governor's words will never disagree with the King's words or bring a message that is contrary to them. He will remind us of what the King has already said and what he desires, and he will also speak prophetically of the future of the kingdom.

SANCTIFIER

Paul wrote to the first-century kingdom citizens in the city of Thessalonica,

> From the beginning God chose you to be saved through the sanctifying work of the Spirit and through belief in the truth.

As Sanctifier, the Governor helps free us from things in our lives that are contrary to the nature of the King and that diminish our capacity to maximize our gifts for the kingdom. Earlier, we saw that to be sanctified or holy means to be both pure (integrated, whole) and set apart. The Holy Spirit therefore eliminates hindrances to our development and progress. It is like separating the chaff from the wheat. The chaff is no good to us. The separation involves some painful "winnowing," but it is for our benefit. The King doesn't want anything to stop us from fulfilling our potential and accomplishing our purpose.

The Governor also sanctifies us in the sense of setting us apart for the service of the heavenly kingdom, and for the day when the King will once more return to the earth to live for-ever with his people with the creation of a new heaven and earth. When the queen of England was going to visit the Baha-mas, the royal governor would require everyone to prepare for it. We would have to sweep the roads, clean the lampposts, and plant trees and flowers. We even had to mow our own private yards, even though the queen would never see them. It is the Holy Spirit's job to prepare every aspect of our lives for the King's coming.

These, then, are the major ways in which the Governor attends to us according to his nature. In the next chapter, we'll take a closer look at the culture of the kingdom that the Governor desires to instill in us.

CHAPTER ELEVEN

THE GOVERNOR'S CULTURE

Your culture reveals your origin.

THE GOVERNOR'S QUALITIES OF THE KING

We should always keep in mind that the culture of the kingdom of heaven is synonymous with the nature of the King. When we talk about the characteristics of the Holy Spirit and his culture, we are talking about the qualities of the King himself. Since the role of a governor is only to represent the king, we should be able to look at a governor's temperament and the way he acts, and conclude what the king is like. Likewise, since the Holy Spirit reflects the qualities of the heavenly King, his characteristics are the personification of the King's nature.

This concept is familiar to us from everyday life. If we sit down to eat in a restaurant and the waiter is rude and inattentive, it will negatively reflect our perception of the whole environment of the restaurant. However, if we go into a shoe store and find an extremely knowledgeable and patient salesperson who helps us find exactly what we need, we will have a favorable attitude toward the company he represents. The manner in which a person serves on behalf of another person, business, or institution inevitably contributes to the perception we have of that person, business, or institution.

THE KING'S CHARACTER DETERMINES THE STATE OF THE KINGDOM

A country's culture may be summed up as it *national character*. It is the combination of its beliefs, attitudes, values, conventions, practices, and characteristics. In a kingdom, the monarch's character and characteristics were vastly important because they influenced and often determined the state of the environment over which he ruled. They created what life was like in the kingdom. The wise King Solomon wrote,

> Like a roaring lion or a charging bear is a wicked man ruling over a helpless people. A tyrannical ruler lacks judgment.

> When the righteous increase, the people rejoice, but when a wicked man rules, people groan.

In other words, when the character of a leader is a certain way, it can affect the experience of his whole country. We see this played out in the history of the nation of Israel in the Old Testament, which eventually split into the kingdoms of Judah and Israel. The character of various kings influenced the people for evil or for good. For example, in the first book of Kings, we read, "Nadab son of Jeroboam became king of Israel…, and he reigned over Israel two years. He did evil in the eyes of the LORD, walking in the ways of his father and in his sin, *which he had caused Israel to commit.*" The epitaph about Jeroboam was that his actions "provoked the LORD, the God of Israel, to anger." Jeroboam had caused the people of Israel to worship idols rather than the Lord, and he had appointed as priest anyone who wanted to be one, rather than appointing only Levites, as God had commanded. His son Nadab clearly followed in his footsteps.

We also read in the first book of Kings that another king,

Ahab...did more evil in the eyes of the LORD than any of those before him. He not only considered it trivial to commit the sins of Jeroboam...but he also married Jezebel daughter of Ethbaal king of the Sidonians, and began to serve Baal and worship him. He set up an altar for Baal in the temple of Baal that he built in Samaria. Ahab also made an Asherah pole and did more to provoke the LORD, the God of Israel, to anger than did all the kings of Israel before him.

The things that Jeroboam had done, which had so angered the Lord, Ahab considered trivial, and he did more evil than any of the kings who had preceded him! Evil leadership continued through the line of the kings of Israel, and the people also continued to do evil. The second book of Kings reports that the people experienced only misery as a result: "The LORD had seen how bitterly everyone in Israel, whether slave or free, was suffering; there was no one to help them."

In Judah, however, we see the example of King Hezekiah, whom the second book of Kings describes in this way:

He did what was right in the eyes of the LORD, just as his father David had done....Hezekiah trusted in the LORD, the God of Israel. There was no one like him among all the kings of Judah, either before him or after him. He held fast to the LORD and did not cease to follow him; he kept the commands the LORD had given Moses. And the LORD was with him; he was successful in whatever he undertook.

The book of 2 Kings gives an account of how the Lord delivered the people of Judah from a boastful, vengeful enemy, and how the people listened to Hezekiah when he told them how to deal with the situation. If they hadn't trusted Hezekiah and his example of faithfulness to the Lord, they would have fallen into their enemy's trap.

The key to a successful kingdom is the good character of its king. Likewise, the character of the heavenly Governor determines the environment of the kingdom of God on earth. Again, his character is exactly the same as the character of the King. He represents the nature and manners of the King in the colony.

The King wants us to understand the nature of his kingdom, so that we can trust it and what it means to live in it. This is one reason why Jesus kept giving his followers descriptions of what he is like. He would say things such as these:

I am the good shepherd. The good shepherd lays down his life for the sheep.

I am the bread of life. He who comes to me will never go hungry, and he who believes in me will never be thirsty.

Come to me, all you who are weary and burdened, and I will give you rest. Take my yoke upon you and learn from me, for I am gentle and humble in heart, and you will find rest for your souls. For my yoke is easy and my burden is light.

Jesus wanted to emphasize his nature because other kings and leaders of his day exhibited the opposite character. For example, his disciples were once disputing about which of them was the greatest and deserved the highest honors. Jesus used this argument as an occasion to explain the nature of the heavenly kingdom. This is his statement from the book of Matthew:

> You know that the rulers of the Gentiles lord it over them, and their high officials exercise authority over them. Not so with you. Instead, whoever wants to become great among you must be your servant, and whoever wants to be first must be your slave—just as the Son of Man did not come to be served, but to serve, and to give his life as a ransom for many.

In this way, and in many other ways, Jesus kept trying to teach them that the kingdom of God was radically different from the kingdom of darkness they had been living under. He wanted to express the qualities and characteristics of the King to thoroughly acquaint them with their benevolent Ruler.

The key to a successful kingdom is the good character of its king.

The whole idea of knowing the nature of the King is critical to Jesus' statement, "The kingdom of heaven is near." He is inviting us to become citizens of a specific kingdom, and he wants to reassure us of the nature of this kingdom.

THE QUALITIES OF THE HOLY SPIRIT: GROWING KINGDOM CULTURE

Paul desired to instill the nature of the heavenly kingdom in the lives of its first-century citizens, who were learning what it meant for them to be realigned with the King. In his letter to kingdom citizens in Galatia, he made a list of essential qualities that make up the character of the King:

- Love
- Joy
- Peace
- Patience
- Kindness
- Goodness
- Faithfulness
- Gentleness
- Self-control

Any true manifestation of the kingdom of God on earth will have these characteristics. Paul referred to these qualities as "the fruit of the Spirit." He was saying that, wherever the Governor was, these qualities should be evident, indicating that the culture of the King was present.

Paul used this particular analogy of fruit because fruit doesn't appear overnight; it develops over time, and he wanted them to know that they would have to *cultivate* the culture of the King in their lives, under the example and leading of the Governor. First, the Governor teaches us the nature of the original government in heaven. Then he shows us that, because he lives within us, we have this original nature and need to manifest it in our lives.

When you receive the Holy Spirit, you also receive the seed of kingdom nature. You develop this seed by putting into your life the kingdom elements that allow it to grow. For example, an apple tree doesn't have to "work" to produce its fruit. The seeds of the fruit are within it, and eventually, through a process of maturity, enabled by elements such as the nutrients in the ground and sunlight, what is on the inside of the tree becomes manifested on its branches. The spiritual nutrients that enable the fruit to grow in our lives are maintaining a continual connection with the King, learning the Constitution of the kingdom, which is the Scripture, and yielding to the direction of the Governor in our lives.

Just as apples are a natural outgrowth of apple trees, the fruit of the Spirit becomes a *natural* development in the life of a kingdom citizen because he is reflecting the *nature* of his King. For example, one of the fruits of the Spirit is goodness. It is therefore natural for us to be good if we're in the kingdom. If we are

> *The King-Father's culture is characterized by love, joy, and peace.*

not good, we are unnatural. The Governor connects us to our original nature, which is true life for us as human beings.

The qualities or fruit of the Spirit embody the King's culture so that, first of all, we see that it is a culture of love, a culture of joy, and a culture of peace. Imagine a culture filled with all the qualities in the above list! It's our culture to be faithful—to be loyal to our commitments. It's our culture to be gentle. We're never brash or rude with other people. As Jesus said, "Blessed are the meek, for they will inherit the earth." It's our culture to be self-controlled. We never lose control of our tempers or our desires. No matter what happens in our lives, we still live out and exhibit all these qualities.

When we have the Royal Governor resident within us, therefore, he renovates our lives by enabling us to reflect the nature of the King. He changes our personal culture by giving us a new perspective on life and a new "kingdom educational curriculum"; he causes us to have the mind-set of the King. He retrains us in how to think, how to talk, and how to walk.

CULTURE REVEALS ORIGIN

Your culture should reveal your origin. The way you behave, the way you respond to others, the way you react to problems, and the way you deal with disappointments should all reveal the culture of heaven. The qualities of the Spirit within you define the uniqueness of your nature. Your unique nature then links you to your heavenly heritage.

Earlier, we talked about how people's distinct mannerisms and traits lead us to instantly recognize what country they are from. You see someone and you say, "That person is an Australian." The same thing is true for citizens of any country. There are certain things that only Australians would say or do in a certain way. People should have the same experience in regard to those who represent heaven on earth. They should look at our behavior and be able to say, "You come from the heavenly kingdom." Jesus said, "By their fruit you will recognize them." Being in the kingdom is a matter of dynamic change into the nature of the King. If the Governor lives in you, you cannot enjoy living in rebellion against the King. Doing so feels uncomfortable and unnatural.

CULTURE CLASH

When you become realigned with the kingdom of heaven, you essentially now live in two worlds or kingdoms. The invisible kingdom of God lives within you through the presence of the Governor. The human kingdom, the kingdom of darkness fueled by Lucifer, is all around you. In addition, remnants of the rebellious nature are still present in your life and need to be rooted out.

We are therefore faced with a choice of which kingdom and its culture we are going to yield to. Paul encouraged the first-century kingdom citizens in Philippi to keep their focus on the heavenly kingdom because "our citizenship is in heaven." Following his list of the fruit of the Spirit, he told the Galatians, "Those who belong to Christ Jesus have crucified the sinful nature with its passions and desires. Since we live by the Spirit, let us keep in step with the Spirit." The disciple John encouraged Jesus' followers, "The one who is in you is greater than the one who is in the world." In other words, the power of the Governor within you exponentially exceeds the power of the kingdom of the world around you.

We often experience a clash of these cultures, especially within our own families. Let me illustrate with another example from kingdom and colony. The majority of the people who live in Caribbean nations are black. Many are related because their ancestors came from the same villages in Africa when they were brought to the Caribbean as slaves. People from the same family were often separated, sold to owners in different colonial kingdoms. So you have people who belong to the same family, but depending on what kingdom they fell under, they took on the language and customs of that kingdom so that, today, the descendents of a single family can't even communicate with one another. They don't know each other's language.

While this was a tragic consequence of colonialism, you may have a similar experience when you enter the kingdom of God and take on an entirely different culture. Because you exhibit the evidence of a changed life, your own family members—people you grew up with—may no longer understand you or why you act in the way you do. They notice that you've changed your language, your attitude, and your friendships. They see that you've stopped doing things that are against the heavenly kingdom. The proof that you are in the kingdom is that you are living the lifestyle of a different culture.

LIVING BY THE SPIRIT

Sometimes, we try to have one foot in the kingdom of heaven and one foot in the kingdom of the world. We want the Governor to look the other way while we behave according to a culture that is foreign to the King's. Yet Paul wrote to the Galatians,

> Live by the Spirit, and you will not gratify the desires of the sinful nature. For the sinful nature desires what is contrary to the Spirit, and the Spirit what is contrary to the sinful nature. They are in conflict with each other, so that you do not do what you want. But if you are led by the Spirit, you are not under law.

Paul went on to catalog the culture of the rebellious nature:

> The acts of the sinful nature are obvious: sexual immorality, impurity and debauchery; idolatry and witchcraft; hatred, discord, jealousy, fits of rage, selfish ambition, dissensions, factions and envy; drunkenness, orgies, and the like. I warn you, as I did before, that those who live like this will not inherit the kingdom of God.

The word *inherit* here implies living in or experiencing the kingdom. The culture of heaven and the culture of the world are opposites; you cannot experience the kingdom of heaven if you are living according to a foreign culture.

Since the Governor's role is to convert the citizens to live as the King does, when we act according to the culture of darkness, he rebukes and corrects us. He does this in two ways. First, he uses the internal warning system of our consciences. Second, he reminds us of the teachings of the King. He brings to our minds what is recorded in the Constitution of the kingdom, or the written record of the King's words and ways, the Scriptures. Paul wrote that we no longer live "under law." In other words, our trying to follow strict *do*s and *don't*s doesn't work. Only a changed nature causes us to live as the King lives. And the Governor gives us this new nature and enables us to follow it.

> *Only a changed nature enables us to live as the King lives.*

Remember "The Speech from the Throne," through which the royal governor would read the queen's will for the Bahamas for the coming year? The Scriptures are a major component of The Speech from the *Heavenly* Throne, and as we become familiar with them, the Governor teaches and reminds us of the King's will. He tells us, "You're planning to do this, but that's not what the King says is good for you. That's not written in the Speech from the Throne." The Holy Spirit will only speak in accordance with what is in the Speech because it's the King's mind. And again, our job is to say, "Not my will, but yours be done." Jesus said, "The Spirit gives life; the flesh counts for nothing. The words I have spoken to you are spirit and they are life."

You must remember that you are under a new Master Teacher, Jesus Christ. You are under a new philosophy of life. You are a student of a new curriculum. You are a steward of a new ideology. You have abandoned all other schools and have submitted yourself totally to the kingdom school. And the Governor is your private teacher, enabling you to internalize and manifest the teaching of the King. He is like a royal tutor, instilling the nature of the kingdom into the king's children. We have to be trained in what it means to be heirs in the heavenly kingdom.

The Governor begins by teaching us to relate to the Creator as our Father again, so that we can call him, "Abba, Father," just as the King-Son did. This relationship enables us to be remade in the image of our Creator. It is because of the rebellion that we lost our capacity to manifest his nature. That nature has been distorted in us because of our former association with the kingdom of darkness. The Governor has the challenging job of teaching us to be what we were originally created to be.

> *The fruit of the Spirit are not only what the King does; they are what he is.*

The qualities or fruit of the Spirit that we have been looking at are not only what the King *does*; they are what he *is*. The King doesn't only *act* in love; he *is* love. He doesn't only *demonstrate* peace; he *is* peace. And every aspect of the King's nature is what we are to be in our essence, as well. This is what Jesus meant when he said, as recorded in the book of Matthew, "Be perfect, therefore, as your heavenly Father is perfect."

Realizing that we are to reflect the nature of our King-Father causes us to watch what we allow to enter the personal culture of our spirits, souls, and bodies. Paul wrote to the kingdom citizens in the city of Corinth, "Do you not know that your body is a temple of the Holy Spirit, who is in you, whom you have received from God? You are not your own; you were bought at a price. Therefore honor God with your body." Paul was saying, in effect, "Don't you know that your body is the Governor's mansion? He is holy, and he lives in you; therefore, you need to keep the residence clean for him and in accordance with his nature. Jesus paid for the redemption of your spirit, soul, and body, so that the Governor could live within you. Therefore, as steward of the Governor's mansion, you should honor it by taking care of it."

Jesus taught, "Your eye is the lamp of your body. When your eyes are good, your whole body also is full of light. But when they are bad, you body also is full of darkness." The culture of the world enters our lives through our eyes and ears. Whatever we watch on television or the Internet, or read in a book, affects the quality of our inner, personal culture. Whatever we keep listening to influences our lives. We must not allow a destructive culture to invade and destroy our lives and our work for the heavenly kingdom.

Being a kingdom citizen requires that we exist in some degree of tension because we live in the midst of a culture of rebellion and death. Our old culture is fighting with the demands of the new culture. Yet we live here for the purpose of spreading the kingdom of light and pushing back the kingdom of darkness. This is why Jesus prayed to the Father, just before he died, "My prayer is not that you take them out of the world but that you protect them from the evil one. They are not of the world, even as I am not of it....As you sent me into the world, I have sent them into the world."

Even as we live in this tension, therefore, we live in the reality of the love, joy, peace, patience, kindness, goodness, faithfulness, gentleness, and self-control of the heavenly kingdom. Paul wrote to the kingdom citizens living in Ephesus,

> You were dead in your transgressions and sins, in which you used to live when you followed the ways of this world and of the ruler of the kingdom of the air, the spirit who is now at work in those who are disobedient. All of us also lived among them at one time, gratifying the cravings of our sinful nature and following its desires and thoughts. Like the rest, we were by nature objects of wrath. But because of his great love for us, God, who is rich in mercy, made us alive with Christ even when we were dead in transgressions—it is by grace you have been saved. And God raised us up with Christ and seated us with him in the heavenly realms in Christ Jesus....For we are God's workmanship, created in Christ Jesus to do good works, which God prepared in advance for us to do.

Though we live on earth, we are also seated in the heavenly realms with the King who has brought us to live in his heavenly kingdom, and we have all the resources of this kingdom to enable us to live out the culture of the kingdom on earth. Jesus told his disciples, "Let your light shine before men, that they may see your good deeds and praise your Father in heaven."

THE GIFTS OF THE SPIRIT: THE POWER OF KINGDOM CULTURE

When the Spirit was poured out on the day of Pentecost, kingdom citizens were given the Governor's power, with various kingdom abilities, to promote kingdom culture on earth.

These abilities are known as "the gifts of the Spirit." The *fruit* has to do with the character of the King. It is the development of the King's nature within us. The *gifts* have to do with the power of the King. One is character, the other is ability, but both are necessary for the kingdom life. Some of these abilities are the gifts of wisdom, knowledge, faith, healing, miracles, and prophecy. We will take a closer look at these gifts in chapter thirteen. However, we should note here that while character develops over time, ability-power from the Governor can be received immediately after a person realigns with the King and receives the outpouring of the Spirit in his life.

With these gifts of power comes great responsibility. Character is more important than power because it protects our use of that power. It keeps us from using it for the wrong motivations and purposes. It prevents us from using our power to hurt others rather than to help them. Everyone wants power, and when we are offered it, we don't often think about the need to regulate it. Many people seek the power without realizing how critical it is for them to develop the essen-

> *It is easier to receive the gifts of the Spirit than to develop the fruit of the Spirit.*

tial qualities of the kingdom at the same time. It is easier to receive the gifts of the Spirit than it is to develop the fruit of the Spirit. It is easier to obtain the power of God than it is to develop the character of God. Therefore, we must develop the qualities—such as love, kindness, and self-control—because they will moderate our use of the gifts.

Both the qualities and the gifts are important, therefore, but the qualities are vital because power without character is dangerous. A balance between the two is a challenge for all kingdom citizens. I believe this is why Jesus spent three-and-a-half years teaching his disciples how to live, how to think, and how to act as kingdom citizens. He trained them first, and then they received the power of the heavenly government through the outpouring of the Spirit at Pentecost. He also told them that, after he had returned to the Father, the Governor would continue to train them because being transformed into the culture of the kingdom is an ongoing, lifelong process.

THE INFLUENCE OF CULTURE

Ultimately, culture is spread through influence, and the qualities and gifts of the Spirit are the influence of the kingdom on earth. As we allow the Governor to transform our lives into the nature of the King, and as we demonstrate his power, our lives will have an effect on others. This is how the kingdom of heaven will spread on the earth. When Peter explained that the outpouring of the Spirit at Pentecost was the fulfillment of the King's promise, the impact on the people who had gathered there was powerful:

> Those who accepted [Peter's] message [about the kingdom] were baptized, and about three thousand were added to their number that day. They devoted themselves to the apostles' teaching and to the fellowship, to the breaking of bread and to prayer. Everyone was filled with awe, and many wonders and miraculous signs were done by the apostles. All the believers were together and had everything in common. Selling their possessions and goods, they gave to anyone as he had need. Every day they continued to meet together in the temple courts. They broke bread in their homes and ate together with glad and sincere

hearts, praising God and enjoying the favor of all the people. And the Lord added to their number daily those who were being saved.

That is quite a picture of cultural transformation! The public impact of the believers' love, sharing, teaching, and demonstrations of kingdom power, as a reflection of the culture of the kingdom, led to their having favor with all the people who witnessed their new kingdom lifestyle. And the influence of the kingdom of heaven on earth grew daily.

As vice governors under the Royal Governor, we serve as ambassadors of kingdom culture. Kingdom influence will grow from personal commitment to community transformation to national impact to worldwide conversion. But it begins with one person who exchanges the culture of darkness for the kingdom of life and light. With which kingdom are you aligned right now?

PART 4

THE ROLE AND IMPACT OF THE GOVERNOR

CHAPTER TWELVE
MANIFESTING KINGDOM CULTURE

The absence of an internal government always demands more external law.

As we have seen, every nation manifests itself in unique cultural and social expressions. There are specific ways that people from certain countries act, speak, and look, so that you can recognize, "That's a Bahamian," "That's an Italian," or "That's a Russian." After you have been around people from various countries or regions long enough, you begin to recognize their distinguishing mannerisms, attitudes, and speech.

The previous chapter emphasized that, as citizens of the heavenly kingdom, we should begin to take on the distinguishing characteristics of our new country. While we are still surrounded by the kingdom of darkness, we are to live from the *inside out* rather than from the outside in. Since we're not used to living in this way, we depend on the Governor to instruct and empower us in all the ways of the kingdom—its mind-set,

229

lifestyle, and customs—so that what is within us can be manifested in our attitudes, words, and actions.

In this chapter, I want to explore an aspect of kingdom culture that is vital to all other aspects of it; in fact, it often leads to and is associated with the gifts of the Spirit, which we will discuss in more depth in chapter thirteen.

To begin, let's look at the characteristics of all human nations, or kingdoms.

CHARACTERISTICS OF ALL NATIONS

There are certain characteristics that nations must have to become established and to maintain themselves as nations. They must have…

1. Land (territory)

2. Culture (what the nation stands for; its ideals)

3. Values (the standards the people of the nation live by)

4. Language (a common form of communication)

For example, what makes the United States of America a nation is not a particular ethnicity or standard of living. It is the land, the foundational beliefs and tenets found in its Constitution and other important national documents, the values that are drawn from those foundational beliefs, and its common language, English.

THE POWER OF LANGUAGE TO A KINGDOM

Of the above four characteristics, *language* is the primary and greatest manifestation of a nation's culture.

Why is language so important to a nation?

Language Is the Key to National Identity

First, language is the key to national identity. When the British Empire took over the Bahamas, the first thing they did was make the people learn to speak English. Language is powerful because it gives people a shared perspective not only on life, but also on how that life is expressed. It could be said that culture is *contained* in language, because it shapes it. If you and I can't speak the same language, we can never have the same culture because we can't communicate with one another. So the key to community is language. A country is really not a country until all the people speak in the same tongue.

Language Creates National Unity

Second, language creates national unity. When a nation doesn't have a common language, the unity of the people begins to break down. In fact, the United States is currently facing a challenge with this issue. Some of the people want the nation to be officially bilingual because of the many immigrants who have come from Spanish-speaking nations. A number of these immigrants don't seem to want to learn English, so signs and literature are being printed in Spanish.

In past generations, when immigrants came to America, such as those from Ireland and Italy, there were also segments of the population who spoke another language. However, most of these immigrants wanted to learn English, and they wanted their children to speak English, too, so the situation was somewhat different. They were not asking that their languages be recognized officially but were interested in assimilating into American culture by learning English. The current question of a bilingual nation has prompted some in the Congress of the United States to propose legislation declaring English the official language.

Historically, Americans have agreed that their language is English, the French have agreed that their language is French, and people from Spain and Latin American countries have agreed that their language is Spanish. If you emigrate to another country, it's supposed to be your responsibility to make sure you adopt the country's language. Otherwise, it encourages disharmony. Therefore, every nation embraces a common language because it is the key to unity.

LANGUAGE IS THE KEY TO EFFECTIVE COMMUNICATION

Third, language is the key to effective communication. National culture, values, history, goals, needs, and desires can be transmitted only if a nation's leaders and citizens are able to effectively communicate these things to each other and subsequent generations. A common language is essential to accomplish this, especially in helping to ensure the accuracy of the transmission.

LANGUAGE IS THE KEY TO EFFECTIVE EXPRESSION

Fourth, language is the key to effective expression. You won't be able to articulate what you desire to say if you lack the words to do so. Such a lack makes it difficult for people to participate in a nation as full-fledged citizens.

LANGUAGE SIGNIFIES A COMMON HERITAGE

Fifth, language is the key to common heritage. It identifies the original home country of those who speak it. For example, if a man from Portugal met a man from Brazil, they would recognize their common heritage because they both speak

Portuguese, even though there might be regional differences in their respective expressions of the language.

LANGUAGE IS THE KEY TO GENERATIONAL TRANSFER

Sixth, language is the key to generational transfer. When families emigrate from a nation, and the parents preserve the language and customs of the home country but their children do not, you eventually have situations in which grandchildren are unable to speak with their grandparents and lose contact with their heritage. This means that, if I want to pass along my values, beliefs, and family traditions to my children, I have to be able to communicate with them in a common language. Language therefore preserves family heritage throughout generations.

LOSS OF UNITY AND COMMUNICATION WITH THE KINGDOM

These points about the power and value of language have implications for kingdom culture on earth. When human beings rebelled against their King and lost the Governor, the clear lines of communication between the heavenly kingdom and the inhabitants on earth were disrupted. In this sense, we could say that heaven and earth no longer had a "common language." Human beings then tried to use their human language to further disassociate themselves from the King. Let's examine how this transpired.

The book of Genesis records, "Now the whole world had one language and a common speech. As men moved eastward, they found a plain in Shinar and settled there." We learn in Genesis 3 that after Adam and Eve were expelled from the garden of Eden, the entrance to the eastern side of the garden was specifically guarded so they couldn't return there. Apparently, they left from the east side, and humanity continued to move eastward as the earth's population grew.

In Genesis 11, we find that the people were still spreading out eastward, and that they had retained a common language. This is the chapter that describes how the people decided to build a city with an immense tower. The incident shows the power of language. The people wanted to build a tower that would reach to the heavens, and they said, in effect, "We will build a tower and make a name for ourselves." God's response was, "If as one people speaking the same language they have begun to do this, then nothing they plan to do will be impossible for them." Note that he said, "If as one people *with the same language*," indicating that a key to power is language.

> *The King wants us to build the dreams in our hearts that he put there.*

The people's desire to build, however, was an indication of their separation from the home country. When you build something just for your own honor and purposes, even while using the mind, talent, and material the King gave you, and you call it your own, this is the same as idol worship. Anything that is more important to us than the King is an idol. So the people were about to build a tower that was more important to them than their Creator-King was.

The King was not against people building cities or towers. In fact, he wants us to build the dreams that are in our hearts, which he put there. Rather, he was against their selfish pursuit of fame, and their arrogance. We are to do everything for the

234

sake of the King's glory, not our own. If it's not for his glory, it will eventually be to our detriment.

Again, the key to their ability to build this tower was their unified language. "If as one people speaking the same language they have begun to do this, then nothing they plan to do will be impossible for them." The power of language is its ability to produce. Today, we see that the language barrier prevents many countries from working together on projects, and it can cause communication problems for companies who try to build in other nations.

Since the whole world at that time had one language, we can say that the whole world had powerful potential. But they used that power of language to build something for themselves, and the King said, in essence, "This is wrong. Everything you're using is mine. The ground is mine. The water is mine. The straw is mine. The nails and the hammers are all made from materials I created." And so, his response was, "Come, let us go down and *confuse their language* so they will not understand each other." He didn't say, "Let us destroy the tower," because that wasn't necessary. If they couldn't talk to one another, the tower couldn't be completed.

The Genesis account continues, "That is why it was called Babel—because there the LORD confused the language of the whole world." This incident is where we get the word *babble*. *Babble* means "confusion."[1] When we say someone is babbling, we mean that what he is saying is incomprehensible. The tower was not originally called the Tower of Babel. That was just what it was called after the King destroyed the people's ability to communicate with one language.

Confounding humanity's language was the King-Father's way of protecting us until he would one day restore our unity and communication with him and one another through the return of the Governor. Expelling human beings from the garden had protected humanity from eating from the Tree of Life and living in an eternal state of rebellion and separation from God, with no hope of redemption. Similarly, confusing humanity's language helped to guard human beings from the self-destruction of pursuing their goals only for selfish pursuit. The action was for their ultimate good.

If the key to power is one language, then the key to weakness is many languages. I believe this is one reason why the United Nations is so ineffective. Different languages, and the cultures they create, inevitably promote misunderstanding and disunity, and it isn't possible to change this fundamental issue, even through well-meaning organizations.

The rebellion of human beings, therefore, damaged their unity and communication with God and one another until the King-Son could put them back in the position to reconnect once again through the Governor. Significantly, this restoration of communication and unity was characterized by a capacity to speak in heaven-given languages, an ability given by the Holy Spirit. Once again, we can see why the key to bringing back kingdom culture to earth is the Governor.

HEAVEN-GIVEN LANGUAGES

One of the first things the Governor gives us after we receive his infilling is the ability to speak in heaven-given languages. He may give an earthly language that the speaker does not understand. Or he may give a heavenly language that is unknown on earth. Through heaven-given languages, the Governor enables human beings to once more share a "common tongue," so to speak, with the heavenly King, showing they belong to his kingdom. After Jesus had accomplished his mission of restoration, he told his disciples, "You will receive power when the Holy Spirit comes on you." But he also said, "These signs will accompany those who believe: In my name they will drive out demons; *they will speak in new tongues*;... they will place their hands on sick people, and they will get well." Jesus was outlining the evidence of lives that have been connected to the heavenly kingdom.

The promise of the Father was not just for kingdom *power*, therefore, but it was also for kingdom *language*. According to Jesus, when you receive citizenship, you receive "new tongues." The Governor gives you languages from the heavenly kingdom. Let's review what happened when the Spirit was poured out on the day of Pentecost:

When the day of Pentecost came, they [the one hundred twenty followers of Jesus at that time] were all together in one place. Suddenly a sound like the blowing of a violent wind came from heaven and filled the whole house where they were sitting. They saw what seemed to be tongues of fire that separated and came to rest on each of them. All of them were filled with the Holy Spirit and began to speak in other tongues [or languages] as the Spirit enabled them. Now there were staying in Jerusalem God-fearing Jews from every nation under heaven. When they heard this sound, a crowd came together in bewilderment, because each one heard them speaking in his own language. Utterly amazed, they asked: "Are not all these men who are speaking Galileans? Then how is it that each of us hears them in his own native language? Parthians, Medes and Elamites; residents of Mesopotamia,

Judea and Cappadocia, Pontus and Asia, Phrygia and Pamphylia, Egypt and the parts of Libya near Cyrene; visitors from Rome (both Jews and converts to Judaism); Cretans and Arabs—we hear them declaring the wonders of God in our own tongues!"

"All of them were filled with the Holy Spirit and began to speak in other tongues as the Spirit enabled them." Suddenly, those one hundred twenty people, who had gathered together to worship the King-Father and wait for the outpouring of the Spirit, were enabled by the Governor to speak in other languages. In this particular case, the God-given languages included human languages that the international crowd could understand. The King was communicating his plan of restoration through a special gift of language given to his kingdom citizens. This was a sign of the fulfillment of his promise. It showed that the communication lines between heaven and earth were open once more through the return of the Governor. It was also an indication that God desires to restore unity among the people of the world.

> *When the Governor indwells our lives, we're supposed to hear his presence, not just see it.*

Peter told those who witnessed their speaking in tongues, "God has raised this Jesus to life, and we are all witnesses of the fact. Exalted to the right hand of God, he has received from the Father the promised Holy Spirit and has poured out *what you now see and hear.*" When the Governor indwells our lives, we're supposed to *hear* his presence, not just see it. It's supposed to be manifest in the evidence of language.

Let's note the beauty of this occurrence. At the incident of the Tower of Babel, God confused the people with multiple languages so he could weaken them. Here, he gave his people the gift of languages in order to strengthen them in their new kingdom life and enable them to communicate the promise of the Spirit to other inhabitants who needed to hear this message. This gift of languages also served to unite kingdom citizens as one people belonging to the King-Father.

I have traveled to over seventy countries, mostly to speak at conferences but sometimes to visit. I don't understand the languages of many of these nations. However, when I have attended conferences in a number of these places, something unique has happened that illustrates the oneness between people that comes from receiving heaven-given languages.

For example, I was recently ministering in Ukraine, where twenty thousand people had gathered in an auditorium. I don't understand Ukrainian. However, we started worshipping, and the whole place seemed to explode with heaven-given languages. When I heard twenty thousand Ukrainian-speaking people begin to speak in tongues, and I joined them, I thought, "We're one now!" I suddenly felt at home. This reminded me again that the power of unity is in language.

In a similar incident, my wife and I went to Germany some years ago, and we went to a Pentecostal church where I was to speak. Of course, everybody was speaking German. Then they started worshipping and speaking in tongues. All of a sudden, I had that same feeling of being home. To hear them speak in tongues was to feel, "We are one family." The barriers dropped away. We realized that we are all citizens of the kingdom, and that we have a common heritage. It was tongues that did it. Then, when the worship portion ended and the people began to speak in German, I didn't understand a word anymore and I felt more like a stranger again. Heaven-given languages are more powerful than many of us realize.

PURPOSES OF SPEAKING IN TONGUES

The purpose of the Governor is to train us in the ways of our home country; and language, as we've seen, is the most crucial characteristic of a country. Let's review several ways in which speaking in tongues is important to us.

PROVIDES KINGDOM IDENTITY

Speaking in tongues is a key element of our kingdom identity. Again, following our reconciliation with the King, our being given the ability to speak in heavenly tongues means the Governor is enabling us, as it were, to share a common heavenly "language" with our King-Father.

GIVES DIRECT COMMUNICATION WITH THE KING

Tongues also enables humanity to once more communicate directly with the King-Father. For example, there are times when we find it difficult to express our desires and needs to the heavenly government while speaking in our earthly languages. Paul wrote that, at these times, the Governor speaks for us and through us to the Father, through spiritual communication.

> In the same way, the Spirit helps us in our weakness. We do not know what we ought to pray for, but the Spirit himself intercedes for us with groans that words cannot express. And he who searches our hearts knows the mind of the Spirit, because the Spirit intercedes for the saints in accordance with God's will.

The Governor provides us with heaven-given languages so that, along with other communication, it becomes possible for us to express our crucial needs and requests to the King.

A SIGN WE ARE CONNECTED WITH THE KING

When Jesus' followers first spoke with "new tongues" as the Holy Spirit was poured out upon them, it was a sign to the thousands of people gathered for the feast of Pentecost that these disciples were connected to the heavenly kingdom. As Paul taught, "Tongues, then, are a sign, not for believers but for unbelievers; prophecy, however, is for believers, not for unbelievers."

AN EVIDENCE OF OUR CITIZENSHIP IN THE KINGDOM

There is an incident in the book of Acts where the Holy Spirit was poured out on new kingdom citizens in the city of Caesarea as Peter was explaining the gospel of the kingdom to them. Peter and the other believers recognized that these were fellow citizens, "for they heard them speaking in tongues and praising God." Their speaking in tongues was clear evidence of their citizenship in the heavenly kingdom.

COMMON QUESTIONS ABOUT TONGUES

Inevitably, in a discussion about tongues, people have certain questions, such as...

√ Are tongues real?

√ Were tongues only for the time of Jesus and his early followers?

√ Is it necessary to speak in tongues in order to live the life of a kingdom citizen?

Let's address these questions.

ARE TONGUES REAL?

Tongues are actual spoken communications between heaven and earth. Many people wonder if tongues are real because speaking in tongues has been put into a context of something that is strange or abnormal. The early followers of Jesus spoke in tongues, as Jesus had said they would. Kingdom citizens throughout the last two millennia have spoken with the King using this means. If we realize that tongues are what comes natural to citizens of the kingdom, their strangeness disappears and their true purpose becomes clear.

> *Because heaven-given languages are a powerful unifier, Lucifer fights against them.*

WERE TONGUES ONLY FOR THE TIME OF JESUS AND HIS FOLLOWERS?

Tongues were given to kingdom citizens to assist them in kingdom purposes, and we are still living in a time when we need this assistance on earth. Their value to the first-century kingdom citizens is their value to us today—communication with the King-Father as we carry out his will in the world.

Yet some misunderstanding and conflict between people concerning speaking in tongues is not surprising. We read in the Genesis account concerning the tower of Babel,

> The LORD said, "If as one people speaking the same language they have begun to do this, then nothing they plan to do will be impossible for them. Come,

let us go down and confuse their language so they will not understand each other." So the LORD scattered them from there over all the earth,

As we just discussed, when people don't understand each other, they tend to separate themselves. We all like to be with people we understand. This is why, generally, all the English-speaking people group together, all the French speakers stay together, all those who speak Spanish join together, and so on. Language creates differences, and differences can create feelings of competition, pressure, and conflict. When you come down to it, war is often created by language differences.

Therefore, when some kingdom citizens don't understand the value of the gift of tongues and have not received it, then conflict and misunderstanding inevitably occur between them and other kingdom citizens, and this is regrettable. I believe that heaven-given languages are a powerful unifier among those who have received them, and this is why Lucifer fights against the baptism in the Holy Spirit and the outpouring of heavenly gifts to the children of the King. He encourages some kingdom citizens to create doctrines against the gift of tongues; in this way he tries to make sure that not all kingdom citizens will speak a common, unifying "language." This is, to a large degree, why we have theological positions against tongues, such as that tongues are not real or that they were only for the first followers of Jesus. We have seminaries that teach that these God-given languages don't exist anymore. Unfortunately, these schools are teaching ignorance. But the real damage is that this opposition to the baptism in the Spirit and tongues prevents some citizens of the King from having all the power they need to exercise the kingdom life.

The devil knows that he is in trouble when we start speaking in tongues. Tongues are our key to overcoming obstacles in many areas of our lives. For example, I used to be F student. After I started speaking in tongues when I was in high school, I became a top student in the school and even graduated at the head of my class. Tongues, therefore, are given for renewing the lives of individual kingdom citizens and enabling them to exercise power for kingdom purposes.

IS IT NECESSARY TO SPEAK IN TONGUES TO BE A KINGDOM CITIZEN?

You can be a kingdom citizen without speaking in tongues. However, you will have problems communicating with the kingdom and, as I said, you will lack the power you could have in living the kingdom life. Here is an illustration to show you that the gifts of the Spirit, and tongues, in particular, are very practical.

In my church, I have members or visitors who come from a variety of countries. There are people from the Philippines who speak Filipino. There are people from Haiti who speak Creole. There are people from Mexico who speak Spanish. If a woman from the Philippines prayed the Lord's Prayer in Filipino, most of us wouldn't understand her. However, would she be making sense? Yes, to other people from her original country. If a man from Haiti spoke a psalm in Creole, he wouldn't make any sense to us, but he would make sense to people in Haiti. The same thing would apply to someone from Mexico who spoke in Spanish.

Now, just because we wouldn't understand them, would that make their languages invalid? Would you be able to say that their languages weren't real? Or, would your belief or disbelief in what they said change the fact that their languages were genuine? No. Whether we understood or agreed with them, the languages would still be authentic. Paul wrote,

> Undoubtedly there are all sorts of languages in the world, yet none of them is without meaning. If then I do not grasp the meaning of what someone is saying, I am a foreigner to the speaker, and he is a foreigner to me.

Now, suppose one of those church members or visitors learned English. Since it is not his country's language, when he picked up the phone to call relatives at home, he would shift into his country's tongue. Therefore, if he wanted information from the Bahamas, he would speak English, but if he wanted information from home, he would speak the language of his homeland.

> *We need a direct line to heaven, and tongues are that direct line.*

In a similar way, when you speak in tongues here on earth, it's as if you've picked up a phone to call your home country and are speaking in your original language. The Scripture says, "For anyone who speaks in a tongue does not speak to men but to God. Indeed, no one understands him; he utters mysteries with his spirit." In regard to prayer, we are to pray in tongues more than we pray in our human languages. This is because we don't want a weak communication of our intent when we're speaking to heaven. The Scripture tells us that the Governor knows the mind and will of God. Therefore, when we pray in the Spirit, we know that the King hears us and that we have the things we have asked him for, because the Governor helps us to pray according to the will of the government. We need a direct line to heaven, and tongues are that direct line. When you are filled with the Holy Spirit, you can speak in tongues at any time of the day, any time you need to communicate with your King-Father. This is why you and I should earnestly *desire* spiritual gifts, as Paul said. They are important resources from the heavenly kingdom.

Some people refer to speaking in tongues as babbling. In fact, the reverse is true. Heaven-given languages communicate the thoughts and requests of the heart more clearly than any earthly language. With tongues, we're not speaking with our minds but through our spirits, and the Spirit communicates every need. For me, speaking in English can interfere with my ability to pray. That's why I pray in tongues much of the time. I love praying in tongues because my prayers don't have to be "translated."

I would even conclude that speaking in tongues is not really an option for a citizen of the kingdom of heaven. Perhaps you grew up in a church where speaking in tongues isn't believed in or practiced. Your theology or your church doesn't give you a relationship with God, however. It is the sacrificial work of Jesus and the Holy Spirit within you that enable you to have this relationship. The Holy Spirit brings you into the kingdom and gives you the ability to speak in tongues so that you can communicate with your King-Father.

DIFFERENT MANIFESTATIONS OF TONGUES

Two distinct forms of tongues are described in Scripture. These differences only demonstrate the versatility of language, as well as how communication changes depending on those with whom we are communicating.

FOR DIRECT, PERSONAL COMMUNICATION WITH THE KING

For the most part, what we have been discussing in this chapter is the first type of communication in tongues, which is for direct, personal communication with the King. Paul wrote, "Anyone who speaks in a tongue does not speak to men but to God. Indeed, no one understands him; he utters mysteries with his spirit [or, by the Spirit]."

FOR HEAVENLY COMMUNICATION TO OTHER KINGDOM CITIZENS

The second type of communication in tongues is not for personal but corporate communication. Paul taught the first-century kingdom citizens that ministry spiritual gifts, in contrast to personal spiritual gifts, are for the building up of *all* those in a local gathering of kingdom citizens. They include the public declaration of the King's will in a heaven-given language(s), with accompanying interpretation in the language of the people who are gathered, to assure that everyone understands the message. Paul wrote,

> Now to each one the manifestation of the Spirit is given for the common good. To one there is given through the Spirit the message of wisdom...to another speaking in different kinds of tongues, and to still another the interpretation of tongues.

> Now you are the body of Christ, and each one of you is a part of it. And in the church God has appointed first of all apostles, second prophets, third teachers, then workers of miracles, also those having gifts of healing, those able to help others, those with gifts

of administration, and those speaking in different kinds of tongues. Are all apostles? Are all prophets? Are all teachers? Do all work miracles? Do all have gifts of healing? Do all speak in tongues? Do all interpret?

When you come together, everyone has a hymn, or a word of instruction, a revelation, a tongue or an interpretation. All of these must be done for the strengthening of the church. If anyone speaks in a tongue, two—or at the most three—should speak, one at a time, and someone must interpret.

For this reason anyone who speaks in a tongue should pray that he may interpret what he says.

Paul was teaching that a special gift for communicating the will of the King through heaven-given language is given to someone whom the Governor helps to speak the mind of the King, in order to present it to the citizens. Notice that Paul said this gift is for the "common good" rather than individual edification. It is to help all the citizens to know

> *Tongues are an integral part of the manifestation of the Governor's presence in our lives.*

the will of the King and to be comforted and encouraged by his words. Paul concluded, "Therefore, my brothers, be eager to prophesy, and do not forbid speaking in tongues. But everything should be done in a fitting and orderly way." We should encourage public declaration of tongues and interpretation, as long as it is done according to the guidelines set forth in the Constitution of the kingdom.

Ten Reasons to Speak in Tongues

There is more to being filled with the Spirit than speaking in tongues, but tongues are an integral and important part of the manifestation of the Governor's presence in our lives. Speaking in tongues is a flowing stream that should never dry up. It will enrich and build up our spiritual lives. In my experience, speaking in tongues is a critical key in releasing and using other gifts of the Spirit. This, of course, applies to the gift of interpretation of tongues, but also to the other gifts, particularly prophecy, wisdom, and knowledge because they involve language.

Let's briefly look at ten reasons why every kingdom citizen should speak in tongues.

1. A Sign of Connection to the Kingdom

Tongues are often the initial supernatural evidence of the indwelling and filling of the Spirit. We see this first in the experience of the followers of Jesus at Pentecost. We also see it in the kingdom service of Paul of Tarsus. The physician Luke wrote, in the book of Acts, "While Apollos was at Corinth, Paul took the road through the interior and arrived at Ephesus. There he found some disciples."

Notice that they were called *disciples.* They were actually followers of John the Baptist, and Paul said to them, in effect, "You are on the right track, but you need to hear about Jesus, the one whom John was referring to, and you need the promise that he provided for you. You need the baptism in the Holy Spirit."

These disciples had said to Paul, "We have never even heard of the Holy Spirit." They are not very different from many people in churches today whose theology has excluded the active working of the Holy Spirit in their lives. They believe in the King and his kingdom, but they are unaware of the full role of the Governor in their lives.

When these disciples heard the gospel of the kingdom, which John had pointed them toward, and which Paul fully explained to them, they were baptized in water in the name of the Lord Jesus. When Paul placed his hands on them and prayed for them, the Holy Spirit came upon them, and they immediately spoke in tongues and prophesied.

An evidence that we are connected to the home country is that we receive heaven-given languages.

2. FOR EDIFICATION

Speaking in tongues builds up, or recharges, our spirits. We are personally strengthened as we interact with the King through the Governor. As Paul wrote, "He who speaks in a tongue edifies himself." Tongues are given to us so that our communication with God can be as it was for Adam—with no interference.

3. TO REMIND US OF THE GOVERNOR'S INDWELLING PRESENCE

Tongues make us aware of the indwelling presence of the Holy Spirit, and when we are conscious of his presence, we are encouraged and comforted. Jesus said,

> And I will ask the Father, and he will give you another Counselor to be with you forever—the Spirit of truth. The world cannot accept him, because it neither sees him nor knows him. But you know him, for he lives with you and will be in you.

4. To Keep Our Prayers in Line with the King's Will

Praying in tongues will keep our prayers in line with God's will and prevent us from praying in selfishness. As I quoted earlier from the writings of Paul,

> In the same way, the Spirit helps us in our weakness. We do not know what we ought to pray for, but the Spirit himself intercedes for us with groans that words cannot express. And he who searches our hearts knows the mind of the Spirit, because the Spirit intercedes for the saints in accordance with God's will.

5. To Stimulate Faith

Praying in tongues stimulates faith. When we know the Spirit is fully communicating our needs, we are enabled to trust God more completely. Having faith also *leads* to praying in tongues as we go to the throne of the King-Father in purpose and confidence. The author of the New Testament book of Jude wrote about faith and speaking in tongues: "But you, dear friends, build yourselves up in your most holy faith and pray in the Holy Spirit."

6. To Keep Us Free from Worldly Contamination

Tongues keep us in constant connection with the culture of the kingdom, even as we live in the midst of the culture of the world. We can speak to the King-Father when we are on the job, at home, or anywhere. Our connection with the King through the Governor helps to keep our minds and actions pure. We can also encourage not only ourselves, but also others in the ways of the kingdom through heavenly communication. Paul

251

wrote, "Speak to one another with psalms, hymns and spiritual songs. Sing and make music in your heart to the Lord."

7. TO ENABLE US TO PRAY FOR THE UNKNOWN

The Spirit knows things we know nothing about; therefore, through heaven-given language, we can intercede with peace and confidence. Again, "we do not know what we ought to pray for, but the Spirit himself intercedes for us with groans that words cannot express."

8. TO GIVE SPIRITUAL REFRESHING

Tongues are a type of spiritual therapy for anxiety, turmoil, and perplexity. Paul wrote,

> Do not be anxious about anything, but in everything, by prayer and petition, with thanksgiving, present your requests to God. And the peace of God, which transcends all understanding, will guard your hearts and your minds in Christ Jesus.

9. TO HELP US IN GIVING THANKS

Tongues help those who are unlearned in spiritual things—and all of us, in fact—to offer the kind of thanks and praise to the King that he deserves. A combination of praying in human and spiritual language helps our minds and spirits to express our gratitude, in addition to other communication, to the King. Paul wrote, "I will pray with my spirit, but I will also pray with my mind; I will sing with my spirit, but I will also sing with my mind."

10. TO BRING THE TONGUE UNDER SUBJECTION

Last—but not least—speaking in heaven-given languages places our tongues under the control of the Spirit of God, something that is much needed in all of our lives. We read in the New Testament book of James, "But no man can tame the tongue. It is a restless evil, full of deadly poison....Out of the same mouth come praise and cursing. My brothers, this should not be. Can both fresh water and salt water flow from the same spring?" Only as the tongue is yielded to the Governor can it be controlled to speak words of life in keeping with the King and his kingdom.

Tongues Are Meant for the Entire Human Race

To conclude this chapter about the manifestation of kingdom culture, I want to emphasize that speaking in tongues does not "belong" to charismatic or Pentecostal Christians. It is meant for the whole world because it is a gift the King-Son came to provide for all the inhabitants of the earth. It is intended for the close to seven billion people on earth

> *Speaking in tongues is as natural as speaking your own native human language.*

right now. It is meant for all ethnic groups—Chinese, French, Sudanese, Australians, Danes, Mexicans—no one is excluded from God's intentions.

At Pentecost, Peter said, "The promise is for you and your children and for all who are far off—for all whom the Lord our God will call." It is our job as kingdom representatives to help people from all backgrounds enter the kingdom of heaven so they may receive this gift and other gifts from the Governor, which will enable them to live the kingdom life on earth.

Remembering the Purpose of Tongues: Communication

Tongues are beautiful, but they've sometimes been made into a doctrine, a denomination, even a whole religion. We've lost sight that tongues are heaven-given languages that are a means to an end: providing communication between heaven and earth.

We've been treating tongues as if they are a religious issue when they are really a *governmental* one in terms of the kingdom of God; through tongues, the Governor communicates our requests to the King, and the King's will to us. We can't pray effectively without the Governor, because he knows the mind of the King and how our requests fit with the purposes of the kingdom.

Speaking in tongues is as natural as speaking your own human language, whether that is English, Spanish, French, or Swahili. Paul spoke in tongues frequently. He said, "I will pray with the understanding, and I will pray in the Spirit." As citizens of the kingdom of heaven, we are to do the same.

CHAPTER THIRTEEN

THE GOVERNOR'S ADMINISTRATION

The need for government is evidenced in humanity's failure to manage itself.

The primary responsibility of a governor is administration over the territory entrusted to him. Likewise, the heavenly Governor is responsible for governmental administration over the colony of earth. He is present to train kingdom citizens on how to have dominion in the territory, because that's our official function under his leadership.

As we saw in chapter ten, the gifts of the Spirit are the delegation and distribution of powers by the Governor to kingdom citizens, in order to execute government business in the colony. They are for the purpose of *impacting* the earthly environment. When the King-Son was on earth, he healed people, cast out demons, did miracles, and even turned water into wine to help out the host of a wedding. He did *practical* works on earth. He was out solving people's problems through the power of the Governor. And this is the work he continues in our lives today through the Holy Spirit.

AUTHORIZED POWER IS GIVEN AS THE GOVERNOR WILLS

In an earthly kingdom, the governor was given power by the king to appoint various people to governmental posts in the colony. The same is true concerning the heavenly government. Paul, after listing various gifts of the Spirit, wrote, "All these are the work of one and the same Spirit, and he gives them to each one, *just as he determines*." What gifts, and to whom he delegates them, are his prerogative and responsibility. We need to learn how to use the authority and power of the Governor in the right way so we can deliver his wonderful works to the world and bring about a change of kingdoms on earth.

Paul listed a number of gifts of the Spirit in his first letter to the kingdom citizens living in the city of Corinth:

> Now about spiritual gifts, brothers, I do not want you to be ignorant....To one there is given through the Spirit the message [or, "word"] of wisdom, to another the message [or, "word"] of knowledge by means of the same Spirit, to another faith by the same Spirit, to another gifts of healing by that one Spirit, to another miraculous powers [or, "the working of miracles"], to another prophecy, to another distinguishing between spirits [or, "discerning of spirits"], to another speaking in different kinds of tongues, and to still another the interpretation of tongues.

AUTHORIZED POWER IS GIVEN FOR THE SERVICE OF THE HEAVENLY GOVERNMENT

Any authority and power that we receive from the Governor is for the service of the heavenly kingdom; it is not for our private benefit. As the Governor delegates kingdom authority to us, he teaches us, directly and through the Constitution of the kingdom, how to administer his gifts correctly and effectively. He shows us that administration has to do with serving others, not lording it over them. Peter wrote, in his first book, "Each one should use whatever gift he has received *to serve others*, faithfully *administering* God's grace in its various forms." Likewise, Paul affirmed,

> *Any authority and power that we receive from the Governor is for the heavenly kingdom.*

> There are different kinds of gifts, but the same Spirit. There are different kinds of service [or "administrations"], but the same Lord. There are different kinds of working, but the same God works all of them in all men. Now to each one *the manifestation of the Spirit is given for the common good.*

Unfortunately, there are some disturbing trends today in regard to the use of spiritual gifts. Some people are using their gifts to make money off fellow kingdom citizens. They're "selling" healings by telling people they will become well if they send money to them. Or they're abusing their gifts by using, for example, a gift of prophecy to intimidate others by claiming to have a message from God that condemns rather than restores or builds up.

The purpose of true government is to serve its citizens. Therefore, if the Governor of the heavenly kingdom gives you a gift, you are to use it in service to your fellow kingdom citizens. It is not for making money, boosting your ego, or giving you control over others.

Authorized Power Is Not Personal Property

In an earthly government, if a governmental employee is given a car or a computer to carry out his duties, this is not his personal property to use in whatever way he chooses. It is to be used only to help fulfill his official responsibilities. The car or computer doesn't belong to him; he has to return it if the government requests it or he leaves his employment. His use of such things is a privilege, not a right.

The same thing is true of spiritual gifts given by the heavenly government. Some kingdom citizens, however, start to believe that the power they have been authorized to use by the Governor actually comes from their own abilities. This leads to the problem we just discussed, that of using this power for their own purposes. This is dangerous for both the person abusing the power and the ones he is supposed to be serving. He fails to fulfill his call, and the ones who are meant to benefit from his service go without the help they could have received.

The Authorization of Power Addresses All the Needs of the Colony

The Governor, in conjunction with the King-Son, delegates power to kingdom citizens in order to address all the needs of the colony for the greatest impact of the heavenly kingdom on earth. Paul wrote to the kingdom citizens in the city of Ephesus,

It was [Jesus] who gave some to be apostles, some to be prophets, some to be evangelists, and some to be pastors and teachers, to prepare God's people for works of service, so that the body of Christ may be built up until we all reach unity in the faith and in the knowledge of the Son of God and become mature, attaining to the whole measure of the fullness of Christ.

Here Paul talked about spiritual gifts in terms of specific roles, which are for building up all citizens in the kingdom. Thus, the kingdom shows its presence by its influence on the people and environment of the world. The authorized power given by the Governor to kingdom citizens also equips them to deal with conflict and opposition from the kingdom of darkness, which exists not to benefit, but to destroy, the inhabitants of earth.

MANIFESTING THE AUTHORIZED POWER OF THE GOVERNOR: THE GIFTS OF THE SPIRIT IN KINGDOM TERMS

Let us now explore nine gifts of the Spirit, as listed by Paul in his first letter to the Corinthians. We will look at them in terms of specific administrations of the Governor on earth. There are three categories of gifts listed:

√ Three of them *say* something.

√ Three of them *do* something.

√ Three of them *reveal* something.

The three that "say" are gifts of utterance: prophecy, different kinds of tongues, and the interpretation of tongues. The three that "do" are gifts of power: faith, miraculous powers or the working of miracles, and gifts of healing. The three that "reveal" are gifts of revelation: the message or word of wisdom, the message or word of knowledge, and distinguishing or discerning between spirits.

259

While there are a variety of gifts, they have a unity of purpose—serving citizens of the kingdom by enabling them to take on the nature of the King and use the power of the kingdom to transform the earth into the image of heaven. We begin with the revelation gifts, which address things such as facts, events, purpose, motivation, destiny, and whether something is human, whether it is of the kingdom of heaven, or whether it is of the kingdom of darkness.

THE AUTHORIZED WORD OF WISDOM

"To one there is given through the Spirit the message of wisdom." The message or word of wisdom is a supernatural revelation by the Holy Spirit concerning the mind and will of God and his divine purposes. It is authorized power from the Governor that gives kingdom citizens the ability to know the best thing to do in difficult or perplexing situations. For example, when you need legal advice, you contact a lawyer, and he gives you legal wisdom that is appropriate to your situation. The word of wisdom is special instructions from the King, through his Governor, about what to say or what to do in a particular instance.

> *Gifts serve kingdom citizens by enabling them to transform the earth into the image of heaven.*

There is natural wisdom that can be gained through a knowledge of the Constitution of the kingdom. For example, in the Old Testament book of Joshua, God encouraged Joshua, Moses' successor, to apply what he learned from the Scriptures in order to have success in life: "Do not let this Book of the Law depart from your mouth; meditate on it day and night, so that you may be careful to do everything written in it. Then you will be prosperous and successful."

A word of supernatural wisdom is different from natural wisdom, however, in that it comes directly from the King to a citizen (or citizens) through the Governor, enabling him to deal judiciously in the affairs of life. Scriptural accounts reveal that this wisdom may come in the form of a vision, a dream, an angel (messenger) from the King, or a word or impression given to a kingdom citizen by the Governor. For example, in the life of Paul...

√ The Holy Spirit spoke to kingdom citizens in the city of Antioch, instructing them that they were to set apart Paul and Barnabas for the work of the kingdom to which they were called.

√ When Paul was being taken prisoner by ship to Rome, and the ship encountered a violent storm, Paul received a message of hope and encouragement for all who were on board:

I urge you to keep up your courage, because not one of you will be lost; only the ship will be destroyed. Last night an angel of the God whose I am and whom I serve stood beside me and said, "Do not be afraid, Paul. You must stand trial before Caesar; and God has graciously given you the lives of all who sail with you." So keep up your courage, men, for I have faith in God that it will happen just as he told me. Nevertheless, we must run aground on some island.

Paul's encouragement, which he received from a messenger of the King, showed them how they were to respond to this life-threatening situation.

A word of wisdom may apply to the person who receives it, or it may apply to someone else. In both instances, the kingdom government is teaching its citizens regarding how to best apply governmental policy and purposes in the colony of earth.

THE AUTHORIZED WORD OF KNOWLEDGE

"To another the message of knowledge by means of the same Spirit." While wisdom is about application, knowledge is about having the *information* you need to make the best decisions in executing delegated authority in the colony. It refers to the government providing you with the ability to understand its policies; but especially, it gives you the ability to understand what the King is thinking; it is supernatural revelation by the Governor of certain facts in the mind of the King.

The King has all knowledge, but he doesn't reveal everything to his citizens. The word of knowledge gives them part of what he knows—what they specifically need to know to carry out their assignments. Some human governments give their employees classified information on a "need to know" basis, which is only what they need to know to fulfill their responsibilities. The word of knowledge operates in a similar way.

> *The word of knowledge is given on a "need to know" basis.*

The word of knowledge may be manifested through an inward revelation, the interpretation of tongues, a word of prophecy, a vision, or an angel. Again, this is not natural knowledge that can be gained from experience or information, or even a profound acquaintance with the Scriptures. It is supernatural, meaning it is something we would not ordinarily be able to know and cannot learn on our own. For example...

√ Jesus demonstrated a word of knowledge when he talked with a woman he had just met and told her she had had five husbands and was currently living with another man. This demonstration of knowledge was for the purpose of gaining her attention and building faith in the King so she and others would understand how to be reconciled to the heavenly government.

√ A prophet named Agabus was given a word of knowledge that a severe famine would afflict the entire Roman world. (In a demonstration of the relationship between the word of knowledge and the word of wisdom, the kingdom citizens took this knowledge and applied it [wisdom], deciding to send relief to kingdom citizens living in Judea.)

√ Peter was given supernatural knowledge that a couple named Ananias and Sapphira were lying about the money they donated to the church.

√ Through a vision, the disciple John was given knowledge of the inner spiritual conditions of seven assemblies of kingdom citizens in Asia, so that he could give them messages of warning and encouragement from the King.

Through the word of knowledge, therefore, the Governor may communicate a message from the King to his citizens, saying, "This is what is going wrong here," or "This is what's going right in the colony; keep up the good work." He may also reveal important information to a kingdom citizen, so that he can convey to another citizen what he needs to function properly in the kingdom.

THE AUTHORIZED POWER OF FAITH

"To another faith by the same Spirit." The authorized power of faith is a supernatural belief or confidence. It is the government providing its citizens with special ability to believe in its policies so they will take action to carry them out.

Every kingdom citizen has faith. In fact, the author of the book of Hebrews wrote, "Without faith it is impossible to please God, because anyone who comes to him must believe that he exists and that he rewards those who earnestly seek him." The gift of faith, therefore, is not the same as the faith with which we enter the kingdom through belief in the sacrifice of the King-Son on our behalf, and the forgiveness we receive as a result. *That* faith comes through belief in the Constitution of the kingdom. As Paul wrote, "Faith comes from hearing the message, and the message is heard through the word of Christ." Neither is the gift of faith the same thing as the fruit of the Spirit known as "faithfulness." Nor is it the faith by which kingdom believers daily live as they trust the King to carry out his purposes through their lives and to bring them encouragement and peace. Again, such faith can be increased through exposure to and application of the King's Word.

Instead, the gift of faith is a special authorization by the government to a kingdom citizen so that he knows, without a doubt, that a particular outcome will ultimately be manifested for the purposes of the kingdom. Some examples of this kind of faith follow. As you review them, note the close relationship between the gift of faith and the working of miracles. (In this context, one Bible commentator referred to the gift of faith as "wonder-working" faith.)

√ The belief of three Hebrew men, who were governmental officials in the ancient kingdom of Babylon, that God could deliver them even if they were thrown into a blazing furnace.

√ Jesus' confidence that Lazarus, who had been dead for four days, would be raised to life.

√ The unwavering belief of Peter and John that a man who had been crippled from birth would be healed in the name of Jesus.

The gift of faith is therefore the Governor motivating kingdom citizens to trust in the promises and power of the heavenly government. The Governor encourages the citizens to courageously carry out their assignments in the belief that he will take care of everything that needs to be done to accomplish the work.

THE AUTHORIZED POWER OF HEALING

"To another gifts of healing by that one Spirit." Gifts of healing are supernatural cures for disease and disability. No natural means are involved, whether medical science or other forms of the application of human knowledge. In terms of the administration of the heavenly government on earth, healing is the King's commitment to the welfare of his citizens, as well as his program for securing that welfare.

This healing power is mentioned in the plural—*gifts* of healing. The word *healing* is sometimes used in the plural in this context, as well: "*gifts* of *healings*." The plural usage refers to the ability to heal different kinds of diseases. The book of Matthew records, "Jesus was going about in all Galilee, teaching in their synagogues, and proclaiming the gospel of the kingdom, and healing *every kind of disease* and *every kind of sickness* among the people."

The gifts of healing address a variety of sickness, both mental and physical, that bring us into disharmony with ourselves, other people, or the King-Father. This would include things such as fear, loneliness, and depression. Gifts of healing are for the restoration of the whole person.

We should recognize that all healing ultimately comes from God, whether it is through a doctor's care or the body's natural healing processes. The gifts of healing do not negate doctors. However, we should be aware that supernatural healing, a physician's care, and the body's natural ability to heal are distinct channels of healing. The first comes from another world, the second only *assists* the healing ability that our Creator has placed within our own bodies, and the third is an inbuilt capacity. In addition, there is a distinction between gifts of healing and our receiving healing by exercising faith in Scriptures that state the King's desire to heal us. A person may be healed by applying to himself statements such as this one from the first book of Peter: "He himself bore our sins in his body on the tree, so that we might die to sins and live for righteousness; by his wounds you have been healed." Yet gifts of healing are manifested through a kingdom citizen to whom the Governor gives a special administration of healing; they occur through the activity of a kingdom citizen as empowered by the Governor.

> *Gifts of healing are for the restoration of the whole person.*

We should also understand that we cannot make gifts of healing, or any of the gifts, operate according to our own wills. They are given only according to the will of the Governor, and we should maintain an open mind to receive whatever gift he may give us.

The following are some examples of healing that go beyond medical help and were administered through the intervention of a person empowered by the Governor:

√ A man's shriveled or withered hand was completely restored; a centurion's servant who was paralyzed and on his deathbed was cured; a man who was born blind was given his sight; a woman who had suffered from a hemorrhage for twelve years—and who had been to many physicians without help—was made completely well. Each was healed by Jesus working in the power of the Spirit.

√ Through Peter's ministry, a man named Aeneas, who was paralyzed and bedridden for eight years, was made totally well.

√ Paul healed a man on Malta who suffered from apparently recurring bouts of fever and dysentery.

It has been said that healing and compassion go hand in hand. Sympathy alone is ineffective. Sympathy means that you feel sorry for the person, empathize with his illness, and want to help him. Compassion, however, is an almost irresistible urge to free a person from the sickness or problem afflicting him. There is true passion in com*passion* that alleviates suffering.

In the administration of the kingdom of heaven on earth, therefore, the gifts of healing are the Governor's authorization of kingdom citizens to free others from being invaded by anything that is abnormal to the kingdom. In this way, the government shows evidence that it is present and can address negative conditions in the colony. In the kingdom of God, healing is executing justice. The Governor confirms the rights of the citizens to live in wholeness.

THE AUTHORIZED POWER OF MIRACLES

"To another miraculous powers." In one sense, all gifts of the Spirit are miracles because they are beyond our natural experience. But miraculous powers or the working of miracles are specific acts that defy human understanding. They "blow the mind." As such, a miracle is a supernatural intervention in the ordinary course of nature, a temporary suspension in the accustomed order of things by an act of the Spirit of God. Some examples of this gift include...

√ Moses' parting of the Red Sea, which allowed the Israelites to escape the pursuing Egyptians on dry ground.

√ The continual flow of a widow's supply of oil and flour during a famine, through the intervention of the prophet Elijah.

√ Jesus' feeding of more than five thousand people by the multiplication of just five small loaves and two fish.

√ Jesus' raising of Lazarus from the dead.

√ Peter's raising of Dorcas from the dead.

√ The temporary blinding of Elymas the sorcerer, who opposed Paul's proclamation of the gospel of the kingdom.

Interestingly, the Greek word for miraculous or miracles, in reference to this gift, is *dunamis,* the same word used for the power that Jesus said would come upon his followers when the Holy Spirit was poured out upon them.[1] Miracles are an "explosion" of kingdom power; they are wonders that bring astonishment to people who witness them.

In the administration of the kingdom of heaven on earth, then, miracles are the government providing for the special needs of people. Whatever the miracle is, whether it is supplying food, raising the dead, or something else, it is provision. Miracles are not entertainment; they are the result of the Governor, through citizens under his authority, performing actions that confirm the presence of the kingdom and its ability to transform the environment of the colony.

THE AUTHORIZED POWER OF PROPHECY

"To another prophecy." Prophecy is a message from the King, supernaturally given, in an earthly language known to the hearer or hearers. It is the heavenly government giving its citizens confirmation about information the government has previously told them.

Paul wrote this concerning the gift of prophecy:

Pursue love, yet desire earnestly spiritual gifts, but especially that you may prophesy. For one who speaks in a tongue does not speak to men, but to God; for no one understands, but in his spirit he speaks mysteries. But one who prophesies speaks to men for edification and exhortation and consolation [or, "comfort"]. One who speaks in a tongue edifies himself; but one who prophesies edifies the church. Now I wish that you all spoke in tongues, but even more that you would prophesy; and greater is one who prophesies than one who speaks in tongues, unless he interprets, so that the church may receive edifying.

The purpose of prophecy, Paul said, is for edification, exhortation, and consolation or comfort. He indicated that prophecy is the most important gift of all because it edifies kingdom citizens. The word *edification* in the Greek means "'the act of building'...in the sense of...the promotion of spiritual growth."[2] It therefore signifies strengthening or building people up in the ways of the kingdom. The Greek word translated *exhortation* means "'a calling to one's side'; hence, either 'an exhortation, or consolation, comfort.'"[3] *Comfort* means "'a speaking closely to anyone,' hence denotes 'consolation, comfort,' with a greater degree of tenderness" than exhortation.[4] I think of this word in the sense of calming people down in the face of difficulty and bringing peace to them.

Paul specifically said that the gift of prophecy should be earnestly sought, for the betterment of others. As the prophet Joel said, "Your sons and daughters will prophesy," and "Even on my servants, both men and women, I will pour out my Spirit in those days, and they will prophesy."

> *The purpose of prophecy is edification, exhortation, and comfort.*

Prophecy is obviously a vital gift to kingdom citizens, but it has been too often misused. Here are some guidelines in using this gift:

1. Prophecy is not one-sided. It must be confirmed by giver and receiver.

2. Prophecy usually confirms something already known by the receiver, rather than being the means of giving direction to that person.

3. Prophecy speaks to the intellect and understanding.

4. Edification, exhortation, and comfort may be delivered through a biblical teaching from a leader in an assembly of kingdom citizens.

5. The gift of prophecy should not be rejected. Paul wrote, "Do not quench the Spirit. Do not despise prophecies."

6. Prophecy should be tested rather than automatically accepted. Paul also said, "Test everything. Hold on to the good," and "Two or three prophets should speak, and the others should weigh carefully what is said."

7. Someone who gives a prophecy is not "under the control" of the prophecy. He has a choice whether or not to speak it and can decide when is an appropriate time to speak it. When someone receives a prophecy, he must draw on the qualities or fruit of the Spirit, exercising self-control in regard to its use. As Paul said, "For you can all prophesy in turn so that everyone may be instructed and encouraged," and "The spirits of prophets are subject to the control of prophets. For God is not a God of disorder but of peace."

We should also note that there is a distinction between the gift of prophecy, which all citizens are encouraged to seek, and the office of prophet, which is given by the Spirit to certain kingdom citizens. We can think of the distinction in this way: the gift of prophecy is about *forth*telling, or declaring the will of the King, while the office of prophet also includes *fore*telling, or the government giving a citizen the ability to receive news before it happens. This may be an announcement of what the King plans to do in the future. A prophet usually has other revelation gifts operating in his life, as well, such as the word of knowledge or wisdom, or the discerning of spirits.

If someone exercises the gift of prophecy, this doesn't necessarily mean he has the office of prophet. In other words, this may not be his regular position or responsibility on behalf of the heavenly government. It just means he has been given special information from the King at that particular time. Some people witness others exercising the office of prophet and decide that they'd like to foretell the future, too. If they try to prophesy in an unauthorized way, this leads to confusion and an abuse of the gift. Each person should function only in the gifts the Governor gives him.

The following are some examples of prophecy:

√ The disciples at Ephesus "spoke in tongues and prophesied" when they received the baptism in the Holy Spirit.

√ Philip the evangelist had four daughters who prophesied.

√ Agabus the prophet predicted the famine in the Roman world as well as Paul's being taken prisoner to face Caesar in Rome.

The authorized power of prophecy, therefore, is the Governor providing a kingdom citizen with information that supports and encourages his fellow citizens in the life of the kingdom. For example, when the Bahamas was still under the kingdom of Great Britain, we would receive various communications from the government, such as, "A storm is coming, but we have a plan in place to address any problems that may arise. If something should happen, here's what the government will do." Similarly, a prophecy from the heavenly kingdom might be, "You're going through a tough time, but we're sending help to address the problems and relieve your distress."

In this way, prophecy is a reminder to kingdom citizens that the heavenly government is still at work on their behalf, no matter what they might be going through. After we have received a prophecy, even if we don't see it immediately manifested, we can know that everything we need is on the way— whether it's deliverance, freedom, peace, or healing.

THE AUTHORIZED POWER OF DISCERNMENT

"To another distinguishing between spirits." Distinguishing between spirits or the discerning of spirits gives a kingdom citizen insight into the supernatural world and its workings. Its revelation is focused on a single class of beings, spirits, and should not be confused with discernment that comes as a result of a word of wisdom. It is not a kind of spiritual mind reading, psychic insight, or mental penetration. Neither is it the discerning of other people's character or faults. It concerns nonhuman spiritual entities. Some believe it only has to do with discerning *evil* spirits; however, it refers

> *Discernment enables us to identify communication from the King.*

to discerning both good spiritual beings, who are part of the heavenly kingdom, and evil spiritual beings, who are part of the kingdom of darkness. Paul wrote, "Satan himself masquerades as an angel of light." We need to be able to tell whether messages or impressions we receive are from the King or his enemy.

One example of the authorized power of discernment is the ability to discern the visible likeness of God.

√ Moses was given this capability, as he recorded in his second book, Exodus:

Then the LORD said, "There is a place near me where you may stand on a rock. When my glory passes by, I will put you in a cleft in the rock and cover you with my hand until I have passed by. Then I will remove my hand and you will see my back; but my face must not be seen."

√ Isaiah the prophet was given this capacity through a vision of the holy King of heaven. He wrote,

> In the year that King Uzziah died, I saw the Lord seated on a throne, high and exalted, and the train of his robe filled the temple. Above him were seraphs, each with six wings: with two wings they covered their faces, with two they covered their feet, and with two they were flying. And they were calling to one another: "Holy, holy, holy is the LORD Almighty; the whole earth is full of his glory."

Another example of this gift is the revelation of the source of a supernatural manifestation:

√ Paul discerned that the slave girl who had a spirit of divination, or the ability to predict the future, was under the control of the power of the kingdom of darkness, and he cast the demon out of her.

√ A centurion named Cornelius recognized that the angel who appeared to him in a vision was from God, and he acted on the instructions he was given in that vision, so that he and his family and friends were connected to the heavenly kingdom.

The authorized power of discernment often works in conjunction with the word of wisdom or the word of knowledge. In terms of kingdom administration, this gift is the government giving a kingdom citizen sensitivity to the supernatural environment around him. For example, if you are experiencing difficulty in an area of delegated authority and can't seem to accomplish your assignment, the authorized power of discernment may enable you to see that you are under attack from agents of the kingdom of darkness, and tell you what you need to do to overcome them.

THE AUTHORIZED POWER OF SPECIAL OR DIFFERENT KINDS OF TONGUES

"To another speaking in different kinds of tongues." Different kinds of tongues are supernatural utterances given by the Holy Spirit in languages not necessarily understood by the speaker or hearer. They are either expressions from the Governor to the King on behalf of the citizens, or expressions from the King through the Governor in response to the citizens.

In the previous chapter, we talked about tongues as the initial evidence of a kingdom citizen being filled with the Holy Spirit. The emphasis was on heaven-given languages that every believer may receive. The purpose of speaking in these tongues is for individual communication with the King-Father. It is mainly a devotional experience through which we praise and worship him and offer him requests. While devotional tongues is usually private, and has to do with oneself, the gift of different kinds of tongues is public, and is in regard to others.

We may therefore call the gift of different kinds of tongues the public ministry of tongues, as opposed to the personal expression of tongues. The gift of different kinds of tongues is manifested within a gathering of kingdom citizens. Paul wrote, "Do all have gifts of healing? Do all speak in tongues? Do all interpret?" He was referring to specific and special gifts given by the Governor to whom he wills, for the benefit of all citizens.

Paul gave an example of how this gift is to be used in a gathering of kingdom citizens:

When you come together, everyone has a hymn, or a word of instruction, a revelation, a tongue or an interpretation. All of these must be done for the strengthening of the church. If anyone speaks in a tongue, two—or at the most three—should speak, one at a time, and someone must interpret. If there is no interpreter, the speaker should keep quiet in the church and speak to himself and God.

When the gift of tongues is in operation in a gathering of kingdom citizens, it is not to be expressed continuously or at exactly the same time as others who are speaking in tongues. It is done in sequence, and it involves only two or three people. Paul wrote that if no one is available to interpret, tongues should not be spoken out loud in the gathering. This is his reasoning: "If you are praising God with your spirit, how can one who finds himself among those who do not understand say 'Amen' to your thanksgiving, since he does not know what you are saying?" Paul also indicated that a person can pray to receive an interpretation of the tongues he is receiving, so that it can be spoken to the assembly. "For this reason anyone who speaks in a tongue should pray that he may interpret what he says."

Apparently, there are times when the King will want us to know exactly what we are praying in tongues, and other times when he will choose not to reveal it to us. When he does not provide means of revealing it, we should not speak it in the assembly.

How might you know if the gift of tongues is working in you? You may feel an intense interest in and compassion for the people around you. Some of the words may start forming in your mind. You might even almost be able to "see" the words in your mind's eye, or "feel" the words coming. You then speak them on the basis of your faith in the government's communication and your yieldedness to the Governor's prompting.

A person who receives an interpretation shouldn't wait for another to speak it (unless someone else is already speaking), but should faithfully deliver the interpretation so as not to cause others to miss a word from the King. Also, when a word is truly from the King, it will build up his citizens, not condemn them or cause them to be discouraged. Like prophecy, special tongues is usually a confirmation, rather than a new direction, regarding something. And a prophecy may sometimes follow tongues.

Again, anyone who exercises this or any other spiritual gift has to subject himself to self-control and the evaluation of the assembly. This is for the purpose of keeping order and peace among all kingdom citizens. We must remember that tongues and other gifts are not given because of who we are or how "spiritual" we are, but because the King loves us and our fellow citizens and desires to communicate with us.

> *When a word is truly from the King, it will build up his citizens.*

Finally, the gift of special tongues sometimes takes the form of earthly language(s) that those outside the kingdom can understand, and by which they can be drawn to be reconciled with the King. Therefore, tongues are the heavenly government giving a kingdom citizen the ability to communicate its policies, wishes, and intents to both citizens of the kingdom and other inhabitants of the earth.

THE AUTHORIZED POWER OF INTERPRETATION OF TONGUES

"To still another the interpretation of tongues." The power of interpretation of tongues is manifested when the Governor reveals to a kingdom citizen the meaning of an utterance spoken in special tongues, and the person speaks that interpretation to the assembly. I believe the word *interpretation* is important in this context. This is not a word-for-word translation but an interpretation that makes the communication comprehensible in the human language of the citizens.

For example, when we are dealing with human languages, there are some phrases and idioms in one language that cannot be translated into another language on a word-by-word basis and still convey their essential meaning, especially if colloquialisms are involved. This might occur when, for example, we take something spoken in English and interpret it for French-speaking people. For this reason, there may be a difference in length between the original statement and its interpretation. The same thing applies in the interpretation of tongues. An utterance in a heaven-given language may lead to an interpretation of longer or shorter length than the original utterance.

Interpretation of tongues obviously does not operate as an independent gift; it is dependent on the gift of tongues. Its purpose is to render the meaning of tongues intelligible to the hearers so that the whole assembly of kingdom citizens can be instructed, warned, strengthened, or encouraged by it. As Paul wrote, "He who prophesies is greater than one who speaks in tongues, *unless he interprets*, so that the church may be *edified*."

EFFECTIVE SERVICE

All these examples of authorized power are very practical and have to do with effective service on behalf of the heavenly kingdom in the colony of earth. Each gift comes from and is working for the same Spirit. Again, the gifts exist to show evidence of the presence of the government in the colony and to reveal the benevolent nature of the King and his desire to give the best to his citizens. All are given by the same Governor, who delegates them as he chooses. He may cause someone to exercise a gift just one time or he may enable him to continually manifest it. We must be sensitive to the ways in which the Governor is working and not try to force something he isn't doing or quench something he is doing.

RECEIVING THE BAPTISM IN THE HOLY SPIRIT

Authorized power comes through the baptism in the Holy Spirit. All kingdom citizens need this baptism in order to live victoriously on earth and fulfill their calling as ambassadors of the King. As we have seen, receiving the new birth is the first step; being baptized in the Holy Spirit is the second step. Without the baptism, we're not prepared to live on earth and serve the kingdom of heaven as well as we could. Many believers have entered into a relationship with the King but have experienced

> *The gifts are given by the Governor, who delegates them as he chooses.*

little of the power of the King, which is necessary for kingdom life to be fully and effectively expressed.

Spiritual power is the privilege of every believer who seeks to be filled to overflowing with the presence of the Governor. We receive the legal right or authority of the King when we receive the new birth. John the disciple wrote, "But as many as received him, to them gave he power to become the sons of God." But Jesus said we would also receive a different kind of power, a power of enablement, an explosive power: "You will receive power when the Holy Spirit comes on you." Again, the

Greek word translated power here is *dunamis,* or "miraculous power," from which we get the word *dynamite.*[5]

This enablement is present to some degree in conversion, but its fullness is received with the baptism in the Holy Spirit, and as we continue to walk in the Spirit. We receive the *person* of the Holy Spirit in the new birth, and we receive the *power* of the Holy Spirit in the baptism. We need the person of the Holy Spirit to enter into the kingdom of heaven, but we need the baptism in the Spirit to live victoriously on earth.

First, this power gives us the ability to witness to the nature and purpose of Jesus Christ in reconciling the world to the King-Father. Second, this power is available at all times and in all places. Before the outpouring of the Spirit at Pentecost, Jesus' disciples experienced kingdom power when he commissioned them to heal the sick and cast out demons in the towns of Judea. Yet this power was not a permanent presence in their lives. However, because Jesus has returned to the Father and poured out his Spirit into our lives, this power can now remain within us.

The King-Son has placed his plans for redeeming and healing the world in our hands through the administration of the Governor. Enabling power is imperative for us if we are to fulfill this role. But we must also understand the nature of this power. I know some people who have been baptized in the Holy Spirit without really understanding the gift they have been given. At some point, they need to understand the baptism or its power will never be fully realized in them, or they will abuse it.

I would therefore like to close this chapter with some guidelines for understanding and receiving the baptism in the Holy Spirit:

The Governor's Administration

1. Know that the Holy Spirit, the Governor, is a gift to be received, not earned.

2. Put yourself in a position to receive the outpouring of the Spirit. The new birth, or salvation, is a prerequisite. The disciple Peter said, "Repent and be baptized, every one of you, in the name of Jesus Christ for the forgiveness of your sins. And you will receive the gift of the Holy Spirit." (Please reread the end of chapter eight if you have not yet entered in to the new birth.)

3. Ask the King-Father for the outpouring of his Spirit, and do not be afraid that you will receive something false. Jesus said, "Which of you fathers, if your son asks for a fish, will give him a snake instead? Or if he asks for an egg, will give him a scorpion? If you then, though you are evil, know how to give good gifts to your children, how much more will your Father in heaven give the Holy Spirit to those who ask him!" We can be sure that our King-Father will not give his children a counterfeit when they ask to receive his Holy Spirit.

4. Expect to speak in tongues. The Holy Spirit will give you the words, but you will do the speaking. Some people wait for the Holy Spirit to "take over" their tongues. Yet the whole experience is a cooperative act between the divine and the human. Allow your spirit, not your intellect or previous experience, to lead you.

5. Continue to walk in the Spirit. We remain filled with the Spirit and ready to be used by the King-Father in the world as we daily seek the Governor, yield to him, and obey his directions. Since the Spirit works through the Word of God, we must read the Scriptures continually to understand the mind and heart of the King and to be ready to combine his will with his power for fulfilling it.

The baptism in the Holy Spirit is a release of heavenly power—in and through you. Praying in tongues is an interpersonal experience between you, the Holy Spirit, and the Father. Therefore, as you experience a release of God's power in your life, and as you pray to the Father in a heaven-given language, you may experience emotion. This is not emotion for emotion's sake, but emotion that is related to God's power and truth. Though the experience can be emotional, God expects us to have a proper handle on our emotions. Paul taught, "The spirits of prophets are subject to the control of prophets." In this way, we won't be carried away with our own desires and plans, rather than God's.

May the King bless you as you administer his nature and will on earth through his kingdom power.

CHAPTER FOURTEEN

WHY THE WHOLE WORLD NEEDS THE GOVERNOR

*Any effective and appropriate help for our world and its plight
cannot come from the world itself.*

As the millennial clock struck, measuring and recording
the passage of time on planet earth, ushering us into
the uncharted waters of the twenty-first century, everything in our world and generation seemed to begin to unravel.
All the secure foundations of our long-established institutions
have been shaken to the core.

With the advent of global terrorism; economic uncertainty
and insecurity; escalating oil prices and fuel costs; the reemerg-
ing threat of nuclear weapons; ethnic, cultural, religious, and
racial conflicts; political and diplomatic compromise; moral
and social disintegration; and a global upsurge in human fear,
the spirit of despair among earth's planet dwellers is becoming
a norm.

This fear is compounded by the attempts of humankind,
with its limited appreciation for human beings' inherent
defects, to address these global conditions through intellectual,

religious, scientific, philosophical, and political systems. Perhaps the greatest evidence of humanity's failure in this regard is the seemingly impotent effects of primary human institutions and coalitions, such as the United Nations, the International Monetary Fund, the World Bank, the World Trade Organization, and the Group of Eight.

If one is to be honest, perhaps it may be realistic to conclude that any effective and appropriate help for our world and its plight cannot come from the world itself. We need help from another world. It is my conviction and experience that humankind cannot and will not solve its self-generated problems. Humanity must look to another world for assistance. My conviction of this fact was the foundation for, and became the essence of, this book. Our natural world needs relevant, practical, and effective help. We need our governing institutions to be governed by a higher, more superior government.

> The kingdom of heaven is infinitely higher than any earthly government, yet it is immediately relevant to our world.

This is why the whole world—each individual in it, as well as the world collectively—needs to acknowledge and experience the return of the Governor. We have seen that the restoration of the heavenly kingdom on earth can come only through the life and power of the King, given to us through the Governor. This kingdom is infinitely higher and more powerful than any government on earth, and yet it is immediately relevant to the world we live in.

Nations are only as good as their communities, and communities are only as good as the families that comprise them.

Families are only as good as the individuals of which they consist. Therefore, the quality of a nation is determined by the quality of its people. This is especially true and critical in regard to the leadership of a nation. Often, as the leaders go, so goes the nation. The values, standards, and moral consciences of our leaders frequently determine the decisions and laws of our nations, and they influence the lifestyles and cultures of the people.

It is imperative, therefore, to understand that if the people of our nations, the individuals we appoint as leaders over us, and the institutions of our societies do not have a higher source of reference for their convictions, beliefs, morals, values, and standards, then we will continue to be victims of our own corrupt nature.

This is why the Creator's design for humankind's life on earth requires that human beings be filled with the very Spirit of the Creator himself—the Holy Spirit—the Governor of heaven. In essence, national community and global life on earth was intended to be lived through and by the Holy Spirit, the Governor. The person and role of the Holy Spirit is not a religious issue, but a social, economic, cultural, and political concern. The Holy Spirit is therefore a national and international issue and must be seen and presented as such.

INDIVIDUAL PURPOSE AND FULFILLMENT

As individuals, each of us needs the Governor for true life, purpose, and effectiveness. The breath of the Spirit that originally ignited life in the first human being did so in three distinct ways: (1) in the invisible spirit of man, made in the image of God; (2) in the soul of man—the total human consciousness of mind, will, and emotions; and (3) in the physical body of man, the living vessel housing his spirit and soul. While Adam's soul and body gave him an awareness of his earthly environment, the Spirit of God within him gave his spirit a consciousness of his Creator-King and the ability to communicate directly with the heavenly government.

> *The King wants the world to receive the Governor again and to be rid of pain, sorrow, and death.*

Human beings must return to this life and wholeness again. We were created to express the nature of God, and we can relate to and reflect his nature only if we actually have his nature within us through his indwelling Spirit.

The meaning of our individual lives—living out our purposes and exercising our full potential—is therefore totally dependent on our receiving the Governor.

A WORLD COMMUNITY OF KINGS AND PRIESTS

While our King communicates with us individually, it is not his intention that the citizens of his kingdom live in isolation. His plan is a *community* of kings and priests who will reign on earth. The Governor is the key to life for *all* of humanity. The world community therefore needs to be led by the Governor if it, also, is to become what it was created to be.

Corporately, the world has rejected the presence and influence of the Governor. This is why we experience wars, natural disasters, and social crises on earth.

The King wants the world to receive the Governor again. He wants the earth to be rid of the pain, sorrow, destruction, and death that are plaguing it. The restoration of the heavenly government reinstates humankind's ability to affect and control circumstances on earth through the Holy Spirit.

When a community of kings and priests works together for the right reasons—honoring and expressing the nature of our King—and acts in genuine unity, we will have powerful potential to influence the earth with the nature of the kingdom.

It will enable us to encourage and create...

√ social stability.

√ economic development.

√ environmental soundness.

√ educational advancement.

√ physical health and wholeness.

√ scientific innovation.

√ political honesty.

√ governmental justice.

√ intercultural understanding.

A BENEVOLENT RULER

Who wouldn't want to function under a government that provides for, encourages, and enables the fulfillment of the greatest individual and corporate potential in life? The prophet Isaiah described this heavenly government, under the rule of the King-Son through the Governor:

> Power and peace will be in his kingdom and will continue to grow forever. He will rule as king on David's throne and over David's kingdom. He will make it strong by ruling with justice and goodness from now

on and forever. The LORD All-Powerful will do this *because of his strong love for his people.*

Again, this rule is a reality only because of the King's great love for his citizens, and his desire for their highest good in life.

The Scriptures, however, also talk about the very real presence of another, malevolent ruler and his cohorts who seek to control this world:

> The ruler of the kingdom of the air, the spirit who is now at work in those who are disobedient.

> Our struggle is not against flesh and blood, but against the rulers, against the authorities, against the powers of this dark world and against the spiritual forces of evil in the heavenly realms.

> For false Christs and false prophets will appear and perform great signs and miracles to deceive even the elect—if that were possible.

The ruler of this dark world is Lucifer, or Satan, the treasonous former general and worship leader of heaven who has attacked the good of humankind since the very beginning of our existence. He would like to perpetuate the sorrow and darkness of the world so that he can continue to control it. He desires to consolidate the people of the world under his harsh rule so they can never become free.

This is why it was essential that the King-Son came to destroy Satan's power over the world, transferring us from being under the darkness of a corrupt world into the light of the heavenly kingdom. The prophet Isaiah wrote,

The people living in darkness have seen a great light; on those living in the land of the shadow of death a light has dawned.

While Satan is described in terms of darkness and death, Jesus, the King-Son, is described in the Scriptures in terms of light and life:

[He will] shine on those living in darkness and in the shadow of death, to guide our feet into the path of peace.

He was with God in the beginning. Through him all things were made; without him nothing was made that has been made. In him was life, and that life was the light of men. The light shines in the darkness, but the darkness has not understood it.

Jesus spoke of himself in these terms:

I am the light of the world. Whoever follows me will never walk in darkness, but will have the light of life.

I have come into the world as a light, so that no one who believes in me should stay in darkness.

Jesus told the theologian-apostle Paul,

I am sending you to [the world] to open their eyes and turn them from darkness to light, and from the power of Satan to God, so that they may receive forgiveness of sins and a place among those who are sanctified by faith in me.

Paul taught first-century kingdom believers,

For you were once darkness, but now you are light in the Lord. Live as children of light (for the fruit of the light consists in all goodness, righteousness and truth).

For he has rescued us from the dominion of darkness and brought us into the kingdom of the Son he loves, in whom we have redemption, the forgiveness of sins.

The nations of the world urgently need the light and life of the kingdom, which comes only from the Son-King through the Governor. The presence of the kingdom of heaven on earth, through the Holy Spirit's return, is the message of the Scriptures, and it is the message of Jesus. The story of humanity—and therefore of all of us—is inextricably tied to this kingdom. Exercising kingdom dominion on earth, under the guidance of the Governor, is our collective purpose and calling.

> *The King-Son came to transfer us from darkness into the light of the heavenly kingdom.*

As we yield to the Governor's presence and work in our lives, we will spread the kingdom of God on earth. Change will take place in all areas of life and in people of all national and ethnic backgrounds, East and West; and from all social and economic circumstances. The CEO, the teacher, the artist, the financial analyst, the health care worker, the farmer, the scientist, the economist, the seamstress, the governmental leader, and the homemaker will be transformed according to the heavenly kingdom, so that life, and not confusion, stress, and death, will be the result.

The Spirit gives *life* to the world, in the fullest extent of the word. Whatever comes into being through the influence of the Spirit will eventually bring life to people, and can reach whole countries and influence the world community. For example, if all the judges in a nation are under the guidance of the heavenly Governor, and if their minds are immersed in the philosophy of the kingdom, you will not have to wonder what kind of judgments they will hand down, nor

> *The Spirit gives life to the world, in the fullest extent of the word.*

will you have to suffer under unjust laws. A culture influenced by the Spirit will be a culture that preserves and protects life. "The mind controlled by the Spirit is life and peace."

THE COMPLETE TRANSFORMATION OF THE EARTH INTO THE KINGDOM

The world is ultimately moving toward complete transformation into the King's image and nature. This plan will climax in the creation of a new heaven and earth. In effect, heaven and earth will become one, so that there will be no essential distinction between the two, and God himself will live among his people.

The disciple John described the earth's total transformation into the kingdom of heaven's nature, mind-set, and values. In the italicized words in brackets, I describe what I see as the implications for kingdom life:

> Then I saw a new heaven and a new earth, for the first heaven and the first earth had passed away [*the earth is totally aligned with the heavenly kingdom, with no trace of the kingdom of darkness*]....

291

I saw the Holy City, the new Jerusalem, coming down out of heaven from God, prepared as a bride beautifully dressed for her husband [*the citizens of the kingdom are totally pure, set apart, and integrated; they are one with the nature of God and in harmony with themselves*]....

And I heard a loud voice from the throne saying, "Now the dwelling of God is with men, and he will live with them. They will be his people, and God himself will be with them and be their God." [*The Governor continues to dwell within the King's people, and there is nothing to separate the King from his beloved children.*]

He will wipe every tear from their eyes. There will be no more death or mourning or crying or pain, for the old order of things has passed away. He who was seated on the throne said, "I am making everything new!" [*The kingdom of darkness has been completely destroyed, and the kingdom of life and light totally reigns on earth.*]

The creation of a new heaven and earth will be the apex of the plan of the King for the coming of the Governor, which he had in mind from the beginning. The people of earth will be a true world community of kings and priests living out the kingdom life in its fullness.

CITIZENS OF THE KINGDOM

The disciple Peter wrote the following declaration to the kingdom citizens of his day, which applies to us, as well.

But you are a chosen people, a royal priesthood, a holy nation, a people belonging to God, that you may declare the praises of him who called you out of darkness into his wonderful light. Once you were not a people, but now you are the people of God; once you had not received mercy, but now you have received mercy.

The Holy Spirit is the key to the world; he is the most important person on earth because he brings us the presence and power of the kingdom of heaven. May you be reconciled to your Creator-King, receive the Governor into your life, and live as the royal kingdom citizen you were always meant to be!

> *The Holy Spirit is the key to the world; he is the most important person on earth.*

A WORD TO THE THIRD WORLD

N ations of the Third World face some of the most difficult challenges of any countries on earth. They desperately need to be free from perpetual poverty, disease, epidemics, and political and social tyranny from government officials who want to hoard the nations' wealth for themselves. For this reason, Third-World peoples perhaps feel a lack of heavenly kingdom influence in their nations most keenly.

The problems and challenges of Third-World nations have been addressed through politics, legislation, and humanitarian aid. These methods certainly have their place, and many good people and programs are currently doing their best to alleviate suffering. For powerful and lasting solutions, however, I think that we have been focusing on the wrong things.

There is a need for something immeasurably greater, something I will call a "national baptism," or an invasion of the Holy Spirit's influence and power in the lives of Third-World peoples. Each Third-World nation must have a countrywide encounter with the Governor of heaven if order and soundness is to return to them and their leaders.

This baptism is one of both philosophy and power. It is where the Holy Spirit infiltrates a whole nation, from the leaders to the children. We have seen that to have a true kingdom philosophy, we must align ourselves with the leadership of the King of heaven, and we must transform our entire outlook so that it is united with his mind-set.

For a nation to experience this kind of transformation, the Governor must, of course, come to live within its people. After the Creator gave human beings his own nature, he (1) gave them physical bodies so they could function in the physical world he had created and prepared specifically for them, and (2) breathed His very Spirit *into* them, animating and empowering them to fulfill their calling on earth.

Four billion people live in countries designated as Third-World or developing nations. Third-World Nations have a unique calling in this world, but they can fulfill their potential only if they receive the power and the mind-set of the heavenly Governor, because the Governor is their connection with the kingdom of heaven.

Only our Creator God, through the working of his Holy Spirit on earth, has the necessary authority, ability, and desire to address the needs of the Third World. No one has more love and concern for developing nations than he does. And he wants to enlist you, as a Third-World resident, to transform your community and nation into a replica of the kingdom of heaven. When you are realigned with God through his Son Jesus Christ, you are not only a member of a Third-World nation; you are also a citizen of the wealthiest, most powerful kingdom in the universe, with all the rights and privileges that correspond with your citizenship.

Earthly leaders can disappoint or abuse us; and even well-meaning friends may not be able to provide the answers we need. We can, however, depend on the Governor of heaven to work on our behalf, and also to work within us, providing supernatural gifts and abilities to overcome the problems we face in our individual and national lives. We can receive help, strength, and answers from the Spirit of the King.

Everything in your life that can seem out of your control, such as who manages your destiny, how you will raise your income level or start a business, how to receive adequate health care, or even where you will get the next meal for yourself and your family can be given into the care of the Governor. You can place yourself under the perfect rule of a benevolent Creator who has your interests, welfare, and fulfillment in mind.

A restored relationship and communication with the Creator-King through the Holy Spirit is vital for the optimum development of Third-World nations and their future in the world community. Third-World, developing nations need to be free from a culture of corruption, poverty, and despair. They must allow the Governor to direct and guide them in valuing the life of every person in the nation, and to provide heavenly kingdom wisdom for knowing how to use their national wealth and resources for the good of the people.

My prayer and challenge for all peoples of Third World, developing countries—for their generation and their nations— is to welcome the Holy Spirit into their personal lives, and then into the lives of their national cultures, allowing him to transform the values, morals, standards, social consciousness, and economic conditions of their countries, as only the all-powerful and compassionate Governor from heaven can do.

NOTES

Chapter One

1. *Thomas Nelson's New Illustrated Bible Dictionary* (Nashville: Thomas Nelson Publishers, 1995, 1986), s.v. "Colony," 287.
2. *Merriam-Webster's 11ᵗʰ Collegiate Dictionary*, s.v. "Colony."
3. Attributed to Harry Thurston Pecks, *Harper's Dictionary of Classical Antiquity*, 1898 <http://en.wikipedia.org/wiki/Apoikia. (June 9, 2006)>

Chapter Two

1. See, for example: <http://helios.gsfc.nasa.gov/qa_sp_gl.html> <http://starchild.gsfc.nasa.gov/docs/StarChild/universe_level2/galaxies.html.> <http://hypertextbook.com/facts/2000/MarissaWagner.shtml/> <http://curious.astro.cornell.edu/question.php?number=31> <http://curious.astro.cornell.edu/question.php?number=40> < http://curious.astro.cornell.edu/question.php?number=510> (All sites accessed July 28 2006)
2. <http://nasaexplores.nasa.gov/search_nav_9_12.php?id=01-079&gl=912 (November 6, 2006)>
3. See W. E. Vine, Merrill F. Unger, and William White, Jr., eds., *Vine's Complete Expository Dictionary of Old and New Testament Words* (Nashville: Thomas Nelson Publishers, 1996), Old Testament Words, s.v. "Statue," 244.
4. Ibid, Old Testament words, s.v. "Likeness," B. Noun, 137.
5. Attributed to Harry Thurston Pecks, *Harper's Dictionary of Classical Antiquity*, 1898 <http://en.wikipedia.org/wiki/Apoikia. (June 9, 2006)>

Chapter Four

1. For a broader discussion on the origin and usage of the word *holy* in this context, see W. E. Vine, Merrill F. Unger, and William White, Jr., eds., *Vine's Complete Expository Dictionary of Old and New Testament Words* (Nashville: Thomas Nelson Publishers, 1996), Old Testament Words, s.v. "Holy," A. Adjective, 113–14.
2. See *Strong's Exhaustive Concordance*, #H4467.
3. See *Strong's*, #H3068.

Chapter Five

1. See the *New American Standard Exhaustive Concordance of the Bible* (*NASC*), The Lockman Foundation, #G3341. Used by permission.

2. See *Strong's Exhaustive Concordance*, #G3101.

3. See *Strong's* and *NASC*, #G4680; #G5384; #G5385; #G5386.

4. See *Strong's*, #G3860, and W. E. Vine, Merrill F. Unger, and William White, Jr., eds., *Vine's Complete Expository Dictionary of Old and New Testament Words* (Nashville: Thomas Nelson Publishers, 1996), New Testament Words, s.v. "Yield," No. 5, 691.

Chapter Seven

1. *Merriam-Webster's 11th Collegiate Dictionary*, s.v. "Receive," "Re-."

2. See *Strong's Exhaustive Concordance*, #G4005.

3. See *Strong's*, #G3187, and the *New American Standard Exhaustive Concordance of the Bible* (*NASC*), The Lockman Foundation, #G3187. Used by permission.

Chapter Eight

1. See *Strong's Exhaustive Concordance*, #G1411, and the *New American Standard Exhaustive Concordance of the Bible* (*NASC*), The Lockman Foundation, #G1411. Used by permission.

2. See *Strong's*, #G3142.

Chapter Nine

1. See *Strong's Exhaustive Concordance*, #G4395, and the *New American Standard Exhaustive Concordance of the Bible* (*NASC*), The Lockman Foundation, #G4395. Used by permission.

2. See *Strong's*, #G1849, and *NASC*, #G1849.

3. See *Strong's*, #G1411, and *NASC*, #G1411.

4. See *Strong's*, #H1870.

Chapter Ten

1. See *Strong's Exhaustive Concordance*, #G3875.

2. See *Strong's*, #G1484, and the *New American Standard Exhaustive Concordance of the Bible* (*NASC*), The Lockman Foundation, #G1484. Used by permission.

Chapter Twelve

1. See *Strong's Exhaustive Concordance*, #H894.

Chapter Thirteen

1. See *Strong's Exhaustive Concordance*, #G1411, and the *New American Standard Exhaustive Concordance of the Bible* (*NASC*), The Lockman Foundation, #G1411. Used by permission.

2. See *Strong's*, #G3619, and W. E. Vine, Merrill F. Unger, and William White, Jr., eds., *Vine's Complete Expository Dictionary of Old and New Testament Words* (Nashville: Thomas Nelson Publishers, 1996), New Testament Words, s.v. "Edification, Edify, Edifying," A. Noun, 194.

3. See *Vine's Complete Expository Dictionary of Old and New Testament Words*, s.v. "Comfort, Comforter, Comfortless," A. Nouns, No. 1, 110; see also *Strong's*, #G3874; and *NASC*, #G3874.

4. See *Vine's Complete Expository Dictionary of Old and New Testament Words* (Nashville: Thomas Nelson Publishers, 1996), New Testament Words, s.v. "Comfort, Comforter, Comfortless," No. 2, 111.

5. See *Strong's*, #G1411, and *NASC*, #G1411.

Scripture References

(All emphasis in the Scripture quotations is the author's.)

Introduction

p. 17: "Since the creation of the world…." (Romans 1:20)

p. 17: "So we fix our eyes not on what is seen…." (2 Corinthians 4:18)

p. 18: "My kingdom is not of this world…." (John 18:36)

p. 19: "By him all things were created…." (Colossians 1:16)

Prologue

p. 21: "In the beginning was the King's Word…." See John 1:1–5.

p. 21: "In the beginning, the King created…." See Genesis 1:1–2.

Chapter One: The Power of Influence

p. 38: "As they stretched him out to flog him…." (Acts 22:25–29)

p. 41: "The time has come…." (Mark 1:15)

Chapter Two: The Adamic Administration

p. 44: "In the beginning God…." (Genesis 1:1)

p. 44: "the blessed and only Ruler…." (1 Timothy 6:15–16)

p. 45: "There's nobody keeping this universe in order." See Psalm 14:1; 53:1.

p. 45: "The universe was formed at God's command…." (Hebrews 11:3)

p. 47: "Let us make man in our image, in our likeness…." (Genesis 1:26–27); ["have dominion"]: (Genesis 1:26 NKJV]

p. 48: "the compassionate and gracious God…." (Exodus 34:6)

pp. 48: "The LORD God formed the man…." (Genesis 2:7)

p. 50: "The God who made the world…." (Acts 17:24)

p. 50: "Do you not know that your body is a temple…?" (1 Corinthians 6:19)

pp. 50–51: "Then God blessed them, and God said to them, 'Be fruitful….'" (Genesis 1:28 NKJV)

p. 51: "You are free to eat from any tree…." (Genesis 2:16–17)

p. 52: "For who among men knows the thoughts…." (1 Corinthians 2:11)

p. 53: "The highest heavens belong to the LORD…." (Psalm 115:16)

p. 54: "The LORD God took the man…." (Genesis 2:15)

Chapter Three: Declaration of Independence

pp. 56–57: "Now the serpent...said to the woman...." (Genesis 3:1–7)

p. 58: "After [the Creator-King] drove the man out...." (Genesis 3:24)

p. 59: "You are free to eat...." (Genesis 2:16–17)

p. 63: "realized" (Genesis 3:7) or "knew" (Genesis 3:7 NKJV)

p. 64: "Rule over...all the earth." (Genesis 1:26)

p. 65: "Cursed is the ground...." (Genesis 3:17–19)

p. 65: "Some paths in life seem right...." See Proverbs 14:12.

p. 66: "For all have sinned and fall short...." (Romans 3:23)

p. 68: Jesus describing Lucifer as the "father of lies" and a "murderer." (John 8:44)

p. 68: "The thief comes only to steal...." (John 10:10)

p. 69: "I will put enmity between you and the woman...." (Genesis 3:15)

Chapter Four: The Promise of the Governor's Return

p. 75: "You will be for me a kingdom of priests...." (Exodus 19:6)

p. 75: "holy unto me" (Leviticus 20:26 KJV)

p. 76: The Creator King describing himself as a "holy" God: See, for example, Leviticus 11:44–45.

p. 76: "Be perfect, just as your [King-Father] is perfect." (Matthew 5:48)

p. 78: The Offspring would "crush the head" of the serpent: See Genesis 3:15.

p. 78: "For to us a child is born...." (Isaiah 9:6)

p. 78: "Sacrifice and offering you did not desire...." (Hebrews 10:5)

p. 79: Account of Noah and the flood: See Genesis 6:5–9:1.

p. 79: "Then God blessed Noah...." (Genesis 9:1)

p. 80: Promise to Abraham regarding having a child who would become a great nation, and its fulfillment. See Genesis 15:1–6; 17:15–21; 18:2–19; 21:1–7.

p. 80: Noah and Abraham's right standing with God. See Genesis 6:8; 15:6; Romans 4:3; Galatians 3:6; Hebrews 11:7–12; James 2:23.

pp. 80–81: Jacob chosen to carry on the lineage of the coming Messiah/name changed to Israel: See Genesis 25:21–26; 28:10–15; 35:10–12.

p. 81: The twelve sons of Jacob/the origin of the tribes of Israel: See Genesis 35:22–26; 49:1–28.

p. 81: Judah chosen to carry on the lineage of the coming Messiah: See Genesis 49:8–12.

p. 81: The twelve tribes in Egypt/preserved through Joseph: See Genesis 37; 39:1–47:12, 27.

Israelite people: See Daniel 10:1–12:13.

p. 92: Daniel being delivered from the lion's den: See Daniel 6:3–23.

p. 92: Mistreatment of the prophets: See, for example, Matthew 5:11–12; Matthew 23:29–37.

p. 92: The Spirit of God leaving the temple: See Ezekiel 8:1–11:23.

p. 93: "For to us a child is born...." (Isaiah 9:6–7)

pp. 93–94: "There was a landowner...." (Matthew 21:33–40, 43)

p. 94: "He will turn the hearts...." (Malachi 4:6)

p. 95: "Afterward, I will pour out my Spirit...." (Joel 2:28–29)

p. 96: "day of the LORD" (Joel 2:11)

p. 96: "See, I will send my messenger...." (Malachi 3:1)

p. 96: "Turn the hearts of the fathers...." (Malachi 4:6)

p. 97: "In those days John the Baptism came...." (Matthew 3:1–3)

p. 97: "I baptize you with water...." (Matthew 3:11)

Chapter Five: The Rebirth of a Kingdom

p. 102: "God sent the angel Gabriel...." (Luke 1:26–30)

pp. 102–03: "You will be with child...." (Luke 1:31–35, 37–38)

p. 103: "The life of every creature is its blood." (Leviticus 17:14)

p. 104: "The one who *comes from heaven* is above all...." (John 3:31, 34)

p. 104: "He will baptize you with the Holy Spirit...." (Luke 3:16)

p. 104: "If you love me you will obey...." (John 14:15–20)

p. 105: "The next day John saw Jesus...." (John 1:29–34)

p. 105: "In Christ all the fullness of the Deity...." (Colossians 2:9)

p. 106: "In the beginning was the Word...." (John 1:1)

p. 106: "The time has come...." (Mark 1:15)

p. 106: "day of the LORD" (Joel 2:11)

p. 107: "The earth is the Lord's...." (Psalm 24:1)

p. 107: "The thief comes only to steal...." (John 10:10)

p. 107: "How can one enter a strong man's...." (Matthew 12:29 NKJV)

p. 108: Jesus the "last" or Second Adam: See 1 Corinthians 15:45.

p. 108: "Our Father in heaven, hallowed...." (Matthew 6:9–10)

p. 108: "A kingdom of priests and a holy nation." (Exodus 19:6)

p. 108: "Repent, for the kingdom of heaven is near." (Matthew 4:17)

p. 109: "Jesus went throughout Galilee...." (Matthew 4:23)

p. 109: "But if I drive out demons by the Spirit...." (Matthew 12:28)

p. 109: "The kingdom of heaven is like a king...." (Matthew 18:23)

p. 109: "The kingdom of heaven is like a landowner...." (Matthew 20:1)

p. 109: "The kingdom of God will be...given...." (Matthew 21:43)

p. 110: "The devil took him to a very high mountain...." (Matthew 4:8–11)

p. 111: "baptism of repentance": See, for example, Mark 1:4.

p. 111: "the company of the prophets": See, for example 2 Kings 2:3; 4:1.

p. 113: "You should be the teacher, not me!": See Matthew 3:13–14

p. 113: "After me will come one more powerful...." (Mark 1:7–8)

p. 113: "Let it be so now; it is proper...." (Matthew 3:15)

p. 114: "The next day John was there...." (John 1:35–40)

p. 115: "As soon as Jesus was baptized...." (Matthew 3:16–17)

p. 115: "This is my Son, whom I love. Listen to him!" (Mark 9:7)

p. 115: "Follow me": See, for example, Matthew 4:19.

p. 115: "No one can serve two masters...." (Matthew 6:24)

p. 116: "baptize...with the *Holy Spirit* and with *fire*." (Matthew 3:11)

p. 116: "As a person thinks within himself, so he is." See Proverbs 23:7 (NKJV).

pp. 116–117: "My thoughts are not your thoughts...." (Isaiah 55:8–9)

p. 117: "full of the Holy Spirit,...." (Luke 4:1–2)

p. 117: "Jesus returned to Galilee" (Luke 4:14)

p. 117: "From that time on Jesus began to preach...." (Matthew 4:17)

p. 118: "My teaching is not my own...." (John 7:16)

p. 118: "These words you hear are not my own...." (John 14:24)

p. 118: "My Father is always at his work...." (John 5:17)

p. 118: "I and the Father are one." (John 10:30)

p. 118: "I tell you the truth, the Son can do nothing by himself...." (John 5:19)

p. 118: "Do not believe me unless I do what my Father...." (John 10:37–38)

p. 118: "If God were your Father...." (John 8:42)

p. 118: "I came from the Father...." (John 16:28)

p. 118: Jesus healing the sick: See, for example, Luke 7:2–10.

p. 118: Jesus delivering someone possessed by an agent of Lucifer: See, for example, Mark 5:2–15.

pp. 118–119: Jesus feeding thousands by multiplying small amounts of food: See, for example, Luke 9:11–17.

p. 119: Jesus raising people from the dead: See, for example, Luke 7:11–15.

p. 120: "The reason my Father loves me...." (John 10:17–18)

p. 121: "Do you not know that as many of us as were baptized...." (Romans 6:3–4 NKJV)

p. 121: "I am the good shepherd...." (John 10:14–16)

p. 121: "This is what is written [was predicted by the King's prophet]...." (Luke 24:46)

p. 122: "It is finished." (John 19:30)

p. 122: "Father, the time has come...." (John 17:1–5)

p. 122: "The earth will be filled with the knowledge...." (Habakkuk 2:14)

p. 123: "For the sinful nature desires...." (Galatians 5:17–18)

p. 123: "Not my will, but yours be done." (Luke 22:42)

pp. 123–24: "If you love me...." (John 14:15–16)

p. 124: "Remain in me, and I will remain in you...." (John 15:4–6)

p. 124: "My grace is sufficient for you...." (2 Corinthians 12:9)

p. 124: "When I am weak, then I am strong." (2 Corinthians 12:10)

p. 125: "He lives with you and will be in you." (John 14:17)

p. 125: "I am going to send you what my Father has promised." (Luke 24:49)

p. 127: "He will baptize you with the Holy Spirit and with fire." (Matthew 3:11)

p. 127: "The Spirit of truth...lives *with* you and will be *in* you." (John 14:17)

p. 127: Jesus walking on water: See, for example, Matthew 14:23–33.

p. 127: Jesus causing an extraordinary catch of fish: See Luke 5:3–11.

p. 127: Jesus cleansing a leper: See, for example, Mark 1:40–42.

p. 127: "Everything I'm about to suffer...." and "I'm going to leave you, but don't panic or worry....": See John 14.

p. 128: The curtain in the temple torn from top to bottom: See, for example, Mark 15:37–38.

p. 129: "When the time had fully come...." (Galatians 4:4–7)

p. 129: "When the Counselor comes...." (John 15:26)

p. 129: "I am going to send you what my Father has promised...." (Luke 24:49).

p. 130: "We have no king but Caesar"/Pilate's choice to crucify Jesus: See John 19:12–16.

p. 130: "gave up his spirit" (John 19:30)

pp. 130–31: "And if the Spirit of him who raised Jesus...." (Romans 8:11)

Chapter Six: A King's Love for His Citizens

p. 133: "For God so loved the world...." (John 3:16)

p. 134: In order to live, one had to die to oneself; in order to be strong in kingdom power, one had to be weak in oneself: See for example, John 11:25–26; Matthew 5:3.

p. 135: "being in the form of God...." (Philippians 2:6–8)

p. 135: "And I will ask the Father...." (John 14:16–20)

p. 135: "For you know the grace of our Lord Jesus...." (2 Corinthians 8:9)

pp. 135–36: "I tell you the truth, the Son can do nothing by himself...." (John 5:19)

p. 136: "Father, glorify me in your presence...." See John 17:5.

p. 136: "Jesus took with him Peter, James and John...." (Matthew 17:1–5)

p. 137: "When the time had fully come...." (Galatians 4:4–5)

p. 137: Jesus submitted himself to the requirements of the law so he could fulfill them: See, for example, Matthew 3:15; 5:17.

p. 137: "I will give them an undivided heart...." (Ezekiel 11:19–20)

p. 137: Jesus asking for a drink of water: See John 4:5–7.

p. 137: Jesus stopping to pick fruit: See Matthew 21:19.

p. 137: "neither slumbers nor sleeps": See Psalm 121:4.

p. 137: Jesus asleep in a boat in the middle of a violent storm: See Luke 8:22–25.

p. 138: Jesus took away the sting of death from humanity: See 1 Corinthians 15:55–57.

p. 138: It pleased the King-Father for the King-Son to suffer and die: See Isaiah 53:10–11.

p. 138: "The wages of sin is death...." (Romans 6:23)

p. 138: "By his power God raised...." (1 Corinthians 6:14)

p. 138: "God made him who had no sin to be sin...." (2 Corinthians 5:21)

p. 139: "For God so loved the world...." (John 3:16)

p. 139: "I am the good shepherd...." (John 10:14–15)

p. 140: "Now I am going to him who sent me...." (John 16:5–7, 16)

p. 141: "My going away....The Governor is *with* you now....": See John 16:7; John 14:17.

p. 141: "If I go to the cross....": See John 12:32.

p. 142: "If you then, though you are evil...." (Matthew 7:11)

p. 142: "Your Father has been pleased to give you the kingdom." (Luke 12:32)

Chapter Seven: Restoring the Connection

p. 143: "He lives with you and will be in you." (John 14:17)

p. 143: "'As the Father has sent me,...." (John 20:21–22)

p. 144: "The LORD God formed the man.... (Genesis 2:7)

p. 145: "In my former book...." (Acts 1:1–3)

p. 145: "Once, having been asked by the Pharisees...." (Luke 17:20–21)

p. 146: "I tell you the truth, some who are standing...." (Mark 9:1)

p. 146: About one hundred twenty disciples present when the Holy Spirit was poured out at Pentecost: See Acts 1:15–2:3.

p. 146: "After the Lord Jesus had spoken...." (Mark 16:19)

p. 146: "And I will ask the Father...." (John 14:16–17)

p. 146: "The Counselor, the Holy Spirit...." (John 14:26)

p. 147: "I am going to send you what my Father has promised...." (Luke 24:49)

p. 147: "On one occasion, while he was eating with them...." (Acts 1:4–5, 8)

p. 148: "on high" (Luke 24:49)

p. 148: "When the day of Pentecost came...." (Acts 2:1–4)

pp. 148–49: Disciples of Jesus given the ability to speak in a variety of languages: See Acts 2:5–11.

p. 149: "And these signs will accompany...." (Mark 16:17)

p. 149: "Why are you speaking like this....?" See Acts 2:12–13.

p. 149: "Fellow Jews and all of you...." (Acts 2:14–18, 32–33)

p. 151: "My kingdom is not of this world." (John 18:36)

p. 151: "I tell you the truth, anyone who has faith in me...." (John 14:12)

p. 151: "And I will do whatever you ask in my name...." (John 14:13)

Chapter Eight: Reinstating the Governor

pp. 153–54: "Whoever drinks the water...." (John 4:14)

p. 154: "Now it is God who makes...." (2 Corinthians 1:21–22)

p. 154: "Now it is God who has made us...." (2 Corinthians 5:5)

p. 154–55: "And you also were included in Christ...." (Ephesians 1:13–14)

p. 155: "Consequently, you are no longer foreigners...." (Ephesians 2:19)

p. 156: "I tell you the truth, whatever you bind on earth...." (Matthew 18:18–20)

p. 156: "I tell you the truth, no one can enter the kingdom...." (John 3:5–7)

pp. 156–57: "Be imitators of God...." (Ephesians 5:1–2)

p. 157: "You will receive power...." (Acts 1:8)

pp. 157–58: "If anyone is thirsty, let him come...." (John 7:37–38)

p. 158: "By this he meant the Spirit...." (John 7:39)

p. 159: "If I drive out demons by the Spirit of God...." (Matthew 12:28)

p. 177: "For the sinful nature desires...." (Galatians 5:17)

p. 177: "Live by the Spirit, and you will not gratify...." (Galatians 5:16)

p. 177–78: "We demolish arguments and every pretension...." (2 Corinthians 10:5)

p. 178: "My thoughts are not your thoughts...." (Isaiah 55:8–9)

p. 179: "If anyone is in Christ, he is a new creation...." (2 Corinthians 5:17)

p. 179: "'This is the covenant I will make....'" (Hebrews 10:16–17)

p. 179: "righteousness, peace and joy in the Holy Spirit" (Romans 14:17)

p. 179: "Let us draw near to God...." (Hebrews 10:22)

p. 179: "Do not conform any longer..." (Romans 12:2)

p. 180: "He who has seen me has seen the Father." (John 14:9)

p. 180: "You, dear children, are from God...." (1 John 4:4)

pp. 180–81: "My friends, do not be afraid of those who kill the body...." (Luke 12:4–8)

p. 181: The King has not given us the spirit of fear: See 2 Timothy 1:7 (NKJV).

p. 181: "For we are God's workmanship...." (Ephesians 2:10)

p. 184: "Let us then approach the throne of grace...." (Hebrews 4:16)

p. 185: "Who among men knows the thoughts of a man...." (1 Corinthians 2:11)

p. 185: Jesus often went off by himself to pray: See, for example, Mark 1:35; Luke 5:16.

p. 185: "*When* you pray...." See, for example, Matthew 6:5–7.

Chapter Ten: The Nature of the Governor

p. 191: "But when *he*, the Spirit of truth, comes...." (John 16:13–14)

pp. 191–92: "A great and powerful wind tore the mountains...." (1 Kings 19:11–13)

p. 192: "being in the form of God...." (Philippians 2:6–7 NKJV)

p. 193: "The Holy Spirit will come upon you...." (Luke 1:35)

p. 193: "I and the Father are one." (John 10:30)

p. 193: "If anyone loves me, he will obey...." (John 14:23)

p. 193: "God is spirit, and his worshipers...." (John 4:24)

p. 193: "*another* Counselor" (John 14:16)

p. 193: "When the Counselor comes...." (John 15:26)

p. 194: "I tell you the truth, all the sins...." (Mark 3:28–29)

pp. 194–95: "As the Holy Spirit says: 'Today, if you hear....'" (Hebrews 3:7–8)

p. 195: The Scriptures speak about God as longsuffering: See, for example, Exodus 34:6 NKJV; Romans 2:4 NKJV.

p. 196: "Do not grieve the Holy Spirit of God...." (Ephesians 4:30)

p. 198: "The Spirit of truth," Jesus said, "...will not speak...." (John 16:13–14)

p. 198: "But the Counselor, the Holy Spirit...." (John 14:26)

p. 198: "And I will ask the Father...." (John 14:16)

p. 199: "In a little while you will see me no more...." (John 16:16)

p. 199: Analogy of a shepherd looking for one lost sheep: See, for example, Luke 15:4–7.

p. 200: "But when he, the Spirit of truth...." (John 16:13)

p. 201: "The Spirit of the LORD will rest on him...." (Isaiah 11:2)

p. 201: "The Spirit of the Lord is on me...." (Luke 4:18–19)

p. 202: "the earth will be filled with the knowledge...." (Habakkuk 2:14)

p. 202: "go and make disciples of all nations...." (Matthew 28:19–20)

p. 203: "For we are God's workmanship...." (Ephesians 2:10)

p. 203: "No eye has seen...." (1 Corinthians 2:9–10)

p. 204: "We have not received the spirit of the world...." (1 Corinthians 2:12)

p. 204: "The man without the Spirit...." (1 Corinthians 2:14)

p. 205: "When he comes, he will convict the world...." (John 16:8–11)

p. 206: "I led them with cords...." (Hosea 11:4)

p. 206: "He will not speak on his own...." (John 16:13)

p. 207: "From the beginning God chose you...." (2 Thessalonians 2:13)

Chapter Eleven: The Governor's Culture

p. 210: "Like a roaring lion...." (Proverbs 28:15–16)

p. 210: "When the righteous increase...." (Proverbs 29:2 NASB)

pp. 210–11: "Nadab son of Jeroboam...." (1 Kings 15:25–26)

p. 211: "provoked the LORD, the God of Israel, to anger." (1 Kings 15:30)

p. 211: Jeroboam causing the people of Israel to worship idols and appointing priests who were not Levites: See 1 Kings 12:26–33; 13:33–34.

p. 211: "Ahab...did more evil in the eyes of the LORD...." (1 Kings 16:30–33)

p. 211: "The Lord had seen how bitterly...." (2 Kings 14:26)

pp. 211–12: "He did what was right in the eyes of the LORD...." (2 Kings 18:3, 5–7)

p. 212: The Lord delivered the people of Judah from a boastful, vengeful enemy: See 2 Kings 18:13–19:37.

p. 212: "I am the good shepherd...." (John 10:11)

p. 212: "I am the bread of life...." (John 6:35)

p. 212: "Come to me, all you who are weary...." (Matthew 11:28–30)

p. 213: "You know that the rulers of the Gentiles...." (Matthew 20:25–28)

p. 213: "The kingdom of heaven is near." (Matthew 4:17)

p. 214: List of the essential qualities that make up the character of the King: See Galatians 5:22–23.

p. 214: "the fruit of the Spirit." (Galatians 5:22)

p. 215: "Blessed are the meek, for they will inherit the earth." (Matthew 5:5)

p. 216: "By their fruit you will recognize them." (Matthew 7:16, 20)

p. 217: "our citizenship is in heaven." (Philippians 3:20)

p. 217: "Those who belong to Christ Jesus...." (Galatians 5:24–25)

p. 217: "The one who is in you is greater...." (1 John 4:4)

p. 218: "Live by the Spirit, and you will not gratify...." (Galatians 5:16–18)

p. 218: "The acts of the sinful nature...." (Galatians 5:19–21)

p. 219: Internal warning system of our consciences: See Romans 2:14–15.

p. 219: The Governor reminds us of the teachings of the King: See John 14:26.

p. 219: "Not my will, but yours be done." (Luke 22:42)

p. 219: "The Spirit gives life; the flesh counts for nothing...." (John 6:63)

p. 220: "Abba, Father." (Romans 8:15; Galatians 4:6)

p. 220: The King doesn't only *act* in love or demonstrate peace; he *is* love and peace: See 1 John 4:8, 16; Ephesians 2:14.

p. 220: "Be perfect, therefore, as your heavenly Father is perfect." (Matthew 5:48)

p. 221: "Do you not know that your body is a temple...." (1 Corinthians 6:19–20)

p. 221: "Your eye is the lamp of your body...." (Luke 11:34)

p. 221: "My prayer is not that you take them out of the world...." (John 17:15–16, 18)

p. 222: "You were dead in your transgressions and sins...." (Ephesians 2:1–6, 10)

p. 222: "Let your light shine before men...." (Matthew 5:16)

p. 223: "the gifts of the Spirit." See, for example, 1 Corinthians 12:7–11.

pp. 224–25: "Those who accepted [Peter's] message [about the kingdom]...." (Acts 2:41–47)

Chapter Twelve: Manifesting Kingdom Culture

p. 233: "Now the whole world had one language...." (Genesis 11:1–2)

p. 234: The entrance to the eastern side of the garden of Eden guarded: See Genesis 3:24.

p. 234: The full incident of the Tower of Babel: See Genesis 11:1–9.

p. 234: "We will build a tower and make a name for ourselves." See Genesis 11:4.

p. 234: "If as one people speaking the same language...." (Genesis 11:6)

p. 235: "Come, let us go down and *confuse*...." (Genesis 11:7)

p. 235: "That is why it was called Babel...." (Genesis 11:9)

p. 237: "You will receive power...." (Acts 1:8)

p. 237: "These signs will accompany those who believe...." (Mark 16:17–18)

pp. 237–38: "When the day of Pentecost came...." (Acts 2:1–11)

p. 238: "God has raised this Jesus to life...." (Acts 2:32–33)

p. 240: "In the same way, the Spirit helps us...." (Romans 8:26–27)

p. 241: "Tongues, then, are a sign...." (1 Corinthians 14:22)

p. 241: "for they heard them speaking in tongues...." (Acts 10:46)

pp. 242–43: "The LORD God said, 'If as one people....'" (Genesis 11:6–9)

p. 245: "Undoubtedly there are all sorts of languages...." (1 Corinthians 14:10–11)

p. 245: "For anyone who speaks in a tongue...." (1 Corinthians 14:2)

p. 246: Paul of Tarsus's statement that we should earnestly desire spiritual gifts: See 1 Corinthians 14:1 (NASB).

p. 247: "Anyone who speaks in a tongue...." (1 Corinthians 14:2)

p. 247: "Now to each one the manifestation of the Spirit...." (1 Corinthians 12:7–8, 10)

pp. 247–48: "Now you are the body of Christ...." (1 Corinthians 12:27–30)

p. 248: "When you come together...." (1 Corinthians 14:26–27)

p. 248: "For this reason anyone who speaks in a tongue...." (1 Corinthians 14:13)

p. 248: "Therefore, my brothers, be eager to prophesy...." (1 Corinthians 14:39–40)

p. 249: "While Apollos was at Corinth...." (Acts 19:1)

p. 249: "You are on the right track...." See Acts 19:2–4.

p. 249: "We have never even heard of the Holy Spirit." See Acts 19:2.

p. 250: The Ephesus disciples being baptized in water, the Holy Spirit coming on them, and their speaking in tongues and prophesying: See Acts 19:5–6.

p. 250: "He who speaks in a tongue edifies himself." (1 Corinthians 14:4)

p. 250: "And I will ask the Father...." (John 14:16–17)

p. 251: "In the same way, the Spirit helps us...." (Romans 8:26–27)

p. 251: "But you, dear friends, build yourselves up...." (Jude 20)

p. 252: "Speak to one another with psalms...." (Ephesians 5:19)

p. 252: "we do not know what we ought to pray for...." (Romans 8:26)

p. 252: "Do not be anxious about anything...." (Philippians 4:6–7)

p. 252: "I will pray with my spirit...." (1 Corinthians 14:15)

p. 253: "But no man can tame the tongue...." (James 3:8, 10–11)

p. 253: "The promise is for you and your children...." (Acts 2:39)

p. 254: Paul spoke in tongues frequently: See 1 Corinthians 14:18.

p. 254: "I will pray with the understanding...." See 1 Corinthians 14:15 (NKJV).

Chapter Thirteen: The Governor's Administration

p. 256: "All these are the work of one and the same Spirit...." (1 Corinthians 12:11)

p. 256: "Now about spiritual gifts...." (1 Corinthians 12:1, 8–10); "word of wisdom," "word of knowledge," "the working of miracles," and "discerning of spirits": (NKJV)

p. 257: "Each one should use whatever gift...." (1 Peter 4:10)

p. 257: "There are different kinds of gifts...." (1 Corinthians 12:4–7); "administrations": (KJV)

pp. 258–59: "It was [Jesus] who gave some to be apostles...." (Ephesians 4:11–13)

p. 260: "To one there is given...the message of wisdom." (1 Corinthians 12:8)

pp. 260–61: "Do not let this Book of the Law depart...." (Joshua 1:8)

p. 261: The Holy Spirit giving a word of wisdom setting apart Paul and Barnabas for the work of the kingdom: See Acts 13:1–4.

p. 261: For background on Paul's being taken prisoner by ship to Rome, and the ship encountering a violent storm, see Acts 27:1–21.

p. 261: "I urge you to keep up your courage...." (Acts 27:22–26)

p. 262: "To another the message of knowledge...." (1 Corinthians 12:8)

p. 263: Jesus demonstrating a word of knowledge regarding the woman who had had five husbands: See John 4:5–42.

p. 263: Agabus receiving a word of knowledge about a severe famine: See Acts 11:27–30.

p. 263: Peter receiving words of knowledge that Ananias and Sapphira were lying about money they donated to the church: See Acts 5:1–11.

p. 263: John being given words of knowledge, through a vision, concerning the spiritual conditions of seven assemblies of kingdom citizens in Asia: See Revelation 1:1–4; 2:1–3:22.

p. 264: "To another faith by the same Spirit." (1 Corinthians 12:9)

p. 264: "Without faith it is impossible to please God...." (Hebrews 11:6)

p. 264: "Faith comes from hearing the message...." (Romans 10:17)

pp. 264–65: The faith of three Hebrew men who trusted God to deliver them even if they were thrown into a blazing furnace: See Daniel 3:1–28.

p. 265: Jesus' confidence that Lazarus would be raised from the dead: See John 11:1–45.

p. 265: The faith of Peter and John that a man crippled from birth would be healed: See Acts 3:1–8.

p. 265: "To another gifts of healing by that one Spirit." (1 Corinthians 12:9)

p. 265: "*gifts* of *healings*": (1 Corinthians 12:9 NKJV)

p. 265: "Jesus was going about in all Galilee...." (Matthew 4:23 NASB)

p. 266: "He himself bore our sins in his body...." (1 Peter 2:24)

p. 267: A man's shriveled hand restored: See Mark 3:1–5; a centurion's paralyzed and dying servant cured: See Matthew 8:5–13 and Luke 7:1–10; a man born blind given his sight: See John 9:1–7; a woman suffering from a hemorrhage for twelve years made completely well: See, for example, Mark 5:24–34.

p. 267: A man named Aeneas, paralyzed and bedridden for eight years, made totally well: See Acts 9:32–35.

p. 267: A man on Malta healed from apparently recurring bouts of fever and dysentery: See Acts 28:7–8 (NASB).

p. 268: "To another miraculous powers." (1 Corinthians 12:10)

p. 268: Moses' parting of the Red Sea: See Exodus 14:5–31.

p. 268: The continual flow of a widow's supply of oil and flour during a famine: See 1 Kings 17:1–16.

p. 268: Jesus' feeding of more than five thousand people with just five small loaves and two fish: See, for example, John 6:5–14.

p. 268: Jesus' raising of Lazarus from the dead: See John 11:38–45.

p. 268: Peter's raising of Dorcas from the dead: See Acts 9:36–42.

p. 268: The temporary blinding of Elymas: See Acts 13:6–12.

p. 269: "To another prophecy." (1 Corinthians 12:10)

p. 269: "Pursue love, yet desire earnestly spiritual gifts...." (1 Corinthians 14:1–5 NASB); "comfort": (NKJV)

p. 270: "Your sons and daughters will prophesy." (Acts 2:17)

p. 270: "Even on my servants, both men and women...." (Acts 2:18)

p. 271: "Do not quench the Spirit...." (1 Thessalonians 5:19–20 NKJV)

p. 271: "Test everything. Hold on to the good." (1 Thessalonians 5:21)

p. 271: "Two or three prophets should speak...." (1 Corinthians 14:29)

p. 271: "For you can all prophesy in turn...." (1 Corinthians 14:31)

p. 271: "The spirits of prophets are subject...." (1 Corinthians 14:32–33)

p. 272: The disciples at Ephesus "spoke in tongues and prophesied." See Acts 19:1–7.

p. 272: Philip the evangelist had four daughters who prophesied. See Acts 21:8–9.

p. 272: Agabus the prophet predicted the famine and Paul's being taken prisoner: See Acts 11:27–28; 21:10–11.

p. 273: "To another distinguishing between spirits." (1 Corinthians 12:10)

p. 273: "Satan himself masquerades as an angel of light." (2 Corinthians 11:14)

p. 273: "Then the LORD said, "There is a place near me...." (Exodus 33:21–23)

p. 274: "In the year that King Uzziah died...." (Isaiah 6:1–3)

p. 274: Paul of Tarsus discerning a spirit of divination in a slave girl: See Acts 16:16–18.

p. 274: Cornelius the centurion discerning that the angel who appeared to him in a vision was from God: See Acts 10:1–48.

p. 275: "To another speaking in different kinds of tongues." (1 Corinthians 12:10)

p. 275: "Do all have gifts of healing? Do all speak in tongues....?" (1 Corinthians 12:30)

pp. 275–76: "When you come together, everyone has a hymn...." (1 Corinthians 14:26–28)

p. 276: "If you are praising God with your spirit...." (1 Corinthians 14:16)

p. 276: "For this reason anyone who speaks in a tongue...." (1 Corinthians 14:13)

p. 277: "To still another the interpretation of tongues." (1 Corinthians 12:10)

p. 278: "He who prophesies is greater..., *unless he interprets....*" (1 Corinthians 14:5)

p. 279: "But as many as received him...." (John 1:12 KJV)

p. 279: "You will receive power when the Holy Spirit comes on you." (Acts 1:8)

p. 280: Before Pentecost, Jesus' disciples experiencing kingdom power to heal and cast out demons: See, for example, Luke 9:1–6, 10; 10:1–20.

p. 281: "Repent and be baptized...." (Acts 2:38)

p. 281: "Which of you fathers, if your son asks for a fish...." (Luke 11:11–13)

p. 282: "The spirits of prophets are subject to the control of prophets." (1 Corinthians 14:32)

Chapter Fourteen: Why the Whole World Needs the Governor

pp. 287–88: "Power and peace will be in his kingdom...." (Isaiah 9:6–7 NCV)

p. 288: "The ruler of the kingdom of the air...." (Ephesians 2:2)

p. 288: "Our struggle is not against flesh and blood...." (Ephesians 6:12)

p. 288: "For false Christs and false prophets will appear...." (Matthew 24:24)

p. 289: "The people living in darkness...." (Matthew 4:16)

p. 289: "[He will] shine on those living in darkness...." (Luke 1:79)

p. 289: "He was with God in the beginning...." (John 1:2–5)

p. 289: "I am the light of the world...." (John 8:12)

p. 289: "I have come into the world as a light...." (John 12:46)

p. 289: "I am sending you to [the world]...." (Acts 26:17–18)

p. 290: "For you were once darkness...." (Ephesians 5:8–9)

p. 290: "For he has rescued us...." (Colossians 1:13–14)

p. 291: "The mind controlled by the Spirit is life and peace." (Romans 8:6)

pp. 291–92: Then I saw a new heaven and a new earth....[ff] (Revelation 21:1–5)

pp. 292–93: "But you are a chosen people...." (1 Peter 2:9–10)

ABOUT THE AUTHOR

Dr. Myles Munroe is an international motivational speaker, best-selling author, lecturer, educator, and consultant for government and business. Traveling extensively throughout the world, Dr. Munroe addresses critical issues affecting the full range of human, social, and spiritual development. The central theme of his message is the transformation of followers into leaders and the maximization of individual potential.

Dr. Munroe is founder and president of Bahamas Faith Ministries International (BFMI), an all-encompassing network of ministries headquartered in Nassau, Bahamas. He is president and chief executive officer of the International Third World Leaders Association and the International Third World Leadership Training Institute. Dr. Munroe is also the founder, executive producer, and principal host of a number of radio and television programs aired worldwide and is a contributing writer for various Bible editions, magazines, and newsletters, including *The Believer's Topical Bible, The African Cultural Heritage Topical Bible, Charisma Life Christian Magazine,* and

Ministries Today. He has earned degrees from Oral Roberts University and the University of Tulsa, and he was awarded an honorary doctorate from Oral Roberts University, for which he is an adjunct professor of the Graduate School of Theology.

Dr. Munroe and his wife Ruth travel as a team and are involved in teaching seminars together. Both are leaders who minister with sensitive hearts and international vision. They are the proud parents of two children, Charisa and Myles, Jr.

The Principles and Power of Vision
Dr. Myles Munroe

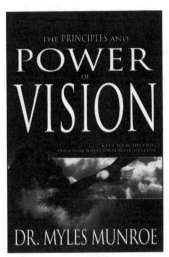

Whether you are a businessperson, a student, a homemaker, or a head of state, best-selling author Dr. Myles Munroe explains how you can make your dreams and hopes a living reality. Your success is not dependent on the state of the economy or what the job market is like. You do not need to be hindered by the limited perceptions of others or by a lack of resources. Discover time-tested principles that will enable you to fulfill your vision no matter who you are or where you come from.

Revive your passion for living, pursue your dream, discover your vision—and find your true life.

ISBN: 978-0-88368-951-6 • Hardcover • 240 pages

The Spirit of Leadership
Dr. Myles Munroe

After personally training thousands of leaders from around the world, best-selling author Dr. Myles Munroe reports that while all people possess leadership potential, many do not understand how to cultivate the leadership nature and how to apply it to their lives. Discover the unique attitudes that all effective leaders exhibit, how to eliminate hindrances to your leadership abilities, and how to fulfill your particular calling in life. With wisdom and power, Dr. Munroe reveals a wealth of practical insights that will move you from being a follower to becoming the leader you were meant to be!

ISBN: 978-0-88368-983-7 • Hardcover • 304 pages

---

www.whitakerhouse.com

THE ISLANDS OF THE
bahamas

For Information on Religious Tourism
Email: ljohnson@bahamas.com

1.800.224.3681

www.worship.bahamas.com

Nonverbal Communication for Business Success

Nonverbal Communication for Business Success

Ken Cooper

A Division of American Management Associations

Library of Congress Cataloging in Publication Data

Cooper, Ken.
  Nonverbal communication for business success.

  Bibliography: p.
  Includes index.
  1. Success.   2. Nonverbal communication.   3. Business.
I. Title.

HF5386.C78   001.56   78-25971
ISBN 0-8144-5500-X

First Printing

To Sue, Jeff, and Dan

Acknowledgments

I wish to thank:

Elmer Kowal for his photographic assistance.

Monsanto Company for the use of its facilities in the photograph sessions.

Shirley Dingler for obtaining permission for the sessions.

Don Verbeck for making all session arrangements.

Jim Jones of IBM and Juanita Carter, Kathy Lowes, Dr. John Mason, Frank Miller, George Panian, Bernie Phillips, Jim Spinks, Bob Stuckey, Don Verbeck, and Iniss Taylor—all of Monsanto Company—for posing for the illustrations.

Karen Gentles for manuscript preparation.

Dr. John Gentles for thoughtful analysis of the manuscript and suggestions.

And all those friends and strangers who so graciously and patiently allowed me to experiment with them and observe them.

Preface

I always save writing the preface to a book for last. As I sit here and glance over the completed manuscript, freshly stacked in its box, I feel a strange sense of loss. *Nonverbal Communication for Business Success* contains some of my best material, up to now saved only for my consulting clients. But I feel it represents a milestone in the application of nonverbal communication to business. Nonverbal communication involves the study of all parts of the communications process *except words*—body appearance and position, body movements, possessions, surroundings, and voice characteristics. I have used nonverbal communication to advantage both in my career as a computer salesman and now as a management consultant.

There have been two main types of books about nonverbal communication: the technical research volume and the "secrets of body language" book. The technical books are filled with fascinating studies identifying behavior and causes, but they are written for the academic community in language unintelligible to the average reader. The "secrets of body language" books have been immensely popular, but they make a fatal error in assigning specific meanings to individual body signals out of context. There are a few books that present the valuable research in a readable format, and up to now no books have been designed primarily for use by the vast working public.

Nonverbal Communication for Business Success is that book. You will learn three visual "scans" that will help you systematically observe and analyze nonverbal information. The scans will enable you to determine whether many different signs *agree* before you make a decision. You can find out how to choose a restaurant for a business lunch, learn why you should look away briefly when you meet someone, and see why wearing high heels ruins your walk.

The information presented in this book is the result of nearly seven years of research into the professional literature and an equal number of years of research and experience as a teacher and management consultant. It is not an abstract theory, however; no concept has been included unless it has been proven to me in personal practice.

The book is not limited to those who work. It also contains chapters on effective voice traits and developing a successful personal image. In the chapter on image, for example, you can see how important appearance was in the 1960 and 1976 presidential debates. I have even had students use the image-building process as parents and spouses.

Now is the time for you to find out what you have been missing. Now is the time for you to transact a little "body business."

Ken Cooper

Contents

1

Nonverbal Communication and Business

It would be wonderful if a secret Eastern society existed to teach us the mysteries of effective communication. We might tear out a small coupon in the back of our favorite magazine, mail it with "only $2.99," and wait expectantly for the Ancient Wisdom Parchment to arrive.

Knowing help was on the way, we could endure our communications failures. At last, the scroll would be sure to save us. Opening the plain-wrapped package with nervous anticipation, we would finally have the answers to the most perplexing problems in human relationships.

What would the message be?

Most likely, the parchment would not offer any deep secrets to successful communication—because there are none. Instead, it would probably contain certain commonly known communications basics that researchers in the field agree on.

This book provides such basics for a special category of communications: *the nonverbals*. Much of what you read here may be intuitively obvious, some information will be new, and some will seem to contradict what you always thought to be true.

For information you already know, you will learn more effective applications. For new information, you will find that you have been watching a color TV program in black and white. Where the forest is alive with sound, you have heard only the clump of your own footsteps. For contradictions, you will experience growth in your ability to communicate effectively.

In all three cases, you will learn the *why* of communications principles. You will become a conscious participant in a process that has been a subconscious part of your behavior every waking hour. That is, you will learn to analyze the nonverbal signals being sent to you and to modify or control the nonverbal information you project.

Most people who have attained even moderate success in the business world have some ability to observe and evaluate nonverbals. For example, examine the three pictures in Figure 1–1. In each case, with whom is the salesman speaking?

A salesman in my office invariably assumed these three postures when talking on the phone, never realizing that each one indicated clearly whether or not he was working. He adopted the first pose with a customer or another employee; the second, with a friend or casual business acquaintance, such as his broker. The third was usually reserved for one of his "intimate friends," since he was a bachelor. (If you said "business associate" for the first pose and "wife" for the second, I want to know who the third person is!)

As this phone example shows, we can make fairly accurate observations in a simple social situation. In more complex settings, however, we may become confused about nonverbal signals. As a first step in overcoming this difficulty, we should examine some of the communications basics from our secret Asiatic missive.

Communications Basics

If we were holding that folded piece of paper, we would find four key concepts that can help us better understand any communications process. The first is that we communicate *with* some-

Figure 1–1. Phone conversation positions.

one, not *to* someone. Communication is not necessarily taking place just because one person is talking to another. We frequently assume that it is, until we find that our listener is a million miles away. In an article in *Reader's Digest* Carol Burnett tells such a story about a conversation with her seven-year-old daughter after a spanking:

> "At bedtime, she was still sniffling," Carol recalled. "So I went in and put my arms around her saying, 'Now, you know I love you very much.' And then I talked about character and what she did that was wrong, and she listened—never taking her eyes from my face. I began congratulating myself—boy, you are really getting through, she'll remember this when she's 40.
>
> "I talked for 20 minutes. She was spellbound; we were practically nose to nose. As I paused, searching for the clincher, she asked, 'Mommy, how many teeth do you have?'"

There's a punch, of course. The person who deserves to be punched in this type of story is frequently us. However, the humor fades when a raise is lost, a key employee quits, or a sale goes to a competitor. Communication is always a team effort between speaker and listener.

The second basic is that communication is separate from information. Communication is an *act;* information is the *content.* The medium is *not* the message, and expression of a message should not be confused with the message itself.

The third basic is that communication is nonrepeatable. There is never a chance for an identical second exchange after the first attempt. Even with writing or a film, readers or viewers change from day to day, from week to week, and are no longer the same people they were when the first exchange occurred. There is the added factor of the miscues in the first trial affecting the encore. A good example is the classic Unveiling the New Dress scene:

From the bedroom, the husband hears, "Close your eyes, hon, I want to show you something I picked up today."

If he's not thinking, the husband says, "Okay." If he's awake, he puts down his paper, mumbles a short prayer, and replies, "I'm ready!"

The rustle down the hall is punctuated by a Loretta Young

swirl as the wife asks the surely dazzled husband, "How do you like it?"

Unmoving after a short, controlled pause, he states with hopeful enthusiasm, "I really like it!"

"You don't like it! I can tell."

"No, listen, it's really a dynamite dress."

"You hate it, Harold. Any time you say 'really,' I know you're not being truthful."

"Look, what do you want me to say, 'I worship the dress'?" he replies with a rising voice. "I *like* it. I wish we had been married in it. If there was another in the store in a smaller size, I would buy it for my mother. What more do you want, a notarized oath?"

"You don't have to get sarcastic, Harold. You don't like the dress and that's all there is to it. You're never satisfied with anything I do. And speaking of your mother and a smaller size—"

"Stop! Dear, go back in the room and come out again. I *do* like the dress and I'll do whatever you want me to do."

Poor Harold isn't living in the Twilight Zone, but he might wish he were so he could get another shot at commenting on his wife's new dress. That's because communication is not repeatable. Next time, he'll be ecstatic just to protect himself. If he fumbles that opportunity, he won't get another chance then either.

The fourth communications basic is that we should consider the total message whenever we speak. People who write about NVC often promote the idea that we are continually communicating "hidden nonverbal messages" that disagree with our verbal messages. This idea may sell a lot of books and seminars, but it just isn't true. Catchphrases like "What is your body *really* saying?" and "Are you missing the opportunities on those lonely business trips?" merely titillate us. In general, there are very few discrepancies between the overall communications message and NVC. Most people just aren't good enough actors and actresses to carry it off.

As an exercise in my college classes, I have students give a two-minute talk in which all their gestures and movements conflict with what they are saying. For example, they may stomp in, slam their books to the floor, and scream in agony, "I'm glad to be here!" I limit these talks to two minutes because it takes a great deal of practice to choreograph the movements to each phrase and coordinate them in a talk.

There is a danger in taking a single NVC sign out of context. I discovered this quite by accident when I made a call on one of my regular customers, a utility executive. I naturally had tried to observe his mannerisms for any useful information, and he had one habit that drove me to distraction. Whenever I presented an idea to him, either one on one or in a presentation, he always listened with his hand covering his mouth. All the NVC literature states that this is a strong sign of disapproval or disagreement. One day while we were having a casual discussion about a communications column I wrote for a local paper, he asked me if I "used" NVC on him and if I had noticed anything unusual.

"You know, Ken," he said, "I hope I haven't given the wrong impression when I listen to you fellows. Have you noticed anything unusual about me when I listen?"

Sensing I should dig more, I said, "No, Bob. Why would you ask?"

"I read a book that told me I shouldn't put my hand over my mouth when I'm listening. Have you noticed I do this?"

"I noticed it, Bob, but I wasn't sure what it meant," I said. It *had* been bothering me, but I wasn't about to let *him* know that.

"As you can see, my face is deeply lined," he began. "I was riding the bus one day and just happened to be sitting in a seat where that large convex mirror by the rear door shot my reflection right back at me. I glanced up and saw my face looking grotesque and distorted, glaring back with an enormous frown. The lines on my face made me look terribly negative. It left such an impression on me that I decided to be certain I didn't accidentally make someone think I was angry or unhappy when I was really just listening. Now I always cover my mouth when I listen so that I won't turn the other person off."

That little confession made me breathe a sigh of sales relief. It also taught me a valuable lesson, and unlike most valuable lessons, it came relatively cheap: *No single NVC sign can be read accurately out of the context of the entire communications process.*

Nonverbal communication consists of three steps: reading, evaluating, and controlling body signals. Accurate and timely reading of nonverbal information is necessary because of the nonrepeatability of the communications process. There is no second chance. Evaluation is necessary to separate information from expression and to better identify the total message. Controlling NVC is necessary because communication is an active process, whether people are listening or speaking.

The Checklist Approach

As a firm believer in effective time management, I have written this book to be efficient and practical in its presentation of ideas. Special emphasis is given to "checklists" of nonverbal signals to help you observe and apply them in social situations. Up to now there has been no structured approach to NVC, much less to NVC in business. Yet NVC can play a major role in improving your business image and increasing your chances of success.

A WINNER WITH NVC—JOE B.

Joe B. is a prime example of how people can be winners with NVC. Before his recent retirement, Joe was one of the foremost architects in a large Midwestern city. Extremely talented, he was known as a supersalesman who always won competitive bids. This success was especially remarkable in view of the way organizations select architects. When a company decides to go out for bids, it will schedule marathon sessions during which any qualified architect, solicited or otherwise, is allowed to present ideas. On the appointed day the architects assemble outside the conference room like a bevy of shotputters, flexing their muscles and trying to psych out their opponents. They sit with their drawings rolled up under their arms and nervously wait their turn.

Joe's success was so legendary that when he merely walked into the waiting area, half the architects immediately got up and left without presenting. Joe was an exceptional architect, but he was not that far ahead of his rivals in technical skills. What gave Joe the edge was his superiority in communications skills. He was so superior, in fact, that his competitors began to assume he would win.

In a long conversation with Joe one sunny afternoon, I asked him about his secret. He had a very simple method. "When I go into the room," he said, "I look for two people. The first is the Star, the big boss. He is the key decision maker. I make certain I sell to him and get his commitment. I also look for the Heel. This is the negative guy, the one who will make trouble for me when I present and when I'm out of the room. I make sure I either put him in his place or draw out his criticisms so I can respond to them before I leave."

"It all sounds simple enough," I commented, eager for some juicy tips, "but how do you tell who is the Heel or Star?"

Giving the answer I feared, he responded, "Oh, you can just tell."

Therein lies the excitement of NVC—and the frustration. NVC can increase your chances of business success, but only if you have a systematic technique for learning its vocabulary and applying it in business. The NVC checklists in the first three chapters of this book will give you a framework for learning the vocabulary you need. The three NVC checklists follow the standard pattern of observation: where you put your body, its appearance and what you put around it, and what you do with it once it is there. The remaining chapters will help you gain fluency.

1. **Body Position and Status**	Territorial space
	Height might
	Tread spread
	Size prize
	Seating dynamics
	Office etiquette
2. **Indicators**	Personal
	Shared
	Public
3. **Body Movement**	Center
	Head
	Posture
	Hands
	Legs

With practice, you will be able to make these NVC scans automatically, taking only a few moments to size up a new person or situation. The time is always available, even if you are speaking. Scientists estimate the speed of conversational thought at 750 words per minute; yet average speech is only 150 words per minute. This leaves you with 80 percent of your mental capacity to do other things. Frequently, you may daydream or plan your next response with this time. What you ought to do is become a better "listener" with your eyes.

NVC in Business

You may be curious about how much information you will gain if your eyes do become better listeners. Albert Mehrabian conducted a series of tests to determine how much body, voice, and words contributed to the communication of attitudes. Take a moment to fill in your estimates of the proper percentages. (Remember, the percentages should reflect the communication of *attitudes*, not ideas.)

BODY	%
VOICE	%
WORDS	%
	100 %

The results of Mehrabian's research were body, 55 percent; voice, 38 percent; and words, 7 percent. The percentages are, of course, highly dependent on the situation measured. After asking my audiences this question for seven years, I obtained the following averages: body, 60 percent; voice, 30 percent; and words, 10 percent. Our attitudes are communicated silently. This is the message that most people miss.

If you don't agree with my percentages—if you believe that words are far more important—you can do a little research on your own. Try this experiment when you come home from work tomorrow. As you walk in, tell your loved ones that you do, indeed, love them. Run over to them, shake your fist, and sweetly say, "I love you!" Then walk away snarling, with a horrible grimace on your face, while you clench and unclench your fists. If words are truly more important than gestures, your loved ones will come over to you with outstretched arms and sweetly respond, "Why, thank you, honey. What a nice surprise. We love you too."

If you survived that experiment, you can follow up with a test on words versus tone of voice. When you come home from work *two* days from now, wait for your loved one to ask, "How was your day, dear?" Then walk over, maintaining as pleasant an expression as possible, and say in a loud voice, "I had just a wonderful day!" with as much sarcasm as you can muster. Once again, if the response is anything other than "That's nice, dear," voice is the dominant factor. Your experiments will have to stop here if you don't want your loved one to develop a nervous tic when you arrive home. If the responses were calm and oriented solely to your words, you can forget this book. You've somehow landed Mr. Spock from *Star Trek*.

President Franklin Roosevelt was particularly aware of NVC. Standing in a boring receiving line one evening, he decided to have a little fun. As each guest came up and said, "Good evening, Mr. President, how are you, sir?" he responded warmly with a pleasant smile, "Fine, thank you, I just murdered my mother-in-law." Not one person going through the receiving line reacted to his comment. It's doubtful people even heard it.

You are now ready to flex your communications muscles at the office. As you walk down the hall tomorrow, try an FDR. When you're asked, "Howya doin'?" cheerfully bubble, "Pretty bad, and you?" Keep count of how many of your fellow workers even hear your words. If *anybody* hears them, he or she is unusually attentive. Most of those you meet will be paying attention only to your nonverbals.

Obviously, words are important and necessary for conveying *ideas* or detailed information. If that weren't true, this book might be a film. (Not a bad idea!) In general, your body is the best indicator of *purpose* and your voice is the best indicator of *importance*.

NVC and Success

NVC has an important impact on all of us. Every President since John F. Kennedy has been tutored in NVC. These politicians realized the tremendous effect of NVC on people's perception of a candidate and on their voting decisions. Your NVC can drastically affect the decisions of your voters—those people in authority who hold your career in their hands.

The animal kingdom, dealing with its human masters, is much more successful than most of us are in using NVC. Even the youngest members are quite adept at seeing into us. If you have ever trained a puppy, you've seen an advanced NVC-reading organism at work.

When you train a puppy, sooner or later you find a "mistake of the second kind" (solid). As you're kneeling there in resigned disgust, your nice canine bumbles by. You call it, using your kindest, sweetest doggy voice. "Here, Thorndyke! Come here, sweet puppykins. Your faithful and kind owner wants to pet your lovable doggy hide."

Does Thorndyke come? Of course not! He knows full well that you plan to beat the daylights out of him with today's news, slam his nose in what he did, and throw him out in the cold, lonely backyard. He knows because he can read your NVC even though you were trying to appear as kind and nice as possible. You even reinforced his feelings by carrying the paper in your hand.

The first recorded NVC professional was not even human. He was a wizard by the name of Clever Hans who could perform *any* mathematical computation at all. Hans was a horse who lived in Germany in the early 1900s, touring the countryside and giving sellout performances at each stop. He would answer any question from the audience that could be represented by the tapping of a hoof. For a year and a half, audiences were baffled, swearing that there had to be a trick. The show conditions got tougher and tougher, but Hans never missed a question.

Then, after 18 months of success, Hans flopped for the first time. He missed a question that was asked by someone out of his line of sight and kept secret from his trainer. Clever Hans's hoof tapped right past the correct answer. For the first time in his career, Clever Hans was no longer clever.

The reason was simple. On his own, Hans had learned that if he stopped tapping his hoof at a certain point, he would get a reward. Hans was nothing more than a psychologist's rat responding to a stimulus. The stimulus Hans responded to was the tension in his trainer! He found that if he stopped tapping just as the tension eased—that is, just when he had tapped out the answer—he was rewarded. When the question was given to him from someone out of his sight, and kept secret from the trainer, there was no tension to "read."

Hans made his career from NVC, and so have many others in various ways, like Joe B. You too have the talent and the ability—if you just take the time to learn the vocabulary of NVC —to improve your business image by bettering your communications skills. For the first time in your life, you will have the knowledge to interpret some of the massive nonverbal data that used to be summarily shunted to the brain's roundfile. It's time you added the title Nonverbal Communicator to your business credentials.

2

Relative Body Location

Our language recognizes the importance of NVC with such body-oriented phrases as:

Cold shoulder	Face up to it
Shake it off	Chin up
Get it off your chest	Grit your teeth
Stiff upper lip	Shoulder a burden
At arm's length	Glad-hander

These phrases are almost more than we can swallow. You've got to hand it to me, though, the ones I dug up are real eye-openers. I can keep them coming hand over fist, until your knees buckle. But don't let your spirits droop; I promise to quit slinging these out before you turn your back in disgust.

The term *body language,* popularized by Julius Fast in his book of the same name, refers to the portion of NVC relating solely to physical communication, excluding voice. Body language is actually the study of three concepts: proxemics, indicators, and kinesics. *Proxemics* (derived from the Greek word meaning "to approach") covers the analysis of body locations. *Indicators,* a sociological term, refers to the objects we gather around us. *Kinesics* is the study of physical movements.

In coming chapters we will not only examine these three areas, but also cover vocal traits, environment, and image as key nonverbal signals of attitude. This chapter introduces the checklist for evaluating body position and status:

Territorial space
Height might
Tread spread
Size prize
Seating dynamics
Office etiquette

Territorial Space

The first questions you should ask yourself in any business situation is "Where are people located and why are they there?" The distance we maintain with others is related to our feelings toward them and indicates something about our relationships. This distance is called *territorial space*. There are four basic zones of territorial space: intimate, personal, social, and public.

INTIMATE SPACE

Intimate space includes distances up to about one and a half feet. It is used for such activities as lovemaking, comforting, protecting, and family greeting. It is also used for wrestling, basketball, sitting in movie theaters, and standing in elevators or on crowded streetcorners. Intimate space is usually reserved for people who have the right to be that close to us. Such familiarity and relaxation of normal distances most often require time and a deepening of relationships. Sometimes this is not always possible, as in an elevator, where closeness to strangers makes most of us feel uncomfortable.

The importance of maintaining my own intimate space was brought home to me one afternoon. A salesman and I were having a casual conversation about the poor economy when I began to get nervous. The salesman kept shifting closer to me as we talked, stopping at a distance of a foot, which put our faces all of nine inches apart. I decided to try a little experiment, partly out of interest and mostly out of self-preservation.

Fortunately, we were at his desk, out in the middle of a large room, so I had plenty of space to work with. As we talked, I slowly backed around the desk, leaning forward all the while to "wean" him off my face. As I stood upright, he unconsciously took a step around the desk, and I was back in his clutches. I performed the maneuver again, so that I was now on the opposite side of the desk from where we started, but the results were the same. I was trapped!

Deciding it was time for more serious measures, I slowly shifted around him and eased over to our starting point, leaning over the desk until I arrived. When I stood upright, he immediately walked around the desk without slowing his conversation. In what I thought to be a flash of brilliance, I sat on the desk so I could put my knees between us. When he moved to stand between my legs, I became desperate. In a last-ditch effort, I leaned back on my hands as I sat. He then leaned forward until I yelled, "Stop! I give up! I give up! You win!"

"What do you mean?" was the quizzical, unmoving reply.

"Don't move a muscle, Mike," I said, as I put my thumb on my nose and touched his nose with the little finger of the same hand. "You're just too damn close for my personal comfort! You are only *that* far away from my face," I said, showing him my outstretched hand. "My *wife* and I don't even converse at this distance!"

"Well, that's your problem, Cooper!" he returned, stomping off in a huff. Later Mike came back to me and mentioned that several customers he had asked admitted they felt as I did. You can't use intimate space unless you have earned the right to be there.

Police purposely use space invasion. One of my students, a county police officer, talked about using this approach in questioning suspects. Leaning forward, he would draw his chair up to the seated suspect until his knee touched the chair between the suspect's knees. He and the other officers would trade off the questioning stints, never letting the suspect regain his territorial space. As the officer put it, "Who needs rubber hoses when I can crowd them as long as I like?"

PERSONAL SPACE

Personal space includes distances of one to two and a half feet. Personal distance is normally maintained between two friends in conversation—for example, at a small lunchroom table. Office workers standing around the water cooler will often maintain this distance, as will people at a cocktail party who know each other. Reduce the distance to intimate space, and your acquaintance will become very uncomfortable, most likely moving away to restore the personal space.

One of the oddities of TV is that the actors often have to talk almost nose to nose to be included in a closeup shot. A humorous example is the "medicinal elixir" commercial where a pleasant young couple stands against a black backdrop and the husband says something like, "This is my wife and I love her. Because she knows she's important, she takes Killital to maintain our love." The ridiculous part of this commercial is that the man and woman are right on top of each other. He is breathing hotly on her forehead and she is craning her neck to smile and look up to him with love. Real people, no matter how intimate, do not talk to each other three inches apart. Even at rip-roaring drunken brawls, at least personal distance is maintained (for conversation, naturally).

SOCIAL SPACE

Social space is approximately four to seven feet. Phrases such as "stand back so I can see you" and "keep him at arm's length" reflect our need for social space. In business, the prime protector of social space is the desk. It automatically puts the heads of the people seated on either side about seven feet apart. The same goes for a conference table, dining table, or counter in a store. Studies of trends in office furniture have shown that status-conscious top executives are getting rid of their desks, files, and drawers, figuring they are above all that. But they are replacing their desks with tables of approximately the same size, in order to maintain control of the social space around their chair.

Strangers thrown together at a party will initially form circles of social space. At social gatherings I often try to determine who already knows whom and who just met by observing how far apart people are standing.

Recently I had a half-hour discussion with a man who knew I was an NVC consultant. He spent the time arguing that NVC is hokum and a complete waste of time. I was happy to let him ramble, because as we were talking I moved closer and then farther away. He unconsciously shifted his position to maintain his own comfortable social space. In the course of the conversation, we meandered up and down a hall and in and out of two offices, ending up where the hall met the office areas. After he finished one particularly long tirade, I said, "Look, I'll buy what you said about NVC if you can answer one simple question for me."

"Sure," he sneered. "What is it?"

"Tell me," I returned, "why have you and I been in and out of a hall and two offices at least twice in the past half-hour?"

He stared at me for a moment and stomped off. I may not have gained a convert, but I won an argument nonverbally.

Public Space

Public space, usually ten feet or more, is reserved for strangers whom we don't care to notice or interact with. People waiting in the lobby for an elevator will mill about at this distance. Even on a busy streetcorner people will try to maintain this space. Watch public places such as lobbies, transportation terminals, reception areas, and museums for how strangers maintain public space.

The importance of public space was illustrated by an experiment performed at a college library. A graduate assistant went to the library when it was relatively empty and purposely sat at an occupied table. Responses varied from complete indifference, to dirty looks, to disgusted stares. Yet in 80 trials, only one person asked her to move. The assistant finally asked to be replaced in the experiment because the subjects in the library made her feel so guilty for intruding.

CONTROLLING TERRITORIES

There is a wealth of information to be gained from observing how attendees mill about before a meeting or "shoot the breeze" around the cooler. It is easy to determine which person is the leader in a group. When a superior is talking with a number of subordinates, the configuration often takes on a "choir effect," as shown in Figure 2–1. The leader, at the top of the diagram, is given more space; the others are facing the leader in a semicircle. The "choir" will usually stand attentively, rarely turning to leave unless someone else arrives to fill the gap.

In a leaderless group, it is apparent who is "in" or "out" by their physical position. In Figure 2–1 the person on the lower left has walked up to a conversation and been recognized but not

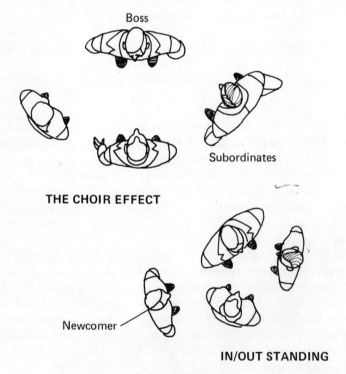

Boss

Subordinates

THE CHOIR EFFECT

Newcomer

IN/OUT STANDING

Figure 2–1. Standing positions.

admitted to the group. Notice how the two people on either side of the newcomer have created a small gap, but not enough to give the newcomer equal space. All of us have been in this predicament at one time or another and often walk away with no small feeling of rejection.

The territorial space characteristics of an office are indicative of its owner. An executive may want to crowd visitors to his or her office by placing the desk about a third of the way between the door and the back wall. This way, the executive has ample space to lean away from the desk, put his feet up, or swivel. The visitor has little space, which connotes less importance or dominance. A client of mine laid out his office in this manner. He placed a large tree on the visitor's side, so that there was just enough room between the desk, tree, and wall for a chair. I can't cross my legs in the chair, much less be comfortable. Of course, my client always apologizes for the smallness of the office, but I've heard he has had the opportunity to move and has refused several times.

The amount of available space can also affect the success of a meeting. I always avoid a small classroom in my training sessions, because the audience is much more argumentative and harder to control. The same holds true for a business meeting. If there is not enough space for the participants, the meeting has a much smaller chance for success as time passes.

We often use objects to mark our territorial space, much as a dog "anoints" a new backyard to indicate its territory. People sitting on a bus or plane will fill the other seat with their belongings to "claim" the space. On the *Tonight Show,* actress Angie Dickinson mentioned that she prefers to read during a flight rather than talk to other passengers. So she always puts her carry-on luggage and accessories in the seat next to her until right before departure to discourage anyone from sitting there. Walls can also be used to define territorial space. Members of a department will fill the walls within their boundaries with pictures, contest posters, or other paraphernalia to indicate the department's physical territory.

Sometimes, we have to claim our territory personally. At a "husbands and wives too" office party, an executive I know was having an animated conversation with his young secretary. They were sitting on the couch and she was touching his arm as they talked, holding his eyes with a steady gaze. Suddenly his wife came over, sat down beside him, smoothed his collar, and listened without saying a word. The move was a show of possession, reminding the secretary of the wife's "territory." The message was not lost on the secretary, because the conversation ended soon afterwards and was not resumed that evening.

Men use the same sort of maneuver at social gatherings to demonstrate possession of their wives or women friends. A man comes up to his woman and casually slips an arm around her waist. In effect, he is saying to the other man, "She's mine, remember?"

Territorial space can be manipulated to gain control, as in the police interrogation example described above. Intruding on people's space is one of the most common forms of domination in business. Some people can make us feel like a rabbit at the wolves' convention by talking close to us, as Mike did. The effect can be intensified by offensive personal habits. If you have a tough meeting coming up, schedule it in a small conference room and anticipate it with a big, garlic lunch. Rope-sized cigars made from buffalo chips are another executive weapon in the discomfort race. Chest poking (the female version is arm punching), nudging (remember Monty Python's "Nudge, Nudge" sketch?), and backslapping are further insults to our sense of space. After 20 minutes of one of the above, most of us are ready to agree to almost anything.

If you want to hold an efficient, spirited meeting, keep the space tight. This can help shorten the duration better than any schedule. Small spaces also intensify conflict. In making recommendations to management negotiators at a large chemical plant, I suggested that they meet with the union local in a "cozy" little conference room. This was to take advantage of the well-known antagonism between the young union president and an old-line vice-president. Although the negotiating sessions were prolonged, the union's inability to present a united front was beneficial to the company.

If you wish to reduce conflict in a session, provide more space. Spread everyone out around a large table in a spacious room.

Become aware of others' needs for territorial space. By moving closer or farther away during a conversation, see if you can determine the space your business associates and acquaintances require. As you grow more familiar with the uses of territorial space, you will be able to continue conversations others are trying to break off by keeping within conversational distance. (I have moved with people as much as 50 feet in a ten-minute chat they wished to break off.) You will learn to stay farther away from people who are trying to control you and to get closer to those you wish to dominate. You will discover that territorial space is both an indicator and a tool in effective NVC.

Height Might

Height has long been associated with the desirable, with success. Up is good and down is bad. Our language is full of phrases like "look up to him," "raised to peerage," "put on a pedestal," "on top of the world," "rise to the occasion," and "high and mighty." No self-respecting god would ever be caught down low, in Death Valley or the Bonneville Salt Flats. They live in places like Mt. Olympus and Valhalla.

Height is a symbol of power and superiority. The winner stands highest on the Olympic awards platform. A judge's courtroom bench is always elevated. Victorious football players put the coach on their shoulders and carry him off the field. Raymond Burr (as Perry Mason) never went up to the judge's bench to argue an objection. How could he appear intimidating if he stood there like a youngster filching cookies off the counter? That was okay for a little villain like Hamilton Burger, but not for our Perry!

Lack of height has always been a sign of inferiority. We can "fall short" of a goal, "think small," be "shortsighted," or be "looked down on." Being lower is a sign of servility. In ancient

Figure 2–2. Height might.
(Copyright © 1977 King Features Syndicate Inc.)

times, vanquished soldiers were forced to pass under a chest-high arch of spears in front of the conquering general. Anyone who refused to bow down was allowed to wear a spear home, buried in his chest. Even today we don't like anyone to "lord it over us."

We consistently favor people with a height advantage, as Figure 2–2 shows. In this century only two presidential candidates who were shorter than their opponents have been elected, and these only recently in the times of TV campaigning. The first was Richard Nixon (5'11½") "over" George McGovern (6'1"); the second was Jimmy Carter (5'9½") "over" Gerald Ford (6'1"). Business also rewards height. A 1972 study of University of Pittsburgh graduates showed that those in the 6'2" to 6'4" range received 12% higher starting salaries than their fellow graduates, independent of any other factors.

The dominance of height is no secret to today's business executive. Everyone knows the importance of standing up to address a meeting in order to gain control.

Many executives choose their office furniture so they can dominate visitors. They sit on large, high-backed, elevated desk chairs while offering their visitors low-slung lounge chairs that are almost impossible to get out of, much less sit up in. A woman who runs a very successful resume service has an office designed this way. Many clients have complained about the low chairs and her obvious attempt to dominate with height. But she denies any purpose to the layout, claiming she merely used the furniture that was available to her. It is interesting to note, however, that despite client complaints she hasn't changed anything.

You can't saw the legs off of someone who is taller than you or modify your office furniture in secret, but there are ways to minimize a height disadvantage. This is particularly important to women in business, since women as a group are shorter than men. As I pointed out in the section on territorial space, distance is a good counteragent for domination. A 6'4" executive who is overwhelming up close is almost completely neutralized at public distances. Sitting at opposite ends of the table, talking from the door of his office, and getting up and moving while you talk will all help you stay even.

A 5'9" IBM sales training manager claimed that he could minimize height might in tough sales calls on any tall executives. Just when the customer was bearing down the hardest, leaning over the desk and slamming points home, the manager would get up and walk over to a window and begin gazing out thoughtfully. He would continue the conversation with, "Now, you've made several good points here. Let me see if I understand them." As he restated the customer's position, occasionally glancing back toward the desk, the customer would often calm down and begin to agree or amplify. Sometimes the customer would even follow him to the window. Then the conversation would continue more rationally as both men pondered the outdoors. Only when the meeting was back on an even basis would the manager return to his chair, successful in escaping a tough situation.

Another way to minimize height differences is to carefully control the location of any conversation or meeting. Like the spider, you should conduct business safely in your web—the office. Adjust the height of your desk chair if needed. Find visitors' chairs that are soft and comfortable, but not so low as to be obvious. Some executives have even had hidden platforms constructed behind their desks. Make your office the one place where you can be in control. Save important conversations for times when you can invite your boss in as he is walking by your door. If he's smart, he'll suggest you follow him to his office. If he's not, you can trap him in yours by saying, "I've got something important to discuss with you," and walking over and closing the door. Once that door is shut, he's psychologically locked in.

When you can't arrange a conversation in your office, at least hold it outside of your associate's office. Talk over lunch if you must. It is almost impossible for an associate to be domineering when special sauce is running out the corner of his mouth or when he's munching a hard luncheon roll with crumbs bouncing from plate to lap. In addition, being in public limits the tactics your associate can use. Other places where height advantage is relatively meaningless are in a car or airplane, in a bar or lounge with deep chairs, and in a crowd.

Being outnumbered also tends to neutralize height might. One of my former managers used to crowd subordinates into his small office for weekly team meetings. I made a point of coming in last when all the chairs were taken. The only spot left was a heater module, which was about desk high and somewhat behind the manager's chair. When I sat on it I was head and shoulders above him and to his rear. The first few meetings I did this he was slightly uneasy but accepted my excuse about no place to sit. The third meeting he *ordered* me to get a chair. This still wasn't acceptable, because he was surrounded. Even if he had stood up, his height dominance would have affected only the people he was facing. He could not address the people at his sides without twisting like a physical fitness expert. This "screaming Mongolian horde" approach can help you make up in numbers what you may lack in physical size.

A final approach to minimizing height advantages is to act aggressively. An administrator in a sales office felt he was being treated unfairly, but he knew he would be lost if he went in to talk with the office manager. The manager was a tall man and a smooth, persuasive talker. Deciding on an aggressive approach, the administrator worked himself into a suitable "mad" and stormed into the office. He strode up to the manager's desk and began telling him what was wrong, pounding the desk to emphasize his points. This continued for a few minutes until the manager slipped in during a pause and said, "Jack, Jack! Sit down and we'll talk about it."

Jack responded with, "I can't sit down, I'm too upset!" and continued to talk. The manager finally broke loose from the onslaught by standing up, at which point Jack abruptly said, "I'm sorry I've gotten so worked up. We'll have to talk about it when I get myself calmed down," and walked out to lunch. The story ended happily when the problem was later resolved, which Jack insists was due solely to his aggressive tactics.

If you are among those of us who won't be getting that 12% higher starting salary, you now have several techniques to use against those who will. Being "one up" is often little more than being physically up, a situation you can handle by using the information in this chapter to "stand tall" with others.

Tread Spread

A variation on height dominance, and the third item on the body position and status checklist, is walking position. Like being "on top," being a "front-runner" is an indicator of status and power. (Why else do we speed up when a VW tries to pass?) In a military inspection, the highest-ranking reviewing officer always walks in front. In a procession of royalty, the monarch is always at the head. I have never seen a picture of former President Ford and former Secretary Kissinger when Kissinger was not sensitive enough to remain in the background. In pictures of Kissinger with his wife, Nancy, she is usually behind her husband. (After all, "*behind* every successful man, there is a woman.") Some cultures require people of lower status to walk at least one step behind their superiors. State department officials closely examine all photos showing dignitaries of "closed" countries such as Russia and China. In pictures of a group walking, power or status is shown by how near the front of the pack an individual is.

Can you imagine the top executive of your organization walking down the hall leaning over your boss's shoulder? Ridiculous. Yet the chances are you've seen a subordinate of the executive walking in that position. One of my students, a bank vice-president, remarked, "So that's why I always end up walking through the bank sideways like a sand crab, talking to one of my people. I've even mentioned it to a few of them, but we still end up this way."

Observe walking position in meeting a new group or sitting in a strange office. I used to watch groups of my customers come out of the elevator, walk up to the reception desk, then arrange themselves around the sign-in table. The boss would usually lead the way. In the instances where he trailed, the others would wait for him to do the talking and sign in first. If one person defers and lets another go ahead, that is further proof of status. An underling does not usually defer to the boss; the boss goes ahead as a matter of course. The subordinate never had the privilege of being ahead in the first place!

I'm frequently asked, "What about a man who opens the door for a woman? What does that mean?" With many men, this is merely a courtesy. In a *business situation*, it is an acknowledgment of dominance. Ignoring the differences in sex, wouldn't you be nervous if, during a long stroll through your office building, your boss carefully opened *each* door for you? You might think, "I've got to stop letting him do this. He'll think I'm lazy or insensitive!" You end up rushing to the next door to usher him in first so that you don't get too far into his psychological debt—the position a woman is in by continuously accepting this "courtesy."

It's time to step out and become a front-runner. One of the hardest things to do is to take initiative. Foursomes bumble at the reservations desk, indecisive about which couple should ask for the reservations. If we are in between two others walking along the street and are forced to crowd down to two wide because of people coming the other way, we are the ones who step into the evasive tap dance trying to save our shins as we fall behind. We are part of that pack milling around the reception desk or hesitating self-consciously at a doorway.

New Yorkers never hesitate. If you stand in front of a pedestrian in New York, you will go home with hundreds of footprints on your body. In the Midwest I did the face-to-face dance many times in order to get by someone coming toward me. Now, when faced with someone coming directly at me, I stop and let the other person move aside or alter his course.

In your office, stop walking behind your bosses. Stay even, or walk in front of them occasionally. Women, open the door for men as the opportunity arises. You may earn a few "libber" grumbles, but if you make the gesture matter-of-factly, the comments will die down. These little changes in walking position can go a long way in building confidence and showing your power. If "it's what's up front that counts," then you had better get there and stay there!

Size Prize

Another variation on height might is size prize, or physical bulk. Our society idolizes size. The most obvious obsession is with the female figure. Ever since an image was first captured on film, America has made a succession of no-talent "femmes énormales" famous and rich. The Playboy empire was dedicated to ferreting out "les glandes grandes." No wonder some women risk serious medical complications to be enhanced by silicone. Size and success are nearly synonymous.

One of my customers, a small airlines company, had the usual flight attendant training system in its home office. It never ceased to amaze me that, while it took a memo three days to go across the hall, it took only 30 minutes for the whole company (male and female) to know that there was a top-heavy young beauty in the current crop of trainees. Mondays at the training area were always busy enough, but once the word leaked out there was a never ending stream of employees just "going by" at break time. Let the poor young woman venture out of the training nest, and the carpets would practically wear out as she stood there.

The respect and love of bigness is *everywhere*. My son watches a Saturday morning cereal commercial that praises the stuff solely for its size. A group of kids in a beat-up wooden hideout sing, "Honeycrumb's big. Big, BIg, BIG! Got a big bite. Right, RIGht, RIGHT! Honeycrumb's a big mouthful, it tastes just right!" Who cares if it's nutritional or if it tastes like outdoor rug glue, as long as it fills up your mouth?

Many consumer products focus on bigness. If your soap isn't

selling, bring it out in a new, larger container. The words "big" and "large" have become so overworked that companies have come up with "family size" and "industrial size" just to announce even more bigness. After all, where else but in America could a fast-food franchise succeed on the strength of a product named the Whopper?

Movies also have to be big. Papers are filled with ads like:

> See *Tidal Jaws: The Towering Earthquake Adventure, 1932.* With a cast of billions. See the destruction of the entire earth in Sound-abound. Feel, breathe the panoramic majesty of massive death. Thrill to the biggest galaxy of stars since the Crab Nebula in a glut of cameo roles. Watch as Ralph, the mechanical earth, a 100 percent scale model, self-destructs, bringing the entire studio down with it.

Even our activities have to be big. "This is the biggest thing that ever happened to this town." One of the most popular books last year was a collection of world records on "the biggest." Heavyweights are the only boxers most sports fans follow. Even the most ardent collegiate football fan probably has no idea that there is a lightweight football league in the Northeast.

Physical bulk is an enormous advantage in today's business world. Several years ago, my office had a chance to interview the graduating captain of Notre Dame's football team. Even though he was a fine offensive tackle, he felt he would have a hard time making it in the pros, so he was interviewing for a position through the college placement office. He was a giant—your average, run-of-the-mill Notre Dame offensive lineman. To his credit (and against his stereotype), he owned a high gradepoint average and had excellent leadership qualities. But what do you think the comments from management were?

"Did you see that guy we had in here today? He could have bent my arm with one hand and tossed me through the window with a flick of the wrist! And he's even qualified."

"Man, if we land that hulk, we'll have a real superstar on our hands."

"He can't miss. Can you imagine letting him call on (customer name deleted)? He'd eat that little pipsqueak alive."

To the football player's credit, he turned down a very lucrative offer, one, I suspect, higher than any other trainee received. For some reason, everyone in the office acted as if we still carry clubs. Evidently we do, only they are psychological clubs.

Remember the University of Texas football slogan of the late 1960s? "If you've got it, flaunt it!" If you are blessed with physical size (not fat, we'll discuss that later), maximize its effect. Maintain closer territorial spaces, dwarf everything you come in contact with. Have a smaller desk and keep the chairs tightly grouped. If you have a large office, jam the furniture into one small area and decorate the empty space or turn it into an unused "casual setting."

Emphasize your physical bulk. Give iron handshakes, talk loudly, slap backs, and punch shoulders. Tell people you play in an adult hockey league for the physical contact. Rugby is even better. (Every rugby player I ever met thought a minor injury was one where you could at least get up before the game was over. A major injury has never been defined.)

One of my customers was an enormous man who would rather crush your hand than look at you. Though I have a fairly large, powerful hand, I was still on the edge of agony every time I greeted him. I was careful to remove my college ring before making any calls on him. He had the habit of pulling his hand back slightly so that my knuckles were in his grasp and my second and fourth fingers were crushed against the unyielding ring. It was impossible to be assertive with this man while nursing a mutilated paw.

Another man in our office let it be known that he had been a heavyweight boxing champion in his youth and used to earn extra money by staying in the ring three rounds with carnival knockout artists. He managed to get into a bar fight every year or so to reinforce his reputation. All he had to do at a meeting was to begin to get a little agitated or start pounding the table, and the others would back off. Although there had never been the hint of a disturbance in his business career, he used this veiled threat successfully for years.

If you are small or slight, you can minimize your lack of size by manipulating your environment. Get a massive desk. Use large, high-armed, heavy office chairs that cannot be moved easily and place them slightly away from your desk. Large bookshelves, enormous paintings, giant displays or charts, all serve to minimize size differences between people. Imagine two men standing under the Gateway Arch in St. Louis, one is 6'4" and the other 5'8". Size becomes unimportant because they are both dwarfed by their surroundings.

Don't worry about drawing attention to your size with this approach, particularly if you have a large office. If your office is small, use lighting to help achieve the same effect. Don't use bright ceiling lights. Take out several ceiling bulbs at night if you have to. Keep the room a comfortable brightness, like a family room, and use an attractive desk lamp for working. Bright light brings out the details of size, making a room and everything in it look smaller. Softer lighting minimizes any negative feature, such as a bad paint job or worn furniture. The more ornate and impressive your trappings are, the less your physical bulk will matter. Is it any wonder that the mousy boss Mr. Foofram in the "Hi and Lois" comic strip has a big, fancy office?

The key to overcoming lack of size is to battle the problem subtly. Small people in business face a strange double bind. If they are aggressive and successful, they are accused of having a Napoleon complex; they are "overcompensating." Remarks such as "She's a tiger for such a little girl" and "He's a real bantam rooster" abound. These are negative compliments of the worst kind. If small people are organization-minded, compliant, and helpful, they are regarded as poor little folks who never made up for size. The truly successful small person in business must develop a style that does not let the question of size ever become a concern. Even if some of the funds must come from your own pocket, make your office the one place where your personal features are maximized. Don't go in for elevator shoes or a Napoleon personality. Let competence speak for you.

One of the most dynamic small people I have ever met also has one of the best corporate styles I have ever seen. He started as the proprietor of a small hardware store and built it into a chain of retail sales and rental stores. After retiring at 32 for two years, he decided to re-enter business and is now vice-president of a large construction firm. If you are familiar with the construction industry, you know it has the biggest collection of hardnosed, burly brutes in the working world. There is no room for the meek or mild. But this executive has the complete respect and cooperation of everyone who works for him. I have never heard any of the short-guy putdowns, nor have I heard any Napoleon remarks. He works with overwhelming, inarguable competence. He never has to raise his voice. He never makes rash judgments. Because there is so little doubt about him as a businessman, there is also little doubt about him as a man. True competence, controlled competence, is the only way to escape the small person double bind.

A woman in business faces the same sort of problem. She may have to deal not only with an inferiority in bulk but also with an attitude of "natural inferiority" ingrained in her male associates. Her double bind is that of being "just a woman" or, if she begins to succeed, of being a "pushy broad," who is trying to become "one of the boys." The answer for her is the same as for the small businessman: competence.

One of my evening college students was a department manager in a large retail store. Only 21 years of age, she was the first "executive level" manager ever to reach that position without a college degree. A tall, imposing young woman, I asked her secret.

"I was very lucky when I was younger," she revealed, "because both my parents were imposing and thought I would be too. They made a point of making me proud of my size, even during those years when being large was the dating kiss of death. So many of my female friends who are large slump and act ashamed of what should be an advantage."

As an experiment, I included this question on the classes' midterm exam: "How should a large woman manage her proxemics (body location) for maximum effect?" Four out of six women and all seven men in the class assumed that she should *de-emphasize* her size advantage. If you are blessed with natural size advantages, don't make the same mistake. You've got it; use it!

Seating Dynamics

Ever since Howard and Cosell, the first two cavemen with the dawning of intelligence in their eyes, decided that there must be something better than working doubled up on the ground like a duck, people have vied for status through seating position. Howard probably found a flat-sided rock and rolled it over to the cave for Cosell to see (which is not easy to do with a flat-sided rock, but then again they were cavemen). One of them, undoubtedly Cosell, suddenly had the bright idea of laying it flat side *up*, and in a flash the table was born. The little scene surely ended with an argument over who would get to sit at the narrow end of the rock.

The locations we choose for sitting are loaded with nonverbal data. Remember the Paris peace talks on ending the Vietnam war? Diplomats spent several *years* trying to determine the seating arrangements for the various delegates. Seating arrangements are no less important in business.

Association Approximation

Certain seating positions are conducive to different types of interaction. By observing those positions, we can begin to draw fairly accurate conclusions about relationships. Figure 2–3 shows four variations in seating dynamics.

Cooperation is best when people are sitting next to each other. When a teacher is tutoring a student or an office worker is showing a replacement how to do a certain job, they usually sit next to each other so both can work from the same document.

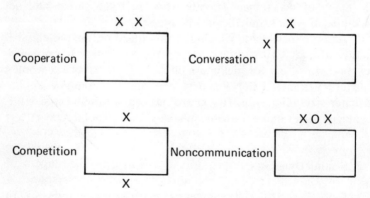

Figure 2–3. Sitting positions.

Conversation is facilitated when people are sitting at adjacent corners of a table. The company lunchroom is a good place to observe this. (If the table is small, though, conversation may be uncomfortable because of insufficient territorial space. In this case, the two people will sit across from each other.) Conversation requires closeness, but not to the same degree as sharing reading material.

Competitors often confront each other face to face, like Western gunslingers. Opponents in a meeting tend to sit across the table from each other, either at the middle or at each end. This way, each one can "keep an eye on" the other. Their underlings or support personnel frequently choose the seats on either side of their "gunslinger," much like lining up for the showdown at the corral. If there is to be no fight, the opponents may choose the noncommunication position, with someone sitting between them. The more people between them, the harder it is to converse. The effect is similar to trying to talk to a relative at the Thanksgiving table with a hearty eater bobbing up and down between you. You end up leaning back and forth like an antenna in the carwash.

Table Status

You should be familiar with the dominant and subordinate positions around a rectangular business meeting table. The dominant positions are the ends. The middle of the table is a secondary dominant position and is usually used for active defense or for disagreement with the leader on the end. The weakest positions are in between the powers, in the "dead zone" of status.

The first table in Figure 2–4 shows the normal primary and secondary positions of power and opposition around a rectangular table. This arrangement is common in meetings of a committee of equals with an appointed chairman, or in meetings where the chairman has a higher position. The second table arrangement is likely when the meeting contains a hierarchy of personnel. I have noticed this pattern frequently in military meetings, where the general sits at the head of the table and those along the side

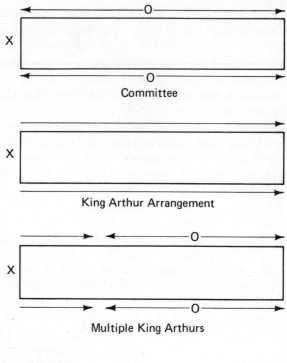

Key:

X = Dominant Positions
O = Secondary Dominant Positions
→ = Direction of Decreasing Status

Figure 2–4. Table status.

are arranged by rank, with the lowly lieutenants sitting meekly at the far end. This is sometimes called the King Arthur arrangement, in honor of the round table, which supposedly had no status. (Instead, the knights fought to see who could sit closest to King Arthur.) The third table in Figure 2–4 shows a multiple King Arthur arrangement where each executive has grouped his minions around him. In this situation, relative status is determined by the number of chairs between a person and his or her King Arthur. See if these observations about seating behavior hold in your organization. You may find that this is one of the primary indicators of power.

REAR FEAR

There is a special case of seating dynamics called rear fear, which may date back to the wild, wild West.

"Okay, you cowpokes and gunslingers. What's the one rule to follow when you're sipping your favorite firewater at the Longbranch? That's right, tenderfoot, never sit with your back to the door! You never know when some filthy varmint will come up and plug ya' in the back." Today, people will first fill the restaurant tables along the wall and may even leave rather than sit in the middle of the dining area.

People do not like to sit with their backs to the door because it makes them feel exposed. Less than one percent of the offices I have seen are arranged facing away from the door. One that was, the office of a principal in a CPA firm, caused people to sit down in the *occupant's* chair instead of the visitor's chair, which faced the door. Even though the layout of the office was clear, the visitor could not imagine that the principal would sit with his back exposed. Another office arranged "backward" had a beautiful view of St. Louis' Gateway Arch, which the advertising-executive occupant could not bear to miss.

Your relationship to the door is also important in meetings or negotiating sessions. If you wish to feel more secure, try to sit with your back to the wall. If you don't want to overpower others, let them sit facing the door. Sitting with your back to the door can be very disruptive, because frequent noises from outside may drive your curiosity to the breaking point. Some negotiators use a noise in the hall or interruptions such as a secretary coming in to ask, "Is George Finster here? There's been a terrible accident," to unsettle their opposites. There may not even be a George Finster, but everyone will go crazy wondering what the "accident" was. Start noticing what is behind you and others, be it a wall or a door, and try to determine how it is affecting your sense of security and comfort.

ZONES OF ATTENTION

Where we sit can greatly affect our attentiveness at a meeting, presentation, or lecture. In college, I knew many students who forced themselves to sit in the front row because they knew they would learn more there. We have all been in the position of arriving late and having to go to the front of the room for the only available chairs, watched every step of the way by the audience and speaker! Once settled, there we sat, uncomfortably exposed to the probing eyes of the lecturer. Afraid to show our attention lagging, we hung on every word, no matter how dull.

People in this "front and center" position give the most attention to the speaker. Those in the middle section pay the next highest amount of attention and ask questions next most frequently. The middle zone is a good, safe area, with people comfortably surrounded by others. Attention and interaction decrease as the listener sits farther back in the room. The side zones are even less responsive and attentive.

The worst listening area is filled with "balcony Baptists." I once had an elderly neighbor who would sit in the balcony of the local church and sleep. It was a very considerate sleep, though, since he learned to hold his head at an angle that would reflect the chandeliers' light from his glasses into the pulpit. That way, he felt he wasn't insulting the pastor by blatantly sleeping through the sermons. In any meeting room, remember: "If you want to see them sleep, sit them deep!"

It's better to arrange the seats a little deeper than wider, after going beyond the first few rows. Try to keep a depth-to-width ratio of about 3 to 2 before lengthening the rows. This way, you will keep more people involved. Also, don't ignore the territorial space needs of your audience. It's better to have 80 percent of the crowd present, comfortable, and attentive than to have 100 percent of your audience crowded and unruly. (The missing 20 percent will be told you were wonderful anyway, which is better than hearing you and leaving it to chance.)

If you can set up a lecture room, keep the door to your side or back. That way, if there is an interruption, you can control it, resolve it in front of your listeners so they can satisfy their curiosity, and continue without waiting for people to turn around again and settle in their seats. If you are plagued with latecomers, such as at an after-dinner speech or early morning meeting, arrange the chairs with the door in the rear and leave four or five chairless rows in the back as a noise buffer zone. Don't overstock the room with chairs before your audience arrives. People will sit as far back as you let them. Set up a few chairs in the buffer zone at the beginning of the meeting; otherwise you'll have half the audience sitting back there from the start.

If you are attending a meeting, find out who else will be there ahead of time. Arrive early enough (without being the first) to have your choice of seats if possible. Let others have their backs to the door if it suits your purpose. Sit there yourself only when you *choose* to. Find out if you are part of a King Arthur competitive group. Sit close to your king if you can, but not too close to the head of the meeting, unless he or she is also your king. If you're one of the kings, determine ahead of time who is in control and what your attitude is toward the leader. Then choose your position accordingly. If you are the leader, you should be picking out your Stars and Heels, like Joe B. did in Chapter 1.

Finally, note the relative positions of the group. Who can you talk to easily and comfortably with no one else in the way? Who "opposes" you across the table? If the meeting has no formal leader, who has picked the leader's position nonverbally? If you wish to gain control, are you in the proper position for it? If you ask yourself these questions each time you sit down at a meeting, you will be well on your way to using seating dynamics successfully.

Office Etiquette

The moment enclosed offices are established in any organization, an unwritten procedure develops for entering an office and responding to a visitor. As a salesman, I enjoyed sitting in a reception area and watching the private offices while I waited for a customer. The relative status of the office occupant and the visitor was apparent the moment the visitor stepped up to the door.

For example, someone comes up to an office door, hesitates with a single brief knock, then proceeds in. The occupant looks up and waves the visitor to a chair. Who has the higher status? The visitor is most likely of a slightly lower status or an immediate underling who has a casual relationship with the superior. The two key points in this scene are the pause at the door and the boss's recognition of the subordinate.

If your home is your castle, then your office is your fortress. In general, a subordinate respects this and will pause at the door before entering. In the case above, the pause was almost negligible, connoting a close relationship or status. The longer the visitor waits at the door, the lower the status. If there is *no* wait—if the visitor strides in without pause—then the visitor has a *higher* status, showing no respect for a subordinate's office. The response of the office occupant is another indicator of relationships. The faster the occupant stands up, the higher the status of the visitor. In the case above, the occupant didn't stand up, but merely waved the subordinate to a chair. Had it been one of the organization's higher-level executives, the manager would have jumped from the chair!

NONPEOPLE

There is a small category of people who can break office etiquette without fear. A secretary can walk in and out of the boss's office without knocking. So can the maintenance personnel. The reason is that they are *nonpeople*, people having no status. In my seminars on professional development for women, only about 10 percent of the secretaries say that their boss introduces them by name (rather than as "my secretary") in a meeting. A maintenance man can enter a meeting room to replace a light bulb and the meeting will go on without a pause, as if he weren't there. Waiters and waitresses fall into this same category.

The invisibility of waiters is illustrated by a famous Groucho

Marx story. Groucho usually went to Chasen's for dinner after his *You Bet Your Life* show. One evening, some people were celebrating a birthday in an alcove right behind Groucho's booth. When waiters wheeled in a cake, Groucho got up, waved them away, and proceeded to cut the cake himself. He served the cake totally unnoticed by anyone in the alcove, came back to his table, and sat down.

"Hello. I'm Ken, and I'll be your waiter for this evening."

"Hello!" you respond, never bothering to introduce yourself. If people introduced themselves to you on the street, would you return the favor? Possibly. You certainly would in a business environment. The next time you are in a restaurant, introduce yourself back to the waiter or waitress and see what happens. You will have made a "person" out of both yourself and the employee serving you. In the business world, someone you convert from a nonperson to a person will pay back your thoughtfulness tenfold.

Treat your office with respect. One of my former bosses had a curious practice that stripped him of all office status. He kept a jar of candy sitting on a table by the door for anyone to take. People popped in and out, no matter what was going on, mumbling, "Just wanted this," "Thanks," or "Excuse me." Everyone had an excuse to enter his office at will, and people did, disrupting anyone else who was in there with him. He gained no status from his office. As a result, he had to close the door frequently, turning away legitimate visitors. He could have stopped the distractions more effectively (and saved some money) by killing the candy dish!

Start noticing your behavior when you enter any office in your organization. Do you uphold "office etiquette"? Are there subordinates who don't recognize yours? If you are vying for promotion with one of your contemporaries, who has a more casual relationship with your boss? Whom does your boss respect more? If you visit other offices as a consultant, auditor, or internal adviser, can you determine the relative status of people before you meet them and learn their names? These are all questions office etiquette can help answer.

Summary

This chapter illustrated the checklist for observing, analyzing, and controlling body location. The checklist shows you how to begin observing NVC by asking the questions:

1. What are the interaction distances? (TERRITORIAL SPACE)

2. What are the height relationships? (HEIGHT MIGHT)

3. Who is leading the group? (TREAD SPREAD)

4. Who has the psychological advantage of physical size? (SIZE PRIZE)

5. Where is everyone sitting and why? (SEATING DYNAMICS)

6. What respect is shown at the office? (OFFICE ETIQUETTE)

With practice, you will begin to ask these questions automatically, taking only a few moments to accurately size up a new situation. Start finding out how these nonverbal signals apply to your organization. It may seem as if you are looking at your company for the first time, seeing a whole new level of communication. You are, because you are now learning the vocabulary of NVC.

3

Indicators

So far, you have learned to observe and analyze where people put their bodies and why. The second NVC scan involves noting information about people's appearance and environment, including their possessions and ornaments. These points of observation are called *indicators*.

Duration of Indicators

Indicators vary in how long they remain consistent. The first time you meet someone, you will notice a number of pieces of information that you will not need to notice again because they will remain unchanged in later communications sessions. Other indicators will be consistent for only a single communications session. (Remember nonrepeatability from Chapter 1.) Still other indicators will not be consistent through even a single communications session.

It is important to separate the indicators you see by their consistency. If you assume a man will always have a mustache and use it to remember his name, you may be in trouble when he shaves it off. A woman student wore a different colored wig and a drastically different outfit the second day of one of my memory classes. Nearly two-thirds of the class had no idea who she was!

ENDURING INDICATORS

Enduring indicators do not change from communications session to communications session. Examples are physical items such as buildings, monuments, and terrain and personal items such as uniforms. Sometimes, these are more important than the people themselves.

Have you ever been in a hardware store in a suit or dress and had someone come up to you and ask about the location of an item? After you stop and explain that you are shopping too, the customer walks off glancing over his shoulder with a look that says, "Well, what were you standing there looking like a clerk for?"

Many stores have gone to the trouble and expense to outfit their salespeople in order to avoid the confusion. One local hardware chain made a big advertising campaign of having "orange-coated experts" in each of its departments. Their experts were the same old clerks in easily identifiable orange hunter's coats.

A police uniform confers automatic authority on the wearer. At one "enlightened" university, school officials abandoned the campus patrolman uniforms and the seldom-used weapons in favor of stylish blazer outfits. Within a few weeks almost the entire force resigned. The men felt that the blazers made their job harder. They stood out less in a crowd and had less control in a conflict situation. Supervisors felt that the uniforms had given the men automatic power and focused crowd attention on them, forcing the officers to act. The school quickly returned to the standard police-style uniform.

Consider the "nonperson" waitress from the last chapter. We often forget which waitress is ours because her uniform helps make her a nonperson, just as the maintenance man's getup makes him a nonperson to office workers. I've decided the best way to commit a crime unrecognized is to wear a McDonald's hamburger clerk shirt and pants and sing, "We do it all for you!" Guaranteed, witnesses will see only what I wear and not who I am. Unusual physical features, such as facial scars, can have the same attention-focusing effect. "What color was the hair, officer?" "Gee, I don't know. But he did have this horrible scar!"

Physical characteristics may or may not be enduring. The McDonald's disguise and scar are not going to last long after the crime. Hair color, hairstyle, weight, and even facial features may change. John Barrymore's profile was enduring for him, but Phyllis Diller's face endured only until her lift. So make certain to sort out what you are likely to see again.

Be alert for a change in the norm. Many a husband has come home and wished that he had noticed that new dress or hairstyle. Don't take anything for granted, in your personal life or in business. One afternoon, I was calling on a regular customer and waited briefly while he handled a phone call. I noticed a new painting on a wall I had seen at least 200 times. This made me curious, so I began to scan the room for anything else out of the ordinary. As I glanced over the large bookcase beside his desk, I noticed a binder with a competitor's name on it, a binder that I had not seen before. It turned out that the customer's entire staff had been to a competitive demonstration covering something I had recently proposed. I questioned the customer carefully about the binder's contents and began to compete for my sale. I may have won the order even if I hadn't seen the binder, but my position would not have been as strong.

Temporary Indicators

Indicators can also be temporary, lasting only one communications session. Clothing, hairstyle, weather, health, time of day, and location are usually not consistent from session to session. Weather has a tremendous effect on our behavior. Grade school teachers know well that they are in for a long day when there is a steady rain. People who wouldn't even glance in sympathy at a car in a ditch will be out there helping a motorist in a snowstorm.

Some people prefer hot weather and some prefer cold. A friend of mine is a cold-weather person, can't stand the heat. Put her in a hot room and she will agree to anything to get out. I would much rather be too warm than too cold. I once taught a four-hour college class in a room adjacent to a boiler. While the rest of the building was down to an energy-conserving 68 degrees (to which everyone was accustomed), our room was in the high 70s. Even though I was on my feet lecturing for four hours, I felt fine after class. The students, however, came out looking like they had spent an afternoon inside a punching bag. So always take into account the weather environment of your session.

Time of day is another important part of people's environment. Some of us are evening people and some are day people. I wake up groggy and don't get going until late morning. I have another period in the day, about 4:00 to 6:00 P.M., that I call my "dead spot," when I am again sluggish. I pick up right after dinner and can go full speed until I drop into bed. For example, I wrote most of this book after 7:00 P.M. Anyone wanting to sell me something or get my commitment for action would have a tough time during my dead periods. My wife and family know this and are careful to approach me at my best times of day.

Others are day people. These are the bright, eager-to-work, bushy-tailed folks we early groaners hate. Day people usually close up shop early and use the evening hours for relaxation or light work. I had a sales partner who was like this. As the workload increased, he would get to work earlier and earlier, and want me to be there too. I tried it for a short time but succeeded only in destroying my entire cycle for several days. I contemplated murdering him, figuring I could claim justifiable homicide, but I was afraid I would get a "morning" judge.

Certain times of day are bad for *all* people. How do you feel when you sit in a meeting, class, or seminar after lunch? Doesn't it seem like the world is moving in slow motion? Nothing is more miserable than wanting to fall asleep and knowing you can't. I have spent many a class fighting this feeling for two hours every day. The main reason we get sleepy after lunch is that our stomach is robbing our brain of blood.

Be aware of the time factor in your communications sessions. I know whether all the important people I deal with are night or day people and in what environment they feel most comfortable. If you don't know, ask them. Maybe you have asked the boss for a raise at the wrong time of the day, or when he is uncomfortable or irritable. An eager young management trainee I knew could hardly wait for her boss to get in to begin her appraisal. What she didn't know was that his car air conditioner had failed that morning and he showed up for work blazing in more ways than one. Had she postponed the meeting until another day, or at least until he had cooled off, she would have fared much better. Had *he* been sensitive, he would have postponed it. Don't make either mistake by ignoring the time of day and the environment.

Start noticing how healthy the other person feels. None of us are effective when we don't feel well. Sales have been lost or raises delayed because the customer or boss had a bad cold. A more insidious form of "bad health" is having to go to the bathroom. What may come across as impatience may actually be acute pain in trying to avoid the embarrassment of leaving to go to the bathroom. Many women find it particularly difficult to say, "Excuse me, I have to go to the john," grab their purse, and leave. Men are less likely to have this problem, although some may find it awkward. An executive I know used this bathroom embarrassment as a domination factor. He always had lunch brought up during long, intensive planning sessions so his people had to disrupt the meeting to go to the bathroom. He felt his personal discomfort in "holding it" was worth it to ensure faster acceptance of his ideas, the most important of which he saved until last.

Be aware of the one-time conditions that exist throughout a communications session. Watch and compare what stays constant and what changes. We are influenced by a host of environmental and physical factors, any one of which can have a drastic effect on the messages we send and receive in any given situation. These factors are another reason why communication is not repeatable.

MOMENTARY INDICATORS

Indicators can also be momentary, lasting only part of the communications session. Examples are distractions, changing locale, visual aids, and even doodles. These momentary items or events can drastically change the course of a session for the better or the worse.

Distractions are the most frequent occurrence. The manager

who kept the candy dish in his office was so plagued by distractions that he spent most of his day with the door closed. This only increased the candy traffic when the door was open, which led to more door-closed time, and so on. Because of these constant interruptions, his people either avoided talking to him during the day or sought him out before and after regular working hours when they would have a better chance of seeing him without interruption.

The phone is another common distraction. America has a cultural phone-answering compulsion, undoubtedly fostered from the start by Alexander Graham himself. He was no dummy when he designed the device with a ring mechanism. (As comedian George Carlin points out, "Isn't it nice that the phone wasn't designed by Alexander Graham Siren?") The baby may be screaming, the sink overflowing, the office on fire, but we'll still answer that incessantly ringing little monster.

All executive training should include a session in *not* answering the phone. Many an important meeting has been wasted by a "short" 20-minute phone call. With one of my managers, who was addicted to phone answering, I would walk out of the room on any phone call lasting more than five minutes. I always explained leaving with, "Oh, I saw that you were going to be busy and I didn't want to seem like I was listening in. Besides, I had other things to do until you were free." This attitude has several advantages. First, you aren't reminded of your lowly status by sitting around wasting your time while your boss is handling "more important" work. Second, you are gently urging your boss to stop the practice because you won't "sit still" for it. Finally, you may get a phone call in the meantime that will make the boss wait on you.

There is one effective way to handle a distraction when you are speaking. I was giving a sales presentation training seminar for a group from a large firm. About a half-hour into my talk, a shapely young woman came in and filled in the sole remaining chair. My audience was gone the minute she opened the door. Realizing that the group was thinking about techniques, but not "speaking" techniques, I shut up. The group finally noticed that I had not been talking about three or four seconds after she sat down. Not wanting to miss the opportunity, I asked them, "What do you do during a distraction?'' To a man (and woman) they answered, "Nothing!" If your audience, be it one person or many, is distracted, stop and let yourself be distracted too. When it's over with, the attention will return and your audience will be ready to continue. Like most powerful emotions, curiosity is short-lived. Let it be satisfied before you get back to work.

Beware of changing locale during a session. A young man planned a luncheon date with his boss to discuss his performance and the possibility of a raise. He wisely chose a restaurant where they could talk discreetly, but he made a fatal error in timing. Walking over to the place, his boss innocently asked about the subject of their lunch, and rather than deferring the young man began his prepared talk. You can imagine the results after dropping off their coats, waiting at the receptionist's table, ordering lunch with frequent visits from the waiter (drink order, drinks, lunch order, lunch, and those ever present water and coffee fillers), and chomping on their meals. The program was never allowed to unfold.

Fortunately, in this instance the manager wasn't negative, but the young man accomplished nothing and missed a chance to further himself. The interference of changing location and then eating was too much for the conversation. The ideal time for the conversation would have been *after* lunch. They both would have been relaxed and the manager softened up.

As a rule, don't change locations. If you have to move, always move to a *better* location for communication. A good example is eating dinner then going to a different room for a presentation, or getting someone out of personal territory into a neutral area or into your territory. The best approach is to control the timing of your communications so that the location can become a temporary environment rather than a momentary one.

Any group of visuals, whether formal aids or extemporaneous doodles, are momentary indicators. There is a wealth of NVC material in visuals. A useful trick in meetings is to be the last one to leave so that you can look at the doodles on all the remaining pads. If it is your meeting, make sure there are pads to use and that you leave last. If you are merely an attendee and can't leave last, make sure to take all your papers with you so you don't provide any unplanned information.

Employees of a radio station in Florida were caught by police going through a rival station's trash. Station personnel had managed to piece together an entire promotional campaign from meeting notes taken during planning sessions. Because of the bad publicity generated by the arrest, the station was forced to return the material, but it still gained a marketing coup. Don't let one of *your* rivals do the same.

A visual aid is a special, controlled type of distraction. It takes attention away from you, so you must return the favor to be effective. I once saw visuals so concise that a monkey would have looked knowledgeable using them. The audience realized it and gave due credit to the presenter who developed them. I have also seen visuals that looked as if they had been drawn by a monkey. The audience was equally unimpressed with the speaker using them. Remember that visuals should be used only when words and body alone are not as effective; they are a distraction with a purpose. Make sure you are presenting your visuals instead of vice versa.

Identifying indicators is really an exercise in increasing your skills of observation. Once you are familiar with the important indicators of the people you deal with, you can sort the indicators by their consistency. Some will be constant throughout your acquaintance with the person, some will last only during a session, and a few will vary from moment to moment.

The indicator checklist is divided into three parts:

Personal
Shared
Public

As the names imply, these indicators vary with respect to how large a group they provide information about. Personal indicators apply to individuals; shared indicators apply to a group such as a company or a club; and public indicators apply to a large group, usually related geographically.

Personal Indicators

If there is one common trait exhibited by humanity, it is the overwhelming drive to decorate its nest. I have not been in a single office that was not in some way customized by its occupant. Even in sparsely decorated offices, some form of humanizing has taken place.

POSSESSIONS AND DECOR

My sales office was a good example of the way people personalize their surroundings. All the desks were out in the middle of big, open rooms, set side by side with only two-drawer file cabinets separating them. Each desk was equipped with a phone. (This unappealing environment may have been intentional—to keep the salesmen out of the office—but I suspect that it was also inexpensive.) Despite the antiseptic atmosphere, each desk was in some way personalized. Managers had small name plates posted on the front of their desks, but the names weren't really needed. The belongings and paraphernalia on each desk were enough to immediately identify whose desk it was.

There were bookends with an abundance of work-related books; there were trophies and awards from contests and classes; and there were those miscellaneous little items that are the most revealing. My desk had a chunk of artificial turf with a little Miami Dolphins helmet on it to ward off the St. Louis Cardinal fans. I also had a Ziggy cartoon saying, "Today is a whole new day to screw up in," in honor of my usual status with management. Another cartoon, a reminder of my first commission check, featured Seminole Sam of Pogo protesting that he at one time amassed a fortune of $24.60 in due bills.

Other desks had such things as a soldered-nail basketball player, a plastic Charlie the Tuna radio, plants, United Van Lines toy trucks, mistake erasers, family picture cubes, a toy mailbox, and a boat on a bendable wire. Many items were even useful. I had an artificial turf telephone pad so my phone would sound different from the 20 or so adjacent phones. There was a myriad of phone number holders, appointment books, and phone note holders. Each desk was truly a reflection of its owner. Even the trash around the desk was indicative of the person who used it. Look around your office and you will probably come up with a list of items as wacky as the one above.

Even though the salespeople in my office spent only a small portion of their time at their desks, a great deal of personalizing was still in evidence. There was even more individualization in the managerial offices. In addition to desk paraphernalia, almost every wall and piece of furniture had some personal touch. Paintings and pictures were in abundance. Managers were sure to include anything of status in their gallery of framed pictures. Boat pictures are good, if the boat is big. A picture of the office occupant standing beside his or her airplane is even better. The most impressive personal picture of this type belonged to the chief of pilots of a small airline. The picture showed him standing on the con of a nuclear sub—a duty he had pulled during his reserve summer tour. How many people do you know who have been aboard a nuclear sub *on duty?*

Paintings are also a good source of information about the occupant's tastes. At the very least, they are conversation pieces. Be careful, though, in making comments about a painting or work of art: you can offend even if you intend to compliment. I once stuck my foot in my mouth with incredible grace and speed by trying to be nice. I complimented an executive on a painting he had displayed, only to find out that he had just moved into the office and hated the painting but hadn't had time to do anything about it. Paintings often grow old or stale to the person living in the office. The best thing to do if you want to talk about a painting is to ask a question about it rather than offering a blind comment.

Degrees, certificates, and awards are other effective wall decorations. They will tell you what the occupant's activities are and what he or she is proud of. They usually come in the standard $8^1/_2'' \times 11''$ size and are displayed in clusters. If you wish to display some of these in your office, make certain they create a positive effect. For example, when I left my sales position, I had two plaques and certificates of achievement for making my company's 100 percent quota club. When I left my island desk to set up my own office, I decided to decorate my work area with some of these items. When I put my four items on the wall, they looked naked, almost obscene. I had seen managers with a string of them running from floor to ceiling in their offices. My little display was somewhat underwhelming.

Decorations can be overdone too. I visited a business consultant who had approximately 25 framed documents on his office wall. When I noncommitally mentioned them, he apologized for the number, telling me that there were four more being framed! This display might have been awe inspiring, except that he had obviously mounted every document he had ever received. There were fraternal awards of the kind that are passed out like pancakes (an Optimist Club executive calls them "M&Ms for the troops"). There were also letters of appreciation, certificates of membership, and one or two outstanding meeting awards. The net effect was to appear ostentatious.

I believe the properly impressive number of framed business items is five to eight. The typical mixture might include two Degrees from Somewhere, a couple of Certified Professional Somethings, and a Member of the Year Award from the Affiliated Associates Association. Make sure they are in the same style of frame so that their number, rather than content, is what strikes the visitor.

Unique or bizarre decorations are also status grabbers. Imagine the company president asking you about the African witchdoctor's mask hanging on your wall. How can he top you when you answer, "Oh, I picked that little thing up on my last trip to the continent"? You know all he's had time for is the stockholders' meeting in Attumswa, Iowa.

Items that are totally unfathomable have the same effect. Prominently display some unimaginable object at the front of your desk. Natural curiosity will force your visitors to ask what it is, in which case you are one up on them. If they don't ask about it, idly play with it as you talk. You will at least distract them, giving yourself a further advantage. A hot item with the computer folks was a printer counterweight, a heavy cylindrical piece of metal that slid in and out of a plastic sleeve. It had no reasonable purpose, but its moving parts gave it a high fondle value.

Puzzles are also good for maintaining control over your callers. I had one customer who kept a small block puzzle on his desk for this very purpose. I studiously ignored it, being careful not to even look at it lest that allow my customer to bring it up. One day he caught me when we started talking about a mutual hobby, puzzles. He suddenly told me, "Well, if you like puzzles, why don't you try this one?" and shoved the block at me. Then he held up his arm and started looking at his watch, saying, "I just want to see how long it takes you; don't mind me."

As all of us who have stood before a group in silence know, a minute can be interminable. I managed to get the block assembled after two and a half minutes, which rated, "That's not too bad, Ken." Before I was buried in any more condescending remarks, I cut the meeting short and beat a hasty retreat. Before the next call on this customer, I memorized a set of ten pencil-and-paper logic puzzles. I resolved that if stumped again, I would at least be able to *trade* puzzles. So beware of any desk puzzles you see. They can be used to inflict major psychological damage.

APPEARANCE

We all place a tremendous amount of importance on physical appearance. Not only does it provide basic demographic data on age, sex, height, weight, race, and physical beauty. It also provides a wealth of data on personality. Appearance is so important to us that we have a special term for our initial analysis of it, the first impression.

First Impressions

A first impression is the "love at first sight" of the business world. We know the importance of making a good first impression, since we "never have a second chance to make a good first impression." Yet so few of us know what first impression we give. I use a first-impression fact-finding procedure in my communications classes. As each person introduces himself or herself at the beginning of the class, the students write on a note card five traits they think best describe this person. When the introductions are completed, the cards are distributed to the attendees. They then have a data base of first-impression traits from their peers, given anonymously. Frequently, the cards are quite similar in content and provide a good composite of the first impression the student creates. Grouping similar adjectives, such as intelligent/smart/quick or ambitious/aggressive/go-getter, gives an even better composite picture.

A refinement in this first-impression procedure is to have class members write down what caused them to list a certain trait for a student. This gives the student valuable feedback. For example, a middle-aged female supervisor had a tendency to wear "girlish clothes"—short skirts and puffy-sleeved blouses long out of style. Her image was one of a child skipping home from school. This revelation prompted her to make an immediate wardrobe change, using one of the other female executives for guidance.

Clothing has an enormous effect on the first impression you project. John T. Molloy has analyzed the effect of various types of men's and women's clothing in his books on "wardrobe engineering." Almost all his research methods were based on first impressions. He showed different clothing styles to individuals and then asked them to draw conclusions about the people wearing the clothes. Molloy's *Dress for Success* and *The Woman's Dress for Success Book* offer valuable information on clothing styles in business.

It is well worth your time to find out the first impression you send out. If you don't have an opportunity to use the classroom method of introduction ask one of your close friends to give you a candid assessment. Or have a friend find out for you by informally questioning your associates. Try to tie the impressions back to specific characteristics or traits, and don't be defensive!

Body Styles

You can also benefit by appraising your physical characteristics for data on your appearance. One of the primary appearance factors is body style. This doesn't include hardtop, convertible, or hatchback, but hefty, muscular, or slender.

The Hefty is the round, fat person. He or she is considered to be good-natured and jolly, with an untiring sense of humor. Typical Hefties are Santa Claus or Curley (of the Three Stooges). Hefties have a number of unpleasant image characteristics to fight. They are thought to have overindulged themselves (even when their problem is medical). The thinner members of society think, "Too bad the poor thing doesn't have the willpower to stop eating."

Overweight people often have a difficult time looking neat. Today's styles were not made for the large person to wear comfortably. The ideal style for a Hefty is probably a toga affair draped over the body instead of the close-fitting, complicated clothes that have been in fashion for hundreds of years. On Hefties, shirts or blouses pull out at the waist, pants or slacks ride up as people sit down, and all the constrictions around the neck, arms, and legs accentuate the loose skin. Other areas of the outfit have to be baggy in order to provide enough give without ripping when sitting or turning. It is extremely difficult to look sharp.

There are ways to minimize this problem. People do not have to be fashion designers or coordinators to choose styles that overcome the negatives of too much size. They may have to pay a little more for clothes, but it can be well worth it to have outfits individually tailored for the best possible fit.

A varying weight makes it harder to look neat consistently, though. If weight fluctuates too much, the clothes have to be big enough for the upward swing and will look baggy the rest of the time. One executive on a massive weight reduction program suffered through this process. His clothes were always too big. Since he couldn't afford a new suit every 15 pounds, he had his suits cut down. When he finally reached his target weight, he rewarded himself with a completely new wardrobe and threw out all his old clothes in celebration. The entire office was aware of his weight loss, and the executive actually gained status from the baggy suits, which became a symbol of his willpower and determination. (He also became the best-dressed man in the office.)

Another way to avoid the sloppy look is to primp often. An oversized salesman made a habit of stopping by the men's room in any office building where he was going to make a call. He would straighten himself out after the car ride and then proceed. He made the point that taking this time was important to his image. He never walked into an office with his hair blown, tie crooked, collar up, or shoes muddy. You shouldn't either.

The second body type is the Muscular. These are the people with athletic builds, the kind that adorn our daytime serials and fill up Muscle Beach. When I was in college, there was a standing joke about guys who went out for track, which was my sport. When all the athletes came in to take showers in the afternoon after their workouts, you could tell each one's sport by his behavior. The football players would come in, bend the showerhead pipe to the proper angle, soap themselves up and begin throwing soap at everybody. The basketballers would come in and loop their towels over the water pipes near the ceiling. The wrestlers would come in looking like little Mr. Americas, wishing they could drink the water instead of wash in it. The baseballers would amble in, every pore of their bodies oozing coordination. The skinny, scrawny guys who didn't look like any sort of athletes were trackmen.

The problem for trackmen was that everyone else in the shower, even most of the basketball players, were those disgusting Musculars. They were the ones who best filled out their letter jackets, had coeds hanging off each arm, and had muscles where trackmen didn't even have places.

Don't underestimate the advantage that a Muscular possesses in the world of NVC. In the 1976 presidential campaign, former President Ford proudly stated that he could still hike a football and fire off the line just as he did years ago at Michigan. And the public believed him. Unlike many Presidents, Ford skied, swam, and played golf. He left office as fit as or more fit than when he went in.

Musculars seem more self-reliant, more mature. Can you imagine 1976 Olympic decathlon champion Bruce Jenner begging his wife to let him go out and shoot pool with the guys? Can you picture John Wayne throwing a tantrum when something didn't go his way? Is Billie Jean King stuck at home because Larry won't let her out? Would Tarzan have been of any interest to us if he had looked like a trackman or the Goodyear blimp? Many top executives of major companies are Musculars—perhaps as high as 80 to 90 percent in some corporations. Do they fit this mold in your company? Do you?

If you do, don't destroy it. Put yourself on a diet to fight the mid-20s to mid-30s metabolism change that seems to catch so many people. Don't let an hour and half of eating jeopardize the eight hours per day of work you put into being successful. If you don't fit the mold, try to get there. There is a definite relationship between a sound body and business success. With growth of racquet sports, indoor sports facilities, health clubs, and adult athletic programs, you should be able to find *something* that interests you. Find it and let it develop into a habit!

The third body type is the Slender. Tall, thin, and fragile, Slenders are the kind of people who need ten pounds to look thin. Most Slenders can eat freely and heavily without the slightest weight change. This can be a curse, though, because under many an older Hefty resides a young Slender who couldn't modify his or her eating habits during the metabolism change. If you haven't yet faced this crisis, be prepared to act when that scale indicator begins to drift toward the right.

Being a Slender is not particularly better than being a Hefty, just different. Slenders appear to be tense and nervous. Their gestures are more accentuated because of their thinness, and they appear to be moving faster and less smoothly. Comedian Don Knotts developed this style to perfection in his "nervous" routine. It was a terrible shock to see him on a Steve Allen TV special talking normally.

There are several ways to dispel the slender image. Don't accentuate your thinness with clothing. Ignore form-fit blouse or shirt and pants styles. Stay away from vertically striped fabrics, which give Slenders a beanpole or picket fence look. Coats should be cut fuller (but not baggy). Vests can add bulk. Ties should be as wide as fashionably possible, without making you look like Corky the Clown. Avoid sleeveless sweaters or blouses, since they make your arms look like sticks coming out of a pipe.

Another step is to slow down. Gesture less rapidly, walk slower, and in general give the image of care and forethought. Make your gestures more muted. If you have a nervous habit such as nail biting, finger twisting, or cuticle picking, concentrate on eliminating it. With your body style, the habit will be magnified and reinforce the nervous stereotype.

Slenders too need regular exercise. There is a world of difference between fatless muscle and toned muscle. While few Slenders may be able to turn themselves into Musculars, they can benefit from the positive nonverbal signals that the "in shape" person transmits.

Whatever your body style, be aware of what your physical appearance transmits. Begin to think of body style as a changeable trait, not a permanent feature. If you don't like your current equipment, now is the time to start modifying it. If you don't want to put out the effort to change yourself, at least analyze what you are and minimize any negative effects through clothing and grooming. Give your body real "style" and you will have another NVC plus.

SHARED INDICATORS

Shared indicators include large, immovable, or difficult-to-move objects such as offices, desks, statues, and bookcases. Michael Korda, in his book *Power*, makes a detailed study of the relationships of office location and status. He points out that corner offices reflect the most power and status within an organization. The architect for the Community Federal Savings and Loan building in St. Louis incorporated this idea into the design. To make it a more attractive lease property in the highly competitive St. Louis office-space market, the architect provided more corner offices than the conventional square or rectangular structure. (See Figure 3–1.)

Office size and furnishings are also indicative of status. I have never seen a subordinate's office better furnished than a manager's office if the two are physically close to each other. Even if the subordinate has a larger office, the manager's office is usually better located.

Many companies have a carpeted "executive's row" with limited access through a screening secretary. Most managers would rather take a cut in salary than pass up a chance to join the row. One large utility went so far as to locate its top executives in a different building, a plush office in the downtown business area a mile or so from the main location. The corporate officers and the two executive vice-presidents were the only occupants of the facility and had almost half a floor of space. This was the ultimate in status. Even subordinates at the vice-presidential level had to get in their car, fight traffic, park, and make their way to the executive offices for any meeting. The top executives *never* went to the main office building. In addition, the main office building was constructed with metal walls and partitions. The nicest office in the building still looked like the inside of a refrigerator, while the executive suites had more wood in them than a lumber dealer.

Figure 3–1. Corner-office building.

(Courtesy Community Federal Savings and Loan Association, St. Louis, Missouri)

The working environment reinforced the status of the office occupants.

Desks are another status indicator. At the lower levels, size is the important feature. The bigger your desk, the greater your status. Ideally, I suppose, you should have a desk that looks like a roller rink. At the higher levels, size is often a minor factor, with simplicity taking precedence. As noted earlier, some chief executives are doing away with the business desk and installing ornate tables of the same size. This is similar to the executive who doesn't wear a watch, which says in effect, "I don't have to worry about what time it is. My assistants will keep me informed, or everyone else will have to conform to my schedule regardless of the time." A drawerless table says much the same thing. "I don't have to store materials for retrieval, nor do I do the type of work that requires me to dig into papers all over my desk." This executive will keep a simple office with a clean desk at all times.

Books are another shared indicator that provides a great deal of information about the owner. I recently met with the chairman of a management program in a local university. As I walked in, I

noticed massive bookshelves lining one wall. We were interrupted briefly by the phone after I sat down, so I spent the time
looking at the titles on the shelf. I was surprised that the chairman
of a management program would have so many finance-oriented
books. When our conversation resumed, I opened with, "How
did you manage to switch from a finance professorship to chair a
management department?" He began to answer and suddenly
stopped, asking, "How did you know that?" I explained about
the evidence on the shelves, and he gave me one of Dr. Watson's
frequent comments to Sherlock Holmes, "Oh, that's obvious.
Why didn't I think of it?"

Bookshelf ogling is easy and is an excellent way to learn the
tastes and interests of the owner of the books. It is also a good
way to build rapport with a new acquaintance during those first
awkward minutes. One small warning, though. Don't be tempted
to load up *your* shelves with impressive titles you have never
read. If you are asked about one of the books you've never
opened, you expose yourself as a fake. So choose books you
have read or at least know about, selecting the books to represent
the image you wish to project. If you are a young college grad
trying to project maturity and good judgment, stick to business-
oriented books from well-known authors. If you want to project
intelligence, go heavy on psychology and esoterica with big-
worded titles that no one has ever heard of. Quoting from these
books will also help maintain your image.

One manager I encountered decided to go with the "intelligence" image. He loaded his office with classical paintings,
"heavy" books, strange desk puzzles, and obscure sayings. He
was indeed intelligent and emphasized the point well. Eventually
he was promoted to a job in a development division where intelligence and creativity were requirements for success. He used his
personal and shared indicators to help create the image necessary
for his promotion.

Public Indicators

Public indicators are the things around us that are not only
shared but also open to the general public. Examples are houses,

museums, monuments, shopping centers, highways, buildings, stadiums, and parks. These are indicative of our culture and of our living habits. Certain public artifacts are also good measures of social status and can communicate a great deal about an individual.

For example, where we live is important. A successful executive had very strong ideas about buying a house. He felt he should buy one that he would be better able to afford in three years. The house should be the lowest-priced house in a high-priced neighborhood and big enough so that he would not have to move out unless he was transferred (in which case the company would pay). The house he bought has doubled in value and is worth approximately 75 percent as much as the average house in his area. More important, he lives in *the* neighborhood in his city, one whose average house costs far more than what people at his job level normally pay.

This is a great advantage. The small corporation he works for hired a new president from the outside, over the current line of executives. The new president, unfamiliar with the area and buying within his salary, bought a suitable house in the city. He later found out that our executive had a better house and was located in a more exclusive area. Now the executive loves to entertain his boss and associates in his home whenever possible.

I once interviewed for a position at a manufacturing plant nestled in a mountain valley 70 miles from the nearest city with a population over 50,000. The entire social life of the area centered around the plant activities and a country club with a nine-hole golf course. Membership in the club was restricted (informally, of course) to executives and managers from the plant. I was truly impressed when I was offered a membership if I went to work at the plant, since this was the highest status I could hope to attain in the area. Fortunately for me (as my wife said at the time), I wanted something more than a life centered around work and a nine-hole golf course.

Just as certain areas of a city have more status than others, so some cities are considered more prestigious than others. Anyone born and living outside of New York has felt the patronizing attitude of those inhabitants of the nation's largest city. New York becomes a source of "war stories" for outsiders. Mastering its customs is a rite of passage for the newcomer. A friend of mine who moved there from a Midwestern city was driving like a madman within a year. He would trample crippled beggars without breaking stride and had a wealth of "New York stories" to pass on to us country bumpkins. As proof of the status he'd gained, he would be asked on his trips back to the Midwest, "What's it like up there?"

Other areas are also touted for their prestige. Texas has its cowboy driving a Cadillac with longhorns on the hood, California has its free and easy "space captain," and Florida has its retirees. For varied reasons, people in each of these areas can justifiably look down on others, gaining status in the process.

Summary

Chapter 2 presented the first NVC checklist for observing and controlling where people put their bodies and why. This chapter introduced the checklist for interpreting people's appearance and what they put around them. In analyzing yourself and others for these nonverbal indicators, try to answer the following questions:

1. What are people's possessions and appearance characteristics? (PERSONAL INDICATORS)

2. What items do people have in common? (SHARED INDICATORS)

3. What categories or groups do people fit into? (PUBLIC INDICATORS)

The key to success with all indicators is observation. Take every opportunity to observe the objects around the people you communicate with. Look at the desk, the furniture, the office. Find out where a person lives and why. The more you understand about how a person decorates the nest and why it is located where it is, the better you will understand the person.

The third NVC checklist, in the following chapter, will help you interpret what people do with their bodies once they have settled into a location.

4

Body Movements

The study of body motions, called *kinesics* (from the Greek word for movement), is a relatively new science. Begun in the early 1950s by a researcher with the unlikely name of Birdwhistell and popularized by Julius Fast in his book *Body Language,* kinesics has had little application to the business world. Until now its principles have not been organized into an easy-to-apply method for people in business. Such a method is now available with the five-point body scan:

> Center
> Head
> Posture
> Hands
> Legs

This scan will help you to "hear better with your glasses on." The body scan lets you observe others in an organized "head to toe" fashion.

Although interpretations will be given for various NVC signals, it's important to keep in mind that *each item in the scan must be checked before any conclusions can be drawn.* As the example from Chapter 1 with the customer who covered his mouth showed, movements are not traits. Readable movements must come in clusters, because no one sign in and of itself is indicative of anything (except the sign reader's gullibility). But this is not a particularly severe limitation. Most situations include enough movement indicators to allow you to draw at least broad conclusions—unless people are purposely trying to withhold their feelings. Even that is a nonverbal signal, usually followed by the question "Is there something wrong?"

Center

Imagine a rod going through the middle of your chest to the middle of your shoulder blades. (My wife has wished this were true several times.) Then imagine another rod from armpit to armpit ("underarm" just doesn't seem to have the same impact as "armpit"). Where these imaginary rods connect in your chest is your "center," as shown in Figure 4–1. The center is perhaps the most reliable and important body indicator. It is the only sign that can ever be successfully taken out of context and is a key indicator of how we feel about ourselves and others around us.

The center can be open, closed, aggressive, or submissive. We achieve an open center by standing erect and facing the person we are communicating with. We close our center by buttoning our coat or blazer, slumping, crossing our arms in umpire fashion, sitting with a chair back facing forward, or turning away from the person to talk over our shoulder. Our center becomes

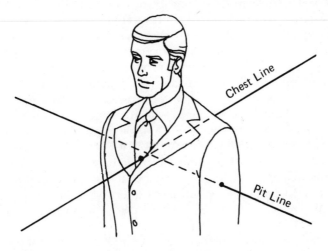

Figure 4–1. The center.

aggressive with our chest out, shoulders back, and chin out, much like a Marine sergeant hazing his "boots." Our center becomes submissive when it is "buried" with bent posture, bowed shoulders, and a downcast gaze.

Occasionally, I'll begin a lecture by walking in front of the group slumped over, picking at my cuticles, and offering in a halting voice, "W-w-well, I'm the communicator. I'm here to teach you how to be effective like I am." You can hear a groan go through the audience as they glance around to spot the doors best suited for an inconspicuous exit. Or I may walk in with body erect, coat buttoned, and arms stiffly held at the sides, announcing loudly, "Hello, I'm Ken Cooper. I am your friend because—I care. You can tell me your problems in complete confidence and know I will help." With this introduction, I can see lips and tongues being bitten all over the room with the thought, "Oh, no, what have I gotten myself into?"

Other times I stride out with coat open, chest thrust out, arms clasped behind my back, and firmly state, "I'm Ken Cooper. You're going to like this class because you need this class. We will have one ten-minute break in the morning and one in the afternoon and that is all because we have a lot to do. Are there any questions?" There never are, of course, because they are too busy trying to see if I am armed.

After each of these shocks, I revert to my normal likable self and begin talking about what my approach made them think about me and the coming talk. My movements, of course, involved more than manipulating my center, but most students later agree that the center is a key indicator. In general, an open center indicates a friendly, positive attitude toward a person. A closed center is negative. Shake hands with someone face to face, and then shake hands with your shoulders pointing at the person looking over your right shoulder. See how less friendly the second position is? Stand in front of a mirror and note how much more informal and open you look with your coat or blazer unbuttoned.

Notice how people orient their centers when sitting at meetings. When two rival executives are placed in adjacent chairs, they will almost always sit with their shoulders angled away from each other, possibly with legs crossed so that their up foot points away from the unfriendly neighbor.

A child psychologist told me he always has both parents come with their child to the first meeting. He observes the parents in the lobby before the appointment. If the parents are sitting with their centers open, possibly with the husband's arm around his wife or at least turned toward each other, the psychologist spends most of the first meeting talking with the child. If the parents are closed to each other as they sit or do not sit next to each other, or if one of them sits with the child while the other sits across from the two, the psychologist spends his time probing to see if there are any problems between the parents that could be affecting the child.

The orientation of the center can also be used to control territorial space. While waiting in a bus station one snowy afternoon, I saw an attractive young woman walk over to one of the few places where there were several seats available and sit down, placing her luggage in front of her. She was immediately spied by one of the denizens of bus stations everywhere, a well-lubricated serviceman (who, like me, had been stranded by the snow). He staggered by the young woman and saw the empty seat next to her. Making as accurate a lunge as he could, he plopped down in the seat and lolled back, looking at her. She visibly tensed, but rather than leaving and risk embarrassing herself or the serviceman, she turned away from him and stared off into another part of the lobby. The serviceman got the message and wandered off for more friendly game. (The young woman noticed some other potential nuisances and put her baggage in the seat next to her to ward off anybody else.)

We can be threatened by an open center when standing next to a stranger. As Figure 4–2 shows, opening our center intensifies our need for territorial space.

A short comment about the crossed-arms method of closing off the center is needed here. Most books report that this is always a negative sign. One researcher went so far as to suggest that it had to do with a teenage girl's embarrassment at her developing chest. Having never been a young woman going through puberty (nor was the researcher), I can't really verify or support this theory. It also does not account for why men do it.

I believe that crossed arms is an overrated sign. Often, it is just a comfortable thing to do with our arms, probably started by

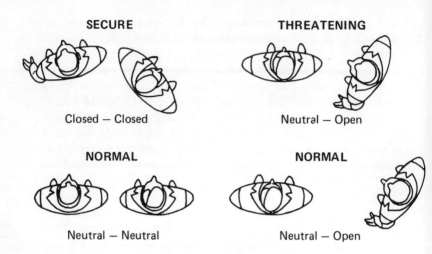

SECURE

Closed — Closed

THREATENING

Neutral — Open

NORMAL

Neutral — Neutral

NORMAL

Neutral — Open

Figure 4–2. Public centers.

one of Tarzan's friends' ancestors and picked up by everyone else with a decent set of arms. I saw an incident that reinforced my opinion when I was downtown shopping during Christmas. A woman was standing at a bus stop with her three-year-old daughter. The mother was posed impatiently, weight shifted to one foot, arms crossed, and an exasperated expression on her face. As I walked down the sidewalk, I saw the little girl, who was standing in the rumpled manner of little people everywhere, look up and study her mother. Glancing quickly back and forth from her own body to her mother's, she slowly crossed her arms, shifted her weight, and when she was certain she "had it right" stood triumphantly with the same imperious look her mother showed. That was proof enough for me of where the crossed-arm gesture comes from and what it means when taken by itself. More than most other NVC signs, it means *nothing*.

Center orientations can also indicate people's relationships in groups. In Figure 2–1, for example, the "choir effect" and "outsider" configurations were indicated by people's centers as well as by their territorial space. The three subordinates encircling the leader all had their centers oriented to the boss. The person "out" of the informal circle was closed off by the people on either side. As you become more aware of centers, you will be able to read people's open and closed attitudes toward others, and their aggressive and submissive attitudes about themselves.

Head

It's rod time again. Imagine a rod going through that open alley your friends claim connects your ears. Then imagine another rod going straight back into your head through the tip of your nose. If you can picture these rods providing an axis of rotation for the head, you can see how the head can nod up and down around the first rod and tilt left and right about the second. As Figure 4–3 shows, the ear rod is your self line, and the nose rod is your others line.

By rotating about these lines, the head can assume four basic positions. If the head is rotated upward around the self line, you

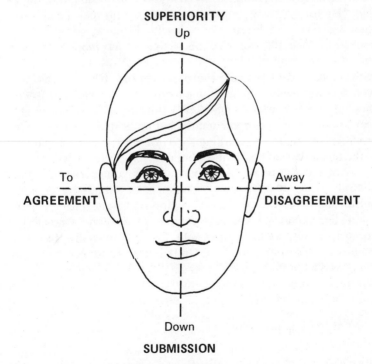

Figure 4–3. Head positions.

are showing *superiority* ("looking down your nose" at someone). William F. Buckley frequently appears to hold this position. If your head rotates downward, you are showing *submission* ("hanging your head"). If your head is tilted around the others line toward someone, you are indicating *agreement*. If it is tilted away, you are indicating *disagreement*.

As Figure 4–4 shows, these head positions can be used in combination during a conversation. At first, the boss is offering criticism in a very concerned manner. When the subordinate responds in too submissive a fashion, the boss returns to a dominant approach. This sparks rebellion in the subordinate and they are both off to the interpersonal races.

Tilting the head with the center open can indicate other things besides agreement. Often it is a sign of *attention*. (Remember King Kong holding Fay Wray with his head tilted, thinking, "Hmm"?) Many people unconsciously tilt their head when they are trying to listen more closely (listening with an "ear cocked"). The tilt can also be a sign of *evaluation* or *deep thought*. As we are thinking, we tilt our head and gaze into space with unfocused eyes while the brain churns. Or at least that's what we want people to think. I sometimes go through this "deep thought" routine after being asked a difficult question in a class. I may know the answer immediately, but my response will be more credible if I seem to be working for it. Besides, it is a compliment to the questioner to honor his or her query with such effort.

Watch how you position your head. Is your normal position neutral? Some of us assume a dominant or submissive position out of habit. As we saw in the section on height might, unconscious habits can influence the way people view us. One clerk I know habitually looks up at people. To my knowledge, he's still waiting for his first promotion. On the other hand, people resent those who have their "nose in the air." "Keep a level head about you" and watch when others don't.

FACIAL EXPRESSIONS

The syndicated column "Fables of the Famous" tells the story about the French novelist Balzac's first visit to Vienna. He was not familiar with either the language or the money and was

MANAGER: *"Your work has not been up to par."*

SECRETARY: *"I'm sorry."*

MANAGER: *"It's not good enough just to be sorry."*

SECRETARY: *"Well, it's not my fault!"*

Figure 4–4. Conversation head positions.

afraid he was being overcharged whenever he traveled by taxi. To make certain that he would not be "taken" on his trips, he developed a simple payment procedure based on the driver's face. Upon arriving, he would hand the driver a single coin. If the driver's hand remained out expectantly, he would add another coin. He kept adding one at a time until the driver smiled. Then Balzac would take back the last coin and depart, confident that he had paid the proper fare and no more!

Our face is the most expressive part of our body—something Balzac's drivers clearly didn't know. Birdwhistell estimated that we can make and recognize nearly 250,000 distinct facial expressions. Most researchers recognize the following as the most common:

> Interest/excitement
> Enjoyment/joy
> Surprise/startlement
> Distress/anguish
> Shame/humiliation
> Contempt/disgust
> Anger/rage
> Fear/terror

Instead of showing these various expressions during the working day, most people wear "masks." Retail clerks have their die-cast smiles and sales personnel have their hearty personalities, no matter how bad the day has been. An old saying warns, "Beware of someone who laughs without a shaking belly." We can mask with muscular control (poker face) or with a prop (toupee, wig, or colored contact lenses). We can choose to accentuate certain characteristics that overshadow others, like Jimmy Durante always posing in profile. (No one seems to have ever noticed the color of Jimmy Durante's eyes.)

When we do show emotions, we often display them in *partials*, reacting with only a portion of the face. I had a regional manager who was the most unconvincing liar I have ever met. He frightened everybody in the office because whenever he praised our sales, he smiled only with his mouth. When he told us how much better we were going to do next year (or else), he showed it with his entire face.

Sometimes we let our emotions out in uncontrollable "flashes." I was sitting at my desk one afternoon when someone from outside the sales office came in to use the phone. I glanced up and, not recognizing the woman, went back to my work. She caught my glance and said, "Well, hi, Ken. I haven't seen you for quite a while."

I looked up again, still not recognizing her, until her voice told me who she was: a customer I had not seen for nearly 18 months. My confusion arose because when I had seen her last, she had carried about 380 pounds on a 5′2″ frame. I had been to her company five times before I ever saw her stand up. The woman I was looking at must have weighed 200 pounds less. Being the cool, suave, controlled NVC expert that I am, I let my jaw drop and managed an unintelligible, "Huh? Wha? Joan?" It took nearly a minute for the shock to pass and my brain to associate the new Joan with the old version in memory. I later apologized for acting so stupid, but she told me, "Don't worry about it, Ken. It's the nicest compliment you could have paid me. Besides, I like to see salesmen speechless occasionally." This was a pleasant, but rather unnerving flash.

Flashes can be negative too, as shown in the famous (and true) High School Reunion Story:

"Well, hon, I sure am looking forward to going to my reunion and seeing how everyone has turned out," Bill told his wife.

"You go by yourself. I'm eight months pregnant and look horrible. I can't sleep, I'm uncomfortable, and the clothes I have hang on me like a sheet."

"Okay, if that's the way you want it, Nancy. I really wanted to go to find out what happened to two old flames I had, one of whom was particularly flamy."

"I'll go, I'll go, you rat. But this is going to cost you a dress!"

Once at the reunion, Bill eagerly looked for his old girl friends without success. Later, while Nancy sat at a table with friends, Bill walked over to talk to some old football buddies. As Bill turned to leave the group, a woman came up and said, "Well, how are you, Bill?" Noticing the confused expression on his face, she continued, "You don't recognize me, do you?"

"Sure I do, Ruth. How are you?" Bill said carefully. He said it carefully because the version of Ruth he saw was carrying 70 more pounds than the attractive teenager he remembered. As they talked on, Bill patted himself on the back for not letting his jaw fall to the floor; then he heard something that told him he was still in trouble.

"I'd sure like to meet your wife," Ruth said.

"Here we go again," Bill thought. "I hope Nancy can hold her surprise too."

When Bill introduced Ruth to his wife, he could tell Nancy had no idea who she was talking to. Then, suddenly, Nancy did a slow pan to Bill with a widening smile.

"I knew Nancy had just gotten six months' worth of ammo," Bill told me later. "All I heard when I got home was, 'Haw, haw, haw. This,' Nancy said, pointing to her belly, 'will go away. That won't. Haw, haw, haw. Wait until I tell your mother.' "

At the reunion, had Bill and Nancy not been able to control their expressions, they could have easily embarrassed or hurt Ruth, just the opposite of what I did to Joan.

One of the reasons expression is so easy to read and difficult to control is that it is made up of eight different factors: forehead, brows, lids, eyes, nose, lips, chin, and skin.

Forehead

The forehead is a great indicator of physical and emotional states. A furrowed brow, read along with other facial features, can indicate puzzlement, deep thought, tension, worry, fear, or concern. A sweating forehead may indicate effort or nervousness. A naturally wide forehead or one due to a receding hairline often adds strength of character to the face. A small forehead or one hidden by hair gives a younger, more casual appearance.

Eyebrows

Eyebrows can be very expressive. They can be furrowed, heavy, light, penciled, soft, and a myriad of other adjectives spelled out in romantic novels. The brows tend to soften or harden a face. John F. Kennedy, for example, had what scientists call "medially downturned eyebrows," which gave his face a concerned look even at rest. Imagine JFK with Everett Dirksen's bushy eyebrows of down-to-earth experience. Thin, penciled eyebrows give a more mature, hardened look to a woman. Arched brows are more dramatic. Light eyebrows on either a man or a woman give the face a softer quality, lacking presence. The vertical line between the brows help form a concerned, worried look.

Eyebrow movement can indicate a variety of emotional states. Our brows may move up suddenly with surprise, fear, or recognition, or they may move down forcefully to indicate concern, worry, or anger. Richard Nixon's overhanging brows give him that brooding, sinister look that cartoonists love.

Eyelids

Eyelids are primarily indicators of alertness or involvement. People who have that sleepy or hooded look are thought to be cool, slow-moving, in control, and detached. An overlong gaze with lids lowered can show sexual interest. Bright-eyed, or wide-eyed people often have a look of alertness, innocence, or wonder. Examples of these two extremes are Charles Bronson and Eddie Cantor. Much of the "inscrutable Oriental" image is created by the epicanthic skin fold (sometimes called the Mongolian fold) around the eye, which gives it a more closed look.

The wink is a useful NVC device. It can mean "Okay" or "Hi, cute person," or it can be a warming personal gesture. Many of the modern "yuk and chuckle" newscasters make this their main tool for exhibiting warmth and charisma. A wink can leer if it is broad enough, or it can point out that the previous statement was sarcastic. A very long wink will almost guarantee a laugh from any crowd because it is a burlesque of the "smooth mover."

Eyes

Important as the eyelids, brows, and forehead are, they all pale in significance compared with the eyes. The eyes indeed have it. Often called "the windows of the soul," they indicate the object of our attention. You know how mad you get when someone wears dark glasses indoors? You are uncomfortable because the other person has the distinct advantage of being able to look anywhere unobserved. Dark glasses allow people to break the unwritten rules of eye contact.

By school age, most children have learned the basic rule of public eye contact: *civil inattention.* Throughout their early years, they have been told, "It's not polite to stare," "Don't look at that poor man while he's eating," or "Keep your eyes to yourself." Civil inattention is the habit of letting your gaze rest momentarily on someone before moving on after a decent period of time. That time can vary from group to group and situation to situation, but it is usually about one second long. As we walk along the sidewalk, our gaze will flicker randomly from face to face in civil inattention timespans, our expression never changing. At a party, civil inattention time is extended slightly as people size each other up.

If we look too long, we are guilty of *immoral looking time.* We can show interest or challenge someone by maintaining too much eye contact. If you walk along the same street resting your gaze for immoral looking times, you can cause people to avert their eyes. Or you may find others challenging your gaze by staring back belligerently as if to say (as in the battery commercial), "You want to start something?"

Sexual interest can also be shown by a lingering gaze. I was walking down the street one afternoon with a bachelor in our office when a young secretary from our building walked by. As we passed her, my friend stopped and turned around, watching her recede. When I asked what was going on, he told me to be quiet for a moment. When she was about 30 feet away, she glanced back over her shoulder, much to my friend's glee. I stood there confused as he exclaimed, "Got her!"

He explained as we walked away, "Whenever I see a good-looking woman walking toward me, I let my gaze linger over her and give her an appreciative smile as I go by. If I get a smile back, I stop to see if it's worth tracking her down. If she turns around, I give her another smile because now I *know* it's worth tracking her down." He had a date with her within two days.

We also practice the *cripple shift* on certain classes of people. One of my students, a woman paralyzed from the waist down and confined to a wheelchair, told me about the way people stare at her. The minute she catches people looking at her, they avert their eyes so "she won't think they are staring." Can you imagine going through life with people instantly looking away from you as you meet their eyes and then trying constantly to sneak a peek when they think you aren't looking? The most human thing to do is to practice civil inattention here too, letting your eyes rest for the normal moment before moving on.

The worst version of public eye contact is the *nonperson stare*. The nonperson stare does not grant the other person enough status to deserve civil inattention. It "looks right through us," as if we weren't there. Examples are the hate stare we give people we are prejudiced against and the blank stare we give waiters or waitresses as we talk at our table and watch them do their jobs. The blank look is a most outrageous insult.

Private looking time is vastly different from public looking time, because eye contact is expected to go up when we talk to people we know. The degree of eye contact in a conversation can often vary from 25 percent to 100 percent, depending on who is talking. Contact is reduced when we are doing the talking and is dramatically increased when we are listening—going from a normal 40 percent to 60 percent for talking to an average 80 percent for listening. Too much eye contact can again become dominating.

A manager I once knew maintained almost total eye contact whether he was speaking or listening. It was as if he came out of a basket to the tune of an Indian flute. If his eyes had spiraled, he could have starred as the snake in Disney's *Jungle Book*. Everyone was uncomfortable in his presence and felt intimidated in staring back at him or in trying to furtively look away. This manager was very tall and had a nonexistent intimate territorial space. Ten minutes with this man standing closely over you and staring into your eyes and you would have admitted to any heinous crime.

Too little eye contact shows a lack of strength or purpose. We have all talked to someone who wouldn't look us in the eye and come away feeling cheated, having no respect for that person. If the gaze moves too quickly we are also concerned, because the person is "shifty-eyed." I was talking to a reporter for a local TV station about a recent mayoral election. One of the candidates, a man running for office for the first time, hadn't learned to ignore the camera. When he was interviewed, he kept shifting his eyes from the reporter to the bright lights and whirring sound. After the interview, the reporter suggested he look at one or the other in the future, because the film was going to show him as a shifty-eyed politician. Unfortunately, there weren't any more interviews and the candidate lost in a landslide.

It's also disconcerting to talk to someone whose eyes are unfocused. This gives a confused, bubbleheaded look to any face. Excessive blinking and eye watering are other negative signs. Blinking makes us look nervous, and watery eyes make us seem overemotional or weak. Many contact lens wearers don't realize the real NVC price of their lenses, as they rub their eyes in discomfort and wipe away the tears with the ever present Kleenex. Other wearers adopt the "contact stare," blinking only when necessary. Often this gives the face a strained, inflexible look, with the eyes locked open like a Shields and Yarnell robot.

Make certain the windows to your soul aren't clouded, giving the wrong information to the people in your life who are looking in. Practice civil inattention with *everybody* no matter what a person's physical condition. Look people in the eye as you listen, and don't be afraid to look away as you talk, it's normal. Keep your eyes on your subject, and your attention will follow.

Nose

Some people can make a career out of a nose, like Jimmy Durante, Bob Hope, and Cyrano de Bergerac. To most of us, the best nose is one people don't notice. There are all types of noses: hawkish curved noses, pixie upturned noses, sharp pointed noses, flat boxer's noses, and noble Roman noses. (When my wife's doctor asked her, "When did you break your nose?" she helped him place his foot in his mouth with the answer, "I never have. I'm Italian!") Each of these is a stereotype that helps define our image regardless of our real personality. Some people find the stereotype so distasteful that they modify their noses. Most of us are content with what we have.

There is really very little to "read" about a nose other than the nostrils. We can be likened to rabbits, nostrils quivering in anticipation, or racehorses, nostrils flared with eagerness. Often we widen our nostrils in fear or anger. Nostrils can provide some information, but why should we pay attention to them with what is waiting below?

Lips

Lips are one of the really interesting parts of the body. Humorist Richard Armour devoted an entire essay to Sophia Loren's lower lip. (I shudder to think how long he would have had to write had he expanded his study.) Lips are also the source of our aggression. "I'm going to give you a busted lip!" "Don't give me any lip!" "Why don't you keep your trap shut?" We even judge character from lips.

Lips can be full or thin. Full lips make a man or a woman look softer, warmer, and more sensual. Thin-lipped women frequently apply their lipstick outside of the lipline to give them a more sensual look. People with thin lips, such as Jack Lord in *Hawaii Five-O*, show more strength, firmness, coldness, and less emotion. Who wants to woo a thin-lipped lover, much less let a career depend on a tight-lipped manager?

Children often thrust their lower lips out in angry defiance. Grown-up lips can pout with petulance or sneer with superiority. (It is my greatest regret as an NVC consultant that I have the right-side sneer, and the "Yech!" double sneer, but I have been unable to develop the left-side sneer.) Lips can also drool with idiocy, part with promise, smirk with certainty, be bitten with nervousness, be licked with worry or anticipation, and have a host of other interesting movements not particularly pertinent to a business book. One of the most common things they do is smile.

Smiling frequency is a learned cultural trait. People in some areas of the country, primarily the South, smile more than others. Studies have shown that Atlanta, Memphis, Nashville, and Louisville residents smile the most. Where do people smile the least? While I resist drawing any editorial conclusions, people in New York smile less than those in any other city.

Every face has a *resting position*. This is the expression we have when our face is in "neutral," not showing any spontaneous or controlled emotion. (This is not a poker face, when we are trying to mask our feelings.) As we work, a large amount of time our face is expressionless (or so we think). Some people have a built-in smile or frown at the corners of their mouths. A vertical line at the lip corners also gives the impression of smiling frequently. As my customer from Chapter 1 who covered his mouth when listening knew, heavy facial lines running from the nose to the edge of the lips give a deep frown. All these resting positions affect how we look to others in our unguarded moments.

As you walk outside or around your building during lunch hour, start watching the faces of the people you pass. You may be surprised to find that the majority have a frowning position. The ones with a truly neutral look or the ones with pleasant expressions will appear much more friendly and warm. Which one are you?

Our lips may adopt a nonresting position when we are emotionless. One of the most difficult distractions I have ever faced in class came when a beautiful woman attended one of my sessions. She was the type that could stop conversation in the company cafeteria when she went through the line. She was very attentive in class, and it was hard to give the other students equal eye contact until I discovered a strange lip movement she had. As she listened, she would run her tongue over her gums as if cleaning her teeth after a big meal. It was not a sexy movement at all, just an earnest tongue polishing her teeth. I told a female associate of mine that I finally had the beauty in one of my sessions and she was driving me crazy! The response was an unsympathetic "I guess that's like marrying Farrah Fawcett-Majors and finding out she snores." Any one of the "active mouth" habits could be worse than a frown.

Chin

The chin is often considered an indicator of personal strength. Whenever we have problems we have to "take it on the chin." Westerns are full of square-jawed young heroes teaming up with lantern-jawed ex-sheriffs to stop those cowardly jowly outlaws. "Faced" with the big gunfight, the old-timer pats us on the shoulder and tells us, "Keep your chin up, kid, these skunks will scatter at the first shot!" We stroke our chin thoughtfully and reply, "Quit jawing at me, pops. I ain't scared." Sticking our jaw out defiantly, we stride off throwing the parting comment over our shoulder, "Besides, I'm going first." This whole important exchange would never have been possible without that wonderful device that holds our lower set of teeth.

The shape and position of the jaw help form our image. Square or angular jawlines are associated with strength; rounded jawlines are associated with warmth and openness. John Wayne, Clint Eastwood, and Kirk Douglas all show strength. Dick van Patton, Dom DeLuise, and Bill Cosby appear more open and people-oriented. Jacqueline Kennedy Onassis shows an angular strength, while Shirley Booth shows her warmth.

The jutting chin can create an aggressive, defiant look. The receding chin suggests meekness or lack of character. It is such a negative factor that it is often used for comic effect.

The skin around the chin is also important. Loose, jowly skin under and around the chin softens the personality and can even suggest weakness. Former Senator Sam Ervin's chin reinforced his easygoing slow-country-lawyer image. On women, this feature often contributes to a warm, grandmotherly image.

In general, the chin is not an item you can "read" for personality information. Instead, you should be aware of what the chin contributes to your image and the impressions you get from others.

Skin

One of the most common things skin does is get red, or blush. This uncontrollable burst of color across our face is a dead giveaway when we are embarrassed or self-conscious. In general, the easier we blush, the less strength and authority we appear to have. This is unfortunate, since blushing is largely an uncontrollable event, usually aggravated by some noxious co-worker who loves the power of being able to visibly embarrass someone. There is no way to "poker face" a blush. We immediately let other people know they have scored.

In addition to color, our skin shows physical depth and firmness. Thin-skinned people, literally and emotionally, appear sensitive, gentle. You have to approach them with finesse and care. Thick-skinned people are tough, in control, and hearty. You can be more direct with them, more open and blunt. They admire forceful, aggressive people. It's tougher to "get under their skin."

Our skin can appear firm and tight or soft and droopy. Romantic literature is full of phrases such as "skin stretched tautly over high cheekbones beneath intense gray eyes" and "bulbous cheeks bouncing hideously as he tore at the turkey leg." Much like the loose skin around the chin, loose facial skin projects a soft personality. Firm skin connotes strength and, taken to the extreme, can indicate a nervous temperament.

Wrinkles are another frequent negative. An article in the December 8, 1977, issue of the *St. Louis Post-Dispatch,* noted that President Carter had wrinkled considerably since his election. The comments ran from Vice President Mondale's "I wish he had more time to completely relax" to Atlanta lawyer Charles Kirbo's "I think he is aging." Commonly thought of as one of the hardest-working Presidents in recent years, Carter was described in the article as "an American executive with workaholic tendencies."

The photo on the left in Figure 4–5 shows President Carter during the campaign; the photo on the right shows him in office. The "new look" Carter was said to have "strain . . . etched in his face and around his eyes." Although the lighting is different in the two pictures, in the later photo the President's brow is fur-

Figure 4–5. President Carter's wrinkles.
(Wide World Photos)

rowed; there are deeper valleys around the eyes and mouth and loose flesh under the chin. This important change in image may hurt President Carter unfairly, since the article also points out that the President's physician pronounced him "in better health than when he entered the White House."

Facial changes can also affect your image of success. You can minimize them by careful emphasis on other features.

HAIRSTYLES AND ACCESSORIES

Hairstyles can play an important role in shaping people's image. John Molloy recommends that men wear their hair like the men in authority they deal with, and that women wear neat styles of medium length without excessive wave or curl. For example, men calling on executives who wear short hair should also wear their hair short. Don't be like long-haired comedian Ricky Jay, who observed, "I perform for people who have spent their entire lives working to earn enough money to get away from people who look like me." This works in reverse too. A friend of mine who is a reservist, and thus has to wear his hair short, worked as a salesman calling on "head shops" (retail stores specializing in drug paraphernalia). Even though he wore appropriate clothes (jeans), store owners were reluctant to trust him and buy from him. He finally had to buy a wig.

In general for men, the shorter the hair, the more conservative the look. The most conservative style is the crewcut. For women, the longer the hair, the more feminine the look; the shorter the style, the more conservative. Hair color can also contribute to people's image. While blonds may have more fun socially, brunettes are considered more authoritative.

Baldness frequently makes a man look more powerful and authoritative. Look at Mr. Clean, Kojak, Daddy Warbucks, and Yul Brynner as the King of Siam. Total baldness is best for showing power. The effect is lost somewhat when there is a halo of hair on the sides or when side hair is combed over the bald spot.

A toupee can have a mixed effect. First, it is an obvious show of vanity in a man, something America's "wooden Indian" concept of masculinity looks down on. It also can be a bad toupee. I remember seeing a graying man with a toupee in a restaurant. He looked like he was carrying a puppy on his head, because the toupee was the color of his long-lost brown hair with the gray showing at the bottom.

Sometimes a man will not be consistent in wearing his toupee. You may see him wearing it one day and several weeks later walk by a bald man without recognizing him. Consequently, the toupee becomes a source of distraction. On the positive side, a toupee is well worth the investment if the improvement in self-image causes a change in behavior for the better.

Facial hair also affects a man's image. One secretary told me that ever since the 1972 Olympics every young executive she sees looks like Mark Spitz. A mustache can make a young man look older, but it has a price. It is very difficult to counteract the natural frown a mustache gives a face, much like the painted frown on a circus clown. The farther away the viewer is, the less the lips appear to be smiling. If the mustache is too long, lunches can get very messy. It's difficult to be impressive with a drop of hamburger grease beading on your upper lip hair. A mustache that is too large, such as a handlebar or Pancho Villa style, can also detract from a man's appearance.

Chin hair is bad at best but should at least be neatly trimmed and fairly short. Long beards are out of style. A businessman wants to look dignified, like Sebastian Cabot, not shaggy, like Hopalong Cassidy's sidekick. Goatees are out, as are scraggly chin whiskers. Goatees just don't seem to look dashing enough without a turban or flowing robe, and lonesome chin whiskers are too goatlike for comfort.

At this writing, sideburns are supposedly going out after their time in the sun. I'm not sure they were *ever* in, considering the way top executives have ignored hairstyles. I may be prejudiced against sideburns, because I can't grow any (I just don't have the follicles). Still, I believe they fall under the category of detractors. The best sideburns are those that when asked of someone, "How long were his sideburns?" you reply, "I don't know; I never noticed." Most men don't want to look like Elvis, nor do they want to have a Little Rascals bowl cut.

Whatever your hairstyle, you should look neat at all times. There is no reason not to stop in a restroom before any important meeting to make an appearance check, particularly after lunch. Comedian Shelley Berman tells of coming home from an unfriendly date one evening to find a piece of spinach plastered on his front tooth. Going directly to any meeting after walking around outside gives us a disheveled nonprofessional look. Don't let it happen to you!

For those of you who are as blind as I am, glasses are a major head accessory. Although you may feel like you are looking at life through two toilet paper rolls, others observe your glasses as part of your image. In general, glasses make people appear more studious and can help give a face authority. This advantage can be reduced, though, if you wear glasses with oversized lenses, flashy colored frames, or those designer glasses with distracting initials on the frame. I wear goggle-shaped wire rims, one size above normal and have been told that they make me look older. For men, heavy plastic or horn rims can have the same effect (although they don't provide as big a field of vision). Glasses can be a big asset for women because they often create a more businesslike and authoritative image. Fashion frames or greatly oversized lenses will undo this advantage, as will half-glasses worn down the nose in the "granny" look.

On the body movement scan, notice a person's head position and features. The position and expression will give you an indication of how people feel about themselves and others, and the hairstyle and accessories will help you analyze their images.

Posture

Posture is very closely related to the center. Stooping closes off the center and pulling the shoulders back makes the center aggressive. *Stooped* or *bowed* shoulders can mean many things, all negative. You may be burdened, self-conscious, unconfident, submissive, beaten, guilty, or afraid. *Retracted* shoulders may make you appear insensitive, angry, impulsive, belligerent, domineering, or mean on the negative side. Depending on your other scan signs, you may also appear forceful, confident, firm, tenacious, and authoritative. *Raised* shoulders usually show tension or even apprehension and fear. *Squared* shoulders generally suggest strength and responsibility.

Have you ever caught yourself driving home from work with your shoulders hunched up around your ears? You probably thought, "I didn't realize I was this tense. I think I'll relax." You drive along a little farther and reflect, "Gee, that worked once. I wonder if it will work again?" So you relax your shoulders a little more. I have driven home from a tough sales day and done that four different times. Each time I thought I was fully relaxed at last, but with the tension of the day and of the evening rush-hour traffic, I couldn't relax all at once. Many of us spend a good deal of our day in this posture, transmitting our worry and tension to the entire office with our shoulders.

Leaning is another facet of posture. The way people lean often indicates how they feel about others. Generally, leaning backward is negative and leaning forward is positive. ("I'm leaning *toward* capital punishment.") When juicy gossip hits the lunchroom table, you can see people lean forward with interest. You go into your boss's office to ask for a raise and the boss leans back in the chair silently as you talk. Leaning affects height relationships. When we lean backward, we gain an artificial height might because we are now looking down at others, even if they are standing and we are sitting. If we lean forward, we pass the advantage to others or at least neutralize it, because we are level or looking up to them.

There is at least one advantage to leaning forward. I recently had a press release photograph taken for use with my seminars and articles. The photographer suggested I lean forward, looking the camera directly in the lens with head erect. Although my face is just so-so (I would rather look like Robert Redford), the pose gave me a more aggressive appearance.

Seating postures are also important. In general, the more relaxed we are when sitting, the higher our status. This makes it easy for Joe B. in Chapter 1 to pick out the Star and Heel in any group. We would never think of going into our boss's office, plopping down in the chair beside the desk in a comfortable slump, and saying, "Howya doin', super cheese?" The boss could easily do this to us, though. Superiority is also shown by relaxed postures such as feet on the desk (if it's your desk, the boss is crowding your territorial space and showing contempt for your possessions), lying back in the chair with hands behind head and legs crossed straight out in front, sitting on your desk (crowding with a height advantage), or sitting turned with a leg over the arm of the chair.

Your sense of presence and authority can also be increased by having what my portrait photographer called a "solid base." He told me that too many PR pictures are posed so that the subject looks like an anvil sitting on a TV tray. He positioned me in a chair turned just slightly away from the camera with my elbows out and hands placed midway down my thighs. This way, my figure was narrowest at the head, angled down to the shoulders, and then angled wider below the shoulders because of the arm position. No part of the background showed through under the arms to spoil the base. A courtroom judge benefits from this look because of the flowing robe. Any clothing of this type—a toga, a dashiki, or a flowing evening gown—adds to our image by solidifying our posture.

Hands

There are four basic areas of the hand: tips, palm, edge, and back. Hand motions involving tips are usually emphatic, as in "making a point." We discipline our children by shaking our finger at them or poking them in the chest. As we turn to leave, they shoot us in the back with the index-finger barrel of their "handgun" smoking in their imagination. At the Cotton Bowl in Texas fans cheer their Longhorns using the famous "hook 'em horns" gesture, with index finger and little finger extended. Uncle Sam looked us in the eye, pointed his finger, and emphatically let us know, "I want *you*!"

Showing the palm is a friendly, peaceful motion. Historians speculate that it originated when people extended their hands on meeting to show they had no weapons. At the altar, the Catholic priest extends his arms, turns his palms out, and intones, "Go in peace, the mass is ended." The rock star acknowledges the cheers of the youthful crowd by waving hands over head with palms out. We wave in greeting; the Indian greets us with steady palm out. The *Star Trek* writers gave Mr. Spock the Vulcan version of the Indian greeting with second and third fingers parted.

Edge-of-hand gestures are very forceful, like karate chops. They add sharp, quick bursts of punctuation to our movements. We wave away a thought we disagree with, we strike the table with the edge of our clenched fist. We use the edge of our hand much like a sword, slicing horizontally and vertically to defend or attack.

The back of the hand shows vitality. It can be aggressive, unfriendly, or negative. The forceful edge-of-hand black-power salute becomes "shaking your fist" at someone just by turning the hand so that the back is out. Nelson Rockefeller showed us the older generation can learn from the young when a photographer caught him with his middle finger thrust defiantly upward at hecklers. The same gesture is not nearly offensive enough if it is given palm out—try it in a mirror and see. In Britain Churchill's victory sign, known the world over, becomes the equivalent of our one-finger gesture if it is shown with the back of the hand outward. We express disbelief by touching our fingertips to our chest and saying, "Who me?"

A closed fist is the universal sign of force. It is rarely positive in a business environment, where it can signal anger, disagreement, fear, frustration, or power. We often employ the fist for emphasis, using it to pound our palm, pound the desk, or pound the other person. A modified version of this requires wearing a ring. An evening student of mine who is on active duty with the Army told me about certain officers known as "ring pounders." These are service academy graduates who seem to develop the habit of pounding the flat of their hand, the one with the graduation ring, on the desk as they speak. It is irritating to the men but helps the officers dominate any meeting they are in.

The service academy ring is a good example of using jewelry to advantage. In general, any hand jewelry other than wedding band and watch can be detrimental to your gestures. Any jewelry that makes noise, such as a bracelet, is reason for justifiable homicide by your fellow workers. One day with a jangling bracelet wearer is enough to make you want to lop off both his or her hands. Your watch should fit your wrist snugly, so that it doesn't bang around. As a side comment, the wedding band can be a plus for both men and women because it reduces the number of "on the make" encounters. Some women wear a band even though they are not married, just to take the social pressure off in business situations. (An attractive friend tells me the only sure way to deflate the incessant wolf is to state, "I only date certain types of people. Are you saved?") Married executives may think they are clever by taking off their wedding ring for business trips, but most single people I know have learned to look at the ring finger carefully. If it has had a ring on it regularly, the finger will show an indentation. (The best way to hide it is to put another ring over it.) In general, additional rings should be kept to a minimum. I wear only a wedding band and an athletics-related college ring. More than one per hand most likely will detract from your business image rather than add to it.

Legs

Although we spend a large amount of our business time sitting, we also have to stand and communicate, if only at the water cooler. A wide stance with feet spread apart is very masculine. We can picture the coach coming out, stopping with a wide base, putting his hands on his hips, and yelling, "Everybody in the pool!" A narrow stance is very feminine. Models are taught to stand with their feet gracefully brought together in a modified T. Imagine the coach coming out, putting his hands on his hips with feet in the dainty T, and mincing, "Okay, now, let's jump in that pool!" Or imagine a woman walking out at the fashion show, and stopping with feet widely placed in the "ten minutes to two" position. This is often considered to be a "loose woman" pose.

We can also interpret how people position their legs when sitting. In almost every tense situation, such as an appraisal or a job interview, a man will cross his ankles in front of him. A woman will usually cross them under the chair. Crossed ankles are a readiness sign, showing self-control. Crossed legs, on the other hand, are a sign of unreadiness, or nonconcurrence. For women, this means the leg-over-leg position; for men, the ankle-on-opposite-knee or "figure 4" position. For some unknown reason, we rarely make a decision when one foot is off the floor.

A special case of leg position is walking. Are you a wall hugger? Then you probably create the impression of being shy and diffident, because you are giving ground and making it easier for others to pass. (Americans hug the right wall and the English hug the left.) Aggressive, dominant people walk down the middle of the hallway, making others push to the side to pass by. If they come face to face with someone, they stop and make the other person step aside so they can pass.

Many NVC experts read too much into walking. One book claims that a springy, bouncy walk shows enthusiasm and a high energy level. I walk this way, but there are many days I'm not too enthusiastic. Essentially, if we walk with our eyes and center, the feet will follow. The first two indicators are more important than the feet.

Women and men who wear high-heeled or platform shoes should realize what they are doing to themselves and their walk.

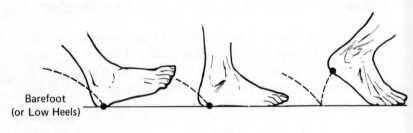

Barefoot
(or Low Heels)

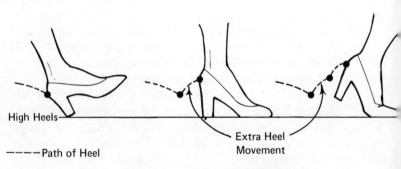

High Heels

- - - - Path of Heel

Extra Heel
Movement

Figure 4–6. High-heeled walking.

There is a reason why their walk is so clunky, and why they have to take little steps. The high heels force an unnatural motion of the heel. Look at Figure 4–6, showing a bare foot stepping down. When the heel touches the floor, it does not move until after the foot has rotated flat. The heel finally rises off the ground as the weight is shifted forward for the next step.

In a high-heeled shoe the foot must continue to move after the shoe heel touches the floor because of its distance from the ground. As the foot rotates flat, the heel moves forward nearly two inches for a three-inch heel. The heel then rises normally for the next step. The only way to reduce the extra two-inch arc is to take smaller steps and come down nearly flatfooted, causing the clunky high-heeled walk. There is no way to walk normally in high heels. For image reasons alone (ignoring the ankle injuries), no businessperson should make very high heels a part of his or her wardrobe.

Summary

This chapter introduced the third NVC checklist, one that helps you evaluate body features and movements. As you observe others, ask yourself:

1. Are people open or closed, aggressive or submissive? (CENTER)
2. What do their head positions, facial expressions, and features show? (HEAD)
3. How do they hold themselves? (POSTURE)
4. What type of gestures are they using? (HANDS)
5. What are their feet doing? (LEGS)

You now have the information you need to systematically read and evaluate someone's NVC. With practice, you can quickly scan body location, surroundings, and body features and movements head to toe. You can also begin to better control your own NVC to improve your business image. To be fully prepared for this, you need to take a more detailed look at gestures.

5

Interpreting Gestures

Arms and hands are second only to the face in expressiveness. They can tell stories in a hula dance or transmit detailed "speech" to the deaf. They can provoke a fight or start a crowd screaming or laughing. They can summon the waiter with a check or control a postgame traffic jam.

Many vocations have special gestures. When I was a rod man on a survey crew during the summers, I learned a complete set of hand signals from the transit man (walkie-talkies were not popular then). If I was not holding the rod vertical, he would put both hands over his head palms together and lean in the direction he wanted me to straighten the rod. If I was laying stakes off line, he would point to the side I should move. The faster his arm pointed and returned to his side, the smaller the distance I should move.

Deep-sea diving, another environment where speech is useless, also has a gesture language for standard or expected situations. Thumbs up or down means ascend or descend. You point in the horizontal direction you wish to go. If you point to your watch, you are indicating it is time to surface because of dwindling air supply. If you point to your compass, you are asking, "Which way next?" A hand extended palm up means, "What next?" Emergency signals include clutching your neck, running your hand knifelike across your throat, removing your mouthpiece, and pointing to your regulator.

Standard Gestures

Standard social gestures are called *emblems*. The hitchhiker stands at the roadside shaking an extended fist with thumb out. If something is satisfactory, we signal okay by putting our thumb and index finger together in a circle. The peace sign is given with palm out and index and second finger extended. For a time, the peace sign was a greeting signal between the young, replacing the wave or handshake.

It seems like every winning football squad on New Year's Day runs off the field with index fingers proclaiming, "We're No. 1." We indicate other numbers by raising up the proper number of fingers. If the number is higher than 5, we open and close the hand for the proper multiple of 5 and give the partial hand count at the end.

We also have gestures that show pictures. I always ask for the check at a restaurant by catching the eye of the waiter and drawing a square in the air with my finger. I have never had this sign misinterpreted. Men often describe a remarkable female shape by tracing the appropriate curves in the air in front of them. Women may similarly describe a man's V-shaped chest. (I have a deep H myself.) We may diagram a football play on our hand or describe the route to our office by tracing the directions on the desk.

I once made a silent movie to be used as a coffeebreak film at a large regional computer sales meeting. An associate of mine played Charlie Chaplin's Little Tramp, and I played a typical young salesman in the early 1900s. One scene called for us to watch an old-time card sorter in action. At the last minute, we were unable to come up with an old enough machine, so we played the scene in pantomime. I walked up to an empty space and proudly pointed out the machine with a wave of my hand. Then I carefully removed the imaginary large cover and folded it up. I gave a brief explanation of the various parts of the machine and loaded in the cards. We were worried that the mature business audience wouldn't accept this bit of make-believe. It turned out the gestures were more than sufficient to capture the audience's imagination, and the film was one of the highlights of the meeting.

Other standard gestures show space relationships. The most common is the fish story. The erstwhile Captain Ahab describes his battle with a Maybe Big Fish, arms getting farther apart with each retelling. We can't seem to keep from giving space relationships even if we are talking about the near miss in the parking lot, or coming "this close" (holding finger and thumb two inches apart) to blowing up at a subordinate. When I tell my classes about my encounter with Mike, the man with no intimate space, (Chapter 2), I always hold up my hand with thumb and little finger extended saying, "this far" to indicate how close our faces were. So the audience realizes how close that really is, I then pick out some poor unfortunate, put my thumb to my nose, and move up until my little finger is almost touching the subject's nose.

We often use gestures to mimic others. A successful insurance agent I know sells seemingly on raw instinct. There is little relationship between his approach and any information the potential client gives him. Still, he has an uncanny success rate of calls to sales. As we were talking about this one night, I asked him to describe his last sales call that day. As he talked about the sequence of events, he began to unconsciously act out the parts. I was seeing a stage version of his sales call. He was able to notice and use the NVC the clients gave him, but better yet he remembered their actions and could apply them in later calls. As the night wore on, I realized that he had to re-create the movements of each customer to be able to tell me about the sale.

We all are natural mimics to some extent; otherwise, we would never have learned to walk or talk. You can watch two people from across the office and often tell what they are talking about by their movements. The storyteller will "conduct" the story in addition to telling it, sometimes performing the solo parts too.

Gestures can be used to trace the flow of a discussion or to list the main points of an argument. We summarize a discussion where we give both points of view with an open palm turned upward ("On the one hand . . . on the other . . ."). The opposing points are counted on the fingers of each hand. We can even tell which side a person is defending by the hand that is used. A right-handed person usually reserves the favored point of view for the right hand; the reverse is true for the left-hander. You can tell which hand a person usually uses by the watch. Except for the small percentage of left-handers, most people wear their watch on the left hand, a fact that has kept mystery writers in plot clues for years.

Touching

We reveal how we feel in many situations by touching ourselves and others. Some touching gestures are important indicators; others are mannerisms that have outlived their usefulness. Rich Little, one of the few comedians to "do" Johnny Carson, told how hard it was to develop a Carson impression. Watching Carson's monologues for several shows, he counted over 20 self-touching mannerisms that were part of Carson's regular delivery —smoothing the coat, touching the face with index finger, straightening the tie, and so on. Although many of these gestures are associated with nervousness, Carson claims that he is not really nervous anymore; he makes the gestures because he is keyed up for each monologue.

I became aware of two unconscious mannerisms of mine when I went out for track in college. Because the frames of my glasses interfered with my vision when I high-jumped, I switched to contacts for workouts and meets. During practice, I found myself punching my forehead between my eyebrows with my middle finger. I also put my hand over my face and grabbed my temples with my thumb and ring finger. I kept wondering why I was doing this, and I'm sure the other jumpers were concerned too. It finally occurred to me that I was pushing up my nonexistent glasses. I had gotten into the habit of doing it unconsciously and had not bothered to let my brain know that I was no longer wearing glasses.

We all have these useless little motions. I'm more aware of some of mine because my college students frequently use me as the subject of their NVC term project. I wipe chalk off my clean hands, push my glasses up my nose even if they are already up, rub the skin on my left hand where a steel splinter resided for

several years, and more. I can only hope none of these mannerisms is too distracting to my classes. My students, however,
know how to "drive me up a wall," sometimes purposely. My
favorite villains are pen clickers, pencil tappers, plastic food
wrap fondlers, head scratchers, and face contortionists. One dou-
ble-jointed student used to absent-mindedly bend her index finger
backward and touch the back of her hand. It made my hands ache
to watch.

Touching is a repressed mannerism in our society. A study of
conversations in outdoor cafés in several countries confirmed our
reserved British heritage. Four cities were observed for touches
(self or others) per hour of conversation. The results were San
Juan, 180 per hour; Paris, 110 per hour; Gainesville, Florida, 2
per hour; and London, 0 per hour. Touching is restricted in our
society because certain areas of the body, on ourselves or others
are considered taboo. Until recently, married couples portrayed
on TV weren't even allowed to sleep in the same bed. Greetings
were confined to gentle busses on the cheek when the husband
came home from work. Today there is a little more realism in the
way married people are portrayed.

In a social or business setting with friends, certain portions
of the body are touchable. The order of the most acceptable to
least acceptable areas for women are hands and forearms, upper
arms and top of head, head and shoulders and feet, and finally
torso and legs. For men it is hands, shoulders and arms, top of
head and upper body and legs, and finally lower body.

Every woman has experienced an unwanted male hand resting softly on her shoulder. Many men have also encountered
female associates whose constant touching makes them feel uncomfortable. With strangers, we prefer no touching. Notice how
salesclerks will jerk their hand back if they accidentally touch a
customer's hand while returning change. Observe how people
will stand as far apart as possible on a crowded bus or elevator,
shrinking back from each other even as they are forced together.
Unwanted touching is the ultimate indignity to territorial space
needs.

Socially, every man knows that he must overcome the touching inhibitions of a new date. If you have ever broken up with a

"steady" and then started dating again, you know how strange a new person "feels" on the first date. The clever bachelor will take every opportunity to contact those acceptable areas to acclimate the woman to his touch. He will help her on with her coat and linger at the shoulders, he will usher her through doors with gentle pressure on the small of her back or shoulders, and he will hold her hand or arm as they walk. I have many testimonials from men that this speeds intimacy, and many women students have in retrospect recognized this technique.

Professionally, men should never touch men other than with a handshake. The handshake is really nothing more than a toned-down embrace. Many a deal has been killed by the hearty back-slap. I don't like business associates punching, pushing, grabbing, or slapping. Generally, men touch men only in sports situations. I remember the crowd reaction when professional football teams started holding hands in the huddle. The crowd was giggly, and you could see that half the players really didn't want to do it. They just wanted to keep their job. Much more acceptable is the massive pile of hands before the game as players gather in a circle and break with a shout of "Let's go!" Strangely, the most accepted form of touch among men is the congratulatory slap on the rump. (Imagine being slapped on the rump by your boss after a good presentation.) Women seem at ease touching their own rear, as in the skirt-smoothing motion. Men would rather have another man do it. The man-to-man seat swat in sports can mean "Good job," "Too bad," "Better luck next time," or "Howya doin'?"

It is better in our society to touch objects. Cigarettes are a common touchable. Most smokers who have tried to quit realize their psychological dependence on the physical ritual surrounding smoking. Stop-smoking clinics suggest that people keep cigarettes in a different location so they become conscious of reaching for them, and that they avoid situations where they habitually smoke. Since the main point is having something in their mouths, and since thumb sucking is socially unacceptable, nonsmokers have had to turn to other objects. The number of chewed pencils in offices would embarrass the beaver population of the world. (I also hope the plastic pens are nontoxic.) We chew the ears on our glasses and nibble on toothpicks, letter openers, or cuticles and fingernails when we can sneak them. I'm always amazed by the number of people I see chomping away on their fingernails as they drive home from work. Mangled fingernails, a tribute to our high-pressure work world, may be the first symptom of ulcers.

Capitalizing on this need to handle something other than ourselves or our associates, fondle factories have produced a variety of touchables. If Captain Queeg can have his marbles, executives can have their paperweights, trophies, toy awards, doodle pads, Rube Goldberg phone directories, and giant erasers. (Ever notice how the giant erasers get dirty long before they are even slightly used?)

One reason jewelry is so popular is that it has a high fondle value. Twirling a bracelet or ring is satisfying and reassuring. Many businessmen who wear vests carry an old railroad watch on a chain instead of a wristwatch. They make a big production of pulling out the watch, snapping open the cover, and noting the time. This is much more elegant than turning the wrist slightly to look at the LEDs shining at you. With some of the more expensive electronic watches, you have to push the stem to see the time. Even though it is impossible to sneak a look at these watches, they sell well, because of their enhanced fondle value.

All these touching signs in our culture are good indicators that a person is seeking reassurance. They can also hint at nervousness, insecurity, lack of self-confidence, impatience, or fear.

Anticipation

One of the most common gestures of anticipation is the open palm of someone expecting a tip. This is often used by only the most aggressive of tipees, the bellhop. Bellhops must get shorted often, because they are so insistent when it comes to receiving a "gratuity." Rather than regarding a tip as an act of appreciation, they turn it into a bribe to make them leave before guilt or irritation overwhelms us.

Waiters often use a more subtle approach. They probably get shorted as frequently as bellhops, but they are much more civil. They linger by your table as you get up, so that if you don't leave a tip, you know that they know it. (All this time you thought they were just being friendly, hanging around to say good-by as you walked away.) If you use a credit card, the pushy waiter will look over the charge slip as he picks it up, so he can register his pleasure or muted disgust. (''Oh, *thank* you, sir.'') A classy operator will merely glance at it to see that it has been signed, and then return your copy.

Another sign of anticipation is the prayer hand position, with palms rubbing back and forth as if to roll out a piece of dough. Without this typical gesture, arch villain Snidely Whiplash could have been played by R2D2. No self-respecting villain would ever snatch even the most insignificant deed out of the freezing widow's grasp without a little gleeful hand rubbing. Diners sometimes make this gesture as they first sight and smell their meal. In a meeting, some executives will ''tip their hand'' by making this gesture when they are about to jump on a mistake. During a sales presentation, I saw that one of the managers was going to break in with just such a point, so I stopped and said to his boss, who had a puzzled look, ''You had a question?'' By the time the boss was done, the manager's point was no longer pertinent and somewhat off the subject.

Anticipation also tends to increase the number and speed of our movements. The rhythm of people's gestures is tied to their speech patterns and emotional state. We need to become aware of any changes in this rhythm. A small child will jump up and down with excitement waiting in line for Santa. A teenage girl will run up and down the stairs and dart from bathroom to bedroom getting ready for that first date. Two parents may pace, fidget, or get into an argument waiting at the airport for their son to return home from the Army.

There are other, more superficial signs of anticipation. We cross our fingers to express hope (originally an early Christian religious sign) or to protect us from lying. We hold our hands together in prayer and look upward for guidance. We ''knock on wood'' to ward off any bad luck in mentioning how good life has been or what misfortune we have avoided.

A sharp intake of breath often indicates anticipation. The karate expert prepares for his blow and shout with a sharp breath.

Spectators at the circus collectively breathe in as a difficult trick is begun, letting out a large "oooooh" when it is completed. To this day I find myself taking an anticipatory breath when I see a child sassing a parent, because in my childhood this was always followed by a quick shot to a spot inducing temporary pain.

Stress

The nonverbal signs of stress are closely related to those of frustration, anger, and worry. Stress gestures often involve the fist: hands in fists at sides, crossed arms with fists, fists resting on a desk, banging the table with a fist. (The child's version is arm waving.) Clenched hands, a modified fist gesture, is also a sign of anxiety. Pictures of disaster survivors grieving for their lost friends or relatives frequently show the subjects in this position. It is almost as if we need to hang on to someone or something, even if it is ourselves in times of stress.

Another stress gesture is hand wringing. One TV advertisement for an office copier was designed to promote the portability of a particular model. The star of the ad talked to us as if we were in the office with him. He pointed out a feature of the copier and then turned away to explain it to us. Behind his back, someone rolled the copier off for other uses. When the actor turned back to the machine and realized it was missing, he made the typical hand-wringing gesture of anxiety. Turning back to the camera, he bumbled out of control until the person returned the machine.

We frequently show stress by rubbing the back of our neck, called *defensive beating*. A popular oil filter commercial features a smug service station mechanic pointing derisively at some poor yuk who is trudging to his car with an obviously large garage bill in hand. The mechanic says something like, "See this little thing? It costs about $5.00. He could have bought one of these and saved himself that big bill. You see, you can pay me now or you can pay me later." The effective part of the commercial is the actor in the background. He walks out to the car rubbing his neck like he's just pulled a muscle, looking at the bill and shaking his head. He gets in the car and just sits there, defensively beating himself until the commercial is over. A bartender reported to one researcher that the defensive-beating gesture was a good indicator of a potential fight. The fights were usually started by the defensive beater.

Many signs of worry or stress involve self-touching. A common one is rubbing the forehead, usually done with thumb on the cheekbone and the first and second finger on the forehead, as if rubbing away the worry lines. It also hints that we have a headache from all the problems. We often rub at our eyes, pull our cheeks, and generally rub our faces in a series of beaten exhaustion moves. We may even stretch slowly and rub parts of our body to psychologically wipe away the strain of the problem.

We also sigh a lot. Without the sigh, our daytime serial actors and actresses would be nearly mute.

(Sigh) "Lance, darling, I don't know what we're going to tell Larry about the results of the tests."

(Sigh) "Rachel, he must be told before Wanda gets to him about the affair."

(Sigh) "Wanda wouldn't do that, would she?"

"You know she's always hated us, Rachel."

(Sigh) "I guess we do deserve it, after testifying about her 'thing' for mint cookies at her incompetency trial."

The sigh says, "Listen to me, I have something more than air to get off my chest." It slows down the conversation; it gives dramatic pause. It gives us a chance to glaze over pained expressions and worried brows without the distraction of words. The sigh often says, "I'm under stress."

Skepticism

Closing off the center is a common indicator of skepticism, suspicion, or secretiveness. Arms crossed tightly over the chest or crossed casually on the desk signal a potential communications problem. Suspects being interrogated by the police frequently use their folded arms to help "clam up," closing their center (and mouth) as tight as a clam shell. A variation in a nonintimidating situation is to put one or both hands over your mouth, as if to say, "Speak no evil."

Scratching the face is another sign of skepticism. Comedian Bob Newhart started his career playing the skeptic in a number of unusual situations, such as being the watchman on the Empire State Building the night King Kong scaled it; being a game manufacturer the day Abner Doubleday called up to talk about baseball; and being a marketing adviser when inventor Herman Hollerith called to introduce his new punched-card sorter. Newhart's standard "You've got to be kidding" gesture is scratching underneath the eye with the middle finger. Some people also pinch the bridge of the nose, as if to say, "I don't believe this!"

We reject ideas by waving them away with a palm-out swipe from side to side as if to say, "Go on!" We use the hand in imitation of the head shake to say, "No, no, no" in a back-and-forth erasing motion. Psychologists theorize that the negative head shake is a relic from infancy when we nursed at the breast or bottle. When we were not hungry, we rejected the nipple by turning the head sharply to the side. Since I've never found a baby willing to talk about it (don't blame me, I've tried), I'm a bit skeptical of this interpretation. I believe that it is another cultural trait learned by imitation. For example, a parent wags a finger at a naughty child. Soon the child is wagging *his* finger at his dog or friends.

Nervousness

We have to move when we get too nervous. A theater audience begins to fidget when one of the characters is about to make a fool of himself. A co-worker tells us she just "can't sit still today." Something is moving all the time in nervous people. Their fingers drum the table, they tap their pencil, they doodle, or they tear paper into little pieces. I remember one customer who used to rub the stickum off transparent tape. (This is not an easy process, as any accomplished tape rubber will attest.)

Many men are terminal coin or key jinglers. I say terminal, because this irritates me so much that I'm tempted to kill them to stop the incessant noise. It's really the fault of pockets. I think the designers who developed the male suit actually hate men. The pockets are relatively useless. They form an unsightly bulge if filled with a handkerchief (especially if it is used), are impossible to get at if a man is sitting down, and are shaped so that the contents fall down to a narrow point that is only large enough for two fingers. With any normal luck, the pockets will wear out long before the suit so that they become a chute for discreetly depositing coins on the street or into a shoe. But since the pockets are there ("Why do I use my pockets? Because they are there."), men use them for miscellaneous possessions, usually metal.

The jingler is unaware of his actions, or else he surely would stop. Even ignoring the noise, it's an annoying nervous habit. I occasionally fall into it, too. To fight its effects, I keep my right pocket (I'm right-handed) empty of everything but my handkerchief. My coins and keys are in my left pocket. Since the pockets seem so irresistible, I have developed the habit of putting only my right hand in my pocket, which is also easier on the suits. Since there is nothing to play with other than a no-fun cloth, my hand stays fairly idle and my pocket-plunging needs are satisfied.

You can fight nervousness by keeping your mouth busy. Smoking is one way, if you're not too hung up about clogged lungs. Whistling is a healthier solution. Anna in *The King and I* found that whistling helped her fight nervousness and fear. Whistling, like yawning, seems to be a community affair. If one person in an office starts whistling, by lunchtime the whole organization sounds like a magpie convention during a spontaneous rally for their favorite bird.

We tend to do a lot of self-repair when we are nervous. Scientists call this *preening,* named after the action of birds who smooth their feathers. We tug at our skirt or pants. We brush at our hair with our hand or straighten our belt or tie. The more we do this and the longer it lasts, the more nervous we are. I have seen some job seekers preen through an entire 30-minute interview.

Self-Assurance and Superiority

One of the most condescending and irritating signs of self-assurance I have ever seen involved sports. When Red Auerbach was head coach of the Boston Celtics basketball team, he had a habit of lighting up a cigar when he felt victory was assured. The earlier he did this in the game, the more insulting he was to his opponent. The crowd and the announcers picked up on it and made it that much more noticeable. Nothing could have been more irritating to an opposing player than to see Auerbach smugly puffing his victory stogie.

The cigar often plays a triumphant role in business. At my old office, new fathers passed out congratulatory cigars. (Being a nonsmoker and a malcontent, I passed out candy. The hell with the men; it sure made the women happy.) Several managers who smoked cigars would light up occasionally after a particularly successful sales call or presentation. One of the engineers used to smoke a Friday afternoon "end of week celebration" cigar.

The cigar lost some of its macho image in our company one afternoon. I was talking to my manager in his office when the branch manager stomped in and shut the door. "Did you see what I saw?" he stormed. One of the new hires, a young woman 5'3" and all of 105 pounds, was nonchalantly smoking an inch-thick "New Baby" gift stogie with a group of salesmen.

My manager, who did most of the interviewing for the office and was more aware of what's fair these days, replied, "So what?"

"We can't have her in here smoking a cigar. What if one of the customers sees her or she does it at a customer location?"

"What are you going to do," my boss countered, "tell her she can't smoke cigars because she's a woman? The men can."

"I guess you're right, but it still bugs me. This would never have happened when *I* was a salesman. Sometimes I think we're going too far."

I can understand the branch manager's feelings at seeing another male symbol going by the wayside. What he didn't know is that it was already on its way out. The cigar has been losing some of its macho image ever since the dainty cigarette-sized cigars came out. "Should a gentleman offer an Armadillo to a lady?'' the ad queries. "Not if he's a man!" the branch manager might answer.

Placing the hands above the shoulders is another superiority gesture. Bruce Jenner threw fists up in victory as he crossed the finish line in the mile finale of the Olympic decathlon. The confident executive sitting in an office may lean back and talk with hands clasped behind his head. This gesture is always a part of a relaxed posture, which, as noted in Chapter 4, usually connotes higher status. The center is very open, almost aggressively open, with the hands in this position. Hands behind the head is primarily a male gesture. A woman who assumes this position will focus attention on her bust, a decided negative in a business situation.

Stretching is another example of the NVC restrictions women face in a male-oriented business world. In my classes all the students need to stretch after sitting for a long period of time. At a break, the men put their hands straight over their head, lean back in the chairs, swing their arms about, let out a grunt, and relax. Any woman who does the "male" version may appear to be provocative. The women go through all kinds of gymnastics to stretch without really stretching. All they are left with is a type of isometrics as they tense and relax their muscles without being able to let out a good stretch.

Putting our hands over our *head* is another sign of superiority. The boxer traditionally clenches his hands over his head. The President acknowledges the cheers of the crowd by waving both hands over his head. The football team chants, "We're No. 1" with hands up in the air, index fingers pointing to the sky. The Nazi salute was a typical superiority gesture.

Psychologists theorize that we raise our hands over our head to raise our height—that this series of gestures is tied to height might. This may be true, but many other self-assurance and superiority gestures don't require increased height. One of the most common is *steepling*. The typical steepling position is to have the hands with opposite fingertips touching (like a "spider doing pushups on a mirror") and fingers spread widely in the shape of a spired church. The elbows are usually on the table, so that the center is somewhat closed and the hands are up around the face. A less overbearing form of steepling is to clasp the hands in a prayer position, elbows on the table, with only the index fingers extended. Sometimes the chin rests on the thumbs and the index fingers are touching the lips.

The next level of steepling is to have the hands clasped with elbows on the table, possibly with the chin resting on the hands. Many businesspeople realize that none of these are good communications postures but unconsciously engage in modified steepling, laying their arms flat on the desk and grasping hands or sitting with hands clasped in their lap.

Hands on hips is another common self-assurance gesture. The Jolly Green Giant towers ominously over his valley standing with legs spread and hands on hips, booming his benevolent "Ho, ho, ho!" Mr. Clean gets rid of dirt and grime and grease in just a minute and, incidentally, stands around with hands on his hips. A mother will confront her child playing in the kitchen drawer with hands on hips, saying, "And what do you think *you're* doing?"

The strongest form of this gesture is to have the fists on the hips. The next strongest is to have the hands open and pointing downward, thumbs on one side of the hips and fingers on the other. Hands in pockets or thumbs looped into the top of pants or the belt loops are weaker versions.

Hands behind the back is a self-assurance gesture often used by leaders. The Army sergeant strides purposefully in front of the green recruits, chest thrust out, arms clasped behind his back. The teacher tells his students how poorly they have done on the midterm exam, hands clasped behind him as he shifts back and forth from the heels to the balls of his feet. (Again, this is not a common gesture for a woman, for the same reason mentioned in stretching.)

Insults and Anger

Consistent with human nature, our gesture vocabulary is full of insults. The most common is one mentioned earlier, the "finger" (or the "bird"), where the middle finger only is extended from the fist and displayed at our target. It is a very taunting gesture, suitable for someone who has just driven us off the road, heckled at our speech, insulted us, or made off with our date. It is being used more and more by both sexes. In the aftermath of the shootings at Kent State, National Guardsmen commented in surprise on the way the women students talked to them and how frequently this gesture was part of the conversation.

Next on the insult list is the gesture made by placing your left fist with palm down on your upper arm near the elbow and bringing the other arm up into a "shaking your fist" position. This says you can take an idea or comment and place it somewhere in the anatomy. The gesture is not nearly so eloquent as the finger, but it is more fun to do. If you need a more socially acceptable gesture, "thumbing your nose" has a certain poetry to it, as you put your thumb on your nose and waggle your fingers in derision. If noise is what you need, the Bronx cheer can show it with a wet "Blblblblbl" (just put your tongue between your lips and blow).

If it's disrespect you're looking for, flapping your ears could be the answer. In imitation of donkey ears, you put a thumb in each ear and wave your fingers. If you don't like to get your chin wet with the Bronx cheer, you can at least stick out your tongue. In a role-playing session recently with a large group of students, I played an argumentative employee and they took turns acting as my manager. When I backed one poor student into a corner and countered her last point, she crossed her arms in desperation, got a very determined look on her face, and stuck her tongue out at me. After the class and I recovered a few moments later, I teased her about breaking role and she replied, "Who broke role?"

We like to insult someone's intelligence by letting them know we think a "screw is loose" or there's "nobody home." The first we do by rotating the index finger near the temple; the second, by tapping the temple with the finger. We make the cuckoo sign (the brain is supposedly going round and round) by circling an index finger around our ear. Sometimes we roll our eyes and look skyward, as if to say, "Oh, Lord, why me?" A Xerox commercial that has run several seasons shows a monk who is told to make several hundred copies of an excruciatingly detailed handwritten manuscript. The enterprising monk sneaks off to his local copy center and comes back with copies the same day. When he presents them to his superior, who in awe mumbles, "It's a miracle!" the young monk rolls his eyes and looks off in disbelief at the superior's ignorance.

Another insulting gesture is the thumbs-down movement,

used to reject another person or idea. This gesture can be traced to ancient Rome, where it was used in audience surveys. When a gladiator was defeated in combat in the arena, the victor had the option of sparing him or killing him on the spot. The spectators could signal death by holding out their fists with the thumb pointing downward. Today we give the thumbs-down sign when someone else is talking and we want to indicate our disagreement without speaking. Thumbs down becomes an NVC "Kill it!" or "It'll never get off the ground, Orville."

As mentioned in Chapter 4, most gestures indicating anger are back-of-hand movements. Giving someone "the back of your hand" is one; shaking your fist is another. Finger pointing and chest poking can also indicate anger, although they are closely tied to frustration. You begin pointing a finger for emphasis in a conversation only when you feel that you aren't getting your point across or that the person is not listening. The more the person argues, the more violently you point.

Another indication of anger is not moving at all. You make no gestures as you talk or listen. This anger sign usually elicits the comment "Is there something wrong?" A teacher will stop talking and stand motionless until a whispering student notices that nothing else is going on in the room. A subordinate will sit rigidly still during the critical part of an appraisal as the boss details the subordinate's shortcomings for the year. Other versions of this are the "silent treatment" and the "cold shoulder." Our lack of NVC signs becomes a signal in itself!

Summary

You've had the chance to learn some of the standard gestures for showing emotions. Since many of these integrate several parts of the body, they were examined in what researchers call "gesture clusters." In the next chapter you will learn NVC behavior clusters for a variety of common business situations. By understanding your environment and making maximum use of NVC in these situations, you can increase your ability to communicate successfully in the business world.

6

NVC in the Office

There are a number of common business situations where you can exercise your new knowledge of NVC. Some, like riding in an elevator, are merely fun to experiment with. Others, like meeting someone in an interview, can help you communicate better.

The Elevator Syndrome

It never ceases to amaze me that the most dynamic people in the world become shy and awkward on the elevator. Riding an elevator has to be one of the most uncomfortable events of our day. Because of this, there is a complete set of unwritten rules in elevator behavior. When you walk in, you punch the proper button, move to the nearest open spot, and turn to face the front. All conversation must stop. As more people get in, you shuffle over (nobody ever *walks* or takes steps inside an elevator) to make room, preferably not touching anyone. If you must touch someone, you keep your body stiff and unmoving at all times as if to say, "Uh, I'm not getting any pleasure out of touching you." As the elevator empties, you again shuffle so there are even spaces between you and the other occupants. If you are in back and need to get out, you mumble, "Out, please" or "'Scuse me" deferentially. At no time do you look anywhere but at the lighted numbers above the door or at the top of the button panel.

I can see the UFO training instructor getting ready for a close encounter of the third kind:

"Today class, we are going to study the archaic human up-and-down box. Now remember, the first rule is *no gronkling*."

A slow student pipes up innocently, "But don't these poor beasts wish to share their discomfort by communicating with each other in their little box?"

"I can see you still don't understand the primitive human animal, Thyroid. It's true that humans crowd themselves into little buglike transportation devices for amusement, pack themselves into a dark room to watch projected images, or attend a sports contest and scream with thousands of their own kind. But they really don't like to be together. It makes little sense, I know, but that's what you've got to keep in mind if you want to pass."

Poor Thyroid didn't realize that the elevator is really an NVC nightmare. All those strangers are shoved into intimate spaces. Sometimes they even are forced to *touch*. (I always seem to end up behind the lady with the beehive or the Afro.) There is no place to morally rest their gaze. And since they are together for such a short time, they have no chance to transform themselves from nonpeople to real people.

There are a number of different approaches to this discomfort. Some people walk on and stand right in front of the button panel. They are out of the way of the door with their backs to a wall where they won't be forced to move as the car fills and empties. Though everyone entering the car has to reach around them to punch a floor button, they maintain the "panel position." Others go straight to the back of the elevator and lean against the rail, even if they are getting off at the next floor. Still others prefer to travel the elevator in pairs, much like women in a restaurant going to the bathroom in tandem. They wait until someone else they know is elevator-bound and then walk on together. Their conversation dies as they enter and restarts in mid-sentence as they depart. What all these people would really like to do is to walk straight to the back of the car, stand facing the wall about six inches away, and over their shoulder say, "Somebody tell me when we get to the fifteenth floor."

You can experiment with your new knowledge of NVC the

next time you ride an elevator. Pick a spot somewhat off to the side (but away from the walls) and don't move as the car fills and empties. This will throw everyone's territorial space gyrations out of kilter. If you end up on the same side with the only other occupant, see how he or she reacts. If you have the fortitude, get on a crowded elevator, push your button, then face the crowd, looking everyone in the eyes. Most of us hate people who do this, so don't get carried away. One executive likes to get on the elevator, face the crowd saying, "You may wonder why I called this meeting," and then turn around. Try it.

Another behavior that makes us uncomfortable in an elevator is loud talking. Mustering your courage one day, get on your elevator and boom to the crowd, "Howya all doin' today? Nice weather we're having, isn't it? How many came in on Highway 40 today?" When nothing happens, say, "C'mon, let's see a show of hands." If you still get no response, start asking them one by one, "Do you drive to work?" This is really fun in the morning when everybody is grumpy and half-awake anyway.

I had an opportunity to experiment with elevator NVC when I was a salesman. My company was located on floors 8, 9, and 10 of our 15-story building. Employees were always going a short hop up or down while the other building tenants were going the full trip to or from the lobby. Another salesman named Jim and I started a quick-thinking creativity game involving weird stories. If I was riding up to 10 from the lobby and Jim got on at 8, the conversation would go something like this:

"Jim! When did they let you out of jail?"

"Oh, the lawyer posted bail in about two hours," Jim would reply, quickly picking up the game.

"Did they ever find the gun?"

"No, but her family is still out looking for it with the police. If they find it, no telling what will happen . . . "

We'd walk off at 10 leaving a carful of people leaning after us as the doors swished closed. The game, of course, was to throw an outrageous opening line at the other person and see who would get stumped or break up first. I like to think we brightened the lives of many of our fellow travelers. (The idea for this wasn't original with us, though. We thought of it when we followed two secretaries all the way to 14 listening to them talk about their dates that weekend. I never did find out what the blonde did after her date stopped the car.)

Greeting Behavior

Part of the problem in an elevator is that we don't have the time to properly greet one another. We've probably all ridden the elevator hundreds of times with people who work on nearby floors without ever meeting or greeting them. The first stage of a true greeting is *orientation*. I once was walking down the hall at one of my major customer's offices when I passed a man who looked very familiar. I must have looked familiar to him too, because we both had a puzzled look on our faces as we passed. We had noticed each other and were in that uncertain area where you don't know whether to say hello and risk feeling foolish or to ignore the other person and risk being insulting. When we were about 15 feet past each other, we both turned simultaneously to look back. When he exclaimed, "Ken!" his name came to me. It was a personnel executive I had talked to six months earlier about putting on a seminar for his division. We laughed about acting in unison in our mutual confusion. We had both noticed each other but had been trapped in indecision over whether we should greet.

When the executive turned, I saw the second stage of greeting: the *eyebrow flash*. After you orient your eyes to someone, your eyebrows move sharply upward. If there is a delay in recognition, there will be a double flash as your eyebrows first move up in recognition, then move higher in greeting. I'm the type of person who likes to sit in hotel lobbies and flash my eyebrows in recognition and greeting at passers-by. That sign alone is enough to make people stop and come over to talk, or at least wave as they continue on.

The third stage of greeting is the *salutation*. It is always a good idea to include a person's name in your salutation. Repeating the name helps you remember it the next time you meet. It is also music to your friend's ears. We all love to hear our name. You can hardly say it too much. Have you ever gone up to someone you thought you knew from behind, tapped her on the shoulder, and said, "Hi, Sally!" only to have her turn around and be someone else? As you slink away looking like a mobile red stoplight, you vow never to make that mistake again. You can take advantage of name sensitivity to avoid such cases of mistaken identity. Go up behind the person and quietly say his or her name. If you get any reaction out of your target, you know you have the right person and can continue in safety.

The fourth stage of greeting is *presenting the palm*. We can do this with a wave. A man will usually wave his whole hand at the wrist by rotating his forearm. A woman will wave by holding her hand up and bending only the fingers or by moving the fingers independently in a ripple motion. If you are close enough for contact, the acceptable business greeting is the handshake. The hand extension for the shake should be well timed. I have seen two men do the "quick-draw boogie" as one put his hand out too early and withdrew it when the other person extended his hand. The longer your hand is extended ungrasped, the greater your embarrassment and insult.

Your handshake is a large part of the first impression you create. Pity the people with cold or naturally sweaty hands, for they have a strike against them. (Breathing on your hand or wiping your hand on your pants or skirt before you shake only makes matters worse.) When I was a salesman, I always wore a warm pair of gloves so my hands didn't feel like ice cubes when I greeted another person. I also made it a habit of keeping my right hand out of my pocket and carrying my leather attaché case in my left hand to avoid a sweaty handshake. If I had to dry my hand, I tried to do it unobtrusively a few minutes before the end of the discussion.

The pressure of a handshake is also important. We've all shaken hands with the "dead fish" and wanted to buy back our introduction. One of the engineers in my office had this type of handshake. Although he was a strong, beefy guy, his handshake was wet toast. When I mentioned it to him, he explained that he had accidentally injured some people when shaking hands. A good "rule of thumb" is to match the pressure used by the person you are shaking hands with.

The politician's handshake, offering the hand in an L shape so only the fingers can be grasped, is poor in business. You should always offer your full hand to someone, unless you are meeting a macho limb crusher. If a crusher gets your knuckles in his grip, you are maimed. The best approach is to thrust your hand fully into his so that your knuckles are past his grip and hope for an early parole.

The last stage of proper greeting is *eye contact*. Most of us have been taught to maintain strong eye contact as we meet—to look another person in the eye and not back down until we are seated and into our conversation. Wrong! When you meet people, especially for the first time, always give them a few seconds to look at you unobserved so they can form that necessary first impression. For example, when a man interviews a woman for a job, he wants to check out what he sees initially (legs, hair, and so on) and then give the woman the once-over, unobserved. While women may not like it, this seems to be a fact of business life. If a man doesn't get the opportunity, he will try to sneak looks during the conversation. This distracts him, at best, from the real job of interviewing. The same is often true with a man being interviewed. I've asked executives what they look for first in a male candidate. While there is no consensus, the most frequently named items are hair length, clothing, pants crease, and shoeshine. Until an executive judges those, he will not be completely relaxed.

You should provide each person you meet with two or three seconds of unobserved eye contact directly after the handshake. In my sales calls, I always did this deliberately. I would look away, turn to put my coat down, lay my briefcase out, take the chair facing the person, sit down, grab whatever papers I needed, and finally look up. Although this took only a few seconds, it gave my customer enough time to observe me in privacy. I once experimented with skipping this part of the greeting, but the potential cost in lost sales was too great for me to continue. My success rate in first-time calls was measurably higher with this pause.

We have another intricate set of procedures for greeting people at distances. When we see a friend coming toward us on the street or down a long office corridor, we quickly look down and keep walking until the person is about ten feet away. As if on cue, we look up in unison, exchange greetings, and then look back down as we pass. (It always amazes me when I see high-level executives walking with their eyes at their feet.) We have to look down because the other person is too far away for us to look at as we approach without extending into immoral looking time.

Just for fun, the next time you are walking along and see acquaintances down the hall coming at you, look at them and greet them the entire time. Keep smiling and waving as you approach; it will drive them crazy. They'll be a basket of potatoes by the time you meet. If you want to bother people, do just the opposite. Keep looking down until you are abreast and then quickly look up as they pass and say hello. You'll be by them and heading away before they have a chance to respond. They are left thinking, "Should I say hello to him?" or "Will she think I snubbed her?"

There are other times when we wish to pass through a group without any contact. Sociologists call this *territorial passage.* The most obvious sign that people want to avoid communication is lack of eye contact. They will pass through the group with their eyes down, mumbling, "Excuse me" or "Pardon me." (I'm sorry I can't pardon you; you'll have to ask the governor.) Their hands will frequently be held down or in front of the body, further showing their desire to pass unnoticed. If someone wishes to join the group, he or she will attempt to move into the circle of discussion. If the group expands and the members open up their centers, the newcomer will maintain heavy eye contact with the speaker and group members and eventually take a verbal "turn."

Conversation

Taking a verbal turn isn't always as easy as it sounds. We have all been in a situation where we "couldn't get a word in edgewise." Worse yet, we've been trapped in a conversation, forced to sit there nodding our head like one of those annoying little dolls in the rear window of an automobile. A student told of being at a gathering with a woman who was a tipsy nonstop talker. Being polite, the student wasted nearly two hours trying to get away from this marathon mouth.

Other people have a habit of interrupting frequently. One of the hardest lessons for a sales trainee is learning when the customer is finished talking. I had one particularly slow-moving (and slow-thinking) customer who would insert long, reflective pauses into our conversations. At first, I assumed he was done and immediately responded to his comments. He would patiently wait for me to finish and then continue where he left off, ignoring everything I had said. This customer still holds my world's record for the longest pause in the middle of a conversation: 60 seconds. Yes, he once sat for a full minute before continuing with his next sentence. In crowds, he is relatively quiet because no one is willing to wait that long for the next thought to drop.

It's simple to determine when someone is done talking. We tend to mark the end of our speeches with physical signals. We look down or away when we are done, breaking eye contact and control of the conversation. Many times a change in posture will accompany the change in speakers. On a recent vacation to the Bahamas I saw good examples of this in the hotel lobby. The tours operating from the hotel required the guests to be out of their rooms by noon on the day of departure. Since the planes did not leave until five in the evening, the lobby was full of guests killing time. Almost as if they had all read the same book, the individual conversations were carefully marked. As one man stopped talking, settling back as he looked away, his companion would lean forward to begin talking. As she finished, she would turn slightly and cross her legs for her listening stint.

When people are not done talking, they will hold their postural position. They will not look down or away and down. They will keep their head and hands up to show a desire to continue. If they are in a group, they may use sounds to maintain control of the conversation. Sounds like "er," "uh," and "ah" keep people talking and force others to appear to be interrupting. Another way to "hold the floor" is to look up and away during pauses. I always joke that there must be a pornographic picture of a man and woman at the point where the wall and ceiling meet in every room because people look there so much. If you want to make a dramatic, reflective pause in your conversation without being interrupted, the wall–ceiling glance is your best bet. Accompanied by a little thoughtful chin rubbing, it will turn you into a surefire intellectual.

Listeners will signal when they want to make a comment to take over the conversation, usually by assuming an erect readiness posture and giving a fast series of agreement nods. Figure 6–1 shows a manager with his secretary. In the top picture, the manager is talking; in the bottom picture, the secretary is responding. Notice that when the manager is speaking he sits as close to the desk as possible and leans forward. He has a slight smile on his face and is palming with one hand. His other hand rests relaxed on the desk. He appears to have a very careful, controlled nature. His coat is still on, and the papers on his desk are neatly arranged in rows. He's obviously a right-hander, with his coffee cup, phone, and pens all lying to his right. The office is in the normal back-to-wall arrangement. The secretary is sitting in a relaxed, slightly slumping posture. Her arms are crossed in a modified closed center and her legs are crossed casually.

In the lower picture, where the secretary is speaking, several changes have taken place. She has uncrossed her legs and arms, moved up in the chair, and assumed an upright posture. One leg is tucked under her chair in a readiness or alertness position. Her chin is tilted up. The manager has assumed an open listening position. His arms are resting comfortably on his chair. He has pushed away from the desk and is leaning back in a superiority posture. His chin has dropped, indicating that he has stopped speaking, but he has not brought his head into a submissive position. His head remains level, a very open sign.

In your conversations, watch for the NVC signs that act as traffic signals for the discussion. If you don't see a marker such as a postural shift, dropped head, or eye contact, be quiet. Your partner will signal you when he or she is finished.

There are a number of NVC signs that indicate whether you are really getting through when you talk. In a good conversation, both parties will often assume the same body position. One salesman in my office did this so often in the casual bull sessions on the sales floor that I couldn't resist trying a small experiment. We

Figure 6–1. Conversation body positions.

started talking at my desk, which was next to a window. When I sat on my desk, he sat on the desk too. I casually moved over to the window and he followed, keeping his normal personal space. I sat on the heater module, tucking one leg under me, and he did the same. I stood up, and within one or two sentences he stood up. I finally put my foot up on the heater module, which was about desk high. He was quite a bit shorter than I am, but he pulled up his pants leg, put his foot on the module, and stood there straining to keep his balance until I felt guilty and moved back to my desk.

While this case is extreme, it does indicate how we signal a deep level of communication by mirroring the body positions of those we are speaking to. Another good indicator of successful conversation is *resonance*. We all tend to move synchronously with someone we are listening to. When the top picture in Figure 6–1 was taken, the secretary was bobbing her crossed leg in time to the boss's right-handed gesture. Sometimes we nod our head in time to a speaker's movements, as if to say, "I agree" or "I understand." We may drum our fingers in time to the pacing of an instructor or sway to the music of a film presentation.

Resonance is also an indicator of relative status. Whoever controls the tempo of the movements is usually the higher-status person, or the NVC leader. If you notice yourself resonating with someone else, change the tempo and see if the other person follows. If you observe two people resonating in a conversation, watch who begins a pattern and who follows, then see if that agrees with their status relationship.

Instructing and Presenting

Instructing or making presentations is a special type of conversation. People who treat instruction as a one-way communications process are making the mistake of communicating "to" instead of "with" their audience. Sometimes people end up communicating the wrong information, which can detract from their real message.

I once ran into this problem in one of my seminars for

women. Midway through the morning, the woman sitting in the front row farthest to my left began to giggle. Fearing the worst, I paused and asked her what she knew that I didn't. She managed to choke out, "You have a safety pin in the seat of your trousers."

I knew at once what had happened. In a class the previous week, I had accidentally sat down on a piece of fluorescent pink chalk. When my wife took the pants to the cleaners, they had evidently put a safety pin on the stain. There are certain things you can't do and be cool, and patting your rear in search of a safety pin in front of 25 women is one of them.

I made a similar gaffe recently just before I was to give an early morning body language speech to a large group of computer salespeople. The meeting was held locally, so I merely had to rise early and drive to the hotel across town. But being a true night person, I felt like a 45 rpm record being played at 33⅓ on the way over. After asking only three people how to find the headquarters room, I walked in to meet my contact. He introduced me to all the people in the room—two women and four men—and then took me to his boss. I remember thinking they were a particularly friendly and cheerful bunch for such an early time of the day, a nice group. My contact suddenly got a strange look on his face and then asked, "Would you like to go to the cafeteria for a cup of coffee?"

Not sensing the urgency in his voice, I replied, "No thanks, I'm not a coffee drinker."

His boss broke in and said, "Then why don't we walk on over and take a look at the auditorium where you'll be speaking? I'm sure you want to get comfortable with the facilities." As we walked over, he quietly said, "Your fly is down."

Now every man has been caught by this joke dozens of times in his life. The secret is not to panic and clutch at your crotch. To be on the safe side, I said, laughing, "This is why I carry a briefcase," and held my leather folio in front of my waist. I took a few more steps thinking, "Why would he pull this one on me?" As I brushed my fingers over the top of my zipper, I noticed a distinct separation. (That jaunt in from the car *had* seemed kind of cold.) I had just walked through a crowded lobby and met some members of my meeting group, fly flapping and white jockey shorts winking brightly through the gap. Thank goodness I hadn't worn my paisley bikini undershorts. (I save those for important occasions.)

Trying to salvage some measure of self-respect after being the body language expert who showed up opened up, I mentioned the old flying joke, "Well, my brother the pilot told me you should never fly if you're the type of pilot who walks out of the bathroom with your zipper down." When that was rewarded with a sincere chuckle, I thanked the boss, "Charlie, I appreciate your not letting me go up there like this. Of course, they would always have wondered if I did it on purpose and I would never have told them."

Appearance is critical in any group communications session. Think of either of these two stories before you rush into a meeting. No matter how late you are, there is always time for a quick 360-degree turn in front of a mirror to spot any irregularities that will destroy your image and change initial respect into derision.

GOOD PRESENTATION NVC

Chapter 2 discussed the importance of laying out a room to give an audience comfortable personal space. One of the problems with many presentations is that there is too much space between the presenter and the audience. In a small conference room holding 20 to 25 people, the lectern may be as far as 15 feet from the first row of chairs. If the attendees, like most people, tend to be "balcony Baptists," the space is even greater.

I always move the lectern up whenever possible. When I can work without notes, I stand as close as possible to the audience without invading the social territorial space of the people in front. This has several advantages. First, the audience is easier to control at closer range. The farther away you are, the easier it is for an audience to whisper, doodle, or doze off. The increased distance gives them a false sense of invisibility. Height advantage is also diminished with distance. If there is an interruption, it is much more difficult to regain your listeners' attention if they are 15 feet away. Finally, your voice may not be able to reach the rear rows of listeners. It is not enough to be heard by those in back; you must be heard throughout your full *range* of speaking to be effective.

It is often helpful to actually "get into" your group during a presentation. During an advanced business seminar that I attended at Harvard Business School one of the professors used this technique. He literally ran up and down the aisles getting to people who wanted to make a comment or ask a question. Although the students were initially amused by the professor's antics, they paid more attention to him than to any other speaker in the course. The class was also much more informal and relaxed.

You can create a more relaxed atmosphere by keeping your center open. I never say a word to a formal group with my coat buttoned, nor do I ever wear a vest to a talk or presentation. Whenever possible, I remove my coat. I do not loosen my tie in a business setting, because I believe it looks sloppy. The loose-tie image is better for after 5:00 P.M. when you are trying to convince your boss that you're working too hard. I believe this informality does not apply as strongly to women. A woman should appear competent and professional to overcome the possible prejudices of the audience. This is hard to achieve if a woman gives a presentation in a relaxed, open manner. A woman can make her presentation more personable through voice and delivery.

A problem that speakers of both sexes have is eye contact. As mentioned in Chapter 4, people normally maintain eye contact less than 50 percent of the time when speaking. In addressing a group, the presenter must break this rule dramatically, maintaining eye contact with *somebody* nearly 100 percent of the time. This total eye contact can be extremely uncomfortable. Many instructors try to solve the problem by looking only at one student, seeing the audience as a sea of impersonal faces or not looking at the audience at all. Some presenters pick a spot slightly above everyone's head in the back of the room and watch it as they talk. This gives the same distracted effect as a TV personality reading teleprompted lines just off camera.

You must develop an "audience scan" technique. The goal is to make all the members of the group feel as if you have looked at them personally during the talk. If you let your eyes sweep across the audience, you are not really making any eye contact. Your gaze must jump from person to person, resting on each one for at least "moral looking time." Anything less is ineffective; anything more is intimidating. You have to be doubly conscious of the edges of the group—front, back, left and right. If your eye jumps in a left-to-right, up-and-back pattern, you will be looking at the edges only half as much as the middle. This is particularly true of the front corners.

I find that simply scanning randomly and concentrating on hitting the edges more often is sufficient to help me maintain better eye contact. I don't follow a specific pattern because I'm afraid to look like a searchlight flashing regularly in the night. This random pattern works effectively for very large groups too, because you can hit more people with a single jump. At a distance of 50 feet, 15 or 20 people will all think you are looking at them individually.

At times you may want to intimidate an unruly listener. A silent, piercing gaze will direct the group's attention to the offender. We've all been talking to someone during a meeting and suddenly noticed that the room was quiet with everyone looking at us. I've always been tempted to scream, clutch my heart, and fall to the ground when this happened to me. (This would be a lot of fun and is a great way to change jobs.)

There is also a rule about gestures in presenting: make some. Many speakers cling to the lectern like a liferaft. If the speaker ever lets go, he or she will drown. The presenter starts with both hands gripping the sides of the lectern. As the speaker moves to the left, the right hand lets go and grabs the left side before the left hand lets go. The process is reversed in moving to the right. Occasionally, the speaker may daringly let go and make a feeble move with one hand before vertigo sets in and the errant hand returns to its permanent roost.

In addition to making gestures, unlock yourself from the lectern. I've found that my listeners are much more responsive when they have a moving target to follow. If you stand in one place, you will lull your listeners into a stupor, similar to highway-stripe hypnosis. Their eyes need to move around in their heads, and their heads need to swivel to keep the brain lubricated. This doesn't mean you have to put on roller skates every time you plan to stand up and say something; but the longer you talk, the more you should provide your audience with a variety of movements for visual stimulation.

When you must stand at the lectern, don't fall into the "Coast Guard sway" shown in Figure 6–2. This is when you tightly grip the lectern on both sides, feet planted widely, and sway left and right toward the side walls as you speak. You had better put Dramamine into the coffee, because the only listeners who won't be seasick in a few minutes are the Coast Guard people. Interact *with* rather than *along* your audience by placing your feet approximately shoulder width apart and putting one foot slightly in front of the other (your "best foot" forward of course). No side-to-side movement is possible in this position. Instead, it will allow you to shift toward the group for emphasis and away from it for reflection. Imagine an old-time preacher leaning low over the lectern and shouting, "You're all going to

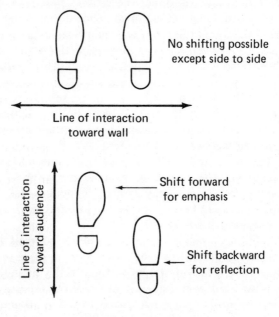

Figure 6–2. Lectern stance.

hell!'' He leans back suddenly upright and softly asks, "What do you think about that?"

These skills can help you make better presentations. You also need to know when you are succeeding and when you are losing in the competition for your audience's attention. I can always tell who hasn't done the homework in my college classes. A student may walk in and claim, "I really liked that Principles of Management book. Yep, I read the first eight chapters and it was *so* engrossing." When I glance down at the student's desk, I notice that the book sits there without a binding gap from being opened. Then when I ask for volunteers to discuss the chapters, the student goes on an eye contact vacation.

One of the sure signs of a lost audience is when you can't find a volunteer. You are suddenly so alone that you may as well take off your clothes. People look down at their papers, pick at their nails, or gaze abstractly into space. I like to just stand there until someone can't take it any more and looks up out of curiosity. I then have my subject, and make a mental note to figure out what I'm doing wrong.

I also like to make a game of calling on students who have questions before they raise their hand. The NVC signals for "wanting to speak" are about 80 percent reliable (though occasionally I've recognized people who are just about to scratch their heads). As in conversation, listeners who want to add to the discussion will usually change positions, sitting alertly as if to say, "I intend to speak when there is a gap." They will also maintain solid eye contact with the presenter in order to attract attention when their turn arrives. Another tipoff is that they will make some kind of noise, such as clearing their throat or saying "er," to verbally get in line behind the current speaker.

Listeners will also signal attentiveness. As noted earlier attentiveness is determined in part by where people sit in a room (see Zones of Attention in Chapter 2). But body position is a much stronger indicator. The King Kong head tilt is a very positive sign of attention, as is resonance with the speaker's movements. Hand-to-side-of-face gestures also show evaluation. Examples of these are forefinger on cheek with thumb and second finger on chin, fingers on cheek, fingers stroking chin, or head on fist. We also sometimes fondle objects such as a pipe or glasses in order to buy time to make an evaluation.

Figure 6–3 shows part of a class that has been kept too late. There is only one positive NVC sign among the three students: the woman's evaluative right-hand position. This is negated by her posture. Like the two men, she is leaning away from the instructor. None of the students' centers is particularly open to the speaker, and two are closed off with either hands or crossed legs. All three have very sober, set facial expressions. The man on the left has a level head position with face turned toward the speaker. The woman also has a normal head position, but her head is turned slightly away from the direction of her gaze. The man on the right has a very negative dominant-disagree head position to go with his closed center and leaning posture. Both men are also gesturing with modified steepling (superiority). This is clearly a negative group of students who are showing little empathy or agreement with their instructor.

Figure 6–3. Losing an audience.

Gestures of boredom or impatience are another sign of losing your audience. I always joke that the best NVC sign that an instructor is "burying" a class is a red spot on a student's forehead after a break. (The red spot is from resting face down on the table.) A shaking or tapping foot is also a consistent indicator of uninvolvement. Drumming fingers, twiddling thumbs, and doodling are other signals. The head-in-hand gesture (not to be confused with hand to side of face) is the worst. If the chin is resting in the open palm with the fingers splayed over one cheek, you can be certain the eyelids will begin to flutter soon after.

As much as I hate to see signs of inattention, they have been of great use to me in teaching. I have very little desire to talk to sleeping people. No matter what my schedule, I'm better off blowing it with several extra breaks than mesmerizing my students in a frantic marathon day. In communicating with an audience, you too should make it easier for people to listen to you and you should "listen" with your eyes for their attentiveness.

Offices and Meeting Rooms

OFFICE LAYOUTS

As mentioned in Chapter 2, an office is an excellent indicator of its owner's personality. Figure 6–4 shows three views of one of the most unusual offices I have ever seen. The top photograph shows the view from the door, the middle photograph shows the view from the plant, and the bottom photograph shows the view from the visitor's chair. This is one of those rare offices with the occupant's back to the door. The executive likes this arrangement because he is "not distracted by people walking past outside the door." Still, it takes a very confident and self-assured personality to ignore rear fear. It also takes a lot of self-discipline not to become distracted by sounds outside the door.

The office is highly individualized. Classical music plays softly in the background. The thriving greenery is not the result of a secretary's zealousness; it has been nurtured with protective concern by the executive himself. The major wall decoration is a *New Yorker* map of the United States, showing all points west of

Figure 6–4. An unusual executive office.

New York City as something akin to the Indian territories. A clock is mounted in prominent view. The shelves display a variety of cards, mementos, and books on many subjects.

The desk is efficiently arranged. In the middle picture, notice the piles of paper in convenient stacks. Necessary tools such as a stapler and staple remover are out on the desk. The pens are neatly laid out directly in front of the executive (to the left of his glasses). The executive appears organized but extremely busy. Compare this picture with the office in Figure 6–1. That executive's desk is much less cluttered and much more organized. No utensils are out; no personal effects show except for the nameplate in the front left corner. The shelves and credenza contain only pertinent books and folders. This office is much more impersonal, giving a serious, "no frills" approach to business.

Figure 6–5 is a diagram of the office pictured in Figure 6–4. It indicates several interesting features in addition to the occupant's chair facing away from the door. First, the office is designed to

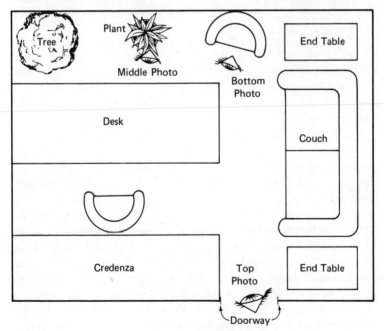

Figure 6–5. Office layout.

minimize a visitor's stay if the occupant desires. The executive has a small office space to work with and evidently wishes to control most of it. The visitor has very little space, being hemmed in by the plant, desk, couch, and end table. As the bottom picture in Figure 6–4 shows, the plant can get in the way of a conversation across the desk. As in the service station commercial, the plant and the visitor "can be *very* friendly."

Although the visitor does not have enough space to feel totally comfortable, the chair is tall enough (and the executive's chair unmodified) so that the visitor is not at a height disadvantage. In fact, the executive will often put himself at a height disadvantage by sitting on the couch to talk to a visitor. In addition to relaxing his guest, this move opens the centers by removing the desk as an obstruction and minimizes the plant's interference. The location of the couch and the executive's willingness to sit "one down" further emphasize his confidence and self-assurance.

FORMAL MEETINGS

I recently examined a government agency conference room with a carefully designed arrangement. The diagram in Figure 6–6 gives the basic features. In this highly structured organization, the seating layout is the basic King Arthur arrangement. At one end of the wide table, the commanding general sits flanked by his chief of staff and deputy. The agency directors sit along the sides in predetermined positions. The greater the director's seniority, the closer he sits to the general. Other meeting attendees sit behind the general in six or seven rows of chairs, with special support staff for a particular meeting sitting in the front row. The closer staff members are to the front row, the higher their status.

Those not seated at the table make their presentations at the lecterns. The left lectern is used if there is only one briefer; both are used if two are speaking. The screen is rear projection, so no audiovisual paraphernalia is exposed. The lighting is uniform, and the heavy drapes over the windows are never opened. The fire door behind the left lectern is always locked from the outside. The main door is behind the rows of chairs, an appropriate distance away from the general's seat to minimize rear fear.

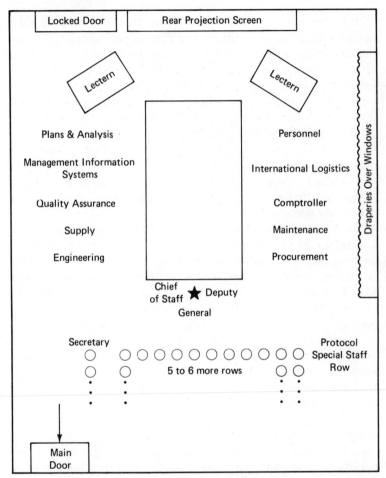

Figure 6–6. Government agency conference room.

INFORMAL MEETINGS

Although we may occasionally attend rigidly structured meetings such as those held in a government agency, we can use NVC to better advantage in more informal meetings. When I was a computer salesman, I discovered quite a lot about one of my customers through a series of informal meetings. The customer had ordered a large computer system upgrade and was having trouble planning and coordinating the physical installation. One of the executives suggested that those involved on both sides begin meeting weekly until the installation was completed. I was the marketing representative for my company and was accompanied by two systems engineers, a hardware maintenance engineer, and a programming maintenance engineer. The customer's representatives included the programming supervisor, the operations manager, and an operations supervisor. I was responsible for leading and coordinating my company's efforts, but the customer had no single person in charge. In addition, no one had been designated to lead the meeting itself.

When I arrived at the conference room about 15 minutes before the first meeting, I found the customer's programming supervisor already seated at the head of the table, facing the door. It was apparent that he intended to run the meeting. I was content to let that happen and decided to mill around until the meeting started and observe how everyone else reacted. The conference room was long and narrow, with two tables arranged end to end the length of the room. Approximately ten people could sit on each side. As people filed in, they glanced about the room and, seeing the programming supervisor at the far end, sat down at the other end near the door. I chose a chair in the middle of the group and sat down, fighting a smile. My hunch was that the programming supervisor was very defensive and was probably isolated from the others because he was not well liked.

The seating arrangement was almost comical. There were at least five empty seats between the supervisor and any other person at the meeting. One of the systems engineers walked in late and, looking around in puzzlement, picked a seat midway between the group and the supervisor ("out of sympathy," as he later told me). The funniest moment was when the supervisor began the meeting by saying, "You know, you don't all have to sit down there. I feel all alone." The participants looked at each other expectantly and shifted in their chairs, like the contestants on *To Tell the Truth* before the *real* person stands up. But they all stayed seated. After an embarrassed silence, the supervisor began the meeting.

As the weeks wore on, I found that my guess about the supervisor and his relationships had been correct. He was not well liked, and people were resentful of his leadership, even though he was the logical person to run the meeting. He sensed the resentment and bolstered his security by sitting with his back to the wall. The attendees retaliated by keeping their distance. The incredible thing was that we sat like this every week for three months. After the first few meetings, people became accustomed to the arrangement and found their ritual locations.

The lessons to me were clear. Whenever I gave a presentation at the customer's location or wanted to control or lead any type of meeting, I arrived early and claimed the end seat *nearest the door*. This let the other attendees sit with their backs to the wall. I also pulled chairs at the other end of the room away from the table and pushed them against the wall. I then spaced out the remaining chairs along the table, leaving no chairs at the far end. This forced the attendees to sit closer to me. I learned never to have more chairs at a conference table than I thought I would need, because people will use the ones that give them the most uninfringed territorial space.

Figure 6–7 is a diagram of another meeting where seating position was important. The meeting was called to market an advanced computer system to appropriate data processing personnel and the potential users of the system. I brought two experts in from out of town along with my systems engineer. The experts sat down first, across from each other at the middle of the table. The first customer to arrive and sit down was the data processing manager. I sat across from him. Although the programming supervisor and the users worked in different parts of the building, they arrived together and picked the positions shown. The systems engineer then sat next to the supervisor. This seating arrangement gave me all the information I needed to plan my sales strategy for the meeting.

On the basis of what you have read thus far, you should be able to answer the following questions:

1. What was the relationship between the manager and his subordinate, the programming supervisor?
2. What was the relationship between the users and the supervisor? The users and the manager?
3. What role did the manager and I intend to play in the meeting?
4. What role did the systems engineer plan to play?
5. How did the users feel about the proposal?

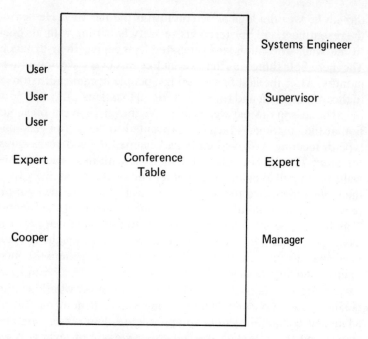

Figure 6–7. Informal meeting.

It was evident that there was no love lost between the programming supervisor and his manager. The supervisor waited until the manager was seated and then chose the one location where it would be almost impossible for him to converse with (or even see) the manager. The three users hovered uncertainly until the supervisor sat down and then sat across from him for easy conversation.

I had no intention of doing anything more than introducing the participants and letting the experts talk to the users. The manager evidently felt the same way, because he too picked a location with little dominance. I later found out he was there just to monitor the meeting and put a stop to any user interest in the marketing presentation. My systems engineer had been working closely with the supervisor and wanted to help him, but he also wanted to get to know the users better. The users were obviously interested enough to come to the meeting, but they were extremely defensive, particularly toward the manager. They made no effort to interact with the manager, although he was primarily responsible for any projects affecting them. And at no time before, during, or after the meeting did any one user ever get as far as ten feet from the other two.

My systems engineer had chosen his seat correctly. If the users were to be influenced, it would have to be through the supervisor, not his boss. I directed the conversation as much as possible to the opposite end of the table, as the systems engineer soon caught on to my strategy and took over. Afterward, I made it a point to engage the users in a technical conversation until long after the manager had a reason to remain. When he left, I scheduled a follow-up session for the discussions. The two experts were directed to a cab out front, content that they had done their job and oblivious to the wealth of information the meeting had revealed.

It pays to watch how participants mill around before a meeting starts. Figure 6–8 shows a small group talking before an informal departmental meeting. The woman and man on the left are supervisory personnel. Their manager is to the far right, and one of his secretaries is shown from the rear. Notice how both men have modified-aggressive NVC signs; the women are much less aggressive. The supervisor in the vest is standing with center open, head confidently cocked looking down from a height advantage, one hand in his pocket, with the other arm "claiming" the cabinet, and weight shifted to one leg. The woman on the left is leaning against the cabinet with center partially closed by her posture and low hand clasp; she is looking up. The secretary is standing stiffly with her center closed off by her clasped arms and slightly bent posture. She has her head in a somewhat submissive downward position.

The most important feature of this conversation is the position of the manager. The three subordinates form the corners of an equal-sided triangle with the manager looking in from the outside. Rather than forming a "choir," the group is oriented away from him. His neutral facial expression contrasts with the pleasant expressions of the others in conversation. Although he is in a dominant position, with hands in pocket and feet widely planted, he is still formally closed with his leaning stance. If you were dealing with this group, you should be alert for problems. It is possible that the manager is aloof or is not generating the respect he deserves with his three subordinates.

Another important feature of the conversation is the difference between the NVC of the two supervisors. While the woman on the left cannot comfortably (or with taste) assume the position of her male counterpart in the vest, she could stand in a more positive manner. The man is her competitor for advancement, and she should not emphasize any disadvantages such as height by leaning or slumping. Begin to watch the men and women in your organization for differences in their NVC.

In Chapter 1 you read the story of Joe B., the architect who could pick out the Star and Heel in any meeting. Figure 6–9 shows a small group listening to a presentation, including two of the people from Figure 6–8. Using the NVC information you have learned so far, try to answer the following questions:

1. Who is the most important person there?
2. Who is the least important?
3. Who is the second most important person?
4. Which one of the two VIPs is the Heel and which one is the Star?
5. Is there anything in the picture that helps you analyze the relationships in Figure 6–8?

If we label the participants Nos. 1–5 from the left, No. 4 appears to be the most important in the right-hand group. No. 5 sits stiffly with fixed gaze, and No. 3 appears to be intent on No. 5's reactions. On the basis of posture alone, No. 5 seems to be the least important. In the other pair, No. 2 is more relaxed and possibly more important. But these two have allowed themselves to be outnumbered and don't appear relaxed enough to offset the apparent show of strength from No. 4. No. 1 shows a more relaxed posture of higher status than either No. 3 or No. 5 and evidently (from his lean) has a good relationship with No. 2.

No. 2 appears to be friendly, and No. 4, the big boss, is the Heel. (Unlike in the Joe B. example given in Chapter 1, there is no "friendly Star," because the Star and the Heel are the same person in this case.) No. 2 is relaxed, upright in his chair, and alert. His center is open (notice the unbuttoned coat), and he has an evaluative tilt to his head. His feet are back under his chair in a readiness position.

This presentation is in serious trouble. The Heel has firmly closed off his center with buttoned vest, tightly crossed arms, and legs crossed away from the speaker (note only the right foot showing). His head is tilted back and away in a disagreement position. He also doesn't have his glasses on (note the glasses case in his jacket pocket), always a bad sign if he needs them for more than just reading. It can be like talking to someone with his hearing aid turned down. The final touch to this negative image is his retracted chin position, much like a turtle drawing back from his enemies. This man's mind will have to be sold over his live body!

A comparison of Figures 6–8 and 6–9 gives a clearer indication of the relationship between No. 2 and No. 3. As noted earlier, the woman works for No. 2, but she is obviously oriented to the Heel in the meeting. Both pictures reinforce the belief that there may be some problem between No. 2 and his subordinates, especially the woman supervisor.

Figure 6–8. Informal office conversation.

Figure 6–9. Executive meeting positions.

Summary

As you have seen, there are many opportunities to use NVC in a business setting. As an instructor or presenter, learn to be the master of your audience. You can control your listeners' receptiveness and responsiveness through proper design of the physical layout. You can begin to "read" their reactions to you and your material. Call on questioners before they raise their hands. Make it a goal to never again interrupt anyone, either in a classroom or in a private conversation, by using NVC. Learn to enjoy greeting people and be comfortable with the rituals that greeting imposes on you.

Use your NVC knowledge of Star and Heel to ferret out your opponents and supporters in a meeting. Determine what they think about themselves and each other by noting what seating positions they take, whom they gather around them, and what body positions they assume. View every office as a carefully controlled informal meeting environment that offers even deeper insights into the character of its occupant.

Finally, use what you have learned in this chapter to brighten at least a small part of your day. Have some fun on that communications torture chamber, the elevator.

7

NVC and Social Business

I had the opportunity to apply NVC under very unusual circumstances several years ago. I was sitting home alone one weekday evening when I received a phone call. It was my wife, who had gone shopping with a friend at the neighborhood market. In a plaintive voice she told me that her purse had just been snatched and that she would be home late. She was waiting for the police to arrive to gather all the pertinent facts.

My wife was much angrier when she finally got home. She and her friend had been pushing their carts out to the car when a teenager ran by and yanked my wife's purse off her arm. She did not have a good view of his face as he went by because of the darkness and the suddenness of the theft. Unthinkingly, she ran after him, only to see him jump in a running car and roar off with two friends. They did not turn their lights on until they were far away, so my wife could not read the license plate. What made my wife angry was that she had absolutely no information to give to the police when they questioned her.

Around two the next morning, we received a call from a juvenile bureau detective asking us to come down so that my wife could make an identification. "We've gotten a confession out of one of the accomplices and would like you to identify the one who took your purse," the detective said. My wife explained that she had no information, but he suggested we come anyway. As we waited at the station for the lineup to be arranged, I asked several questions about what we were going to do. In order to be legal, a lineup must place the suspect with at least three other people of the same race and general appearance. It would not have been acceptable, for example, for the young suspect to be lined up with a group of adults. The police found three other teenagers by putting out a radio call for squad cars to pick up any teenagers fitting the approximate description and bring them in. This point is important in understanding the mental state of the other members of the lineup.

After talking with the detective, we were ushered into a room where four suspects were standing on a stage with bright spotlights shining in their eyes. We sat behind a sheer black curtain so we could look at them unobserved. The first suspect, a short stubby blond, obviously did not fit the description. The other three looked very much alike and behaved in the following manner:

SUSPECT NO. 2 was clearly bored and resentful at being put through the inconvenience at 2:00 A.M. when he was "just out minding his own business." He turned insolently and stood with weight shifted on one leg, hands on hips. His head was tilted back as he rolled his eyes in disgust at each command.

SUSPECT NO. 3 was very matter of fact. He moved with no hesitation; his face was a relative blank. After a while he stood erect with hands clasped loosely in front of him.

SUSPECT NO. 4 was totally intimidated by the process. He stood slumped with head down. The detective repeatedly had to tell him to lift his head so we could see it. The suspect moved in leaden response to each command, squinting in the lights.

We left the room to confer with the detective. My wife told him she could not make a positive identification between No. 3 and No. 4. She did not want to jeopardize any young man's future with an erroneous ID. The detective then requested that she at least pick the one she thought was most likely the culprit:

DETECTIVE: Could you make a guess as to which one you think it was? Although we probably can't use it in court, it could be another lever in questioning, since we already have broken down one of his buddies and he knows it.

WIFE: Well, if I had to guess, I'd say No. 4. I really don't remember the thief having a light mustache, but I might have missed it in the dark. Am I right?

COOPER: No, you're wrong, it had to be No. 3. (If you're going to stick your neck out, do it with confidence.) No. 4 couldn't have done it.

DETECTIVE: Yeah, your wife's wrong; it was No. 3. (Turning to me) Wait a minute, you weren't even there. How did you know who did it?

COOPER: Oh, I could just tell from their body language.

DETECTIVE: (Walking off) Oh, brother.

Although the NVC signs happened to work out well, it did have to be No. 3. What my wife took for guilt in No. 4 (head down and sunken-in center) was really submission. Here was someone who was obviously ashamed and humiliated at being dragged into a "real police lineup." This isn't the behavior of an intentional thief who kept lying to police until one of his friends broke under questioning.

What tipped me off to No. 3 was his lack of emotion. He was the only one under the lights who wasn't showing *something*. I can just imagine what went through his young mind. ("I won't show them a thing; I'll be a blank. They won't read me from the way I act.") But because everyone else had nothing to hide, his conspicuous poker NVC was the most damning evidence of all. When he unconsciously went into a modified closed center at the end of his movement, clasping his hands low in front of him (the only one to do this), I felt certain that he was the suspect.

I haven't had the opportunity to do any sustained research into the NVC characteristics of suspects in a lineup, but I find that my police officer students identify the suspect correctly whenever I use the example in a test. In two years I have had only one officer miss it, and that's because he wouldn't play his first hunch and erased his answer. Police officers are adept at reading people's behavior because it is their business. Their lives are often endangered in family disputes where anticipating people's actions can mean the difference between a calming chat and a brawl with family members.

Although picking out guilty suspects may not be a part of

your livelihood, there are many social situations where NVC can be of value in your career. The most common situation is the male–female ritual called courtship.

Courtship Behavior

I was standing in the noonday line of a downtown burger bar when I saw a fascinating encounter unfold. A young businessman ahead of me, looking to be fresh out of school, was lounging against the wall staring absently into space. I happened to see an attractive young woman notice him (I am always alert to what attractive women do strictly for NVC purposes) and walk over to where he stood. As she neared, she called his name and put on a dazzling smile. He started at the sound of his name, glanced over, and seeing the young woman, proceeded to change in a manner no less dramatic than Clark Kent turning into Superman after a brief visit to a phone booth. As his face displayed the eyebrow flash and smile of greeting, he seemed to grow in height and build before my eyes.

The woman was obviously taken with this new executive, for she stood in the classic "total rapture" position: listening to him from a close distance, standing erect with hands at her sides, and looking up directly into his eyes. They held these positions for several minutes as they conversed in animated fashion, then the woman turned and bounced off to her friends farther back in line. The young businessman watched her go with a smile, then slowly reversed his dynamic transformation, ending in the slumped position against the wall, looking like Lee Marvin's horse in *Cat Ballou*.

Courtship behavior of this type is not confined to men and women who have a dating interest in each other. It is usually indicative of general social interest, such as between a boss and a secretary or a male and female executive. One of the most common courtship indicators is self-touching or preening. Much like a bird smoothing his feathers (in birdland as in business, the males have large egos), we unconsciously arrange ourselves when we are expressing interest. As the young man above slowly stood up, he unthinkingly straightened his tie and hitched at his pants. The woman was in better control: she only smoothed her skirt three times.

There are many indicators of courtship behavior in addition to preening. The man will hold his head high in a proud and confident position, highlighting the neck and chin lines. The woman will give the corner-of-the-eye look made famous by those TV commercial lovelies who slither around in the front seat of a Mercury. The chest will be out and the stomach will be tensed or pulled in. If the woman is sitting, the legs will be in a sexy position, either crossed or with one leg tucked under. If she is standing, the feet will be placed in the model's T position, accentuating the curve of the hips down to a narrow base. In cases of extreme interest, there will be a pelvic tilt. The pelvic tilt rocks the hips forward at the pelvic bone, causing the back to arch slightly and accentuating the stomach and the derrière.

One of the best places to see these poses is in one of the higher-class girlie magazines like *Playboy* (which, as in the case of the young woman, I look at for purely academic purposes). Photographing a playmate is no simple business. It often involves several thousand photographs over a week or two, according to one Playmate of the Year. The poses, in addition to concentrating on obvious physical attributes, are carefully designed to create specific images. The poses fall into two main categories: the tigress and the kitten. The tigress has all the courtship indicators, giving a very aggressive impression for those readers who are attracted to aggressive women. The kitten shows few or none of these signs, often posing in a demure fashion of passive enticement.

It is easy to tell if a man is affected by live or pictorial female interest signs. Researchers found that a man's eyes will dilate when viewing sexually exciting material. A female will most often indicate her interest by showing her palms in feminine gestures—from holding the man's forearm as they converse to coughing coquettishly with the back of the hand to the mouth.

The limp wrist is also a positive sign of female interest. In my lectures, I joke that Sammy Davis, Jr. always sings with his hand away from the microphone limp at the wrist. He has to because of the weight of the diamonds. For some reason, men usually keep their wrists straight. A man will never bend his wrist as he walks arm in arm with his lady friend, but a woman will carry her purse through the office with the wrist limply dangling toward the floor. The more palming and bent-wrist gestures you see during a conversation, the more interest there may be (particularly if the gestures are being watched through dilated eyes).

Male courtship behavior is characterized by overlong gazes (immoral looking time), droopy eyelids, and a slight smile. When I illustrate immoral looking time to my audiences, the women usually blush and the men shift uncomfortably. A male courtship stance is usually fully upright or cockily shifted with the weight on one leg, like Snoopy leaning up against the school building as "Joe Cool." In either case, the chest is out, the stomach in, the chin tucked back, and the head tilted in a relaxed "agree" position. The hands are often held in a dominant and aggressive hip position or a modification with thumbs hooked in the belt or hands in pockets. As the publicity photos of John Travolta in *Saturday Night Fever* showed, pelvic tilt in a man is now acceptable. Every shot showed him in the haughty arched-back position.

At a distance, interest is revealed by smiling, preening, and immoral looking time, as the story in Chapter 4 about my friend looking at passing women showed. Close up, you can begin to spot NVC signs that often indicate more than just interest. A lovers' look, sometimes called a "knowing glance," passes between two people who are sharing intimacies. They may also have "lovers' hands," which break the touching barriers normally present in social situations. Their touch may last a fraction of a second too long, or they may touch normally forbidden areas such as shoulders in too familiar a manner. When more interesting essentials are made available after hours, lovers often forget that touching in the office is limited to obvious nonessentials.

It is also possible to manipulate courtship behavior. Remembering a prank from college days, one of my associates set up a special blind date with one of his friends and a man in our office. Before the date, he had a talk with the man:

ASSOCIATE: You're really going to like this gal. She's very attractive and a lot of fun on a date.

MAN: Okay, what is it? I knew there had to be some problem.

ASSOCIATE: Well, she had a slight accident with one eye as a child, and she's very sensitive about it because sometimes it doesn't track quite right.

MAN: Which eye is it?

ASSOCIATE: Oh, I don't remember, but you can tell if you look closely.

He then went to his friend and told her the same story: "He's really a great guy, but there is one problem that he's very sensitive about. His one eye doesn't track quite right at times, but you should pretend you don't notice." Of course he didn't remember which eye, but he was sure she would be able to tell if she looked closely.

You can imagine what the date was like. Although they had a good time with each other, they spent the entire evening staring raptly into each other's eyes, searching in vain for the "problem eye." With most practical jokes, humor is in the eye of the jokester and not the victim. Fortunately, both parties saw the humor in the situation; and since they had a good time with each other, they postponed the murder until a more convenient date.

I've seen this same trick pulled with each person being told that the other is "self-consciously deaf, so if your date speaks loud, you speak loud back." Couples end up yelling at each other all night, so beware!

Begin to notice the male–female interaction in your working environment (and socially too). NVC can be a good cross-check against the grapevine, and it is often more reliable. Even if you're not in the "pick-up" business, you can pick up on when there is more electricity in the air than in the walls.

Travel NVC

Unfortunately, we cannot spend all (or more) of our time talking to the opposite sex. One of the common requirements of business life is traveling, which is often dreaded and is normally just endured. Traveling is also one of the least comfortable activities of business, ranking right down there with riding in an elevator and getting fired. Flying, for example, consists of a sorry series of events lowlighted by the flight itself.

In a typical trip, you arrive at the airport and park your car in one of the long-term parking facilities conveniently located in the next county. You hike across the lot to the shuttle bus waiting area. If it's summer, the shade is well past the seats in the lean-to. If it's winter, the enclosure is facing *into* the wind. You stand with a group of strangers (or sit, with the metal seat conveying the subfreezing temperature to your posterior) as the biting wind whips over the level parking lot. You bump into the luggage littering the waiting area and stay as far away from other people as possible.

The bus finally arrives, a remnant of the local mass-transit system that the mechanics couldn't revive. You battle your way up the stairs with your luggage, banging knees and bus alike. As the bus fills, you breathe a sigh of relief: there are few enough riders that you won't have to share a seat with anyone else. To make certain, you pile your travel equipment next to you before you sit down. Your nose curls as you smell the stale odors of thousands of travelers before you, mixed with the fumes of a decaying diesel.

The bus is well designed for your NVC needs. Most of the seats face the front, so no one has to look anyone else in the face and worry about immoral looking time. The last seats to fill are the ones facing each other in the front of the bus. The designers, understanding that passengers in these seats must put their eyes somewhere, thoughtfully provided overhead slots for advertisements so people could gaze in moral relaxation. When the bus finally begins its short trip, you notice that the passengers have spaced themselves out as far away from one another as possible.

You clatter off the bus at the airport and walk over to the sidewalk baggage attendant for your airline. You stand around with a group of strangers waiting to give your possessions to another stranger and pay him for the privilege of handling your belongings. You watch your bags sink down to a lower level on the ever present conveyor belt, always an unsettling feeling. As you walk away, you say the traveler's prayer, "Please let them be there when I arrive!"

Once inside the airport, you are assailed by visual and aural stimuli—chattering voices, echoing footsteps, and an array of displays and signs. People are scurrying about in a single-minded attempt to make their flight. You locate your carrier and join the first of several lines. No one traveling alone talks in this line. Talking is left to families or business associates who are familiar enough with the procedures to be relaxed. If you strike up a conversation with anyone, you are viewed as a cross between Jack the Ripper and Mr. Hyde. Reaching the ticket agent, you are greeted with the cold warmness generated by an intensive airline training program tempered from thousands of uncommunicative travelers. You answer the obligatory questions in an uncharacteristic monotone—"Fine," "Chicago," "Nonsmoking"—and go to the waiting area to find a seat that is not surrounded by women and children. You sit back and warily eye the other passengers, hoping to get a plane seat far away from the colicky infant in the next row. Your sense of territorial space has taken a terrible beating, but this is only a hint of things to come in the airplane.

You're no ordinary passenger. You know a few travel tricks. You wait to board until the last minute, avoiding the lines through the electronic detection equipment and entering the plane when the aisles are fairly empty. You walk past the first-class seats in envy (your company's too cheap to go 1-C) to your slot back in the cattle car. Looking up at the row letters and numbers ("Now is 'A' aisle or window?"), you find your seat with a sinking feeling. Sitting next to you is a bulky, sweating piece of beef with arms splayed out over the rests on either side. The poor young man in the window seat is staring fixedly out the window, pressed up against the cold inner wall in discomfort.

You stow your gear top and bottom and plop down, cursing the airplane gremlin who always crosses the belts so that you wind up sitting on them. You squirm in your seat, carefully trying not to touch the overflowing neighbor as you retrieve the proper ends on the correct sides and buckle in. You unconsciously mouth the chief attendant's preflight litany as you sink deeper into your shell of discomfort. Fortunately, your immense companion follows the unwritten rule of grabbing only half the armrest and gives you the back part. You take what you can and slip your elbow into the slot, leaning out into the aisle slightly to keep the proper space. You become almost blind to what is next to you to make up for the lack of distance.

Your territorial space sensibilities are now totally at war.

Like your fellow passengers, you bore inward to create an artificial privacy. The plane is quiet; few conversations between strangers start. The drink cart finally comes rolling up. The airline, quick to take advantage of your need to relax, offers a wide range of liquid desensitizers. You are only mildly aware of the cart as it thumps your shoulder going by. As the drinks are delivered by a teetering attendant leaning over your seat, you realize once more that the aisle seat can have its price if the help is clumsy. As you sip your soothing brew, you suddenly find a rear stuck into your face as the attendant delivers the orders to those across the way. It's just your luck that it is the wrong-sex rear, so there's nothing of interest to contemplate.

Next comes the meal, an airline's version of McDonald's au gratin. Eating on an airplane is something like trying to go to the bathroom with a broken leg in a half-bath with sand-finish walls or making a phone call from a booth containing fighting storks. Your elbows flash like the Three Musketeers battling the Evil Cardinal's men. Even if you have traveled in comfort so far, you now feel totally violated. The meal trays are finally carted off and you just begin to relax again when the back of the seat in front of you comes crashing toward your lap. The weary executive in front has decided on a snore-filled nap. You twitch as the beefsteak next door bumps your knee every minute or so. You finish the flight by rereading the airline's back-patting magazine, the *Rickenbacker Skymaster*, and the French version of the sickie bag instructions.

The flight comes to a merciful end with the jolt of a four-point landing (two landing gears twice). As the plane rocks to a rest, the passengers jump out of their seats even though there is no place to stand. It is better to stand hunched under the overhead storage compartment than remain another minute in the seat. You move forward while the Texas-born flight attendant plastically parrots, "Bah, bah, bah" as you file out. Thinking of the supersonic needle-nosed sound monsters, you muse, "No wonder people are willing to pay three times as much for a ride that is twice as fast!"

You step out of the entry tunnel into the open gate area, really relaxing for the first time since you left your car in the windy lot. It is time to prepare yourself for the baggage gauntlet and hope that your prayers were answered. You pass a bathroom, which reminds you of a not yet critical need (flying seems to do that). Preferring to go on the side of the road rather than in the terminal or on the airplane, you decide to wait. You arrive at the baggage area only to hear a disembodied incoherent voice bubble, "Baggage from flight eye sifteer is now arriving at carousel psst." Passengers space themselves out around the baggage belt, still conscious of the pummeling their territorial space needs have undergone. Just when you are beginning to worry that your bag never made the flight, it appears—lop-eared from having been bounced off the baggage train coming in from the ramp.

Lugging your suitcase through a terminal that looks like it is inhabited by the same people you just left, you examine the new easy-to-read international hieroglyphics that pass for direction signs. Mistakenly finding the rental car area, then the hotel limo desk, you finally locate the taxi stand. You feel a certain surge of power and sense of class as you give the experienced traveler's sign of wanting a cab, raising the hand up casually to say, "Here I am." Unfortunately, there is no one around to see your casually experienced sign; the stand is empty. When a taxi finally arrives, it doesn't even have a roof light or an ad on the rear bumper. The sign on the side says, "Bill's Ride 'n' Pride."

The driver is Bill himself and is usually one of two personalities: Bob Barker or Calvin Coolidge. (Occasionally you will get Hanna-Barbera's Mumbles the Dog, who talks constantly but can't be understood.) Bob Barker regales you with the fascinating aspects of his city and expounds on any current event he happens to think of. All that's required on your part is to stay upright in your seat. (In some cases, you can fall over if you keep your eyes open.) Calvin drives wordlessly but looks at you in the mirror throughout the trip just to keep you loose. The only sound that breaks the monotony is the steady and all too frequent thud of the meter eating up your expense allowance. When you arrive, you give Calvin a good tip because you don't know what to expect if you don't and "it's not worth it with these cabby types."

You enter the antiseptic hotel lobby filled with chairs no one ever seems to sit in and walk to the registration desk. The hotel clerk greets you warmly from behind an imperious counter and acknowledges your status by asking you to confirm that you are alive and independently wealthy. After the forms are signed and witnessed by a consultant with eidetic memory, the key is laid on the counter tantalizingly out of your reach, to be whisked away by that ever present faceless nonperson, the bellboy. (Why he's called a boy when he's often 60 years old and rooming in the VA hospital I'll never know.)

You now get to join the bellboy on a fun trip in the elevator. Your bellboy is nice, so he doesn't try to start a conversation on the way up. He knows you are mad enough at having to tip him to run an elevator and decipher the room-numbering system, which is well indicated with signs on each floor so you can stumble in tipsy and still find your way up. When you arrive, he performs other specialized functions such as unlocking the door, turning on the lights, opening the door to the bathroom to see if there is one, and holding out his hand. At this point in your day, you pay him anything to leave. For the first time since you walked away from your car, you are truly alone and can relax.

As you can see, traveling is one uncomfortable NVC situation after another. Even when I know what to expect, I find travel at least a bother and often downright unpleasant. The negative effects of travel are caused by the inability to adjust to a rapidly changing physical environment inhabited by strangers. The participants all become nonpeople because of the tremendous volume flowing through the system. As hard as the airlines try to personalize their service with nametags for their attendants, brightly designed terminal gates, and giveaway magazines, the impersonal nature of the effort remains.

You can now make your travel more pleasant by analyzing what has been happening to you from an NVC standpoint. Once you understand that the sanctity of your territorial space will be violated for the duration of the trip, you will be much happier. Once you steel yourself to doing business with an array of nondescript strangers (who regard you as a stranger too), you will be much friendlier. Once you start recognizing the NVC information that others are transmitting, you will be much more knowledgeable.

Be more observant in the terminal. When you pass a bank of phone booths, look at the various people sitting or standing and see if you can tell who they are talking to, the way you did with the executive in Chapter 1. If there are benches lining the walls or out in the open, notice how people sit at them. As with all seating arrangements, there are dominant and submissive positions. The person sitting submissively on one end of a bench is saying, "See, you can have the other end of the bench and we won't invade each other's space." The person sitting challengingly in the middle is saying, "I dare you to sit on either side of me where there's not enough space for us to be apart." I once sat that way on a bench near a baggage conveyor during the airlines' pre-Christmas rush. There wasn't a seat to be found in the terminal, yet no one asked me to move. At the end of half an hour, I had made my point and was beginning to feel guilty because of all the people standing. When I left, two people immediately sat down, one at each end of the bench.

On the airplane, watch how the attendants behave. I often get the feeling that they are mentally "slopping the trough." They serve with a machinelike formality that makes the McDonald's clerk repeating cry of "May I help someone?" sound like a marriage proposal. Because attendants have to reach so much, their center is rarely opened to the passengers. They are always facing down the aisle. In addition, the seated passenger is in the awkward position of having to look over and up to the attendant with the protruding headrest bulge at his or her neck. Consequently, eye contact is brief at best. When dealing with attendants, call them by name (last name) and maintain strong eye contact. It will do wonders for your service.

Be aware of the person sitting next to you. He or she is probably as unenthusiastic as you are about the trip. Play the armrest game to win. If you are sitting next to a "rest hog," wait until he or she moves an arm and grab the entire rest, then hold it out of spite until your arm falls off in petrification just to see what the passenger does to retaliate. You may as well have some fun. If you are next to a knee bumper, bring your tray down and start writing, your elbow waggling partially over your neighbor's lap. Change positions often. For your fellow passengers, it's like traveling with a two-year-old. Sigh or make funny noises with your mouth. If you are reading a book, even if it is *Differential Calculus*, laugh out loud every page or so, smiling and shaking your head. It will drive your seating partner crazy.

If the nonpeople next to you show potential, try to involve them in conversation. If they don't want to talk, you will soon find out. I find that most travelers welcome conversation. I've passed some of my most interesting hours seated next to strangers on an airplane. The chances are that the person next to you will welcome a respite from the impersonality of the trip. Watching NVC can make your trip more interesting. Using NVC to change what happens on the trip can make it more pleasurable. The choice is yours.

Restaurant NVC

Another common locale for business dealings is the restaurant. I always prefer to entertain out rather than at home because the environment can be so much better controlled. It never fails that when I've got that important client relaxed and enjoying himself in my living room, the toilet backs up all over the bathroom floor or the dog goes into labor. One time my automatic garage door opener broke with a guest's car inside the garage. It took me nearly 45 minutes to dismantle the attachment from the door to the track. Another nice feature about entertaining out is that you can create the impression of high living at very little cost. You can live in a dump and drive a rust box, but if you own one good outfit you can entertain in style and never lose any social status. The only real negative is that you are no longer able to eat in privacy.

Whenever people eat in public, they pretend they have suddenly gone deaf in order to create the illusion of privacy. Even though a conversation easily carries to the next table, no one shows the slightest reaction to what is being said next door. If a group is particularly loud and boisterous, the other diners will begin glaring their disapproval at the disruption of their illusion.

If you are the one making loud conversation, be careful of loose talk. I was eating lunch once with a group of people from my office when the topic turned to one of our clients. As the client's name was mentioned in a derogatory fashion, my friend Sam nudged me and nodded toward a man at the other table who suddenly looked as if he had grown rabbit ears. He could have been an extra in the E.F. Hutton commercial ("When E.F. Hutton talks, people listen"). There was no way to warn the other salesman without alerting the interested listener, so we quickly shifted the conversation to another subject. On the way out we told the others what had happened and discussed the dangers of loose talk. It turned out that the salesman had been overheard by his customer's immediate superior who relayed the comment directly to the customer.

People often have a hard time pretending not to be listening. I once ate lunch in a customer's cafeteria and eavesdropped on the conversation next to me. A group of executives were reminiscing about a friend who had been transferred. The one story I had the worst trouble "ignoring" concerned an unusual experience this friend had at a downtown motel in a large city. He slept in the nude out of habit and, having a room to himself, saw no reason to change. Getting up in the middle of the night, he staggered to what he thought was the bathroom door, walked in, and turned around to relieve himself. What he saw shocked him. He was standing out in the brightly lit hall absolutely naked and locked out of his room.

At that point, many of us would have curled up into a fetal ball and started crying. This executive was famous for his iron will and control of every situation. Searching the deserted hall, he found an old newspaper and wrapped it around him, tearing it to hold together and leave his arms free. His modesty taken care of, he continued to search the hall for anything else that would be of help. Finding nothing, he resigned himself to going down to the lobby and getting a bellhop with a passkey. In triumph, he found a house phone in the elevator lobby on his floor and called the front desk. The phone was answered by a laughing room clerk who listened to the story patiently, then commented, "I know. We've been watching you on the security cameras for about 15 minutes now. A bellhop is on his way."

The table next to me was in an uproar as the executives retold their favorite story. I was sitting next to them, twitching up and down in my chair, choking on my food, and trying to remain stoically deaf. What made it worse was that they saw I was laughing and began to watch me pretend I wasn't listening.

The next time you are in a restaurant, observe the other

diners as they silently "interact" with their neighbors. People never really eat alone; they merely don't have anyone at their table to talk to.

Restaurant owners understand this privacy problem and arrange their facilities to minimize it. The first thing they do is darken the room. Just as a theater goes dark to allow you to lose track of the people sitting next to you, so the restaurant lowers its lights to enhance the illusion of privacy. It can be overdone, though. Some places are lit so dimly that you feel as if you are eating in a submarine con at night. You stumble through your food in relative secrecy and walk out into the bright daylight snowblind for five minutes. The best level of lighting is one that is as low as possible without making customers say, "Boy, it's sure dark in here!"

Some restaurant owners try to minimize rear fear in their layouts. The local quicky steak factory (I refuse to call it a restaurant) recently added about two miles of partitions to its dining room. I came off the line and felt like a rat starting the maze. At the end, if I was successful, I would be rewarded with an empty table. Even though the dividers eliminated most of the eye contact between tables, they did little to create a feeling of privacy. The tables had been jammed up next to the partitions to preserve the restaurant's seating capacity. Without the partitions, the tables had at least been several feet apart. Now the customers were so close that even a whisper carried past the chest-high divider. Partitions can't maintain sound privacy; they can only create physical separation.

The most common approach to sound privacy is to mask the restaurant sounds with music. Since restaurant owners do not want to waste expensive space on making people comfortable, they substitute an aural potpourri that acts like a pimple coverup. It doesn't make the blemish go away; it just makes it less noticeable. After several minutes, our marvelous brain adjusts itself to tune out all the nonessential sounds and begins to think there really is "quiet"—that is, except for the kitchen.

Wherever I go I seem to end up next to and facing the kitchen. In the event that area is mysteriously full, I am put next to the serving area, replete with spare supplies and dirty dishes. It amazes me that the same restaurant displaying Louis XV antiques will have wide swinging doors that show brief glimpses of sweating cooks retrieving half-done meat from the floor, throwing globs of salad into a bowl, and chewing on their nails. And the requisite for most kitchen help is that they be able to yell like Foghorn Leghorn, so that diners eating in elegant surroundings and atmosphere (defined as old furniture, darkness, and no Muzak franchise) hear snatches of kitchen conversation wafting past the swinging doors. Such exposure to the mechanics of feeding people can spoil even the most careful of efforts in the dining area.

Another factor that destroys privacy is people watching us eat. Many times, the worst offenders are the help. Some of the fancier restaurants will assign a busboy to each table so that the ashtray is whisked away while the ash is still drifting downward. The waiter will hover nearby looking for the merest flicker of an eyebrow or a head poised to rotate in search. This type of service can be annoying at best and stifling at worst. I may be oversensitive to it, but ever since I waited on tables in my college days I haven't been able to view restaurant employees as nonpeople. (My ears did not become plugged the minute my uniform went on, though. Much like standing in the elevator, I frequently heard interesting bits of conversation, mostly between male and female diners.) I don't enjoy a meal when I know each chew is being monitored by two or more sets of eager eyes.

Some restaurants compound the problem by locating the waiting area next to the dining room. This way, the clatter of hungry patrons looking at you like children peering through a pet store window becomes part of your "dining experience." I wonder if owners do this on purpose to speed the turnover, or if they are just careless. On a crowded weekend, you can feel like a depositer withdrawing savings during a bank run under the panicky eyes of those hoping to find money left when they get to the window. I would rather eat in the kitchen than near the reservations desk, hearing the poor hostess squeeze through the crowd and periodically shout, "Johnson party of two? Johnson party of two?"

If feeling like stuffed customer under glass isn't enough to make you speed through your meal, sitting on restaurant furniture probably will. A New York City diner called in a management consultant to help speed its turnover of lunchtime patrons, who tended to linger over their meals. The consultant suggested calling in an orthopedist to solve the problem. The owner took the advice, hired the doctor, followed the doctor's recommendations, and immediately nearly tripled the lunchtime business. What the doctor did was to redesign the seats so that they were comfortable for only about 20 minutes, the average eating time. Early arrivals cleared out before the noon rush and the noon arrivals were finished in time for a new group at 12:30.

In the better restaurants I have visited, comfortable sitting time usually ranges from 60 to 90 minutes. After that, the bottom begins telling the stomach that no matter how good the food and drinks are, it is leaving. Most restaurants prefer tables that are supported in the middle by a single pillar with a wide base. The pillar and base greatly restrict the legroom underneath the table, so that it is impossible for people over 5'8" to stretch out. An hour sitting upright or with the legs bent back under a chair is about all most people can endure before having to stand up. A trip to the bathroom is normally the only respite—unless you are leaving. The normal four-legged table support provides much more leg space, although it does reduce the seating options. (It also stops all those "excuse me's" generated when you step on the base thinking it is someone's foot.)

If you simply want to entertain in a restaurant, one with strong drinks and a quick bar is probably your best choice. If you hope to transact some business during the meal, you should follow several rules. Unless you plan to linger at your table, you had better complete most of your conversation before the food arrives. Once everyone starts eating, the conversation will come to a standstill. Another good reason to get down to business early is that before-dinner drinks dull things a bit. If you need the relaxation, fine. If you don't, you're going to get it anyway. After dinner, the body begins to slow down in accordance with nature's plan. The stomach steals blood from the brain for the digestive process. The combination of booze dumped into an empty stomach and digesting food makes Jack a pretty dull boy. Hit your topics while everyone is still mentally present.

Choose the restaurant with care by asking yourself the following questions:

1. Does it have barely adequate lighting for eating?
2. Does it have sight privacy from neighbors? help? bar patrons? people waiting?
3. Is there acceptable sound privacy for the subject matter to be discussed?
4. Can you be assured of a table away from the kitchen, serving area, busboy station, and reservations desk?
5. Is the help competent but not zealous?
6. Is the furniture comfortable for the length of time you plan to spend there?

Remember that people's impression of a restaurant is more often a result of the time they had there than of how good the food was. So only when all the above questions are answered satisfactorily should you worry about the food. Quality will often vary from dish to dish, night to night, and opinion to opinion. As the above questions suggest, you should never plan an important evening around a restaurant you have never been in. From an NVC standpoint, good restaurants are hard to find, so begin to analyze your favorites and any new places you encounter. It's time you got more out of a meal than a full belly.

Shopping NVC

I am always put off by the customer chaser masquerading as a clerk who says, "May I help you?" and then stands there while you look at the goods. I feel like Linus staring at Snoopy when he is playing vulture up in the tree by his house. I want to grab whatever I am looking at in one arm and start sucking my thumb. Salespeople don't really want to stand and watch customers either, or else they wouldn't ask a question that invites a "no." They're like children who come to your door saying, "You wouldn't really want any seeds today, would you?" When you agree, you can see the relief on the kid's faces as they begin to muster enough courage to go to the next house.

The problem, once again, is our difficulty in dealing with strangers. The rules of moral looking time tell us that we shouldn't be watched, yet the clerk wants to be of help (or stay close enough to make certain we don't cart anything off). We are nonpeople to each other, immediately placed under the headings of clerk and customer. Most of the conversation is very plastic, from the "May I help you?" to "No thank you, I'm just looking," to "Thank you and come again" at the end of the sale.

One retail store manager told me that the best way to break this pattern is to greet the customers as they come into the store. Instead of walking up to them after they have entered the store and asking the "help you" question, his clerks meet each customer at the door with a "Good morning" or "Isn't it a nice day?" They then *leave the customer alone* for several minutes, returning only when it is apparent the customer is looking for a specific item or needs some help. At this point, the clerks comment about the item or ask if they can be of assistance.

The manager also mentioned that the most important employee in the store is the cashier. Many stores make the mistake of placing an inexperienced clerk at the register or handling this step as a mass-production line. The position should be reserved for the brightest and most cheerful personality on the staff. The last person the customer deals with is the cashier. As the old saying goes, "You can have a bad meeting, but make sure the coffee's good so people can at least leave with a pleasant taste in their mouth." The cashier can ensure that any complaints are brought to the surface and that the customer leaves with a positive feeling.

The best retail stores have clerks who know how to be personal with customers. I once went with my wife to buy a dressy winter coat. We ended up in a small specialty shop that, in addition to women's fashions, sold the various antiques that made up the decor. The saleswoman, a native of Israel who was living in the United States, showed us how effective the personal approach could be. She introduced herself and within the first few minutes of conversation gently probed for all sorts of background information. She soon knew how many children we had, where we lived, and what I did for a living, and was getting a good idea of our personalities as my wife and I talked about coats. While my wife was in the back of the store looking at collars, the security guard in the front started discussing sports with me. My wife and I ended up spending nearly 90 minutes in the store, and by that time we were considering buying a hall tree, a cuckoo clock, and an English hunting horn, thanks to the skillful guidance of the saleswoman.

Managing to pin my right hand before it could get to my wallet, I began to think about what had been going on. I realized that the saleswoman and the guard had been treating us as friends, and that we felt incredibly comfortable with them. They had burst through the artificial barriers people erect for strangers, and in doing so had eliminated their own. We did buy the coat, and I'm sure we will shop in the store again, because at no time did we feel like the employees were hovering over us.

A local jewelry firm uses a somewhat different approach to break down normal sales barriers. All its stores are designed with the display cases about desk high. The stores are adequately staffed and equipped with small padded stools. When you stop at a counter to examine a piece, the clerk invites you to sit down and then unlocks the display case. (Even though you can't reach in, the lock is a good touch. "It must be valuable, it's locked.") This is an excellent selling approach, because it forces the customer to relax and gives the clerk more time to sell. Once customers are off their feet, they tend to stay a while. The clerks can service more than one customer at a time as long as they leave no more than one piece out at a time. Seated customers don't seem to mind being left alone as much as standing customers do. The cleverest part of the approach, though, is the use of stools rather than chairs. The stools are designed so that customers can take their weight off their feet, but they are not really comfortable. Like the seats in the New York diner, the stools ensure that turnover doesn't suffer by letting customers feel too much at ease.

Getting customers out of a store isn't really a major concern. Every retail store would love to have that problem. The important chore is to get them *into* the store. This is often done nonverbally with displays that customers see when walking by. The display must somehow say, "Buy me!" It must immediately catch the eye, and if the store is in a shopping center, it must be distinctive from other windows.

Most display windows are elevated so that the merchandise is at eye level. Within the store, goods placed on the upper shelves will sell better than those on the lower shelves. Just as we will write a phone number on the telephone booth wall at eye level, so we notice more when we don't have to look up or down. An old merchandising maxim states that "85 percent of the buy is in the eye." If a display can't catch the eye, it won't catch the sale.

We are also attracted by color. Displays using banners are consistently effective. Christmas windows are easy to do because the colors are bright and garish. Green mice in red stocking caps are perfectly acceptable at this time of year. Good displays involve the observer, encouraging shoppers to mentally put themselves into the scene. In fabrics, for example, where the goods anticipate the seasons by three to four months, a winter window will show a colorful spring scene, or a sunny day at the beach.

Once customers have been lured into the store by the display, advertising, or previous experience, the goal is to make them walk through the entire store. The layout can be cleverly designed to increase store touring. For example, the most expensive goods are usually placed in the front of the store. Most people will not want to spend that much money, but they will be impressed with the quality of the store and its merchandise. They will begin to work their way backward in search of more reasonably priced articles. The rear of the store is the best location for items in greatest demand. Display goods are placed here, because they will sell better than items not on display.

Specialty items should also be in the rear. For example, a fabric store that specializes in hard-to-find drapery material keeps these goods in the floor area farthest from the door. The manager explains, "We're noted for our fine selection of drapery goods, so there's no reason to try to draw people in with a display or to place the goods up front where they are more likely to be seen. My customers will go wherever the goods are located. If I had a basement in the store, I'd put the drapery goods there."

Sale goods require a different approach. Sale items are sometimes placed in the rear of the store, but more often they are spread out over the sales floor. Large discount stores and department stores often send out weekend flyers showing a wide range of goods. If you bought every item in the flyer, you would have to make a complete circuit of the store. These stores also move customers around with nightly specials announced on the PA system. Typically, the store first announces a temporary special in the rear of the store, then announces further short-term sale items located in the opposite corners. The announcement might blare out, "KC Store shoppers, there's a puce-light special over in the Sweatsocks Department. You can get pink argyle ankle wraps for $2.95 for the next ten minutes only." The announcer then cleverly never tells you exactly where the Sweatsocks Department is so that you have to wander around the store a bit. Store directories are usually vague for the same reason.

Another technique to make customers tour the store is to separate the entrance and exit areas. The entrance has a one-way gate so that customers cannot leave the way they came in. The only path out of the store is through the exit lanes, which are on a different wall from the entrance. Stores are also designed to make movement from floor to floor difficult. The elevators are buried in the back of some little-traveled department such as Scouting Clothes and labeled so that you can't see them from more than 20 feet away looking straight ahead. (This is frequently true of bathrooms too.) Escalators are often arranged so that you have to walk around to the other side to continue your way up or down. You are never allowed to walk adjacent to the elevator bank; your path is usually cut off by some department. Indirect pathways guide you past a number of the most interesting departments, such as women's sportswear and shoes. The specialty departments, where most purchases are planned, not impulse, are always located near the outside walls away from the escalators.

Departments are also arranged to fit customers' shopping patterns. Men's and women's departments are placed next to each other, so that if husbands become bored shopping with their wives (or vice versa), they can drift over to something that attracts their interest. For example, the local Target store places hardware next to housewares, and calculators and sporting goods next to cosmetics. All impulse items are placed near the checkout counters or the exit walkway (with a security guard stationed there to reduce shoplifting). All these techniques are designed to get you into other parts of the store.

Within the departments, there are many nonverbal tricks to help you make the decision to buy. One of them—called "pyramiding" in the liquor industry or "stack and sell" in the appliance industry—involves displaying an enormous number of items in a "sculptured" pile. The nonverbal message to many shoppers is that if the store had enough confidence to buy in such quantity, the items must be good. Another approach is to lay a large number of items directly on the floor, with a sign showing only the price. The informal display and lack of promotional hoopla suggest to the customer that the store is offering the items at a good price in order to get rid of them.

The layout within a department is also carefully planned to encourage you to buy. Good display space is never wasted on staple merchandise. Standard best-sellers can be relegated to the walls or placed on lower shelves, since these items do not have to be seen to be bought. In a grocery store, for example, people will go out of their way to find staple items such as soups and canned fruits. The ends of the aisles in any store are prime promotional spaces, because they are high-traffic areas. Customers pass them going up and down the aisles *and* walking from department to department. The most attractive, unusual, or colorful goods are placed here to lure customers over for a closer look. If a department does not have a particularly display-worthy group of goods, or if its merchandise is fairly stable (for example, small appliances), the goods are shuffled from location to location every week so that it appears, to regular customers, that new merchandise has been brought in.

Certain methods of display attract our attention. An executive for an appliance distributor told me that TVs are often displayed incorrectly. They should all be tuned to the same channel and left running with the sound off. As customers walk by the appliance department, they see a whole wall of images in synchronized motion, like a TV screen as seen through the lens of a fly.

Motion is the ideal attention getter. Paper flutters from the vent of an air conditioner. A humidifier runs off a clear plastic tank filled with goldfish; the blown moisture collects on a glass pane and is funneled into the tank below. All the clocks in the home furnishings section are set at a different time so that something is chiming, bonging, or cuckooing every few minutes. In shopping centers automobiles are displayed rotating on a turntable. The sign above the bank spins hypnotically, blinking time and temperature alternately.

Touch is another important attention getter. One of the advantages of running a TV with no sound is that a customer must touch the set to try it out. Once the customer adjusts the sound, a psychological barrier has crumbled and a strange sense of ownership begins to grow. You may pass by a car you test-drove once and still think of it as "your" car. You will search a counter for a ring you tried on several months ago before you look at the other items.

One very successful pet store owner depended heavily on touch in selling. Whenever a man and his son came in "just to look," he would leave them alone, watching the boy's eyes. When the boy spotted a pet, the owner would walk up and ask the father if he could help. The father would reply, "We were just thinking about getting a dog and wanted to see what you had." The owner would stride over to the puppy the boy was watching, get the dog, and hand it to the boy. He told me, "Once I get that puppy in the boy's arms, I'm home free. Most puppies will lick anything that moves. So there's the boy, with a squirming and licking puppy in his arms, looking at his father imploringly. It's almost impossible to resist. If the father is still unsure, I make *him* take the dog out of the boy's arms. I don't let him get away with, 'Now give the man the dog.' The boy glares at his dad and the puppy gets a shot at the father. If I can't close the sale 90 percent of the time when I let both people handle the animal, I'm in the wrong business."

Summary

A wealth of nonverbal information is being transmitted, received, and acted upon in almost every social situation. Observe and enjoy watching men and women play the "oldest game in the world." Be aware of the nonverbal environment when you travel and dine out. The next time you go shopping, notice which techniques the store is using to urge you to make the "buy" decision. There's an enormous amount of body business in social business.

8

Developing an Effective Voice

As we saw in Chapter 1, words—the actual content of our messages—contribute only 10 percent to the communication of attitudes. In Chapters 2 through 7 we examined body movements and positions, which comprise 60 percent of attitude communication. It's now time to examine the remaining 30 percent: *voice.*

Voice is more important than many of us realize. Nixon found out that there was an immense difference between reading a transcript of a conversation and hearing a tape recording of the voices. We aren't aware of listening to a good voice because it gets the job done without calling attention to itself. Only when a voice is ineffective do we notice it. A good example is the "common person" or "celebrity" TV commercial. An immaculately dressed housewife "casually" being interviewed in a laundromat nervously drones, "I love new Green Sheen detergent. Since I started using it, my husband bought me a mink coat because he was so pleased with his underwear." Baseball star Stan Musial gallantly tries to promote the features of a shock absorber in a conversation with a sports announcer on radio. Musial is as out of the announcers' league as the announcer would be trying to take batting practice with "The Man" in an old-timer's game.

Some people make a living from their voice. Mel Blanc, the

actor who played Jack Benny's violin teacher and the Mexican visitor Si ("Sie? See, Sie!"), was the voice behind all the Warner Brothers cartoon characters. (In the movie *Bugs Bunny Superstar*, he talks about some of the voices he was asked to do. The most difficult was having to portray an English horse neighing.) Some actors have very effective voices for commercials. Paul Burke, William Conrad, James Garner, and David Janssen appear both on and off camera in many current TV commercials. The reason they are so much in demand is that they can control one of the most accurate indicators of feelings: their voice.

I use an exercise in my classes to illustrate the many meanings we can give one word with our voice. I invite three students to the front of the room and give them each a card with "Quiet" written on it, along with a description of how the word is to be said:

"Quiet!" (Be quiet!)
"Quiet?" (Is it finally quiet?)
"Quiet." (Sigh. At last it's quiet.)

The class has no trouble identifying the three different meanings of the word.

In addition to feelings, voice can indicate when we are lying. Inventor Allen Bell has developed a device that can determine whether people are telling the truth by analyzing their voice. Unlike the polygraph, the device does not have to be attached to the person. It can analyze tapes, TV transmissions, or phone conversations. Called the psychological stress evaluator (PSE), it measures certain tremors in the voice that are undetectable to the human ear. The voice produces a tremor at the rate of 8 to 14 cycles per second. When a person tells the truth, the muscles that control the voice are relaxed and produce a certain pattern. When a person lies, the effort creates stress and the pattern is altered. We seem to have no control over this process.

Bell first tested the PSE on the TV show *To Tell the Truth* (where three contestants claim to be the same person and the panel must determine which one is not lying). Bell claims the PSE was correct 95 percent of the time. In another trial, three PSE operators analyzed the statements of John Dean and John Mitchell in the televised Watergate hearings. Mitchell showed stress at several points in his testimony—for example, when he said he didn't think Richard Nixon had known about the break-in or cover-up. Dean did not show any stress. As we all know, history proved Dean right and Mitchell wrong.

Dale Carnegie, in his book *How to Develop Self-Confidence and Influence People by Public Speaking,* tells us that "we are evaluated and classified by four things in this world: by what we do, by how we look, by what we say, and by how we say it." You can improve "how you say it" by working on your voice. The muscles of the larynx can be strengthened and toned with practice.

When I first started consulting, I found it difficult to conduct a full day's class without losing my voice. I gradually strengthened my voice so I could do several days in a row with no problem. Getting greedy, I scheduled four days in succession one winter, two in Kansas City and two in St. Louis. Kansas City was in the throes of an ice storm, with the temperature hovering near zero. I was given a classroom next to the heating pipes, which banged with strain throughout the session. After two days of shouting over the pipes, I felt as if my throat had been dragged behind a horse, and I still had two days to go! In St. Louis, blessed with a quiet classroom, I managed to finish the two sessions without incident by using every technique I knew to project my voice with a minimum of effort. You too can develop control of your voice for strength, endurance, and effective public speaking.

Voice Control

We learn to control our voice at a very early age. Newborn babies can make thousands of separate and distinct sounds, but by the age of six months their range of sounds is usually restricted to their native language. English has approximately 50 sounds, each taking nearly .15 second. These sounds are made by a combination of breathing, phonation, resonance, and articulation.

Normal *breathing* is a regular cycle of inhalation and exhalation every three to five seconds. When we intend to speak, we inhale more quickly, then exhale in a controlled manner. Anyone who has played a wind instrument knows the importance of the diaphragm in good breath control. The diaphragm is a muscle between the chest cavity and the stomach. It expands, making more room in the chest cavity for air, and contracts, forcing air outward. Trumpeter Raphael Mendez had such breath control and mastery of his instrument that he could play *Flight of the Bumblebee* through twice on a single breath!

The air is passed into the windpipe and then the larnyx for *phonation*. Housed at the point of the Adam's apple are two vocal folds that produce sound. They are brought together and are set vibrating by the outgoing air. A set of incredibly complex muscles changes the length, mass, elasticity, and hardness of the folds to produce variations in pitch and loudness. The vibrating air is next passed to the nasal passages, throat, and mouth cavities to create resonance. This is similar to the function of the sound box of a speaker in a stereo system. The nasal passages and mouth cavities are of different sizes and shapes and are lined with membranes of different degrees of firmness and moisture content. The size and shape of most of these passages and cavities can be adjusted to modify the voice.

The final step in the speech process is *articulation*. We articulate by positioning our tongue, teeth, and lips properly for each sound. Many of us might say the last sentence, "We articalate by posishning are ton, teethe, and libs proply for eedge soun." This is simply being lazy with our verbal tools. One of the advantages of singing is that it teaches people to overarticulate sounds so that the audience will understand their lyrics. This discipline can carry over into everyday speech.

Dale Carnegie relates the story of a down-on-his-luck Englishman who was stranded in the United States with no money. He went for an interview in a worn suit and scruffy shoes, the only clothes he had. The interviewer was captivated by the man's mastery of the language. Despite his ragged appearance, his speech set him apart as someone special. Although the interviewer didn't hire the Englishman, he arranged for an interview with a business associate who did. By properly controlling your voice, you may affect people the same way.

Voice Codes

Certain sounds, like certain gestures, have universal meaning:

"Tsk! Tsk!"	Disapproval
Wolf whistle	Appreciation
"Augh!"	Frustration (Charlie Brown's cry when Lucy yanks the football away)
"Oops!"	Chagrin (whenever I miss a high pass in basketball I call it an "Alley Oops" play)
Bronx cheer	Derision
"Yea!"	Cheer; approval
Boo! (whistle in Europe)	Displeasure
"Ow! Ouch!"	Pain
Snort	Scorn
Laugh	Humor

Some words function solely as sound imitators—for example, *bang, pop, pow, wham, bop, boom, crash, thud, swish, swirl.* As small children, we used to orchestrate our play with appropriate sound effects from our all-purpose vocal noisemaker. Somehow as adults, we lose this versatility and uninhibitedness in using our voice. We become expressive only when we are emotional and can seldom rise to the occasion on purpose.

The more thought we give to our speech, the less expressive we become. With nervousness and anxiety, we increase our reliance on nonspeech sounds, called *nonfluencies.* The most common of these is the *er-ah-um-uh* family of sounds. When we are making a difficult speech, we unconsciously increase these sounds to give ourselves more thinking time. "Well, ah, there are several different approaches to busing in the large cities which rather, er, affect student performance."

Nonfluencies are often used to keep control of a conversation. As long as there is sound coming out of someone's mouth, it is impossible to say something without seeming to interrupt. Frequently, people will indicate that they wish to continue speaking by making one of these sounds while giving other NVC signs of conversation: head up, eye contact broken, the posture unchanged. A new salesperson trying to make all the sales points before the customer interrupts will try this.

We sometimes let meaningless phrases intrude into our speech. "Ya know" seems to be one of the most popular, particularly among young people and recent school graduates. "Well, ya know, engineers had to take nearly 18 hours a semester, ya know, so it was a lot harder to get out in four years than with another major. Ya know what I mean?" "Ya know" is one of the most insidious of nonfluencies. It's like yawning: once one person starts it, everyone is doing it. I once had a sales partner who was deeply into the "ya know" habit. In a few weeks, I said it as much as he did, as did our support reps and our boss.

Some people interject strange noises into their speech. One of my instructors in school would sip on his upper bridge as he breathed in. Another instructor had a strange "dh" sound that interrupted his sentences. "The next topic we'll cover, dh, is managerial planning." As we listen, we inject nonword verbal signals when we wish to speak. We clear our throat or "harumph" when we have something to say. We also clear our throat if we are getting into a sensitive area of conversation. "Did you have a nice time after the office party, Rhonda?" "Well, ahem, I did stay late and had a few drinks." In my classes I sometime have the students list and then read some of their long-term personal goals. They often read the more innocuous ones first, then signal the important ones coming up with an "ahem."

Other types of nonfluencies are repetition and omission. Repitition can take the form of a stutter or a repeated word. Porky Pig ends each cartoon with "Th-th-th-that's all, folks!" Or we may repeat a word: "I hope you can see—see what I mean." Sometimes we may repeat part of a sentence: "It seems that—it seems that there is no alternative." We can also omit part of a word, a full word, or an end of a sentence. Porky next stutters, "Let's go to di-di-di-di—supper." You may state, "It doesn't seem fair I should have to go!" Someone may reply, "The reason . . . you'll just have to."

Another type of nonfluency is the tongue slip. I once told a class I completed a project in "one swell foop." A student told me, "I haven't had much term this time." (I'm still amazed that no one has complained about cartoonist Gary Trudeau's rock star Jimmy Thudpucker in the Doonesbury comic strip.)

If you have a large number of nonfluencies in your speech, you are definitely hurting your credibility and persuasiveness. The problem with eliminating them is that like most people you are probably unaware of the habit, much as I was with the "ya know" pattern I picked up from my sales partner. What you can do is to set up your own biofeedback on nonfluencies. The brain is a closed-loop system. It can send control signals but depends on feedback from the controlled organs to make corrections. Researchers have found that the brain can control certain bodily functions that were once thought to be uncontrollable. For example, machines have been designed to provide feedback on blood pressure. A light blinking in time to a beep that corresponds to a person's blood pressure can be used to teach the brain to lower the readings.

The biofeedback system I designed to rid myself of nonfluencies revolved around my family. Every time I said "ya know" at home, my wife would quietly say my name.

"Well, Sue, it seems that, ya know—"

"Ken."

"Okay, it seems that Bill is going to be a hard man to convince, ya know?"

"Ken."

The mention of my name was enough to make me consciously aware of the habit. At first, my wife seemed to be doing nothing but saying my name every time I spoke. Even though I didn't have this "service" at work, I managed to rid myself of "ya know" in about three weeks. I then went to my partner and suggested he let me do the same for him. Although his dependence on the phrase was much more ingrained than mine, he too "cured" himself within a few weeks. Don't be afraid to enlist coworkers or customers in your biofeedback program. I've seen whole offices embark on "ya know-icide." It becomes particularly effective if you have to put a nickel or dime into the "ya know" box every time you use the phrase. Some groups have enjoyed a heavily funded "ya know" party from their fines.

Once you have reduced your nonfluencies, look for them to

creep back as you suffer withdrawal symptoms during pauses in your speech. Much like an ex-smoker wanting that after-coffee cigarette, you will want to fill up those gaps in your conversation with a sound, any sound. Tell your biofeedback partner to keep monitoring your speech for any irregularities. Once you have eliminated these undesirable speech patterns you can begin to develop good voice characteristics.

Qualities of Voice

The first voice quality is *pitch*. Every voice has a base pitch, usually described as high ("Hi, there, I'm Glen Campbell") to deep (William Conrad as radio's Matt Dillon). Our pitch changes direction with different types of sentences. Statements end with a drop in pitch and questions end with a rise in pitch. Say, "You've been working here for 12 years" as a statement and a question. One is a simple acknowledgment of fact; the other expresses disbelief that someone has 12 years of experience. The range of our pitch can be narrow or wide. Most Clint Eastwood characters use a monotone with little pitch variation; Radio's Great Gildersleeve used excessive pitch variation for a humorous effect.

Voice pitch can also be thin, tense, or throaty. A tense voice, produced by tightening the throat, is particularly difficult to listen to. I once heard a preacher who deliberately used a tense public-speaking voice in an effort to speak louder. After the first ten minutes of his sermon, the parishioners began to feel a tickle in their throat. Coughs of discomfort echoed through the sanctuary in sympathy for the minister's throat. Toward the end of the sermon, the listeners were offering a chorus of unconscious coughs and throat clearings in empathetic pain. The preacher was trying to speak louder in the wrong way.

Volume is the second voice quality. Varying volume to emphasize certain words is extremely useful in controlling meaning. Read the sentences below, saying the italicized words louder, and note the changes in meaning:

I should mow the front lawn. (I should do it rather than you.)

I *should* mow the front lawn. (I should mow rather than do something else.)

I should mow the *front* lawn. (I should mow the front rather than the back lawn.)

We can even manipulate what people hear by the way we say something. In my classes I use a collection of puzzles that I call a Misdirection Quiz to illustrate how the voice can control listeners. Two samples read:

1. How many animals of each species did Moses take aboard the ark?
2. When in history did California begin with a "c" and end with an "e"?

When I *say* them, though, I emphasize the following words (again shown in italics):

1. How many animals *of each species* did Moses take aboard the *ark?*
2. When in history did California *begin* with a "c" and *end* with an "e"?

As old as the Moses riddle is, nearly two-thirds of the class will miss it. One answer is, of course, that Moses never had an ark. The poor fellow, every time he tried to do something with water, it went bad on him or it dried up. Noah was the ark expert. The California riddle is tricky, and no one in my classes ever solves it. The answer is "always." Reread the sentence aloud, putting emphasis in this manner:

When in history did *California* begin with a *c* (pause) and *end* with an *e*?

California has always begun with a *C*, and *end* has always begun with an *e*. By changing the volume of your voice, you focused attention away from the alternate meaning of the sentence.

Volume is a good indicator of emotional intensity. Loud people are often thought to be forceful and aggressive. Have you ever tried to fight in a whisper? Right after we were married, my wife and I lived in a typical college matchbox apartment with paper-thin walls. Everyone could hear what the neighbors were doing and saying, particularly through the bathroom. We learned to argue in a forceful, angry whisper that more often than not resulted in our breaking up as we showed violent body language signs with whispering voices. When we moved to a duplex with greater sound privacy, we had a terrible time learning to argue in a loud voice. When we did, though, our disagreements were much more satisfying.

The proper way to produce volume is not to work harder, like the preacher, but to work more effectively. This comes as a result using the diaphragm properly. You don't have to run a large amount of air past your vocal cords to be loud. This makes you sound breathy, like a bubblehead sharing personal secrets with the world. You should push the air firmly out of your lungs with your diaphragm. My trumpet teacher would suddenly poke me there while I was playing a passage. If my diaphragm was pushing properly, I would make a slight gulp. If I was shoving air incorrectly through the horn, the gulp would become a blurp.

You can tell if you are using proper breath control with this experiment. As you speak loudly, loosely cover your mouth with your hand. If the sound is almost entirely muffled, you are too breathy. If the sound is only partially muffled, your diaphragm is pushing properly. Another test is to speak loudly without blowing out a match held several inches from your mouth. Volume is properly made with the larynx, a muscle that you can strengthen for louder and more sustained speech.

The third voice quality is *resonance*. Without it, the fullness of a resonant tone, the voice takes on a nasal quality that Dr. Bill Beeners of the Princeton speech department calls "the loveless twang."

Your resonant passages can be blocked by a cold or congestion. In our family, the proof of whether you had a cold was how you said "Pat Boone." If it came out "Bad Bood," you had a cold. You can consciously block off your resonant passages if you wish. Scuba divers learn to do this simply for survival. Most people breathe through their mouth and nose simultaneously out of habit. Under water without a facemask, this leads to choking and eventually drowning. So a diver is able to close off the nose when necessary.

As a hay fever sufferer, I often ran into the problem of having to give speeches when I was congested. I knew I sounded blocked a good portion of the time, especially in the summer. To solve this problem, I practiced my presentation on a tape recorder, using the scuba-diving trick to teach myself to speak without nasality.

When you have a cold, or if your voice sounds as if it is coming out of your adenoids, try one of the following techniques to improve your vocal image. First, speak more slowly and over-enunciate. I used to speak at normal speed or even faster when I was congested, because I tended to mumble with lack of resonance. When I felt I was speaking ridiculously slow and enunciating as if I were a diction teacher, my voice sounded much more normal. Second, let the pitch of your voice play a more important role in your speech. Raise your base pitch a tone or two and increase your pitch range. This will help restore some of the expressiveness to your voice and will draw attention away from your clogged sinuses.

The final voice quality is *tempo*. We can speak quickly or slowly, fluidly or with hesitation. At one time or another in our careers, we have all been around the machine-gun talker. One of my favorite examples is James Cagney in the 1961 movie *One, Two, Three*. In this sophisticated Billy Wilder comedy, Cagney played a Coca-Cola executive in West Germany who continually spewed out numbered instructions to his subordinates. The pace is so fast that you must listen carefully to catch all the one-liners.

Radio comedians Bob and Ray have a routine where they parody *slow* speech with an interview of the head of a national slow-talking society. The "slow talker" speaks at the rate of about 30 to 40 words per minute instead of the normal 150 words per minute. As the conversation progresses, the interviewer becomes more and more impatient, finally shifting in his chair in agony as he waits for the next word to drop. In my classes, I've found that speaking this slowly is third only to running my fingernails across the blackboard and using squeaky felt tip markers in irritating the students.

Fluid, continuous speech is best illustrated by those TV hucksters who do a one-minute commercial without a breath. Usually they are selling something like the Fed 'n' Shredder, which "dices, splices, slices, spices, and ices nices twices. It will size, disguise, revise, resize, liquidize, gourmandize, oxidize, standardize, vitalize, equalize, sterilize, fractionize, tenderize, and pulverize anywise. And it costs only $11.95 with your check or money order, or $512.17 COD." After the address is repeated twice in another marathon sentence, you lean back in your easy chair exhausted from the blitz and breathing heavily as if you were pulling for the announcer to make it to the end.

You have also heard the typical pause-filled campaign speech delivered to a highly partisan crowd. The political analyst for station NACN (National American Columbian Network) comments at the close of the rousing speech, "Well, Frank, the mayor sure had the council in the palm of his hand." To which the anchorman replies, "Yes, Henry, in a ten-minute speech interrupted only 127 times by applause, Floral Oaks Mayor Harly Goodman announced his resignation."

Often, breaks in delivery can add drama to your speech or give emphasis to certain words, such as the "pause" in the California riddle. Taken to an extreme, these pauses, whether for thought or for effect, can greatly detract from your delivery. In my corporate training sessions, we retype an important speech an executive is planning to give (such as an investment broker's summary or a statement to the media) and break the speech up into the most effective voice patterns. President Carter frequently breaks up his sentences in unusual places, a trait that has not passed unnoticed by impressionists. A typical sentence might sound like this: "It is the right of the American people . . . to forgo certain . . . luxuries much . . . as I do. For example, . . . I don't see . . . Billy . . . as often as I should."

President Carter also has an unusual habit of letting his voice drop at the end of his phrases. This hurts his image of credibility and truthfulness (see Table 8–1). The regional manager I mentioned in Chapter 4 who smiled only with his mouth had this vocal trait. His voice merely reinforced his image of toughness and insincerity.

Table 8–1 lists different voice qualities and the images they evoke for men and women. The images are based on my research into the academic literature and on the results of experiments in voice technique. In my voice sessions, I have each student tell a short personal story that is tape-recorded and analyzed by the group. The table summarizes typical reactions to various qualities of voice.

Some voice qualities are open to more than one interpreta-

Table 8-1. Voice qualities and personality traits.

Quality	Male	Female
PITCH		
Base		
high	nervous, artistic,	feminine, emotional
deep	immature, forceful, mature, masculine	masculine, unemotional
Direction		
all up	nervous, high-strung	flighty, high-strung
all down	cold, unemotional, untruthful	cold, unintelligent
Range		
monotone	masculine, cold	masculine, cold
wide	dynamic, feminine, excitable	dynamic, outgoing
Quality		
thin	no significant traits	immature, sensitive, sense of humor
tense	old, stubborn	young, emotional, less intelligent
throaty	old, mature	unintelligent, cold
VOLUME		
Breathy	young, artistic	sexy, attractive, superficial
Soft	powerful	naive, emotional, feminine, attractive
Loud	aggressive, insensitive, boor	forceful, argumentative, masculine
RESONANCE		
Sonorous	healthy, energetic, proud	lively, outgoing
Nasal	many negative traits	many negative traits
Blocked	unintelligent, dull	unintelligent
TEMPO		
Speed		
Slow	careful, cold	unintelligent, lazy
Fast	outgoing, nervous, impatient	outgoing, nervous
Continuity		
Continuous	earnest, confident	confident
Broken	insincere, unsure	weak, uncertain

tion. For example, a soft voice in a man may be regarded as either weak and feminine or very powerful, depending on other factors. Marlon Brando used a quiet, hoarse voice in portraying the *Godfather*. Only men who command power and respect can afford to speak softly and slowly, making others strain to hear and wait for each word. Less authoritative men lose their presence and power by speaking with a soft voice. When a voice quality suggests two or more contradictory traits, only the most frequently cited trait (in this case, "powerful") is shown in Table 8–1.

Voice-Quality Combinations

The real benefit of studying voice qualities is that you can learn which combinations are effective in different situations. Research on this topic was conducted by asking actors to read the same script to an audience using different vocal traits. The listeners were then given questionnaires to evaluate the effectiveness of the messages. The experiment was modified and repeated several times with different audiences to verify the results.

Table 8–2 shows the best combination of voice qualities for projecting credibility, persuasiveness, and other traits. Pitch di-

Table 8-2. Effective vocal traits.

Trait	Base Pitch	Pitch Range	Base Volume	Volume Range	Speed	Continuity
Credibility	up	varying	up	wide	varying	less than normal
Persuasiveness	normal	varying	up	normal	faster than normal	more than normal
Cheerfulness	up	varying, mostly up	up	normal	faster than normal	normal
Satisfaction	normal	upward	normal	narrow	normal	normal
Warmth and Affection	down	slightly up	down	narrow	slower than normal	normal

rection, pitch quality, and resonance are not included in the table, since they do not change for any of the categories. Pitch direction should always be varied, rising and dropping for each type of sentence. A normal pitch quality is always desired, regardless of the situation, as is a fully resonant or sonorous voice.

I use the credibility voice for teaching and speaking. My base pitch is normally two full tones higher when I'm talking to a class than when I'm conversing during a break. I try to make my voice more expressive by using a wider pitch range. This is not only less monotonous for the students over a long period; it also makes me sound more involved. We tend to forget that what is "too much" in a conversation does not seem at all outlandish in front of even a small group. A higher base volume is also an aid in maintaining the listener's attention and reinforces the speaker's passion for a subject.

Increased volume also makes a speaker's soft range more effective. Billy Graham uses this contrast to perfection, following up thundering questions with a feather-soft rejoinder. Your tempo should remain varied. The best way to transmit credibility is to control the continuity of your speech. Well-placed pauses, together with appropriate body signals of evaluation and thought, show you to be a thinking, concerned, careful, and truthful speaker.

Contrary to what most of us think, persuasiveness is different from credibility. Although base volume should be higher for persuasive speech, pitch and volume range should be the same as in normal conversation. Persuasiveness is achieved primarily through the speed and fluidity of the message. The stereotype of the slick-tongued, fast-talking salesman is 100 percent accurate. We have all noticed TV or radio commercials that blare on after a quieter program. These loud commercials make no attempt to be credible through varied tempos and thoughtful pauses. Instead, they focus on being persuasive, bouncing the information off us faster than we can think. We see a bewildering array of characters soaking chalk in ink, ripping shirts in half, throwing their bleach away, or talking to each other through the medicine cabinet. All these unlikely events happen within 60 seconds, yet none of the characters misses a word.

Another useful vocal trait for business is cheerfulness. When

I first went into the real world as a neophyte marketeer, I asked one of the experienced men in our office what I needed to become a good salesman. He looked at me for a second and said, "A thick skin," then walked off. I soon learned what he meant: everybody loves to dump on the salesman, because he can't fight back. (A saleswoman still has it a little better in this respect, since chivalry is not yet dead.) On some days and in some situations, I don't feel particularly cheerful or salesy. But I know that I won't have a second chance to prove to a client or class that a poor performance was just an off day. I must always be "up." One way I do it is by psyching myself, like an athlete before a sports event. Another is by showing all the NVC signs of cheerfulness.

The cheerful voice uses a higher base pitch, with variations mostly in the upper range. The base volume should be louder and the tempo faster, with normal continuity. Volume should be within normal range. Table 8–2 also shows the best combination of voice qualities for projecting satisfaction, and warmth and affection.

Building Your Voice

Once you understand how voice qualities contribute to your image and to your effectiveness as a speaker, you can begin to change for the better. The first step to tape your voice. A low-cost cassette tape recorder can be of value here. Many businesses use them in their training sections, so you may even be able to borrow one for overnight use. Try to tape your voice when you are least aware of the recorder. Most of us become automatons when faced with a humming recorder, its reels spinning like pinwheels. Get a 120-minute cassette and leave the recorder on during a long phone conversation or during dinner when you can forget that it's running. Have a friend tape you while you are making a presentation or speaking at a meeting where there is frequent interaction. The important point is to get a record of your normal voice.

The next step is to rate your voice for the characteristics listed in Table 8–1. Also evaluate your diction. If you are working with a friend, rate each other's voice to get a better reading. We all are so self-conscious about how we sound that it is often difficult to be honest. Listen to your voice until it no longer sounds "horrible." I have heard myself enough times on tape to know what to expect, so I can now listen without pain. In a recent radio interview about one of my clients, I tried to use a lower pitch range. The adjustment gave my voice a more authoritative sound over the radio speaker. Before, I had always sounded a little high and nervous, although I wasn't *that* nervous!

The main problem for most of us is lack of expressiveness. We speak at a consistent volume, pitch, or tempo. There is a lot to be learned from the professional voices we are exposed to each day on radio and TV. Comedian George Carlin jokes that all the announcers sound as if they went to the same school of broadcasting. The reason they sound so much alike is that they have all mastered the techniques of effective speaking. My favorite place to work on vocal expressiveness is in the car (difficult if you are in a car pool). I have heard some commercials often enough to know them by heart, so I announce them right along with the broadcaster. I'll come home and give my children the news and weather report in *Sesame Street* style.

You should treat your voice as another body muscle. It too needs regular exercise to stay in shape. On my way to a customer seminar, I will warm my voice up by singing along with the radio, yelling at the other drivers, and thinking out loud. To the range of my voice, I sing falsetto along with my favorite records (for women, this is the "high soprano" voice) and thump the baseline to those pounding rhythm songs. I might spend a half-hour auto trip yelling my speech. Like any exercise, this is not to be overdone at the start. It took me many months before I could do four consecutive full-day sessions without losing my voice. If you feel a strain in your voice, stop.

Summary

Your voice is one of the most valuable NVC tools you possess. Begin to analyze the voices of other speakers and try to determine what makes them expressive or persuasive. Acquaint yourself with your own voice. It shouldn't be a stranger to you when you hear it, and it certainly should not make you wince. Then, much like a singer in training, extend your vocal capabilities through practice. For the first time, you will begin to manage the other 30 percent of NVC for your benefit.

9

Politics and Image

Most of us underestimate the importance of a good professional image. Politicians are one of the few groups to understand and control image successfully. Rarely is appearance such an important factor as in getting someone's vote. Americans are notorious for their emotional or illogical voting patterns, with candidates at the top of the ballot having a better chance of getting elected than those at the bottom. Americans also seem to shy away from the unusual. A candidate named Grableskew Hraboff is a longshot to win the alternate dogcatcher post. Adlai, Hubert, Wendell, Alf, and Strom have little chance against the likes of Harry, Jack, Dick, and Jimmy. A candidate who looks like he lives under a bridge and eats travelers will never get the nomination.

The importance of appearance was reinforced for me in the 1977 mayoral election in my home town. My family lawyer of many years was running for mayor on the Republican ticket (in a very Democratic community). He had received an impressive write-up in the largest local daily and was evidently well supported by his party. When I mentioned his candidacy to one of my in-laws, she immediately asked, "Is he good-looking? I mean, what kind of image does he have?" She was not asking for her voting information; she was *assuming* that he needed a good image to have a chance at being elected. A good public image is now a prerequisite for success in politics. I doubt that someone like Abraham Lincoln could make it today. Who wants a President who looks like the "before" in a Charles Atlas comic book advertisement?

Today TV plays a critical role in a presidential campaign. Imagine going into a TV debate that will influence an election in one of the most powerful countries in history. The office is one of the two or three most influential jobs in the world. It commands a mighty army. It serves over 200 million people. Running for the office is the result of countless lesser attainments, years of detailed planning. Few of us will ever face an event with as much personal career significance, where so much lies in the balance.

We blanch at the thought of lining up for a last putt that means $20,000. The idea of a $100,000 winner-take-all tennis match (even if the loser gets a "mere" $40,000 less) can freeze the most successful pro. But even these events pall in comparison with a presidential debate. The true effect of TV on a presidential election wasn't fully realized until after the 1960 Kennedy–Nixon debate.

The 1960 Kennedy–Nixon Debate

The 1960 presidential election pitted two experienced pros in a very tight race. Kennedy was the silver-spoon candidate, born to wealth and committed to public service. Nixon was the bootstrap candidate who fought his way to national prominence. Both understood the importance of the debate and worked hard to win it. But the results of the debate were startling to the American people and devastating to Nixon. A survey taken after the debate showed that people who *read* the transcript or *heard* it on radio felt it was a draw or gave Nixon a slight edge. But those who *saw* the candidates on TV—the vast majority of voters—felt the debate was a clear win for Kennedy.

A study asked the voters, "How did the candidates live up to your expectations for the debate?" The results showed that Kennedy and Nixon stayed even in being as concise, fair, and articulate as expected. But Kennedy was rated as more interesting, sharp, active, strong, colorful, handsome, relaxed, calm, deep, experienced, wise, and virile than expected. Nixon appeared more boring, dull, passive, old, weak, colorless, ugly, tense, agitated, shallow, inexperienced, foolish, and sterile. Yet both men were trying to maximize their appearance!

This debate has become one of the most highly studied media events in history. Its surprising results lie in a complex series of unfortunate circumstances, accidents, and misdirected strategies for Nixon, and some careful planning by Kennedy.

The campaigning before the debate had been difficult for Nixon. Because he was behind schedule, he spent the entire day of the debate speaking in Chicago before hostile Democratic crowds. In addition to fatigue, his health had been a problem. He had recently been ill, had lost weight, and was bothered by a knee injury. Kennedy, in comparison, had just completed a California campaign swing and was fit and rested. He spent the day of the debate in a hotel suite planning strategy with his advisers.

The TV producers did their best to guarantee the candidates equal treatment. New picture tubes were placed in all the cameras for clear, sharp transmission. A solid-color backdrop was provided to make the candidates stand out on the home screens. Small spotlights, called inky spots, were placed to shine in Nixon's eyes in order to eliminate the dark shadows caused by his heavy brows. The producers agreed not to show Nixon wiping sweat from his forehead, since that would make him appear worried or beaten. They also agreed to keep screen time as even as possible, so that neither candidate would benefit from a larger amount of exposure.

Nixon was concerned about how his beard would appear on TV screens. Nixon has light skin and a dark, heavy beard. Even though he shaved immediately before the debate, he still had a shadow. Many people have heard about the "makeup" Nixon wore that night. The truth is that Nixon used aftershave powder to hide the beard shadow from the TV cameras. This also came back to plague him.

Figure 9–1 shows the candidates as they appeared on the TV screen. I have used the appropriate NVC checklist items to highlight their appearance differences during the debate.

As you can see, Nixon's appearance suffered. Standing on one leg caused his coat to wrinkle and gap in front. His weight loss made his collar gap, and his clothes did not seem to fit properly. In addition, he did not show up as well as Kennedy on the home screens because of his lighter-colored suit. This was aggravated by the backdrop, which had been drying light even after

Figure 9–1. Kennedy–Nixon debate.
(From Randall P. Harrison, Beyond Words: An Introduction to Nonverbal Communication, *Englewood Cliffs, N.J.: Prentice-Hall, 1974, by permission)*

NVC Cue	Kennedy	Nixon
HEIGHT MIGHT	JFK was taller, although this was negated by the TV coverage.	RMN was slightly shorter, but this was not noticeable and had no effect.
SIZE PRIZE	JFK had a muscular body style. He looked healthy and fit and wore a well-tailored suit.	RMN looked tired and under normal weight. His suit fit looser than normal because of his recent illness.
HEAD	JFK shook his head as he listened, as if disagreeing with RMN's comments.	RMN unconsciously nodded his head as he listened, in apparent agreement.
Forehead	JFK had a narrow forehead.	RMN had a wider forehead due to his receding hairline.
Brows	JFK had "medially downturned" brows, giving a concerned look to his face.	RMN had dark, thick brows, giving him a brooding, negative, frowning look.
Eyes	Heavy-lidded.	RMN had deep-set eyes, which caused dark shadows under his eyebrows.
Lips	JFK had a fuller, sensitive lower lip.	RMN had downturned lips, giving the impression of a frown; deep lines from nose to mouth corners accentuated his negative look.
Chin	JFK had a square, solid jaw.	RMN had a jowly chin, which was more noticeable when he spoke.
Skin	JFK was tanned from his West Coast campaign.	RMN was light-skinned; his beard showed in blotches despite the powder.
Hair	JFK had a softer, fluffy hairstyle.	RMN combed his hair straight back in a style close to the head; his hair shone.
POSTURE	JFK stood erect.	RMN leaned to one side.
HANDS	JFK used his hands when he spoke and took notes when sitting.	RMN gripped the podium tightly to help maintain balance when standing and sat holding his sore knee.
LEGS	JFK used an open stance, weight distributed evenly on both legs.	RMN stood on one leg, resting his knee, and crossed his legs when sitting.

repeated coats of paint. In fact, it was still wet at airtime. As expected, Nixon sweated heavily from the heat of the lights. Unfortunately, this caused his aftershave powder to streak, giving the "smeared makeup" look that became famous and accentuating his beard further.

The media precautions only increased Nixon's problems. The backdrop was just the beginning. The new camera tubes worked against Nixon since they picked up his streaked face clearly and transmitted it to millions of TV viewers. The inky spots didn't do their intended job either: they had been jostled out of line by news photographers milling about the stage before the debate began. Nixon still had those deep, sinister eye shadows the political cartoonists love. There was even one shot of Nixon wiping his brow, although it was from a distance.

Nixon also gave the impression of being in accord with Kennedy. Many of us unconsciously nod our head as we listen, as if to say, "I hear you." On TV, this made Nixon look as if he were *agreeing*. Kennedy shook his head "no" and took notes, supposedly to be used later. An exposure count showed that Kennedy was getting more shots and screen time than Nixon. Yet Kennedy's advisers griped about it to the director during the debate. Yes, *griped!* They complained, "Keep the camera on Nixon. Every time his face appears he loses votes." And he did lose votes. He lost enough votes to swing the election to Kennedy's favor, a result ranked as one of the major campaign blunders in recent history. Even though both men were trying to maximize their appearance and had enormous resources of talent and money to help them, only one was successful. In view of the NVC data being sent out by the candidates, it is little wonder that those who saw the debate felt so differently from listeners and readers. These lessons were not lost on later candidates.

The 1976 Carter–Ford Debates

The results of 1960 were on the minds of the two candidates in the 1976 election. When Jimmy Carter agreed to debate with Gerald Ford, many questioned Carter's wisdom because of the tremendous lead he held in the polls. But 1976 was a curious campaign year. Neither candidate generated much enthusiasm with the voters. Both were said to lack the personal charisma of a Kennedy or the political savvy of a Johnson. The issues were fuzzy in a down economy, and neither candidate was willing to risk being the first one to offer solutions. The arguments of "Why I was a good President" versus "Why I'll be a good President" excited no one. More than any other election since 1960, image alone may have decided the winner in 1976.

A Gallup poll conducted for *Newsweek* magazine asked 517 registered voters across the country who saw all or part of the second debate the following questions:

	Carter	Ford	Neither or Not Sure
All things considered, which man won the debate, Carter or Ford?	50%	27%	23%
Do the following statements apply more to Carter or to Ford?			
1. Seemed well prepared and well informed	42	38	20
2. Seemed nervous and unsure of himself	27	38	35
3. Would be honest and open with the public about his foreign policy	48	33	19
4. Would have good judgment in a time of international crisis	33	45	22

I believe the NVC information these two candidates transmitted in the debates explains the results of the poll and, ultimately, the choice Americans made for their President.

Neither candidate made Nixon's mistake of campaigning the day of the debate. Both prepared in detail in hotel rooms beforehand, memorizing tremendous amounts of information for the debate. Indeed, one of the main reasons each debate was limited to a single topic was to give the candidates this opportunity to stockpile information. We will never know how much of what they memorized was actually used.

Coming into the debates, each candidate had a carefully established image. Ford was the tall, rugged former athlete carrying the power and prestige of the presidency on his broad shoulders. The last two Presidents had aged terribly in office. Ford was the picture of good health after his first year. He was the only one of the previous three Presidents to leave office without being physically and emotionally drained. As the picture of Carter in Chapter 4 shows, Ford may be the only one of the last *four*.

One of my favorite pictures of Ford in office is the one taken when he received his injection during the ill-fated swine flu vaccination program. The picture showed Ford, sitting with shirt sleeve rolled and a needle going into his arm, smiling at the doctor. How many of us even *look* while we get a shot? How many more of us don't flinch? Although I don't know the exact circumstances, there probably were dozens of photographers standing around Ford as he received his shot, praying for the slightest show of discomfort. Then they could blast the embarrassing photo across the country. (Remember the famous Ford ski fall shown on national evening news one winter?) Surely the President of the United States can afford to have a pressure gun used for his injections. No, Ford showed he could defy fear and look a needle in the point, smiling. Whoever set up the swine flu shot knew how to make President Ford look tough.

Carter had a warmer and more sensitive image than Ford. Publicity photos showed him carrying his own clothes on trips, reading the Bible at Sunday school, lounging in blue jeans, and being interviewed in an open-collared shirt (as in the *Playboy* feature). Portraits by Avedon of both candidates when they were asked to pose standing show Ford stiffly upright while Carter is relaxed with one hand in his pocket.

Figure 9–2 shows four typical pictures from the second debate. I have once again used NVC checklist items to identify the different NVC information that the candidates transmitted:

Figure 9–2. Second Carter–Ford debate. *(Courtesy* Newsweek/ *Wally McNamee)*

NVC Cue	Carter	Ford
HEIGHT MIGHT	JEC is of average height.	GRF is four inches taller.
SIZE PRIZE	JEC is fit, with average build showing in a suit.	GRF, former football player, "could still hike the ball and fire off the line at Michigan."
CENTER	JEC kept his center open when talking and turned to Ford when listening.	GRF kept his center open when speaking and listened with closed center.
HEAD	JEC spoke with head tilted, "looking up" to camera; he listened with head tilted.	GRF spoke with head held straight and listened with head tilted away.
Forehead	JEC has normal-sized forehead and wears hair down over one side, a loose strand occasionally falling forward.	GRF has receding hairline, shows large forehead, and wears hair back.
Brows	JEC has bushy brows with vertical "concern wrinkles."	GRF has pale eyebrows, set close to eyes.
Eyes	JEC has wider eyes, outside corners turned down.	GRF has narrow, squinty eyes, often slitlike.
Lips	JEC has thicker lips, slightly downturned in resting position; prominent lines connect nose and mouth corners. He listened with slight smirk.	GRF has thin lips forming tight, level line in resting position; he has a toothy grin that could be interpreted as a grimace. He listened with a tight frown.
Chin	JEC has rounded, slightly jowly chin.	GRF has square jaw, that looks firmly set even at rest.
Skin	JEC's skin has a rough, almost grainy look.	GRF's skin seems smoother; fine wrinkles at jaw, around eyes, and along forehead.
Hair	JEC has coarser hair, arranged slightly over the ears; temples are silvered.	GRF wears his hair straight back in slick look; hair is off ears.
POSTURE	JEC looked more "back on his heels" than GRF. He stood upright but relaxed, and sat down when listening.	GRF looked "up on his toes." He always stood perfectly upright and squared to the podium.
HANDS	JEC held a pen in his right hand and rested it on the lectern; his left hand made palming gestures and rested on his leg when he listened.	GRF's left hand gripped the lectern tightly; his right hand made frequent gestures. He crossed his arms when listening, with hands open.

As the *Newsweek* poll showed, both candidates seemed equally well informed to viewers. Carter seemed much more confident. He also gave the impression of being more honest and open with the public about international policy, a sore point with the American people after the Nixon administration. But the viewers polled felt Ford would have better judgment in times of international crisis. Here was a tough man of positive action. As every football locker room says somewhere, "When the going gets tough, the tough get going."

Both men were well dressed. Neither made Nixon's mistake of wearing a suit that didn't show up properly against the backdrop. Their clothes were well tailored and performed perfectly. That is, they gave the candidates a professional image without drawing attention to themselves. I was teaching a public-speaking course at the time of the second debate. I asked my students to watch the debate and mentioned that I would quiz them on the delivery of the two men. One of the questions I asked was "What color suit and tie was each man wearing?" Not one student could answer, which is the ideal result.

Both candidates were also well prepared, almost too well prepared. Their delivery was about as off the cuff as a computer's. Much was made in the media about the time they spent in their hotel rooms before each debate, and about who came and went and what they said. This extensive preparation may have robbed each candidate of his spontaneity and image of conviction. At times the two seemed to be in a statistics duel.

In seeming honest and open, Carter had many advantages over Ford. Carter carried himself in a much more relaxed manner. He stood comfortably, sat when listening, kept his hands resting on the lectern, and kept his center open. Carter also has a more "human" face. His fluffier hair texture and style, bushy eyebrows, open eyes, thicker lips, rounder face, and coarser-looking skin help make him look people-oriented. He is also blessed with the Kennedy-shaped eyebrows of concern. His habitual hand movement—the preacher-style palming gesture—made him appear concerned, friendly, and relaxed.

Ford was very much the opposite. He was rigid and tight in his stance and never sat down, even during technical difficulties in the TV coverage. He made forceful edge-of-hand or pointing gestures. He closed his center off with his arms when listening and gripped the lectern tightly when speaking. His face showed strength of purpose and resolve. His combed-back hair emphasized his forehead. He stood with square jaw, lips compressed. Here was a man of resolve and action.

Both men also seemed to learn from the mistakes Nixon made while listening to Kennedy. Ford stood with shoulders facing Carter, head cocked in an evaluative listening pose, a slight frown on his face. Carter tried a much more dangerous strategy: the slight smile.

Political analysts had questioned Carter's wisdom in debating an incumbent, because of the limitations on criticizing. Carter could not show a lack of respect for the office of the President of the United States; nor could he be derisive. Instead, he used an understated smile that said, "The current President is doing it again. Let me just have my turn and I'll show people what's wrong with that." The smile conveyed an "I've got him now" or "He's playing right into my hands" attitude.

Whereas Ford showed with his pose that he was not in agreement with Carter, Carter showed disagreement plus the hint that he had a better answer. He looked *eager* to stand up for his rebuttal. Someone should have clued Ford in on his center. If he wanted to look truly negative, he shouldn't have turned toward Carter. Looking over his shoulder would have been much more effective.

Both men also adopted Kennedy's strategy of taking notes during the debate. Carter took notes in a normal manner, as Figure 9–2 shows, but Ford used a curious technique. Often he did not look down while he wrote. Very few people can take notes without looking at the paper. In my career I have met only one person who did this regularly, a personnel manager for a large company. She wanted to maintain eye contact with the prospective employee during the interview, so she developed the habit of writing things down in very large script, using an entire page for about five lines of information. This way she could write legibly without having to look at the paper.

Ford may also have developed this skill, but it was difficult to tell from the movement of the pen whether he was actually writing. Also, he never once looked down at his jottings during his rebuttal of Carter's remarks. It is possible that Ford was taking notes only for show, following instructions from his advisers. "Hey, Jerry, take notes, big guy. It worked for Kennedy and it looks good."

The *Newsweek* poll made it fairly clear what the American people were looking for in their President. Carter was declared the winner by nearly a two-to-one margin.

Ford might have been more successful if he had changed his style a bit to soften his image of physical strength and force. He could have made more use of a relaxed smile in publicity photos. Additional informal shots away from the White House would have helped him appear more like Mr. Average. It's too bad he didn't dig in his garden or play with model trains. He could have softened his gestures during the debate using fewer chopping motions. And he should have released his death grip on the lectern. This is one of the first habits to break in any beginning speaker.

Carter played the smile perfectly. No one was unhappy with his treatment of the President. He could have appeared stronger, at times standing up straighter and gesturing forcefully, with more edge-of-hand and pointing movements. It is not surprising that, two years into Carter's presidency, the major criticism of his administration was the perceived lack of direct, decisive leadership.

Both men hurt their image with their delivery. They spoke in slow, exaggerated tones, as if they were in front of 2,000 people at a political rally and needed to make up for the sound lag. Speaking before a TV camera is much like conversing from across the room. A TV speaker is really addressing people seated ten feet away in easy chairs. Ford and Carter should have backed off the public-speaking techniques and spoken on a more personal level. During the vice-presidential debate both Mondale and Dole used this personalized approach effectively.

You may never face a situation with as much at stake as a presidential candidate, but your image is just as important to your career. The first impression you create at a job interview is often the determining factor in an employer's hiring decision. As you progress in your organization, you have more time to establish yourself both through your accomplishments and through the image you project to others.

Building a Successful Image

An image is a difficult intangible to manage. You can't grab it, beat it, talk to it, or comfort it. You probably can't even get two people to agree on what your image—or anyone else's—is. So most likely you have no idea what kind of image you project, much less how to improve it. For that matter, do you even have an image? Do you have more than one image? Are they similar or do they conflict?

The first rule in successful image building is to be *consistent*. Nobody really likes the unexpected. What does your heart do when you are surprised? It gets mad! It beats in a sprint, pumping blood quickly through your body in case you have to take action. Let someone sneak up on you and startle you, and your muscles will briefly go into seizure, followed by your heart blowing its top. Even when the surprise is pleasant, your body goes through this process.

Management is a lot like your heart. It absolutely hates surprises. A manager once told me that he didn't care what kind of difficulties his people got into as long as he knew what was going to happen. What is known, even if unpleasant, can be managed. What is unknown can be grounds for dismissal.

For managers, the worst kind of subordinate is an inconsistent one. A good performer·is rarely monitored; a poor performer is always monitored, and needs to be. In either case, management at least knows where it stands. But nothing is more annoying to a manager than having to check up on someone who might foul up and then discovering that the checking was needless. It's equally upsetting to have to deal with the inconsistent subordinate's personality. Is the subordinate going to be in a good mood today, or is there going to be fighting or tears?

The same is true of images. Most managers prefer employees whose personality traits can be easily identified. If a subordinate is very inconsistent, the manager becomes wary and guarded, fearful of a potential surprise. You have probably heard someone say of an associate, "He's a strange one; I just can't get a handle on him." This is worse than having negative personality traits. No one personality characteristic is inherently good or bad; its desirability depends on the job. What may be poor in a salesman may be of value in an office manager. If you have *no* obvious characteristics, management has no basis on which to judge you for any job.

Avoid surprises in building your image. Your image should be obvious as well as consistent. This way, the people who make the decisions that affect your career will have something to count on, something predictable. They can then pick and choose among the jobs that are best suited to your traits and that offer you and the company the best chance for success.

The next rule in image building is to make your traits *harmonious*. A businessman I know has a card that lists him as an office products salesman and a marriage counselor. (I've always wanted to have a card that read, "Dr. Ken Cooper, Neurosurgery and Janitorial Supplies.") It is very difficult to carry off a two-sided image—such as being hard-nosed with money but free-wheeling with ideas, or being a smooth talker but shy. The traits you choose to emphasize should agree with each other and fit together in a logical pattern.

People tend to think and talk in clichés, so the closer your image is to a stereotype, the easier it will be to establish that image. A personnel manager for a large chemical company claims she can always recognize one type of person by sight: the IBM office products salesperson. She feels they all look the same, talk the same, and act the same. It is unlikely that IBM is *that* good in selecting a certain type of person for its salesforce. (After all, their selection process *is* barely less intensive than that used by the Rockettes.) Still, the candidates selected quickly fit into a stereotyped pattern of what an IBM office products salesperson "should be."

Other stereotypes include the green-eyeshade accountant, the sliderule-carrying engineer (or is it a calculator now?), the backslapping yes-man, the pushy door-to-door salesman, and the shrinking-violet bookkeeper. These stereotypes are guaranteed to ring true in the minds of others.

If you want a nonstandard image, be careful to make your traits fit logically. In this case though, make certain that you don't come too close to a clichéd image, because that will undo all your efforts to be different. Many an office oddball has found that he is "just like Bob," even though the similarities are superficial. Make certain the cliché isn't still there working with you.

The most important rule in image building is to *be yourself.* As you grew up, you undoubtedly met people you admired and respected. You spent much of your time pretending to be these people and acting out their lives. As an adult, you must take your own talents and traits and maximize them, not try to acquire the traits you see in others. How many people do you know who are "wasted" in their current jobs or are trying to copy someone they are not?

Phonies are easy to spot. Today's young people are particularly adept at sizing up others. If we try to be something we are not, it will be incredibly obvious. If we really had enough talent to keep a fake image alive, we would be actors and actresses instead of businesspeople. Since we aren't entertainers, we had better stick to being ourselves.

That still gives us a lot of latitude. Everyone has many different personalities, with many different traits. Dr. John G. Geier, a consulting industrial psychologist, believes that managers have three separate personalities, defined by how they view themselves, how they feel others view them, and how they act under pressure. Each of these personalities has four major dimensions: dominance, influence, steadiness, and compliance. Geier developed a test to measure these traits in assessing a manager's style and effectiveness. His analysis may be overly restrictive in the personality traits considered, but it does illustrate our varied selves.

We may also have work, spouse, and parent personalities. In fact, we may have a separate personality for every role we play. One of my customers was a particularly hard man to deal with. He was secretive and continually kept me in the dark about what was happening in the account. Consequently, I was regularly surprising my boss with unsuspected problems. As I built up a picture of this customer as a paranoid, power-hungry sneak, I also began to learn about him outside of work. He was a warm, loving father and husband. He had many creative hobbies and was quite friendly and pleasant when he left work. He would have been a much better manager if he had let some of these traits carry over into his workday.

You are most likely the same way. You have many different personalities, depending on the environment and whom you are with. Sometimes your personality is mood-dependent: there is a "happy you" and a "down you." Out of these different selves is the making of a successful "you" that can be projected as your business image.

DEFINE YOUR IMAGE

The first step in building a successful image is to determine what your current image is. You may not be aware of your image, or you may think others don't have an image of you. You are wrong! Picture your friends and associates. As you think of a name, you suddenly get an image of that person. You could give a short summary of his or her personality traits. You may guess fairly accurately at how your friend would react to a certain situation or reply to a particular question. If you can do this with others, they certainly can do it with you. The challenge is to develop an accurate picture of yourself as others perceive you.

Many organizations use employee evaluation surveys to help managers get a handle on their image. One large corporation conducts training classes after managers have been on the job 3 months, and then again after 18 months. A detailed (and confidential) employee survey is used as a training and evaluation tool in both sessions with comparisons made between the survey results. This provides valuable feedback to the new managers.

The manager who is not offered such a program must do a little more detective work. You should start by finding out what traits you transmit to others and why you project these traits. You should be able to get a fair assessment from your spouse and close friends. Let them relay what people are saying about you. Frequently, secretaries are a good source of information, since they are often privy to conversations in the boss's office. Ask your manager what he or she thinks of you and why. This is a valid question and can provide valuable feedback on both your performance and your image. Be open-minded, and don't become defensive. Remember that the opinions expressed about you are *always* valid, if only because the other person feels that way.

Once you have an accurate picture of what others think of you, you can begin your self-analysis. In Chapter 3 you read about environment and physical appearance. You can now evaluate these two nonverbal indicators as if you were a presidential candidate designing or improving a public image.

Stand at the doorway of your office or work area and pretend you are seeing it for the first time. Systematically study it (this may actually *be* the first time). Look at it wall by wall, not missing a single paint chip or ceiling tile. What do you have on the walls— paintings, plaques, diplomas, nothing? Look at the furniture. What does it say about you? Is the office sloppy, or orderly, empty or cluttered, large or small? Where is the furniture located? If you had to draw a character sketch of the person who worked in this area, what would you say? Look at other people's offices or work areas in your company. What do they have in common? What sets them apart? How does yours fit in? In other words, what is your personal work environment telling others?

What about your office clothing? Even if you do not have the resources to modify your current wardrobe, you should at least become aware of how clothing contributes to your image. Does your clothing fit in with those around you? You don't have to become a fast-food clerk and show up every day in uniform, but you should know whether you are different or similar.

Is your wardrobe consistent? A salesman who was proud of his stylishness got caught one day with all his suits dirty or at the cleaners. So he pulled out an old one and wore it to work. That night, his wife came home and, seeing the suit in the wastebasket, asked what had happened. One of the salesman's customers, complimenting him on his taste in clothes, had remarked, "I really like your suit. It's almost as nice as what they're wearing *this* year."

Are you guilty of having a "wedding wardrobe"—something old, something new, something borrowed, something blue? If you are, you surely look like it. You don't have to keep up with fashion's every whim. But make sure your wardrobe says what you want it to say about you and that the statement is not conflicting.

Now is the time to look at yourself. You know how to analyze your body type. You should also analyze your face. What is its resting position? Are you frowning, neutral, or smiling? Aren't a large portion of the people you observe usually frowning slightly? Considering the amount of time your face spends in resting position, it is no wonder that this characteristic can strongly influence your image.

Another important part of your image is your attitude. One of the most basic of human needs is the need to be recognized. This is particularly true in the business world, where our feelings of self-worth so often depend on the feedback we receive from managers and associates. In transactional analysis (TA), the process of recognizing others is called *stroking*, and a unit of recognition is called a *stroke*.

There are positive strokes and negative strokes. Companies and organizations use awards to motivate their people ("M&M's" when the normal method, money, is not available). The training director of a large international organization talked about the problem of motivating leaders who held their posts for a single year. "We use an intricate series of awards," he said, "to overcome the motivational problems inherent in a short-term job. This keeps the leaders working throughout the year." These rewards are all forms of positive stroking.

On the personal level, positive strokes are like coat hangers: they tend to multiply without your noticing them. Suddenly, your whole day is full of good things to say to others and nice things being said in response. A retired executive, consulting with the Small Business Administration, was asked why so many of the companies requested him by name. "There are many secrets to success," he replied, "and I was fortunate to discover one of them early in my career. While I am no more competent than many of my associates, I always try to leave the other person glad to see me again, whether it's on the street or in the office."

The secretary of a college extension office was the opposite, a constant source of negative strokes. She always complained about her boss, the professors, and the working conditions. She couldn't understand why the people around her weren't more pleasant and cooperative. The most positive comment she could make was that someone had not been mean to her.

What if you were to carry a special notepad to work today? Each sheet would be divided into two columns: "plus" and "minus." For every positive stroke you gave others, you would make a mark in the plus column; for every negative stroke, you would place a mark in the minus column. Would your net score be above zero? If not, don't you think this is seriously affecting your image? If your score would be high in the plus column, could it be that you are a little too nice? Keep count one day, or one week, and find out how you rate.

By now you should have a better idea of what your image is. You must build a business image that is consistent, has harmonious traits, and fits your personality. In building this image, you should leave nothing to chance. Everything should be done for a reason.

Your next task in defining an image is to decide what traits you want to project. You may feel that you don't know enough about yourself to determine these traits. One way to find out is to take a battery of personality, interest, and aptitude tests. A number of psychological testing firms and consultants offer these services, but they are usually very expensive. Since many of the tests and testing procedures are standardized, you can often get similar services through an adult education course offered by a local high school. Costs vary, but they rarely exceed $50.

I went through one of these courses after I left college. The first night of the program, we were given a mental ability test and then a personality inventory survey. The second night, we took vocational interest and preference tests. The third night included discussing the test results with a counselor and selecting the aptitude tests we wanted to take to investigate our areas of interest. The fourth and fifth nights involved taking the tests and reviewing the results with the counselor. By the end of the course, we had a much better idea of our interests and abilities, particularly of how our abilities might stack up to others' in the business world. We also had a better idea of our personalities and of what motivated us. We were fortunate, of course, in having an experienced counselor to guide us, but the test results alone would have made the course worth the time and money. The information we gained was invaluable in helping us develop an image that fit our personalities and interests.

RATE YOUR TRAITS

Based on the data you now have about yourself, you can begin to determine traits you have that are beneficial in your current job. Table 9–1 lists 325 personality characteristics. Make several photocopies, then go through the list and circle about 50 adjectives you think accurately describe you. (There are many synonyms, so don't worry about getting every version of a specific trait. That will cause too much work later on in the process.)

Obviously, your self-analysis of personality traits will be somewhat biased. If you want to get a more accurate assessment and can remain nondefensive, have your spouse, boss, and associates rate your traits for you. Then compare the items appearing on their lists with your own. You might even take into consideration the characteristics that appeared more than once on your first-impression test (Chapter 3).

Now divide a sheet of paper into three columns labeled "helpful" (+), "nonessential" (0), "harmful" (−), as shown in Table 9–2. Go down your circled list of adjectives and place them in the proper column, according to how they affect your image and job success. When in doubt, place an item in either the helpful or harmful category rather than in the nonessential column. If you end up with all your traits in the helpful column, you aren't being truthful with yourself. Your plus-to-minus ratio can be as high as two to one, with the nonessential-column size varying depending on the person and the job. You now have one of the most useful tools for career success to come along since having a father who is company president. The three lists should show you what to emphasize in your personality and what to play down.

Keep in mind that the value of a given trait depends on the job. If you are looking to move upward in the company, you may want to make an additional list for the position you aspire to, especially if it involves very different success traits from those in your current job.

Table 9-1 Image traits.

absentminded	anxious	bitter	charming	conceited
active	apathetic	blustery	cheerful	condescending
adaptable	appreciative	boastful	civilized	confident
adventurous	argumentative	bossy	clear-thinking	confused
affected	arrogant	calm	clever	conscientious
affectionate	artistic	candid	coarse	conservative
aggressive	assertive	capable	cold	considerate
alert	attractive	careless	commonplace	consistent
aloof	autocratic	cautious	complaining	contented
ambitious	awkward	changeable	complicated	conventional
cool	defensive	dissatisfied	efficient	excitable
cooperative	deliberate	distant	egotistical	fair-minded
courageous	demanding	distractible	emotional	fastidious
cowardly	dependable	distrustful	energetic	fault-finding
critical	dependent	dominant	enterprising	fearful
cruel	despondent	dramatic	enthusiastic	feminine
curious	determined	dreamy	esthetic	fickle
cynical	dignified	dull	ethical	flirtatious
daring	discreet	easygoing	expressive	fluent
deceitful	disorderly	effeminate	evasive	foolish
forceful	gentle	headstrong	immature	inhibited
foresighted	gloomy	healthy	impatient	initiative
forgetful	good-looking	helpful	impulsive	insightful
forgiving	good-natured	high-strung	independent	intelligent
formal	greedy	honest	indifferent	interesting
frank	guilty	hostile	individualistic	interests narrow
friendly	handsome	humorous	industrious	interests wide
frivolous	hard-headed	hurried	infantile	intolerant
fussy	hard-hearted	idealistic	informal	introspective
generous	hasty	imaginative	ingenious	inventive
irresponsible	masculine	nagging	original	pessimistic
irritable	mature	natural	outgoing	philosophical
jolly	meek	negative	outspoken	planful
kind	methodical	nervous	painstaking	pleasant
lazy	mild	noisy	patient	pleasure-seeking
leisurely	mischievous	obliging	peaceable	poised
logical	moderate	obnoxious	peculiar	polished
loud	modest	opinionated	perceptive	powerful
loyal	moody	opportunistic	persevering	practical
mannerly	moralistic	optimistic	persistent	praising

One of the oddities of business is that people are sometimes judged more on their capabilities than on their performance.

Table 9-1. Image traits (cont.)

precise	quick	relaxed	rude	sensitive
prejudiced	quiet	reliable	sarcastic	sensuous
preoccupied	quitting	resentful	self-centered	sentimental
productive	rational	reserved	self-confident	serious
progressive	rattlebrained	resourceful	self-controlled	severe
protective	realistic	responsible	self-denying	sexy
prudish	reasonable	restless	self-pitying	shallow
pushy	rebellious	retiring	self-punishing	sharp-witted
quarrelsome	reckless	rigid	self-seeking	shiftless
queer	reflective	robust	selfish	showoff
shrewd	snobbish	stern	sympathetic	timid
shy	sociable	stingy	tactful	tolerant
silent	softhearted	stolid	tactless	touchy
simple	sophisticated	strong	talkative	tough
sincere	spendthrift	stubborn	temperamental	trusting
skeptical	spineless	submissive	tense	unaffected
slipshod	spontaneous	suggestible	thankless	unambitious
slow	spunky	sulky	thorough	unassuming
sly	stable	superstitious	thoughtful	uncomfortable
smug	steady	suspicious	thrifty	unconventional
undependable	uninhibited	unselfish	warm	wise
understanding	unintelligent	unstable	wary	withdrawn
unemotional	unkind	vindictive	weak	witty
unexcitable	unrealistic	versatile	whiny	worrying
unfriendly	unscrupulous	vulnerable	wholesome	zany

Someone management feels is a "comer" may be able to explain away poor performance as "the best in a bad situation." Selling this often depends upon how well the person's "next job" image is solidified in the eyes of management. These lists can provide you with guidelines for developing not only an image of competence in your current job but one indicating that you can do the next job as well.

PROJECT YOUR IMAGE

Now that you have a list of your desirable and undesirable traits, you are in a position to project the proper traits. This is the final and most difficult step in building a successful business image. Unfortunately, there is no well-defined system for imple-

Table 9-2. Sample image traits analysis for a specific job (corporate trainer).

Helpful (+)	Nonessential (0)	Harmful (−)
active	affectionate	absentminded
assertive	ambitious	aggressive
confident	candid	anxious
curious	conservative	argumentative
dominant	determined	bossy
energetic	efficient	demanding
enthusiastic	high-strung	forgetful
forceful	individualistic	fussy
good-natured	logical	hard-headed
humorous	methodical	impatient
informal	natural	nervous
intelligent	persistent	opinionated
interests wide	practical	reserved
inventive	sentimental	restless
original	simple	skeptical
perceptive	stable	stubborn
polished	stingy	tense
rational		worrying
self-confident		
showoff		
sincere		
thorough		
uninhibited		

menting your image. Just as no two people's lists will be the same, so no two people will use the same approach in projecting an image. You have been exposed to a large number of NVC signs and techniques, covering where you put your body and what you gather around it. You can now use this information to project your image.

Start with your work area or office. If you want to convey order and precision, have all material neatly filed and labeled. Keep an alphabetized phone pad with all pertinent numbers in it. Your desk should be neat, with the drawers carefully laid out for easy search and storage. Keep personal mementos to a minimum —for example, a single ornate three-part frame of family pictures. If you want to seem busy and productive, keep your desk covered with material, messages piled all around your phone. Have layers of file folders scattered about. Always appear to be hustling; walk quickly through the office even if you are going to get a candy bar. There are hundreds of possibilities, all of which are correct as they are *deliberate,* and convey some trait on your list.

Make your office work to your advantage. Arrange the furniture to best fit your space needs and to gain control over your visitors. Minimize any height disadvantage by adjusting the chairs or rearranging them. Design the layout to maximize your physical size. Make every decoration say something about you: your personality, your tastes, your interests, or your accomplishments.

Take stock of your physical characteristics. Should you lose a few pounds? Start exercising regularly, or take up a sport. When you get your next haircut, go to a good professional and describe what you are trying to accomplish with your appearance. Make every purchase of business clothing fit into your long-range plan and image. Know what you want from the start and let the salesperson help you find the right look. I can't say enough about the value of finding experienced professionals for these personal services. Even if they cost a little more, the advice they offer about style and physical appearance will more than justify the expense. We've all seen the TV experiment where a prominent designer or stylist takes a ragged member of the studio audience and returns the next week with a totally different person. That person could be you!

In his book *Winning Through Intimidation,* Robert Ringer details his methods of success in the income-producing real estate business. When he started out, he was like every other real estate agent, working for any commission he could get from his clients. After being shortchanged time and again, he decided to develop an image that would help him get every penny of the commission he had earned. Ringer developed an image that was so professional, so high level, that clients never thought of skipping out on commissions. He used an expensive book instead of a business card. He traveled with his own secretarial staff and sent his assistants by airplane to fetch any documents he needed. He even walked out on one deal involving hundreds of thousands of dollars in commissions rather than fall back on his old image and agree to less than he deserved.

I recently met a man who achieved success by developing the opposite kind of image. This man is one of the finest theater organists in the nation, but he has achieved national fame as a bumbling collector of antiques. You may have seen him on several network talk shows, displaying his oddball collection of vacuum sweepers, washing machines, and cooking utensils. What makes his visits entertaining is that these contraptions, much to his amazement and confusion, never seem to work properly. The character he presents is strictly a ruse, of course. In an interview on a local radio call-in show he mentioned that he never played the organ during his appearances. How could a confused, bumbling collector have the talent to make such beautiful music come out of an organ? That would totally destroy his image. So he confines his organ engagements to the city where he gained fame as a musician.

It is a constant source of amazement to me that the public can accept someone who says, "Goooollly, Sarjent! Ah jist cain't unnerstan' a thang yewr yellin' aht muhee," and then sings like a Metropolitan Opera star. Yet this is the power of an image in highly visible fields such as politics and show business.

But what about the business world? When I graduated from college, I was in a quandary about what personal business style to develop. I had accepted an offer for a position and had about two weeks to move, buy clothes, and report. A little research and questioning of people I knew revealed that the company had a conservative dress code. So I got a haircut and purchased three suits: dark green, dark blue, and dark brown. I bought five white shirts and seven striped ties that would intermix with the suits. With this dazzling array of drabness, I reported for work.

As I began my long and complex training, I could see myself fitting right into the mold. The clothing made me almost invisible, and the jargon and speech habits of the office were becoming ingrained in my conversation. People didn't work there; they were "on board." I began to think I had signed up for the Navy! My wife remarked on the change in me, not any of it necessarily bad, but a change nonetheless.

After completing almost ten months of training, I had to decide where I wanted to work in the office. Did I want to become a member of a large, well-paid marketing team, where I would be a junior member with reduced responsibility, or did I want to get my own sales territory and have complete control and responsibility for the results? There was another factor. Up to this point, I had been exactly like every other trainee who had come through the office. If I hoped to advance in this highly competitive company, what would I have to do to shed the invisibility I had thus far maintained?

After going through the psychological testing procedure described earlier, I felt ready to begin designing my image. No matter what else, I had to prove that I was different, and that being different made me exceptional. I turned down the lucrative marketing team offer and trained for the sales position, where I would have my own territory in several years. My hair grew back to a more comfortable length, longer than most men's in the office. In replacing my wardrobe, I tried to pick suits that were much less conservative but still businesslike. Eventually, I grew a mustache, one of the first in the office.

In a town that ardently supported the local football team, I stayed loyal to the Miami Dolphins, a team I had followed since living in Florida. My desk had Pogo and Ziggy cartoons taped to it instead of family pictures. I stayed clear of office politics and avoided after-work drinking parties. When one of my managers told me I didn't fit the mold, that I was an individualist, I knew I had succeeded.

I decided to emphasize my creativity. When my unit had to sponsor a meeting for the entire office, I stayed late one night taking pictures for a humorous opening for the meeting. I also volunteered to write promotion party and meeting skits for anyone in the office. While some of these skits took more time than anything my job required, I felt that late hours were worth the exposure.

I worked at developing a reputation as a good presenter. I spent extra time preparing and reworking my visuals and delivery. I taught evening classes at a local college in order to develop a "stage personality," and I let my manager know why I was doing it. While most salesmen dreaded being assigned any in-house presentations, I sought them out as an opportunity to shine to my superiors.

The results may not have been due entirely to image, but by my third year out of college I was earning my age (back before double-digit inflation) and had received my first title promotion, about two to three years ahead of the norm. And I was not the only one using this approach.

John C. had worked in our office for many years, but was an enigma. He was extremely well liked and competent, yet people knew very little about him outside of business. He had no outstanding characteristics or mannerisms; he had not been involved in any unusual events. When it came time to write a promotional skit for him, we were stumped, since we had so little information to work with. Then it finally hit us. His most outstanding characteristic was that he had no outstanding characteristics. We finally wrote a series of skits around that theme; "He's the only man who can walk into an empty room and it's still empty," "He's the only person that the personality meter doesn't have to be plugged in to rate." So everyone has traits that can contribute to a successful image.

Summary

You may not have the resources of a political candidate, but you do have the same requirements for success. Take a lesson from people who are professionals at gaining other people's confidence and commitment. Define your professional image. Identify and rate your personality traits, keeping in mind their relevance to your current job and potential future positions. Then make certain you consciously project your best traits.

You can be your own campaign manager, communications consultant, strategy expert, and planner at a mere fraction of the cost a candidate would pay for those services. After all, no one knows you better than yourself. Since you know who you are, you can now use your knowledge of NVC to let others know who you are too.

Selected Bibliography

Allport, Gordon W. *Becoming*. New Haven: Yale University Press, 1955.

Argyle, Michael, and Dean, Janet. "Eye Contact and Affiliation." *Sociometry* 28 (1965): 289–304.

Argyle, Michael. *Bodily Communication*. London: Methuen, 1975.

Beeners, William J. "Total Communications." Talk given to the IBM Marketing School, Endicott, N.Y., July 20, 1976.

Benthall, Jonathan, and Polhemus, Ted, eds. *The Body as a Medium for Expression*. London: Allen Lane, 1975.

Birdwhistell, Ray L. *Introduction to Kinesics*. Louisville: University of Louisville Press, 1952.

Birdwhistell, Ray L. *Kinesics and Context*. Philadelphia: University of Pennsylvania Press, 1970.

Condon, W. S., and Ogston, W. D. "Speech and Body Motion Synchrony of Speaker and Hearer." In D. L. Horton and J. J. Jenkins eds., *Perception of Language*, pp. 224–256. Columbus: Charles Merrill, 1971.

Davis, Flora. *Inside Intuition*. New York: Signet Books, 1975.

Davis, Martha. *Understanding Body Movement*. New York: Arno Press, 1972.

Darwin, Charles. *Expressions of the Emotions in Man and Animals*. Chicago: University of Chicago Press, 1965.

Dittmann, Allen T. "The Relationship Between Body Movements and Moods in Interviews." *Journal of Consulting Psychology* 26 (1962): 480.

Drillis, Rudolph. "Objective Recording and Biomechanics of Gait." *Annals of the New York Academy of Science* 74 (1958): 86–109.

Duncan, Starkey, Jr. "Nonverbal Communication." *Psychological Bulletin* 72 (1960): 118–137.

Eisenberg, A. M., and Smith, R. R., *Nonverbal Communications*. New York: Bobbs-Merrill, 1971.

Ekman, Paul, and Friesen, Wallace V. "The Repertoire of Nonverbal Behavior: Categories, Origins, Usage, and Coding." *Semiotica* 1 (1969): 49–98.

Fast, Julius. *Body Language*. New York: Pocket Books, 1971.

Fischer, Seymour. *Body Image and Personality*. New York: Dover, 1968.

Goffman, Erving. *Behavior in Public Places*. New York: Free Press, 1963.

Goffman, Erving. *Presentation of Self in Everyday Life*. New York: Doubleday, 1959.

Goffman, Erving. *Strategic Interaction*. Philadelphia: University of Pennsylvania Press, 1969.

Half, Robert. "Shorty in the Oval Office." Interview for the Associated Press, quoted in the *St. Louis Post-Dispatch*, December 11, 1976.

Hall, E. T. "Proxemics." *Current Anthropology* (1968): 83–108.

Hall, E. T. *The Hidden Dimension*. New York: Doubleday, 1966.

Hall, E. T. *The Silent Language*. New York: Premier Books, 1961.

Hare, A. Paul, and Bales, Robert F. "Seating Position and Small Group Interaction." *Sociometry* 26 (1963): 480–486.

Harrison, Randall P. *Beyond Words*. Englewood Cliffs, N.J.: Prentice-Hall, 1974.

Hinde, R. A. *Nonverbal Communication*. London: Cambridge University Press, 1972.

Humber, Thomas, ed., and Akeret, Robert U. *Photoanalysis*. New York: Pocket Books, 1975.

Key, Mary Ritchie. *Paralanguage and Kinesics*. Metuchen, N.J.: Scarecrow Press, 1975.

Knapp, Mark L. *Nonverbal Communications*. New York: Holt, Rinehart and Winston, 1972.

Korda, Michael. *Power*. New York: Ballantine Books, 1976.

Lorenz, Konrad. *On Aggression*. New York: Harcourt Brace Jovanovich, 1966.

Mehrabian, Albert. "Relationship of Attitude to Seated Posture, Orientation, and Distance." *Journal of Personality and Social Psychology* 10 (1968): 26–30.

Mehrabian, Albert. "Significance of Posture and Position in the Communication of Attitudes and Status Relationship." *Psychological Bulletin* 71 (1969): 359–372.

Molloy, John T. *Dress for Success*. New York: Warner Books, 1975.

Molloy, John T. *The Woman's Dress for Success Book*. Chicago: Follett, 1977.

Morris, A. R. *A Handbook of Nonverbal Group Exercises*. Springfield, Ill.: Thomas, 1975.

Nierenberg, Gerald I., and Calero, Henry H. *How to Read a Person Like a Book*. New York: Pocket Books, 1973.

Norum, Gary A., Russo, Nancy J., and Sommer, Robert. "Seating Patterns and Group Tasks." *Psychology in the Schools* 4: 276–280.

Pliner, Patricia, Kranes, Lester, and Alloway, Thomas, eds. *Nonverbal Communication of Aggression*. New York: Plenum, 1975.

Scheflen A. E. *Body Language and Social Order*. Englewood Cliffs, N.J.: Prentice-Hall, 1972.

Scheflen, A. E., ed. *How Behavior Means*. New York: Gordon and Breach, 1973.

Scheflen, A. E. "Quasi-Courtship Behavior in Psychological Therapy." *Psychiatry*. 28 (1965): 245–257.

Scheflen, A. E. "The Significance of Posture in Communication Systems." *Psychiatry* 27 (1964): 316–331.

Sommer, Robert. *Personal Space*. Englewood Cliffs, N.J.: Prentice-Hall, 1969.

Spiegel, John P. *Messages of the Body*. New York: Free Press, 1974.

Stanford, Phillip. "A Different Lie Detector—Your Voice Gives You Away." *Parade Magazine*, January 10, 1977.

Zunin, Leonard. *Contact: The First 4 Minutes*. Los Angeles: Nash, 1972.

Index